MW00426124

STUDIES IN BIBLE AND FEMINIST CRITICISM

Support for the publication of this book
has been provided with admiration, respect, and affection

for

TIKVA FRYMER-KENSKY

by friends at

BETH HILLEL CONGREGATION B'NAI EMUNAH

Wilmette, Illinois

and
by a gift from

SAMUEL PANUSH FRIED

dedicated with love to

GIGI PANUSH FRIED

JPS דור דור
SCHOLAR ודורשיו
OF DISTINCTION
SERIES

TIKVA FRYMER-KENSKY

STUDIES IN BIBLE AND FEMINIST CRITICISM

THE JEWISH PUBLICATION SOCIETY

Philadelphia   *2006 • 5766*

The Jewish Publication Society
2100 Arch Street, 2nd floor
Philadelphia, PA 19103

Composition by Book Design Studio II
Design by Adrianne Onderdunk Dudden

Manufactured in the United States of America

06 07 08 09 10   10 9 8 7 6 5 4 3 2 1

Publisher's Note:
With few exceptions, the articles in this anthology are as they appeared in their original. As a result, there are variations in spelling and language style from piece to piece.

Library of Congress Cataloging-in-Publication Data

Frymer-Kensky, Tikva Simone
  Studies in Bible and feminist criticism/Tikva Frymer-Kensky.—1st ed.
    p. cm.
  "Bibliography of published writings of Tikva Frymer-Kensky"—P.
  Includes bibliographic references.
  ISBN 0-8276-0798-9
    1. Bible. O.T.—Criticism, interpretation, etc. 2. Bible. O.T.—Feminist criticism. 3. Bible—Theology. 4. Middle Eastern literature—Relation to the Old Testament. I. Title

BS1171.3.F79 2006
220.6082—dc22

                                        2005043538

Tikva Frymer-Kensky

To my husband, Rabbi Allan Kensky,
whose loving support nourishes me as much as food and drink;

to my daughter, Meira Kensky,
who has grown into my colleague and my friend;

and to my son, Eitan Kensky,
who is emerging as my friend and as an excellent scholar
who has much to teach me.

I am deeply blessed to have my close, loving family.

Contents

vii

FEMINIST PERSPECTIVES I: GENDER AND THE BIBLE

FEMINIST PERSPECTIVES II: GENDER AND THE LAW

THEOLOGIES I: BIBLICAL THEOLOGY

THEOLOGIES II: CONSTRUCTIVE THEOLOGY

Acknowledgments

It is hard to know whom to acknowledge and thank for help in work that has spanned over thirty years. First, I would like to thank Judith Lawrence, my secretary at the Divinity School of the University of Chicago, and Manuel Cruz, a Ph.D. candidate at the Divinity School, for their extensive efforts in preparing this manuscript and correcting the bibliography. I have been blessed over the years with secretaries and librarians who have been eager to do whatever was needed—and I thank them all for their assistance and encouragement. I have been fortunate to have had the guidance of wonderful teachers, from my undergraduate Bible professors H. L. Ginsberg, Yohanan Muffs, Shalom Paul, Moshe Held, and A.S. Halkin, through my graduate professors in Semitics and Assyriology Franz Rosenthal, Marvin Pope, J.J. Finklestein, and William Hallo. My sincere thanks also to my "adopted" teachers Thorkild Jacobsen and Moshe Greenberg, who have given of their time freely and generously over the years to discuss their work and mine.

In the final analysis writing is a lonely business; but it is not done in a vacuum. I am conscious of my readers and their questions—a consciousness that is not abstract. I would like to thank my students at Wayne State University, the Reconstructionist Rabbinical College, and the University of Chicago, as well as the many participants in adult education courses and lectures that I have given over the years. Little by little their interests have become mine; their questions have shaped the way I look at scripture; and their intellectual needs have urged me to write—to go beyond the lecture or the class.

I would like to acknowledge my colleagues at the places where I have been fortunate to teach and learn. The faculty at the Reconstructionist Rabbinical College was eager to discuss all matters of Jewish learning, and I learned a great deal from them during the years that I taught there. I have been fortunate to have had two stays at the Center for Advanced Jewish Studies of the University of Pennsylvania, a place wholly devoted to facilitating the work of its professors. My sincere thanks to the Divinity School of the University of

Chicago, with its superb professors eager to stretch the boundaries of their knowledge through interdisciplinary work and discussion. I can not imagine a better place for me to work and I am deeply grateful to be there. These people and places have nourished me through the years in which I produced the articles assembled here. I am thankful for them all.

Above all, I have been blessed with a wonderful family. I am grateful for my husband, Allan Kensky, who has stood with me and encouraged me during the times when I felt unstoppable, as well as during the times when I felt ready to give up the difficult struggle. His love, his companionship, and his intellect have nourished me, challenged me, and enabled me to continue. And I am grateful for my children from whom I have learned so much. I have learned from the love that I felt and feel for them, and continue to learn from the questions they pose and the matters they teach me as they demonstrate their keen intellects and accumulated knowledge. They have become my friends and my colleagues.

Which brings me full circle to this book. I would like to thank my congregation, Beth Israel Congregation B'nai Emunah of Wilmette, Illinois, who enthusiastically helped defray some of the expenses entailed in such a project. And I am deeply grateful to the wonderful people at The Jewish Publication Society, without whom this book would never have come into being. First of all, Ellen Frankel, Editor-in-Chief and CEO of JPS, who conceived of the project and, working with her board, named me as a JPS Scholar of Distinction—an honor for which I am sincerely grateful. I am honored and moved by the distinguished company I keep and am happily aware that not only am I the first woman to be so honored, but also the first of my generation of scholars. I now take my place among some of the great scholars who have taught me. Next, my thanks to my wonderful editor, Rena Potok, who collected and selected the articles to be included and who gently nudged me to finish writing the introduction and translating the "Theology of Catastrophe." And finally, Janet Liss, who was in charge of proofing the manuscript and doing everything else necessary to put this book to bed. To these wonderful women, and to all the others whose names I never learned, I am very grateful for and appreciative of their immense contributions to this book.

Introduction: A Retrospective

Sometimes decisions of which you are not even aware can have an enormous impact on your life. The autumn of my second year in elementary school was a traumatic time for me. The public schools in Queens must have adopted the educational principles of John Dewey, because in October the classes were split up and new classes were formed. To me, this meant moving from a class full of bright kids to a mixed class in which I was far and away the smartest child. The move toward an equal treatment of all students extended even to reading groups: instead of the groups reading on different levels, we were all expected to use the same second grade reader and write answers to a list of questions before we could do anything else. If the other students had seen me struggle with my own portion as they struggled with theirs, they might have accepted me. Instead, they saw me finish in just a few minutes and then sit reading my own book for fun while they struggled with the difficulties of learning how to read. I was the "whiz kid," annoying in my smartness and attacked with schoolbags as I left school each afternoon. Going to school became a tormenting mix of intellectual boredom and social anxiety.

There was one oasis in my education: Hebrew school, which I attended for two hours each Monday through Thursday and all morning on Sundays. At Hebrew school, no one appeared to care about educational theory—most of the teachers had never heard of John Dewey. They simply wanted to teach Jewish kids enough Judaism and Jewish history to inoculate us against disappearing into the American "melting pot." These teachers had no ambitions to nurture self-esteem or even social cohesiveness; they just wanted to teach the lesson plan. And they certainly didn't want to cope with the boredom of a very smart, very eager student. So they kept "skipping" me into higher grades, a practice that the public schools had dropped. As a result, I graduated at ten years old together with the thirteen-year-olds in my class. And I was happy. Nobody in class envied or hated me. When they paid attention to me at all, it was with the kind of teasing affection one gives the friends of one's younger siblings. Hebrew school was a joyous spot in my day: I was accepted socially and stimulated intellectually—certainly not most children's reactions to Hebrew school. In Hebrew school I first learned how to conjugate verbs, read about the Crusades, the Inquisition, the revolutionary movements in Europe. It was there that I first began to associate religious studies with intellectual challenge and stimulation.

I don't know what the Hebrew school would have done with me after I "graduated." As it happens, we moved to Israel when I was ten years old. In my public school in Tel Aviv, I was faced with the considerable challenge of learning sixth-grade classes in a language I really didn't know. I loved Hebrew grammar, though, and even before I began to speak Hebrew fluently I could conjugate a verb as well as or even better than most of the Israeli kids in my class; we all laughed at the 98 I got on the first quiz. I also loved my Bible class. Jeremiah's Hebrew was far too difficult for me, but it was also difficult for the Israelis. We all had to learn very slowly, and we spent a lot of time on basic comprehension. To me this meant that after I had finished decoding the language, there was still time to concentrate on the prophet's meaning.

Two years later, my mother and I came back from Israel to join my fifteen-year-old sister, who had returned to the United States alone. I didn't want to forget my Hebrew after I came back and I knew that if I didn't study I would lose it all. I knew far too much spoken Hebrew and had far too much textual knowledge to fit into a Hebrew high school, so I came to Manhattan to seek a place to study. I visited Herzeliyah, a teacher's academy, but at twelve years old, I was not interested in becoming a teacher. Ultimately, I landed in the Prozdor program of the Jewish Theological Seminary. Today, the Prozdor is a formal after-school Hebrew high school. In those days, it was an informal seminar of kids who had passed the entrance exams for the Seminary College but were too young to be admitted. There, we were taught by the brightest of the coming generation of scholars, mostly young rabbis who were advancing in Ph.D. programs. I had found my home. I spent three years in the Prozdor being taught and befriended by Yohanan Muffs, Shalom Paul, Avraham Holtz, and Joel Kramer. During the day I went to an overcrowded public high school with a factory-like atmosphere and lowest common denominator curriculum, spending months studying for everyday quizzes that featured such questions as: "Name five things that David Copperfield saw on his way to London." Then I would take the subway uptown to study with Muffs, who introduced me to the writings of Henry Frankford and Ernst Cassirer. Without having planned to do so, I was duplicating my grade-school experience, being bored most of the day in public school and then coming alive in the intellectually stimulating atmosphere of Judaic studies.

Long before college, even before I had gone to Israel, when I was just ten years old, I decided to teach nuclear engineering in a university. I knew nothing about college life. My only academic relative lived far away and I never visited him on campus. My father, who was a journalist and a Zionist activist, had always dismissed the very thought of the "ivory tower" as irrelevant to the world, but I felt more at home in a classroom and a library than anywhere else, so I expected that I would spend my life there, teaching "the peaceful uses of the atom." I didn't know anything about nuclear science or engineering, but my liberal Jewish heart, seeking its spiritual fulfillment in *tikun olam* (the repair of the world), had been seduced by the heavy public relations message, so popular in the 1950s, of saving the world through "the peaceful uses of the atom." I never wavered in my decision, even in the face of the mean-spirited persecution that the physical sciences teachers inflicted on me, the girl who wanted to go into a "man's profession." Nothing deterred me. Nothing, that is, until my freshman year of college when I took engineering or rather, pre-engineering classes for the first time and discovered that much to my surprise I didn't like calculus and I didn't like engineering. Once again, I was bored all day in general studies courses and came alive intellectually in the evening when I studied Bible and Talmud at the Jewish Theological Seminary College. I finally realized I had my priorities backward: I should read science for fun and study Bible as a profession. And so I began to prepare for a career in biblical studies.

The field of biblical studies was no more open to women than high school physics had been, and I had no female role models. But none of that mattered because I was determined to master it and learn everything I needed to know to answer the questions about the Bible that interested me—questions about law and religion and the relations between them, questions about the development of biblical ideas from prebiblical through postbiblical times. That meant going to graduate school to earn a Ph.D.—not in Bible, but in Assyriology. I had spent eight years at the seminary studying Bible with Muffs, Paul, Moshe Held, and H. L. Ginsberg. Not realizing that there were approaches to the Bible other than the philological and close-reading techniques I had learned at the seminary, I didn't even consider the possibility of a graduate degree in biblical studies. The seminary taught us a kind of arrogance: along with texts, we learned that our professors were the best text readers in the world, and that to the degree that we mastered their techniques we could aspire to grow into their excellence. I couldn't stay at the seminary, which did not have a graduate school and did not admit women to the rabbinical school, so I would have to leave to study elsewhere, but why go somewhere to a pale imitation (we all thought) of the seminary?

There was one method that the teachers at the seminary used heavily but did not teach formally: a comparison and contrast with Near Eastern, primarily Assyriological, texts. I had been hearing about Nuzi, Mari, and Ugarit since I was thirteen, so off I went to Yale to study Assyriology and law with J. J. Finkelstein. At Yale, W. W. Hallo introduced me to Sumerian and Sumerology. I could now go back earlier and earlier, as far back as writing could take us. Sometimes, particularly in law, this meant being able to follow two different legal principles, or to trace changes first between Sumerian and Babylonian polytheism and then between Old Babylonian and later Mesopotamian ideas. But Yale was as adamant as the seminary about the need for careful, meticulous study of the texts. One could not use Mesopotamian texts to illuminate the Bible without first studying the Mesopotamian material as carefully as the seminary had taught me to read biblical texts. Nothing good could be achieved by premature contrast and comparison. So I learned to read Sumerian texts as a Sumerologist and Akkadian texts as an Assyriologist, determined to treat the cuneiform materials with honor, and not simply to go on a treasure hunt to find "tidbits" to highlight the Bible.

Yet, I remained a biblicist at heart, and the questions in Assyriology and Sumerology that interested me all had to do with the development of ideas and institutions of religion and law, or with the intersection of the two, as in oaths and ordeals. Ur III economics or battles and conquests had little interest for me, but I began to work seriously on the vocabulary of crime and punishment, on motifs and myths of creation, and on oaths and ordeals. Ordeals became the focus of my dissertation, and in the years to come, I worked mainly on questions of law and jurisprudence, building my self-image as a careful and meticulous scholar. Most of the legal articles I wrote during that period are technical, and only one, "Patriarchal Family Relationships and Near Eastern Law," is in this volume. Three nonlegal articles come from this period: "Pollution, Purification, and Purgation in Biblical Israel," "The Planting of Man," and "The Atrahasis Epic and Its Significance for Our Understanding of Genesis 1–9." They represent my lifelong interest in biblical metaphysics and especially in Genesis 1–11, which has fascinated me ever since I first began to learn it seriously, and which I have taught ever since my first year of graduate school when I taught it in Hebrew junior high school. Curiously enough, even though I taught in Jewish schools during graduate school (high school, adult education, summer camps, and even first-grade day school), I paid little attention to the impact of ethnicity, religion, or gender on my interests and my work. That would come later.

A funny thing happened to me on my way to publishing my dissertation, "Judicial Ordeal in the Ancient Near East": I became pregnant. At that time (1978), academic women were not supposed to notice their pregnancies. We were to carry on as if nothing was happening, and then take two weeks off and come back as if we had taken a brief trip to view the sites or visit our relatives. I was even advised (by my department chairman) that I shouldn't ask for maternity leave because the tenure committee would not view such a request favorably. I followed all these rules, knowing that something didn't seem right about them; the only time I let myself think about the experience of pregnancy was during my weekly Lamaze class, and that was mainly about breathing.

As my ninth month came, the baby's head did not engage and it became clear to me that I was not going to have the "natural" childbirth for which I was preparing. Thirteen years earlier, a camp counselor, happy and flirtatious after his day off, had danced me around and thrown me across the arena in a wrestling throw. Instead of rubber mats, the ground was covered with gravel, and the impact of my landing moved my spine 99+ percent forward on my sacrum. A massive bone graft secured it, but an X-ray in my fortieth week showed that my spine was jutting out into the birth canal and we couldn't risk labor. If we did, the doctor told me, white as this page, the baby could bash her skull against it. "Go home," he said, "get your things, and come right back. I'm taking the baby first thing tomorrow morning." The doctor seemed panicked, and I went home close to it. But I displaced my emotion: rather than think about the surgery in the morning, I worried about what I would do that evening after my husband left for minyan and was not allowed back. I took along some novels that I had saved for after the birth when (I had been told) I would have time to read (!), the *TV Guide*, and, because of either lunacy or Providence, a folder of Sumerian birth incantations that I had collected. (I had written on the religious significance of water, and birth incantations have a lot of water imagery, for obvious reasons.) That evening, I couldn't get interested in the novels and I didn't want to watch television. I realized that I didn't want to distract myself; I wanted to concentrate and meditate on the birth. I spent a lovely three hours studying the birth incantations, during which time my anxieties melted away into a feeling of being part of a long chain of women giving birth and having difficulty doing so.

Ten months later, after I had recovered fully from the birth and the general anesthesia of the C-section, I began to get angry. Why was it that a woman fairly well trained in Judaism and in Christianity had to go all the way to ancient Mesopotamia to find something to read to focus on birth—and what did the poor women do who couldn't read Sumerian? I decided to teach a course on women and religion and spent the next two years reading everything that was beginning to be written in this new field. Gradually, I gained an understanding of what is now generally acknowledged by many thinkers: that Western religion has been a religion of talking heads; that Christianity turned against the body; and that Judaism had an uneasy relationship with it. With this understanding, my anger disappeared, replaced by a sense that perhaps there was a purpose for which I had learned Hebrew and Aramaic, Greek and Latin, Akkadian and Sumerian; that maybe I could find and reclaim long-neglected readings, like the Sumerian incantations, that would address women's issues. This revelation sent me on the long quest that culminated in *Motherprayer* seventeen years later. I did find ancient readings, which I translated, but they addressed only conception and difficult birth and were mainly focused on the hope for healthy babies and the life of the mother. This perspective was understandable, since half of all ancient women could expect to die of childbirth and infant mortality was so rampant. But the readings did not address the experiences of the mother during pregnancy or the spiritual signifi-cance of the process. I developed what I call "recombinant theological engineering" to address these issues and to create a new theology and liturgy using traditional religious language. The two poems in this vol-ume illustrate some of these techniques: "Shaddai" is a meditation on a passage in midrash Tanhuma, and "Like a Birthing Woman" takes the

Bible's use of the simile "writhing like a birthing woman" and turns it backward to explore more fully how the Bible understands the religious sense of the action of giving birth.

At the same time that I began work on the theology of birth, I also began another long-term project. During the years that I devoted to reading the initial writings in the new field of women and religion, I had been bothered by the publication of the many feminist writings on "the Goddess" and the supposed "reconstruction" of goddess religion. What these writers were saying about goddesses bore absolutely no similarity to the mythological images of goddesses or hymns to the goddesses written when people were actively worshipping them. Nor did the image of monotheism that was being attacked have much to do with the religion of the Bible or of Rabbinic Judaism. These writers had taken everything they disliked about patriarchy and patriarchal religion and projected it as "God." They then reversed this abominable "other" to create a Great Goddess, one who had left no traces in polytheist texts because she existed only in the psyche of twentieth-century women. At first, I was angry, but then I realized there was no reason for me to be angry at the goddess writers—they were creating the religion of their dreams, and if it distorted the actual historical record it was because they did not concern themselves with historical accuracy. Since I did, it was up to me to set the record straight. So, too, many of them were angry at the Jews for "killing the goddess." In my view, they didn't care if their portrayal of monotheism was accurate, and since I cared about Judaism, it was again up to me to set the record straight. I embarked upon a project to understand what exactly it was that goddesses did, what the functions of goddesses were in a polytheist system, and then what happened to these functions in a system that had no goddesses, such as biblical religion.

Because well-meaning colleagues warned me that I would destroy my reputation if I starting writing about goddesses, it was important to me to show that one could apply the same care, diligence, and meticulousness to questions about goddesses that one would use to study ancient law, and that there was nothing inherent to women's studies or to feminism that would prevent the highest standards of scholarship. I knew that these two projects meant I would have to delay the publication of my dissertation, and I would have to shelve my work on ancient mythology and its significance for Genesis 1–11. But these two interrelated projects of *Motherprayer* and the goddesses were vitally important to me both as a woman and as a scholar. Through them, I hoped to expand the cultural history of the ancient world to include questions important to women's history, and to expand current religion and liturgy to incorporate areas of women's concerns. Together, they placed gender studies at the center of my concern and attention. The articles printed here on gender grew out of these concerns.

I discovered that one of the major functions of goddesses in Mesopotamia was to represent societal ideas about gender. This was not surprising, but when I looked seriously at gender in the Bible to see if and how the stories about women served the same function I discovered, much to my surprise, that the Bible did not have a two-gender view of human nature, that unlike Greece and even Mesopotamia, the biblical authors did not think of certain psychological characteristics as "male" or "female." The Bible viewed humanity in gender-blind or gender-neutral ways, an idea I explore in "The Ideology of Gender in the Bible and the Ancient Near East." As for the other functions of goddesses, many of them had been usurped by the male gods during the second millennium B.C.E. and were no longer considered the domain of goddesses. Tracing the result of eliminating goddesses is the main task of *In the Wake of the Goddesses.* But what about the biblical stories about women? The women do not represent gender issues, nor do they inherit the other functions of the goddesses. What, then, are they doing in an admittedly androcentric book from an ancient patriarchal society? This question led me on another scholarly exploration of these stories, from which arose "Virginity in the Bible" and "Reading Rahab," and which resulted in *Reading the Women of the Bible.*

In the Wake of the Goddesses, Motherprayer, Reading the Women of the Bible, and the articles on gender and feminism contained in this volume ended the "digression" into feminism, women, and gender that I began almost thirty years ago. Someday, if I am granted the time, I would like to return to each of the functions I delineated there and use them as my guide into the fascinating issues of biblical theology. Among those are questions of "Jews and genitals" that I began to raise when I realized that goddesses also contribute to an understanding of (heterosexual) sexuality and that the Bible lacks an exploration of the role of Eros in the cosmos. Without the Ishtar-type goddess, there was a vacuum that the Rabbis filled by importing the Greek ideas about gender and sexuality that many find distasteful today. It is important to work toward a Jewish theology of sexuality, but first I am exploring the main issue of biblical theology toward which the goddesses pointed me—the nature of humanity and its role in the universe. The essential difference between monotheism and polytheism is not the number of gods, but the position of human beings—who become God's avatars, partners, and interlocutors in the universe. Along with *In the Wake of the Goddesses,* "The Image: Religious Anthropology in Judaism and Christianity" is a step toward understanding the religious humanism of Judaism, which I hope to pursue further as I return to my studies of Genesis 1–11, and as I continue my explorations into constructing a biblical theology for today.

As I left my earlier studies to pursue my "feminist digression," not only my subject matter but also my mode of working began to change. And the influences on my reorientation came from occasionally surprising sources. Sometimes questions randomly asked by strangers can redirect one's whole thinking. I was fortunate to have two such questions posed to me.

From a career perspective, I should have left my job at Wayne State University as soon as I received my doctorate. But my husband was happy in Ann Arbor and in his congregation, so I stayed in my "starter job" teaching Hebrew and a little Bible long after I should have left. I even stayed on to teach part-time after I was denied tenure because my position was being closed. I was a classic "Mrs. Adjunct," a married woman who is unable to move to where the jobs are and therefore teaches courses all over the place. One semester, I flew round-trip to Hamilton, Ontario, in one day to teach two Bible courses—for the joy of teaching graduate students, and for the paycheck. In those days, one of my steady sources of income was the Midrasha, the institute of adult Jewish education in the Detroit area. One or two nights a week I would drive into Southfield to teach two courses, usually text courses. One December evening, as I was teaching my class on Genesis 1–11, I noticed a young man wearing the black hat of the ultra-Orthodox standing outside the door, listening intently. The ultra-Orthodox community does not learn modern Bible studies, and they do not learn from a woman. But this young man stayed for the entire class and then came in to speak to me. He wanted to know if he could study with me the next semester (when I would be teaching Exodus) and if I would allow him to disagree with me in class. When I replied that I would welcome both his presence and his participation, he asked me a set of questions to test my suitability. First, he asked, did I believe that the Torah was revealed? Having wrestled with this question for years I replied that, yes, there was a (nonliteral) sense in which I believed the Torah was revealed. "Then," he asked, "how about the Oral Torah [the classic Rabbinic texts]?" I replied that there was also a sense in which I believed the Oral Torah was revealed. "Then," he asked, "what about Rashi [the great early medieval commentator to the Bible]? Do you believe that Rashi wrote with the Holy Spirit?" Bingo! That was the question. "Yes," I replied carefully, "but you have to understand that I believe that I too write with the Holy Spirit. After all," I said, "the tradition says that whenever somebody sits to study Torah, the *Shekhinah* [the immanent presence of God] rests upon her or him." The young man was satisfied with that answer, and I told him that I would be happy to teach him, but perhaps he would want to talk to his rabbi first.

I never saw that man again, but his question—and my answer—stayed with me. There is, I realized, a profound difference in me when I study Bible from when I study Assyriology. I read Mesopotamian texts with great love and with an appreciation of their enormous importance for the history of humanity. I study the texts for their inherent interest and, sometimes, for their comparison to or contrast with the Bible. But there is no social component to this study and no spiritual element. When I study the Bible, in contrast, I am aware, somewhere in the depths of my consciousness, of the impact that my study can have on people, of the possible transformations that it can occasionally cause in Judaism and/or in people's personal lives. In this, I find no difference between learning Torah (a traditional religious exercise) and studying Bible. I find the process of studying an exercise in holiness and spiritual meditation. Long ago I rejected the facile dichotomy of my professors who said, "When I pray, I speak to God, and when I study, God speaks to me." I am keenly aware of the voices of ancient writers composing the Bible, and of the hands of the anonymous tradents who preserved it over the ages. The verses in the Bible call me into conversation with them and with other readers through time. And since the authors are trying to make a place for God in this world, they—and I—are engaged in a holy activity. The world has changed, and the old answers can no longer suit the old purposes of improving the life of all human beings or of magnifying the holiness of the world. But the ancient questions, which come from careful attention to both the text and the needs of people, still demand attention. When I study, these ancient authors speak to me and I join them; I bring my contemporary perspectives, my scholarly expertise, and my woman's sensibility into conversation with them; I seek to understand their texts, to see how their texts can become mine, and how my voice can help these texts speak to the modern world. The process of studying Torah is twofold: it is both an intellectual occupation and a spiritual exercise in seeking the multifaceted nature of God, reality, and "truth." Sometimes there is yet a third reward to studying Torah, as the process of learning illuminates some facet of today's world. This reorientation in my thinking made me aware that my studies could have ramifications on the spiritual lives of people who might never even hear my name.

The second question came at about the same time. I went out to Long Island to teach a weekend *Shabbaton* at a synagogue there, in which I presented several of the studies that I ultimately published in *In the Wake of the Goddesses.* The topic of Saturday's talk was the change in gender ideology that entered into Judaism during the Greco-Roman period. I explained my concept that the Bible has a gender neutral or gender-blind notion of the sexes, thinking of them as essentially identical. Women are subordinated socially to men, but they are not inferior in any intellectual or spiritual way, indeed, in any essential way at all. In Second Temple literature, however, we begin to find misogynist stereotypes of women. It is clear that by that point Greek ideas about gender had entered Judaism, ultimately influencing Rabbinic *halakhah*, with its two-gender system that eliminated women from public life, and with its concern about the mixing of the sexes to prevent sexual commingling.

Since the Long Island synagogue was serving Friday night dinner and Saturday lunch, the rabbi's wife took the opportunity to go visit her family. The rabbi, an old friend of my husband, invited a friend of his to spend the weekend at his house, I think as a chaperone for appearance's sake (since I was staying there as well). The friend was an Orthodox man, neither a rabbi nor a scholar but fairly well educated. On Saturday afternoon, the three of us were chatting, and the rabbi's friend said he had a serious question. "If something comes into Judaism from the Greeks," he asked, "is it any less Jewish than something that came in from the Sumerians?" I didn't hesitate with my answer: "Of course not," I said, for I didn't want to fall into the fallacy of assuming that earlier is always better. After all, the Conservative movement's acceptance of women into full participation in public ritual life may only have begun in the 1970s and may have been influenced by American ideas about equality, but full women's participation in synagogues is no less Jewish than are the more old-fashioned synagogues that still keep women as onlookers. But his question raised another one for me: What is the effect of discovering that some idea or concept began with the Greeks?

When I find that the Bible says something different from what the Rabbis have interpreted it to mean, what impact does this have on the way we look at the Rabbinic idea? As I pondered this question, I realized that new understandings of biblical ideas do not have any direct impact upon the Rabbinic system. Still, they show that the Rabbinic "read" is not the only possible read, that there is nothing necessary about it, but that it is a product of Jewish thinking in the Greco-Roman period. Its acceptance is "hegemonic"—it relies on the authority of the Rabbis rather than on evidence or internal logical necessity.

At that point, I became a biblical theologian. Constructive Jewish biblical theology has nothing to do with the Protestant biblical theology of the nineteenth century and the early twentieth. Instead, biblical theology presents an alternative, or sometimes many alternatives, to Rabbinic concepts, for both the individual and the community. As a biblical scholar studying historical theology, my first job is to discover and describe biblical ideas with all their nuances. Without careful biblical analysis, a theologian's use of the Bible descends to prooftexting or to a modern paraphrase of Rabbinic interpretation of the Bible, and a continued use of the Bible as only the fictive center of Jewish ideas. The first step in constructing a biblical theology has to be a modern understanding of the biblical text. Next, we must discuss the importance of each idea to the modern world. Sometimes, I set an idea alongside the Rabbinic system and the medieval developments, maximizing the choices and relevance for today. There are some areas in which the world of the Bible is more like our world than the Rabbinic period. Foremost of these is power: most of the biblical authors wrote in a period of Israelite autonomy in which there was constant fear of losing this independence to the Assyrians and the Babylonians. By contrast, Rabbinic, gaonic, and medieval writings come from periods in which the Jews were constantly under the dominion of others. Our own time is the first period since the Roman era in which Jews have had power: the power of self-government in Israel, and the power of participation in government in the United States. And with the experience of power come the challenges of power, of relative powerlessness toward other nations and God, combined with the power of dominion in the universe. "The Emergence of Jewish Biblical Theologies" is a preliminary attempt to set out the agenda and parameters of the enterprise. "Biblical Voices on Chosenness" and "Covenant: A Jewish Biblical Perspective" are attempts toward understanding a major element in biblical theology, the relationship of Israel and God. "Moses and the Cults: The Question of Religious Leadership," "Revelation Revealed," and "The Sage in the Pentateuch: Soundings" consider the relationship of Israel and its leaders. "Ecology in a Biblical Perspective," "The End of the World and the Limits of Biblical Ecology," and "But in Ourselves" *(In the Wake of the Goddesses)* consider the role of human beings in the universe. "The Image: Religious Anthropology in Judaism and Christianity" and "Homo Sapiens" *(In the Wake of the Goddesses)* explore the relationship between human beings and God. Another group of articles considers the interrelated questions of holiness and pollution, an important element of biblical metaphysics: "Pollution, Purification, and Purgation in Biblical Israel," and "The Theology of Catastrophe." It is to such issues that I hope to return.

I now turn my attention to my commentary on Ruth. It is a kind of transition in my work. It is a book about a female and may even have been written by a woman, thus fitting well into my work of the last thirty years. Moreover, the Book of Ruth wraps in a childlike story a powerful theological statement about the relationship between humanity and God. I would next like to return to Genesis 1–11, which explores the development of human beings and human civilization from its first childlike state into a suitable administrator of the universe and partner to God. Once the earth is filled, God starts a second stage, beginning with having Abram leave Ur of Kasdim (Southern Iraq) to come to Israel and begin an intimate relationship with God. As I work on these two big projects, I continue my explorations of biblical theology, the many topics it addresses, and the fascinating nature of biblical theology itself—which embraces plurality, ambiguity, and uncertainty as the fundamental characteristics of God, the world, Torah, and humanity's relationship with each and with all. With so many absorbing subjects to study, life is never dull.

As I continue to fight my illness, I thank God for the great gifts of my life: my husband and life partner, Rabbi Allan Kensky, my children and fascinating companions, Meira and Eitan, and the Torah itself, which fills my life with interest. May God also grant me fullness of years!

Tikva Frymer-Kensky
Wilmette, Illinois
June 2005

List of Abbreviations

AB   Assyriologische Bibliothek
AfO   Archiv für Orientforschung
AJA   American Journal of Archaeology
BA   Biblical Archaeologist
BASOR   Bulletin of the American Schools of Oriental Research
BDB   Brown Driver Briggs
B. Hag.   Babylonian Talmud Hagigah
Bib   Biblica
BM   Tablets in the collection of the British Museum
BWL   Babylonian Wisdom Literature
CBQ   Catholic Biblical Quarterly
CRRAI   Comptes rendus de la Recontre Assyriologique Internationale
EA   Egyptian Archaeology
HUCA   Hebrew Union College Annual
JAAR   Journal of the American Academy of Religion
JAOS   Journal of the American Oriental Society
JBL   Journal of Biblical Literature
JCS   Journal of Cuneiform Studies
JNES   Journal of Near Eastern Studies
JQR   Jewish Quarterly Review
JSOT   Journal for the Study of the Old Testament
JSS   Journal of Semitic Studies
M. Avot   Mishnah Avot
MIO   Mitteilungen des Institus für Orientforschung
OrNS   Orientalia, Nova Series

PAPS   Publications of the American Philosophical Society
RB   Revue Biblique
RSO   Rivista delgi Studi Orientali
SBL   Society of Biblical Literature
SLTN   Sumerian literary Texts from Nippur
TIM   Texts in the Iraq Museum
TCL   Textes cunéiforms de Louvre
TJ Hag.   Jerusalem Talmud Hagigah

COMPARATIVE CULTURE I: ANCIENT NEAR EASTERN RELIGIONS

Creation Myths

1 / *Atrahasis*: An Introduction
1982

Stories of human creation are often incorporated into larger mythic traditions. Some, for instance, are used in myths which describe the creation of the entire cosmos; others are used to introduce histories of the human race. *Enuma Elish* exemplifies the former idea in which human creation helps put order into the cosmos. Marduk creates the human race in order to relieve the defeated gods of their onerous duties. After this creation, all the gods unite to celebrate Marduk's accomplishments since he has finally stabilized the divine world. (See *Enuma Elish* VI: 1–44.) Likewise, the Israelite Creation Hymn uses a variation on this pattern. The human race is the final step in God's well-conceived plan of a complete cosmos. Human beings are the crowning glory of creation and are given dominion over the earth. (See Genesis 1:26–28.)

Both of these myths, then, place the human race in the scheme of cosmic creation. But another mythic tradition uses stories of human creation as a starting point rather than a conclusion and traces the earliest history of the human race. This tradition usually combines a number of previously independent stories into a continuous account although the sequence of stories may vary from one account to another. Such primeval histories begin, of course, with the creation of the human race. And they often continue with a utopian era in which human beings prosper and a degenerate era which brings divine displeasure. Finally, they end with the gods destroying the human race (frequently by a flood) and renewing it after the destruction.

Like the cosmic tradition, this pattern can be seen in several different cultures throughout the Mediterranean area. The early chapters of Genesis provide the best known example: the human race is created in the story of Adam and Eve (2:4–3:24); the utopian period is suggested by the genealogy of the early patriarch (5:1–32); the decline is found in various places including the story of Cain and Abel (4:1–26); and finally the

5

destruction and renewal are contained in the story of Noah (6:1–9:29). From the Greco-Roman culture, Ovid's *Metamorphoses* also exemplifies this tradition. It begins with human creation, continues through the easy life of the golden age and the degeneracy of the iron age, and ends with a flood and subsequent repopulation of the world.

The Mesopotamian poem *Atrahasis* is the oldest known example of this mythic tradition. Probably written in the early second millennium, the poem presents the same sequence of events as the primeval histories in Genesis and Ovid's *Metamorphoses*. Since it was discovered only a little over a hundred years ago, the text of the poem causes many difficulties. Scholars are still debating the significance of some lines and even the meanings of some words. But perhaps the biggest problems are caused by the many breaks in the clay tablets on which the poem was originally written. They leave large gaps in the story and many incomplete lines whose meanings can only be surmised.

It is fortunate, however, that several versions of the poem have been discovered. The oldest, copied by a scribe a few generations after Hammurabi, is also the most complete. Fragments of other versions, dating as late as 600 B.C.E., are written in various languages including Babylonian and Assyrian. Although these versions often differ from the oldest copy in many details, they help fill gaps in the general plot of the story. (See Lambert and Millard, *Atrahasis*.) The summary which follows gives a general indication of how the story as a whole fits together.

SUMMARY OF THE POEM

Atrahasis begins before the human race existed, but the gods are already organized in an orderly society. Anu, the father and king of the gods, controls the sky; Enlil, second in command, rules the surface of the earth; and Ea (also called Enki) is in charge of the waters. Enlil has assigned many of the lesser gods to do the heavy work of digging canals, and they have been working for forty long years under very oppressive conditions. So they unionize and, late one night, form a picket line at Enlil's house where they set fire to their tools. When Enlil is awakened by the hubbub, he calls a council of the major powers, bursts into tears, and wants to retreat to the sky with Anu. But the ever-crafty Ea has a plan: the birth-goddess Nintu (also called Mami) is to create *lullu*, the aboriginal human being, so that this new creature can take over the backbreaking work on the canals.

Next, the creative process is described in some detail. Nintu mixes clay with the body and blood of a dead god, and the other gods spit on the mixture. Then Nintu boasts of her accomplishments, and the worker-gods join her celebration by giving her the new title "Mistress of all the gods." Finally, fourteen birth-goddesses bring the mixture into the "house of destiny" where Ea treads on the clay and Nintu shapes it into fourteen statues, seven male and seven female. Ten months later, Nintu eagerly plays the role of midwife as the new creatures emerge from the womb. When the birth is completed, she happily exclaims, "I have made it; my hands have made it."

After a large gap in the story, we discover that the situation has changed dramatically. Human beings have been multiplying at an alarming rate for twelve hundred years. Because they are constantly making noise, Enlil is unable to sleep and so tries to cut back the human population by plague and drought. But his attempts are thwarted by Ea, who has befriended the human race. Then Enlil conceives a plan which he thinks Ea will be unable to stop; he decides to destroy the human race with a massive flood which Ea himself must direct as ruler of the waters. Ea, however, is too clever for Enlil and circumvents the commands by warning his human friend, King *Atrahasis*, who then survives the flood in a boat.

After the flood, all the other gods rejoice that the human race has been saved, and they blame Enlil for trying to destroy these creatures in the first place. While the gods are bickering, Ea devises a plan to mollify Enlil and still allow human beings to survive. He commands Nintu to create once again; but this time she will create three new classes of creatures: women unable to bear children, demons who "snatch the baby from the lap of her who bore it," and priestesses who remain celibate. Although it is likely that the poem ends soon after this, the rest of the text is missing.

INTERPRETATIONS OF THE POEM

There are many problems involved in attempting to interpret *Atrahasis.* The summary above indicates that the plot follows the traditional pattern of primeval history, but it does not help us understand the significance of the events. In addition, the missing parts of the main version may have contained important clues to the meaning of the poem as a whole, and the fragments of other versions sometimes contradict the main version. These difficulties are increased by the lack of evidence on the date of the poem's composition. It was probably first written down during the early years of Babylon's rise to power in Mesopotamia (early in the second millennium B.C.E.), but this dating is not certain and at best provides only a general historical setting. Because of these difficulties, any interpretation of the poem must be tentative. But scholars have found several clues within the poem itself which may point to its main theme.

First, the poem concentrates on Enlil as the god who has the most influence over the human world. No matter how much Ea may help human beings in the short run, Enlil's plans and decisions ultimately determine the fate of the human race. According to Thorkild Jacobsen, the poem displays an ambivalence about the character of Enlil. On the one hand, it shows a perverse fascination for the tremendous destruction which Enlil can unleash; on the other, it reveals an awareness that he is an adversary and that his motives are suspect (*Treasures of Darkness*, p. 223). If the poem is in effect a paean to Enlil, it belongs in the same tradition as *Enuma Elish* and Hesiod's *Theogony*, which exalt one god over all the others in their pantheons. But *Atrahasis* would be unique in this group because it glorifies a god who is an adversary of the human race.

Second, the poem frequently explains the origins of various Mesopotamian social practices. In its description of human creation, for example, the poem elaborates on the origin of rituals related to childbirth. But perhaps the most important of these etiologies occurs at the end of the poem when the problem of human overpopulation is resolved by the creation of female sterility, miscarriages, and religious celibacy. These new creatures are useful to Mesopotamian society because they limit the human population and thus avoid further divine attempts to destroy the entire human race ("The Babylonian Flood Stories," p. 36).

Finally, the pattern of primeval history also provides a clue to the poem's meaning. In the Mesopotamian worldview, the original human beings were apparently too wild and barbarous to begin any kind of organized life on their own and were thus dependent on the gods to provide it for them. In Babylonian tradition, seven sages received the gods' instruction on civilized behavior and passed it on to the rest of the human race. The extent of these teachings can be seen in the Sumerian concept of the *mes*. A *me* was any organized segment of human civilization, including the institution of kingship, the building of cities, all occupations and crafts, and even the low life of prostitutes, thieves, and other criminals. It did not matter whether a *me* was legal, helpful, or moral; if it existed in civilized life, it must have come from the gods.

(See Lambert and Millard, pp. 18–21.) The gap in Tablet I of *Atrahasis*, which immediately follows the creation of the human race, may have contained a similar explanation of the development of human civilization. In that case, the first part of the poem would have emphasized not only the hard work which human beings had to perform but also the sanctity and value of Mesopotamian institutions.

THE HUMAN CONDITION

According to Mesopotamian tradition, then, human beings were dependent on the gods for their creation and their way of life. *Atrahasis* follows this traditional belief in the two processes which the gods use to create the human race. In the first process, the gods act as craftsmen as they shape a new creature out of unformed clay mixed with divine flesh and blood. Nintu and Ea cooperate in forming statues of the new creatures and in reciting magic incantations. But even this elaborate procedure is not enough to finish human creation. The creatures must still stay in a womb for the normal period of human pregnancy before being born. This second process indicates how the civilized life of human beings follows divine patterns. The gods set a precedent for later human behavior as they perform various rituals connected with childbirth. These etiologies include many details which are not clear to us, such as the placing of the brick and the beating of the drum. But each of these acts shows how the gods give the human race their first lesson in civilized living, the proper way to handle birth.

The materials the gods use to create the human race also show how human life reflects the divine pattern. Human beings are a mixture of clay, divine spittle, and the flesh and blood of a god "who has rationality." In general, this idea is similar to that in other accounts of the creation of the human race. Humanity is a combination of earthly and divine elements, for example, in the story of Adam and Eve when God takes up some soil and breathes life into it. But *Atrahasis* divides the divine element into four parts. First, the blood of the slain god provides human beings with life just as God's breath does in the story of Adam and Eve. The divine blood gives movement and growth to an otherwise unliving form. Second, the spittle of the gods serves the practical purpose of wetting the clay to make it malleable, but it also provides a further divine element in human nature. Spittle, like breath and blood, is a symbol of life and is often considered to have magical qualities. Third, the flesh of the slain god introduces a spirit which will live on after death. Even though the use of a god's flesh to signify this idea is not found elsewhere in Mesopotamian literature, it is consistent with their belief in a spirit which survives death and can haunt the living (Lambert and Millard, p. 22). Finally, the slain god is characterized as one "who has rationality." Although the meaning of this phrase is not completely understood, it is clear that this characteristic is also passed on to the newly created human beings. Thus, *Atrahasis* attempts to account for the complex nature of human life which shares so much with the divine world.

Finally, the poem suggests that there is an interdependence between the human and divine worlds which grows as human history progresses. At the beginning of the poem, the gods have a simple and clear reason for creating the human race. They find that the hard work necessary for survival causes too much dissension among themselves, so they create a new class of creatures to perform these duties. Human beings, then, are essentially slaves who work so that their masters may enjoy freedom and leisure. Later in the poem, it becomes apparent that the divine plan has not worked, for human beings are making so much noise that the gods cannot rest. Whether this condition is the result of overpopulation or some other cause, the human race has apparently lost many of the civilized values which the gods gave them. Enlil, who rules over the earth, finds the problem sufficiently serious to suggest complete destruction; and the other gods agree that human beings are not worth the trouble which they cause. After the attempted destruction has failed, however, the gods turn against Enlil, for they realize that they need the sacrifices and hard work which the human race has performed for many generations. By the end of the poem, then, the gods have realized that there is an interdependence between the divine and human worlds which gives added stature to humanity. Human beings are originally created as slaves, and their civilization is patterned after the divine world. But the gods are ultimately dependent on the human race to provide them the means of maintaining their freedom and leisure.

This seemingly simple poem, then, contains some very complex ideas about creation and defines human nature in terms of its relationship to the divine world. The poem is in some respects traditional: it uses primeval history as its broad setting and it pictures human beings as a mixture of divine and human elements. But it is also unique in its complex conception of human creation and its great concern for explaining the origins of its native social practices. Its ideas and artistic conventions may appear alien to us, but they can also give us a fresh perspective on the meaning of human life and the idea of the divine.

OUTLINE OF *ATRAHASIS*

A. Creation of Human Race (I: 1–304)*
  1. Worker-gods rebel (I: 1–73).
  2. Enlil is awakened (I: 74–98).
  3. Chief gods hold council (I: 99–177).
  4. Nintu and Enki plan creation (I: 178–220).
  5. Human race is created (I: 221–304).
B. Problems with the Human Race (I: 352–II: iv)
  1. Noise of multiplied human race bothers Enlil.
  2. *Atrahasis* consults Enki about plague.
  3. Enki advises *Atrahasis* about plague.
  4. Famine is described.
C. Flood (II: v–III: iv)
  1. Enki is ordered to flood the earth.
  2. *Atrahasis* is ordered to build a boat.
  3. *Atrahasis* builds and stocks the boat.
  4. Earth is flooded.
D. Aftermath (III: v–viii)
  1. Gods suffer hunger and thirst when sacrifices cease.
  2. *Atrahasis* makes an offering.
  3. Gods descend upon offering.
  4. Enlil and Enki argue.

Starred passages are included in the readings which follow.

ATRAHASIS

Translated by Tikva Frymer-Kensky

Worker-Gods Rebel (I: 1–73)

When the gods, like man,
bore the work, carried the labor-basket—
the labor-basket of the great gods—
the work was heavy, much was the distress.
The seven great Anunnaki   5
caused the Igigi to bear the work.
Anu their father was king.
Their counselor was hero Enlil.
Their "throne-bearer" was Ninurta.
And their sheriff was Ennugi.   10
These are the ones who seized power.
The gods cast lots and divided (the Cosmos):

[Anu] went up to [heaven];
[Enlil had] the earth as his subject:
[the lock,] the snare of the sea,   15
[was given] to Enki the wise.
[After Anu] went up to heaven
[and Enki w]ent down [to the ap]su
. . .
[they caused] the Igigi [to bear the work].   20

[21–36. These lines are fragmentary. Enough is left, however, to reveal that the gods' work includes digging the Tigris and Euphrates rivers.]

. . . Forty more years
. . . they bore the labor night and day.
They [wearied], complained,
[grum]bled in the workpits.   40
"Let us confront the throne-bearer
that he may remove from us our [hea]vy labor.
. . .
come on, let us confuse him in his dwelling,
Enlil, the counselor of the gods, the 'hero,'   45
Come on, let us confuse him in his dwelling."

[47–60. Most of these lines are lost, fragmentary, or repetitious. But it is clear that one of the worker-gods is speaking to the others and exhorting them to rebel. His speech ends with the following:]

"Now, engage battle,
stir up war and hostilities."
The gods listened to his words.
They set fire to their implements,
to their spades [they set] fire,   65
their labor-baskets into the flames
they threw.
They held them [as torches]; they went
to the gate of the shrine of hero Enlil
It was night; at mid-watch   70
the house was surrounded; the god did not know.
It was night; at mid-watch
the Ekur was surrounded; Enlil did not know.

Enlil Is Awakened (I: 74–98)

Kalkal observed and was disturbed.
He slid the bolt and looked [outward].   75
Kalkal awakened [Nusku].
They listened to the noise of [the Igigi].
Nusku awakened [his] lord,
made [him] get out of bed.
"My lord, [your hou]se is surrounded;   80

battle has come up to your gate."
"Enlil, your [house is surroun]ded;
battle has come up to your gate."
Enlil had [his servant] come down into his dwelling.
Enlil opened his mouth   85
and said to his vizier Nusku,
"Nusku, lock your gate,
take your weapon, stand before me."
Nusku locked his gate,
Took his weapon and stood before Enlil   90
Nusku opened his mouth
and said to hero Enlil:
"My lord, these children are your own;
they are your sons; why are you afraid?
Enlil, these children are your own;   95
they are your sons; why are you afraid?
Send [the order]; let them bring Anu down [to earth];
Let them bring Enki into your presence."

Chief Gods Hold Council (I: 99–177)

He sent and they brought Anu down;
they brought Enki into his presence.   100
Anu, king of heaven, was seated.
The king of the Apsu, Enki, was in [attendance];
the great Anunnaki were seated.
Enlil arose . . .
Enlil opened his mouth   105
and said to the great [gods]:
"Against me [have they come]?
They have waged war . . .
Battle has come to my gate."   110
Anu opened his mouth
and said to hero Enlil,
"The matter of the Igigi—
has its reason been brought to you?
Let Nusku go out. . . ."   115

[116–17. These lines are too fragmentary for translation.]

Enlil opened his mouth
and said to [his vizier Nusku],
"Nusku, open [your gate],   120
take your weapon.
In the assembly [of all the gods]
bow down, stand up, (say to them):
'[Your father] Anu has sent me,
your counselor [hero Enlil],   125
your throne-bearer [Ninurta],

and your sheriff [Ennugi].
Who is the one [who instigated] battle?
Who is the one who [provoked] hostilities?
Who is the one [who started the] war?'"   130

[131–58. Most of these lines are either fragmentary or repetitious. It seems that Nusku goes to the rebel gods and repeats Enlil's words as he was instructed. Then, he returns to Enlil with their reply, which he repeats as follows:]

"Every [single one of us g]ods
has started the war.   160
We . . . in the workpits.
Excessive [labor] has killed us;
our wo[rk was heavy], much was the distress;
[and every] single one of us gods
has spoken . . . with Enlil."   165
Enlil [heard] these words
and his tears flowed.
Enlil [heard] these words;
he said [to] hero Anu,
"Noble one, with you in heaven   170
carry your authority, take your power.
With the Anunnaki seated before you,
call one god, let him be thrown to the netherworld."
Anu opened his mouth
and said to the gods, his brothers,   175
"Why are we accusing them?
Their work is heavy, much is their distress."

Nintu and Enki Plan Creation (I: 178–220)

[178–88. There is a small gap in the text here. In later versions of the story, Enki, rather than Anu, is speaking at this time. In those versions Enki reveals his plan for creating the human race. In this version he is probably speaking when the story resumes:]

"While [Nintu the birth-goddess] is present,
let the birth-goddess create the offspring,   190
let man bear the labor-basket of the gods."
They called the goddess and asked [her],
the midwife of the gods, wise Mami:
"You are the birth-goddess, creatress of man.
Create lullu-man, let him bear the yoke.   195
Let him bear the yoke, the work of Enlil;
let man carry the labor-basket of the gods."
Nintu opened her mouth
and said to the great gods,
"It is not properly mine to do these things.   200

This work belongs to Enki.
He is the one who purifies all;
let him give me the clay, and I will do [it]."
Enki opened his mouth
and said to the great gods;   205
"At the new moon, the seventh day, and the full moon,
I will set up a purifying bath.
Let them slaughter one god.
Let the gods be purified by immersion.
With his flesh and blood   210
let Nintu mix the clay.
God and man—
let them be inseparably mixed in the clay;
till the end of time let us hear the 'drum.'
Let there be spirit from the god's flesh;   215
Let her proclaim 'alive' as its sign;
for the sake of never-forgetting, let there be spirit."
In the assembly, "Aye," answered
the great gods,
the administrators of destiny.   220

Human Race Is Created (I: 221–304)

At the new moon, the seventh day, and the full moon,
he set up a purifying bath.
We-ila, who had rationality,
they slaughtered in their assembly.
With his flesh and blood   225
Nintu mixed the clay.
Till the end [of days they heard the drum].
From the flesh of the god there was spirit.
She proclaimed "alive" as its sign.
For the sake of not-forgetting there was a spirit.   230
After she had mixed the clay,
she called the Anunnaki, the great gods.
The Igigi, the great gods,
cast their spittle on the clay.
Mami opened her mouth   235
and said to the great gods,
"You commanded me a task—
I have completed it.
You slaughtered a god together with his rationality.
I have removed your heavy labor,   240
have placed your labor-basket on man.
You raised a cry for mankind;
I have loosened your yoke, have [established] freedom."
They heard this speech of hers;
they ran around and kissed her feet.   245

"Formerly we called you 'Mami.'
Now, may 'Mistress of all the gods' be your [na]me."
They entered the house of destiny,
Prince Ea and wise Mami.   250
With the birth-goddesses assembled,
he trod the clay in her presence.
She recited the incantation again and again.
Ea, seated before her, prompted her.
When she finished her incantation,   255
she nipped off fourteen pieces of clay.
Seven pieces to the right,
seven to the left, she placed.
Between them she placed the brick.

[260–76. There is a gap in the text here. From an Assyrian version we learn
that fourteen birth-goddesses shape the clay. They make seven males and
seven females and align them in pairs.]

[The birth-g]oddesses were assembled;
Nintu was seated.
She counted the months.
At the destined [moment], they called the tenth month.   280
The tenth month came.
The end of the period opened the womb.
Her face was beaming, joyful.
Her head covered,
she performed the midwifery.   285
She girded her loins;
she made the blessing.
She patterned the flour and laid down the brick.
"I have created, my hands have done it.
Let the midwife rejoice in the prostitute's house;   290
where the pregnant woman gives birth,
the mother of the baby
severs herself.
Let the brick be laid down for nine days
that Nintu the midwife be honored.   295
Let them continually call Mami their . . .
Praise the birth-goddess, praise Kesh.
When the bed is laid . . .
let husband and wife lie together.
When for wifehood and husbandhood   300
they heed Ishtar in the house of the father-in-law,
let there be rejoicing for nine days;
let them call Ishtar Ishara.

[304–end. After a gap of approximately fifty lines, the story continues. Twelve
hundred years later, Enlil is trying to destroy the human race because it is

making too much noise. See the introduction to this chapter for a summary of this part of the poem.]

NOTES

Translator's note. This translation follows the edition of the *Atrahasis* epic by W. G. Lambert and A. R. Millard, *Atrahasis: The Babylonian Story of the Flood* (Oxford: Clarendon Press, 1969) and uses the line numbers of that edition. The only significant differences between my translation and theirs are in the section relating to the creation of man, lines 204–230, but there are various lesser differences, and the reader might want to compare the translations. This translation also incorporates several unpublished suggestions by the late J. J. Finkelstein although, of course, the responsibility for the translation is mine.

Note to the text. The passages included here are taken from the first tablet of a Babylonian version dated about 1700 B.C.E. Although many versions and copies exist, this copy is the most complete. Parts of the poem have been known to exist for over a hundred years, but it was not until 1969 that Lambert and Millard edited all the available versions in a bilingual edition. Lambert and Millard's edition also includes "The Sumerian Flood Story," edited by M. Civil. The text of this story is even more fragmentary than that of *Atrahasis*, but both apparently follow the same plot from the creation to the aftermath of the flood.

5. *The seven great Anunnaki.* Anunnaki and Igigi are frequently synonymous collective names for the gods. Here the seven great Anunnaki administer the destinies of all the gods; in other words, they fix and can change the status quo. Thus, they are the gods who impose the heavy work on the other gods.

16. *Enki the wise.* Enki is also named Ea (250) and is the same god who rules the fresh waters in *Enuma Elish.*

18. *To the apsu.* The *apsu* is Ea's home in the subterranean fresh waters. See *Enuma Elish* I: 73–78 for an explanation of the origin of the *apsu.*

73. *Ekur.* Ekur is the house of Enlil.

74. *Kalkal.* Kalkal is Enlil's doorkeeper.

119. *Vizier.* A vizier is an adviser and second in command.

189. *Nintu the birth-goddess.* Nintu is also called Mami (193) and Mistress of all the gods (248). Nintu probably played a larger role in an earlier version of the story.

195. *Lullu-man. Lullu,* a general word for humanity, apparently referred to human beings in the remote past. Here it may indicate human beings in their original state.

210–17. See *Enuma Elish* VI: 1–44, Genesis 2:7, and the Sumerian poem "Enki and Ninmah" for similar ideas about the materials used in the creation of the human race.

214. *Let us hear the "drum."* The drum may refer to a heartbeat here.

216. *Let her proclaim "alive" as its sign.* Although this line is difficult to interpret, it seems to mean that the spirit taken from the slain god is the distinguishing mark of human beings.

233. *We-ila, who had rationality.* The god We-ila is not mentioned elsewhere in Mesopotamian writings. His rationality is emphasized to indicate that it was the characteristic passed on to human beings. See also 239.

259. *Between them she placed the brick.* The brick was apparently a structure on which women would lie during labor. See also 288 and 294.

280. *They called the tenth month . . .* Since the Mesopotamians used a lunar calendar, the normal human gestation period would have been ten months.

2 / The Planting of Man: A Study in Biblical Imagery

1987

There are two distinct traditions about the creation of man in Sumerian literature. In one, man is created from clay, most probably an analogy to the work of potters and sculptors. This tradition is continued in Akkadian literature, where creation from clay becomes the dominant image of the origin of man, and, of course, in Israel, where creation from clay is the only story preserved of man's creation (Gen 2:6–7). In the other Sumerian tradition, man sprouts up from the earth like grass. This concept did not play a major role in Babylonian religion, possibly because it was associated with An and Enlil rather than with Enki.[1] It is, however, a powerful symbol of the nature of man and survived in biblical literature as a pervasive image of man, and more particularly of the people of Israel.

Creation from clay is certainly the most widespread and best known of the Mesopotamian motifs. The major Sumerian source for this idea is the myth of "Enki and Ninmah."[2] In this text, which describes the labor of the gods before the creation of man and their distress, Enki decides to make man and to bind onto him the corvée of the gods. He creates the Siensišar to assist in the birth[3] and tells his mother Ninsun, "After you knead the heart of the clay above the *apsu*, the Siensišar will nip off pieces of clay; after you have given it form . . . [the various mother and birth-goddesses] will assist in the giving of birth." This *abzu*-clay here called "clay above the *abzu*" and elsewhere "clay of the *abzu*"[4] is the material from which Ninmah later fashions her creatures in "Enki and Ninmah," and from which Enki fashions the turtle in "Enki and the Turtle" (UET VI:36). It is known in the later incantation literature as the material from which Enki made the craftsmen gods (R. Acc. 46:6) and from which ritual figurines are fashioned (CT 17 29:30–33). A more oblique reference to this concept is found in Enki's creation of the

19

kalatur and *kurgarra* from the dirt under Enki's fingernails in "Inanna's Descent"[5] and, similarly the creation of the *dimgi* and *saltu,* also from the dirt under Enki's nails.[6]

Babylonian literature contains numerous references to creation from clay.[7] In the creation of Enkidu in the *Gilgamesh* epic, a "special creation" paralleling the original creation of man, Aruru washes her hands, takes the clay and casts it onto the steppe (ii 37–38); in the *Babylonian Theodicy*, Zulummar nips off clay in the *abzu* and fashions man and lesser deities; and in a fire incantation, Ea nips off clay in the *apsu* and creates humankind (fire incantation no. 3 25–27).[8] Babylonian religion also introduces a new concept to Mesopotamia, the idea that man was created from the flesh and blood of a slaughtered god.[9] In the Babylonian *Atrahasis* epic the clay is mixed with the flesh and blood of We-ilu, a god who has rationality, so that man will have a spirit. In *Enuma Elish* the clay is not mentioned, and it appears that man is created entirely from the blood of Kingu. In KAR 4, a bilingual text which may be a scholastic composition (see below), the Anunnaki decide to slay Lamga gods and create humankind from their blood.

The imagery of creation from clay is twofold. In its simplest form the image used is that of potting and sculpting: "nipping off" the clay *(țițam karașu)*, moistening the clay (in *Atrahasis* the god spit on it, in *Gilgamesh* Aruru washes her hands, and in Genesis 2 the first step in the creation of man is the rising of the *ʾed* to moisten the earth), mixing or kneading the clay, and casting it (*Gilgamesh*). This craft imagery is also combined, in "Enki and Ninmah" and *Atrahasis*, with a sexual idea: birth goddesses, mother goddesses, and midwives are called to assist, and in *Atrahasis* the clay undergoes a gestation of nine months before man is "born." The two images are juxtaposed rather than harmonized, for both the creation of man which is analogous to the creation of a statue, and the birth of the first man which is like the births of all subsequent humans, are understood as parallel metaphors.

The second Sumerian tradition about man's creation also draws on a fundamental metaphor of human existence, the parallel between man and plants. This parallel is inherent in language, which speaks of the numun, *zeru, zeraʿ,* "seed" of mankind, and is ultimately related to the idea of "mother earth" and to the relationship between human sexuality and the earth's fertility which is so important to pagan religions. The female, like the earth, is "ploughed" by the "farmer" and "planted" with "seed."[10] The birth of man from woman is thus like the emerging of plants from the fructified earth. This is a profound human symbol, and the "vegetal" model for the creation of man is not confined to the ancient Near East.[11] Within the ancient Near East the image is well developed, and the picture emerges of man being "planted" in the ground.

The tradition of the sprouting of man appears in its simplest form in the introduction to the hymn to the E-Engur, the temple of Enki at Eridu:[12]

a-ri-a nam ba-tar-ra-ba
mu hé-gala₇ an ù-tu-da
ukù-e ù-šim-gim ki in-dar-ra-ba

when destinies had been established for all engendered things,
when An had engendered the year of abundance
when people had broken through the ground like plants.

From the other Sumerian source for this tradition, the "Creation of the Pickaxe" *(en-e ni-du₇-e)*, it is clear that this "sprouting" of man was not an accident, but was intended by the gods, in this case Enlil. The text brings us back to the beginning of finite time, and indicates that the motive force behind the separation of heaven and earth was precisely the creation of man:

^{d}En-líl numun-kalam-ma ki-ta e₁₁-dè
an ki-ta bad-du-dè sag na-an-ga-àm-mi-in-si
ki an-ta bad-du-dè sag na-an-ga-àm-mi-in-si
uzu-è sag mú-mú-dè
dur-an-ki-ka búru? nam-mi-in-lá

Enlil, in order to cause the seed of the land to arise from the earth,
Hastened to separate heaven from earth.
Hastened to separate earth from heaven
In order that the "flesh-producer" might produce the vanguard (of man)
He bound up the gash in Duranki ("the bond of heaven and earth")

The "flesh-producer," uzu-è, is probably the same place as "the place where flesh grew forth," the uzu-mú-a, a well-known sacred area of Nippur, "the bond of heaven and earth."[13] Here Enlil planted man, who thereupon grew out of the ground toward him (1.18–20):

uzu-è ^{giš} al-a sag-nu gá-gá-dè
sag nam-lú-u$_x$-lu ^{giš} ušub-ba mi-ni-gar
^{d}en-líl-šè kalam-ma-ni ki mu-ši-in-dar

Placing the "vanguard of man" in the "flesh-producer" with the pickaxe,
He placed the vanguard of mankind into the mold
Towards Enlil (the people) of his land sprouted up through the ground.

Despite the numerous minor difficulties in reading this passage, it is clear that man was placed (or planted) in the womb of the earth to emerge.

Perhaps because of the highly urbanized nature of Mesopotamian civilization, and possibly because the plant-image was associated with Enlil, this view of the creation of man did not have as much force in Babylonian religion as the clay metaphor. A reference is found in the Sumerian version of *mis pi* (CT III 36:20–21)[14] and in the bilingual KAR 4. As mentioned before, KAR 4 shows many earmarks of being a scholastic text: it concludes with an invocation to Nisaba, patron of scribes, and with a prescription that the wise should teach the mystery to the wise; it contains a lengthy (now fragmentary) description of the duties of man; and it has no dramatic impact. It would therefore probably be wrong to call this text a myth, but it contains many ancient mythic elements, and preserves both the idea that man was created from the blood of a slaughtered god (in this case the Lamga gods) and the idea that "skilled worker from skilled worker, unskilled worker from unskilled worker, they sprouted out of the earth like grain" (1.60–61). Unilingual Akkadian texts, however, do not preserve this image.

In Israel, on the other hand, the agricultural metaphor is very important. The only version preserved of the creation of man is creation from clay (Gen 2:6–7), but the vegetal image survives in numerous metaphors and similes, and in the concept of the Israel-plant. The idea of man as a plant is applied in Israel to the people, and the pervasive image of "plant-Israel" is an important metaphor to understand and express the history of the people.

Part of the plant-people imagery is embedded in the Hebrew language. The word *zeraʿ*, 'seed,' can also mean 'semen' and 'offspring,'[15] the word *perî*, 'fruit,' can also mean 'offspring,' both as *perî beṭen*, 'fruit of the womb,' and simply as *perî*, and many of the verbs used in agriculture, *pry, prḥ, ṣmḥ*, can mean literally 'bear fruit,' 'flower,' 'grow,' or be used in an extended sense to mean 'increase,' 'flourish', and 'grow.' Such parallels as ʿqr, 'to uproot,' and *ʿăqārā*, 'barren woman,' *yônēq*, 'nursling,' and *yônēqet/yônēq*,[16] 'sapling,' 'shoot,' 'tender plant,' are built into the language, and their use is not consciously metaphorical. In addition to these unconscious metaphors, many images from the plant world are consciously applied to mankind. Many of these rely on the fact that the agricultural world was an immediate referent in Israelite life, and the similes would therefore be immediately understood. Hebrew poetry makes abundant use of similes comparing men to various plants (particularly to grass and trees) and to parts of plants.

The tree, of course, is the image of long life: "for the days of my people will be like the days of the tree" (Isa 65:22) and its verdancy is like the virility of man. A eunuch might consider himself a "dry tree" (but should not, Isa 56:3), and Jeremiah's enemies plot against him: "let us destroy the tree in full sap,[17] cut him off from the land of the living, that his name be remembered no more" (Jer 11:19). Grass, on the other hand (*ʿēśeb* and *ḥāṣîr*), although abundant (for which see below) is noted for its fragility and impermanence. It is therefore a prime image for man who "grows like grass in the morning. In the morning it grows and flourishes, by evening it is cut down and dried" (Ps 90:5–6). This simile relies on two characteristics of grass, the ease with which it is cut, and the rapidity with which it can dry up. So too "evildoers will be cut down quickly like grass and wither like green herb" (Ps 37:1–2). The drying up of grass is likened to man's days and heart (Ps 102:5[4] and 12[11]) and those who abandon God are like reeds without water which dry up even before grass (Job 8:11–18). Unlike God's compassion (Ps 103:17), word (Isa 40:8), and power (Isa 51:12–13), man is impermanent and as vulnerable as grass and wildflowers before the wind (Ps 103:15–16):

> Man, his days are like grass,
>   his flowering like that of a wildflower.
> For a wind passes over it, and it is no more,
>   and one cannot find its place.

And the people is like grass in its vulnerability (Isa 40:6–8):

> A voice said "call" and I said "what shall I call?"
> All flesh is grass and all its (deeds of) compassion like wildflowers.
> Grass dies, wildflowers wither,
>   for the Lord's wind has blown on them:
>   just so the people is grass.
> Grass dries, wildflowers wither,
>   but the word of the Lord will stand forever.

So too the beauty of Ephraim, unable to withstand the tempest of God's wrath, is like that of wildflowers withering and blowing away in the wind (Isa 28:1–4). And all of us wither like a leaf blown away by the wind (Isa 64:5 [6]).

The only thing even more impermanent than grass is the grass which grows on roofs *(ḥāṣîr gaggôt)*, which does not even get a chance to grow fully and reach harvest before it dries up: just so will be those who hate Zion (Ps 129:6–7):

> Let them be like roof grass,
>   which dries up before it is fully grown
> that a reaper has not filled his hand with,
>   nor the sheave-binder his bosom.

and the inhabitants of the cities destroyed by Sennacherib are like grass and roof grass (2 Kgs 19:26 and Isa 37:27).

The tree similes rely on the fact that Israel is familiar with the world of nature. The characteristics of the differing trees are well known, and both simple metaphors and extended parables rely on this intimate knowledge of nature.[18] Ezekiel's parable of the "vine-tree" particularly suited for firewood and little else is used as the simile for the inhabitants of Jerusalem (Ezek 15:1–8). The parable of Jotham (Judg 9:7–15) and the parable of Jehoash (2 Kgs 14:9) both rely on the contrast between brambles (Judg 9:15, *ʾāṭād*) and thistles (2 Kgs 14:9, *ḥôᵃḥ*) and other trees, particularly the cedars of Lebanon. The cedar is noteworthy for its luxuriance, height, and strength, and Ezekiel tells an allegory of Assyria as a cedar which grew taller than any other tree, but was ultimately chopped down (Ezek 31). The height of the Amorite is compared to a cedar (Amos 2:9), the righteous are to flourish like the palm and the cedar (Ps 92:3), and the tents of Israel seem to Balaam like aloes planted by God, like cedars on the water (Num 24:26). Trees planted by water are the most fortunate, for they can withstand drought. The man who delights in God's law is like a tree planted by streams (Ps 1:3), as is the man who trusts in the Lord (Jer 17:7–8):

> Blessed is the man who trusts in the Lord,
>   and the Lord is his mainstay:
> For he is like a tree planted near water,
>   that sends its roots toward the stream,
>   that does not fear[19] the coming of heat,
>   for its leaves remain green.
> It does not worry in years of drought
>   and does not fail to bear fruit.

In contrast to the man who trusts in man, who is like a desert scrub that dwells in a salty uninhabited land (Jer 17:5–6). In addition to all these similes using natural aspects of trees, there are four passages in Proverbs that compare wisdom (Prov 3:18), the fruit of the righteous (Prov 11:30), desire (Prov 13:12), and wholesomeness of tongue (Prov 14:14) to the possible mythical "tree of life."

Man is a plant which comes from seed *(zera{c}),* grows, and bears fruit. The root of the man is therefore his foundation and his stability. The man, woman, family, or tribe who turns away from God is a "root bearing gall and wormwood" (Deut 29:17–18); "out of Ephraim came a root against Amalek" (Judg 5:14); "the root of the righteous bear" (Prov 12:12); and the fortunate man (Job in happier times) has his "root opened towards the waters" (Job 29:19). Although Jeremiah complains "you planted them (the wicked) and they took root, they went and bore fruit" (Jer 12:2), in the future the adversaries will not take root (Isa 40:24):

> they (the princes and rulers of the world) will not be planted,
> will not be sown. Their stock will not take root in the earth,
> and he will blow on them and they will dry up and the storm
> will carry them away like straw.

They will not be left "root or branch" (Mal 3:18 [4:1], the evildoers); they will be uprooted (Ps 52:7, Doeg the Edomite; Jer 12:14–15, the evil neighbors of Israel); their roots will become rotten (Isa 5:24, those who call evil good); and the root will be killed (Isa 14:20, all Pelešet, and cf. the root of the Amorite destroyed, Amos 2:9). Israel's messianic hopes are also expressed with this metaphor, for the future king will be "a branch from the stem of Jesse, a stalk from his roots" (Isa 11:1) and the root of Jesse will be an ensign to the nations (Isa 1:10). God will raise up for David a righteous sprout *(semah)* who will rule and be called "the Lord is our victory" (Jer 23:5–6 and 33:15–16), and the one who will rebuild the temple will be called "sprout" (Zech 6:12). Similarly, the "servant of God" will be "like a 'shoot/sapling'[20] before him, like a root from dry ground" (Isa 53:2).

Above all, it is Israel which is compared to a plant, and the plant image becomes a very important way in which Israel expresses its history, the way that God tended it, planted it, will destroy it, and will then replant it. Israel is a leafy olive tree destroyed by lightning (Jer 11:16):

> leafy olive tree,
> beautiful, lovely to behold—

so did the Lord name you.
With a tumultuous noise he sets fire to its leaves[21]
and its branches are shattered.

The classic image of Israel is that of a vineyard (the land) and a vine (the people). The vineyard is noteworthy for the care given it, the choicest grapes planted there, its indifferent yield, and the ease of its destruction. This vineyard image may have originated with Isaiah, who gives it in its most complete form in "the song of my lover about his vineyard" (Isa 5:1–7). In this song God

had a vineyard in a fruitful corner.
He fenced it and removed its stones
and planted it with choice grapes (*śôrèq*)
built a tower in its midst, and also made a winepress in it
and he expected it to make grapes, but it made wild grapes. (Isa 5:1–2)

And this song also seems to be the source for Jeremiah's similar statement of frustrated expectations, "I planted you with choice grapes (*śôrèq*) all true seed; how did you become foul for me, a strange wild vine"[22] (Jer 2:21). The result of the improper yield of the vineyard is its destruction (Isa 5:5–6):

And now I will tell you what I will do to my vineyard;
I will take away its hedge—and it will be for destruction,
break its fence—and it will be for trampling.
And I will lay it waste: it shall not be pruned, or dug,
and there will come up briars and thorns
and I will command the clouds not to rain on it.

The vineyard is an important image in Isaiah and Jeremiah. The vineyard has been corrupted and destroyed by its elders and rulers (Isa 3:14) and is therefore destroyed. The remnant of Israel is gleaned like grapes are plucked (Jer 6:9) and many shepherds devastate it and trample it underfoot (Jer 12:10). In the future, however, God will again plant and tend his vineyard and it will be called a "vineyard of red wine" (Isa 27:2–4).[23]

"The vineyard of the Lord of Hosts is the house of Israel, and the man of Judah is his delightful plant" (Isa 5:7), and the image of the vine can describe an Israel without its land. The grapes existed before they were brought into the land, for God "found Israel like grapes in the desert" (Hos 9:10). The allegory of the "vine out of Egypt" (Ps 80:9–16 [8–15]) describes the process (Ps 80:9–11 [8–10]):

you brought a vine out of Egypt,
you chased out the nations and planted it.
You made room before it, and it took deep root and
filled the land.
The hills were covered with its shade,
and its branches were mighty cedars.
It sent its boughs to the seas and its shoots to the river.

The vine, however, turned into an "empty vine"[24] (Hos 10:1), and the root must therefore dry up (Hos 10:16). The destruction of Israel is depicted as the plucking of the vine in "the vine out of Egypt" (Ps 80:12–13) and in Ezekiel's allegory of the "mother vine" (Ezek 19:10–14). In this poem Israel is conceived as a vine "planted by water, fruitful and branching from the many waters" (Ezek 19:10), but in Ezekial 19:12):[25]

she was plucked in fury and cast to the ground
and the east wind dried its fruit
and her strong limb was broken and dried up,
fire consumed it.

The vine/vineyard imagery can depict many aspects of God's relationship with Israel because it can express the conscious planting, the constant care required, the frustration, the fragility of vineyards, and the ease of their destruction. The idea of an Israel planted by God, however, is not confined to these vineyard/vine allegories, but is rather a very ancient image. Israel's entry into its land is depicted as its "planting" in the "Song of the Sea" (Exod 15), "you brought him and planted him in your 'heritage mountain'" (Exod 15:17); and in Psalms 44:3, "you, your hand drove out the nations and you planted them [Israel]."[26] The destruction of the plant is an important metaphor for the destruction of the people. Israel, found like grapes in the wilderness (Hos 9:10), is smitten, its roots dried up, unable to bear fruit (Hos 9:16). The "Israel-plant" withers, or is uprooted. The image of the "withering" *(nbl)* of the people is Isaian: "for you will be like an oak whose leaves wither and a garden which has no water" (Isa 1:30); "Its [Ephraim's] crown of glory which is on the fruitful valley will be like a withering wildflower" (Isa 28:1); "the land will be emptied, the land will be despoiled, the land will wither . . ." (Isa 24:3–4); "grass dries up and wildflowers wither for the Lord's wind blows on them, just so is the nation grass" (Isa 40:7–8). Uprooting *(ntš)*, on the other hand, seems to be primarily Deuteronomic. Thus in Deuteronomy 29:27, at the covenant in the plains of Moab, the people are told that if they go and worship other gods they will be destroyed, and the nations will be told that "the Lord uprooted them from their land in anger and wrath and great fury and sent them to another land as this day." In 1 Kings 14:15 Ahijah tells Jeroboam "the Lord will smite Israel as a reed moves in the water, and he will uproot Israel from his good land which he gave to your fathers, and will scatter them across the river, because they made the Asherahs which anger the Lord." Jeremiah relates the Lord's word to Baruch (Jer 45:4): "behold that which I have built I am destroying and that which I have planted I am uprooting, for the whole land is mine."[27] And in 2 Chronicles 7:20 Solomon is told that if the Davidic rulers forsake God's commandments, then "I will uproot them [Israel] from my land which I have given to them, and this house which I have sanctified for my name I will cast away from me, and will make it a proverb and byword among all the nations." The concept of uprooting can be extended to other nations, and Jeremiah delivers this message to Israel's enemy neighbors (Jer 12:14–16):

> Behold I am going to uproot them from their land, and root out the house of Judah from their midst. And after I have uprooted them I will once more have compassion on them and return them each to his possession and each to his land. And if they will learn the ways of my people to swear by my name, "by the life of the Lord" (as they taught my people to swear by Baal), then they will be built up in the midst of my people. And if they will not listen, then I will uproot that nation, uproot it and destroyed it.

The plant image is particularly important to describe God's actions at the restoration. As the destruction was an uprooting and a razing, the restoration is a planting and a building (Jer 31:27). This concept is already found in Hosea, "and I will sow her for myself in the land, and I will have compassion on 'not mercied' and I will say to 'not my people,' 'my people' and he will say 'my God'" (Hos 2:25); and in Amos 9:15 (if the passage is original), "and I will plant them on their land and they shall no more be uprooted from their land which I gave to them." Jeremiah is particularly fond of the replanting image (and of the uprooting image), and he sees the restoration as the time when "I will sow (*zrʿ*) the house of Israel and the house of Judah with the seed of man and the seed of beast" (Jer 31:26) and when "I will rejoice over them to do good for them, and I will plant them in this land in truth, with all my heart and with all my soul" (Jer 32:41). Furthermore, to Jeremiah this new planting of Israel (unlike the original planting) will not be uprooted: "I will watch over them benevolently and return them to this land, and I will build them and will not destroy, will plant them and not uproot" (Jer 24:6; so too Jer 42:10 and cf. Jer 31:39 for the non-uprooting of new Jerusalem). Isaiah expresses the idea that the replanted Israel will take root: "And the remnant which remains from the house of Judah will take root below and bear fruit above" (Isa 37:31; cf. 2 Kgs 19:30), "Jacob will take root, Israel will flower and bud, and they will fill the world with fruit" (Isa 27:6). In the eschaton envisioned by Deutero-Isaiah, the people will all be righteous, inherit the land forever, and be the "branch of my planting, the work of my hands to glory in" (Isa 60:21) and "righteous oaks, the plant of God to glory in" (Isa 61:3). This idea of "replanted Israel" is not an empty or fossilized metaphor, moreover, and the agricultural image can be extended to express watering and growth (Hos 14:6–8):

> I will be as dew to Israel and it will flourish like a crocus
>   and cast forth its roots as Lebanon.
> Its branches will spread and its beauty will be like an olive,
>   and it will have a scent like Lebanon.

One of the important aspects of the restoration of Israel is the multiplication of the people, the resettlement of the land with abundant population (e.g., Exod 36:10–11). This hope may be expressed by comparing the people to grass, a recognized simile for abundance. In Psalms 92:8 it is the wicked who flourish like grass, in Psalms 72:16 those of the city will flourish like grass at the time of the righteous king's son; in Job 5:25 Job is told "your seed will be numerous and your offspring like the grass of the earth." In Ezekial 16:7 Jerusalem is told "I made you abundant like the plants of the field, and you grew many and great." In Isaiah 43:3–4 this image is applied to the restored Israel:

> I will pour water on the thirsty and liquid on dry ground.
> I will pour my spirit on your seed, and my blessings on your offspring,
>   and they shall sprout up as among grass, as willows by waterways.

It is in this context that the somewhat problematical verses of Hosea 2:1–2 (1:10–11) become clear:

> And the number of the children of Israel will be like the sands of the sea which cannot be measured and cannot be counted, and instead of it being said to them "not my people" it will be said to them "children of the living god." And the children of Judah and the children of Israel will gather together and appoint themselves a head and "come up from the earth," for great will be the day of Jezreel.

The problem with his passage is the somewhat ambiguous phrase *veˀala min ha-areṣ* which might conceivably be translated "go up from the land" or "come up from the ground." "Go up from the land" does not seem to fit the context, for the children of Israel and Judah are coming back to, rather than leaving the land, nor does it seem necessary to emend the passage.[28] The phrase also appears in Exodus 1:20: "let us outsmart him lest he multiply, and if there should be a war he will join our enemies and fight us *wᵉʿālāʰ min hāˀāreṣ*." The traditional translation "and so get them out of the land" does not make sense, for Pharaoh's worry is not that they should leave, but that they should be numerous and then join the enemies. The new Jewish Publication Society translation "gain ascendancy over the land" makes much better sense, but is philologically difficult.[29] The meaning of the phrase is clear from the context in Hosea 2 which, as shown by Cassuto, is a coherent poem with A-Z, B-Y parallelism.[30] Our lines are thus thematically parallel to Hosea 2:24–25:

> And the land will answer the grain and the corn and the oil,
>   and they will answer Jezreel.
> And I will sow her for me in the land
>   and will have compassion on "not pitied"
> and I will say to "not my people" "my people"
>   and he will say "my god."

The poem begins and ends with a reference to Lo-Ammi ("not my people"), to Jezreel, and to the planting of man. Jezreel itself is a triple entendre: as palace of Ahab and site of the disaster, the name also means "God sows" and the passage indicates that God will sow the people. Thus in vv. 1–2 the people are going to be very numerous, reunite, choose a ruler, and "rise up from the earth" because "great is the day of 'god sows.'"[31] Seen in this context it is clear that the phrase "rise up from the earth," like the phrase "sprout up as among grass" in Isaiah 44:4, is an image of man emerging from the ground, with the implication of the numbers of man. So too in Exodus, the sense of the passage is that Israel, being so numerous, may join the enemies—and he is "popping up all over the place" (to use a somewhat equivalent English idiom).[32] The phrase "rise up from the earth" is thus a continuation of the ancient image, attested in Sumerian literature and so productive in Israelite poetry, of man arising like grass from the earth.

NOTES

1. The relationship between Enlil and Enki is very complex. Much of the mythology known from Babylon is associated with Enki in the Sumerian sources, although in one instance (the *Atrahasis* epic) the role played by Enki in the Sumerian is played by Enlil in the Akkadian. The reason for the greater impact of Enki-stories is not fully known. It may have something to do with the role Enlil (i.e., Nippur and its priests) played in the destruction of Sumer. Another possibility, suggested by van Dijk, is that when the Babylonian dynasties could not gain the approval of the Nippur priesthood, they transferred supremacy to the Eridu cult (van Dijk, "Les contacts éthniques dans la Mésopotamie et les syncretismes de la religion Sumérienne," in *Symposium on Cultural Contact, Meeting of Religions, Syncretism Turku, Finland 1966* [ed. Sven Hartman; Stockholm 1969]: 187; and "L'Hymne à Marduk avec intercession pour le roi Abiᵖesuh," MIO 12 [1966]: 57–74).

2. The myth "Enki and Ninmah" has not yet been adequately edited. A preliminary edition was prepared by Carlos Alfredo Benito, "Enki and Ninmah" and "Enki and the World Order" (Ph.D. diss., University of Pennsylvania, 1969). For texts and studies see the entry in Borger, *Handbuch der Keilschriftliteratur*, p. 155, under TCL XVI 71.

3. The word si₇-en-si-šár is unknown in Sumerian. It is parallel to the *šass-uru* (birthgiver) of the *Atrahasis* epic and possibly related to it.

4. For a discussion of the clay of the *abzu* and its role in Sumerian sources, see Margarte Green, "Eridu in Sumerian Literature" (Ph.D. diss., University of Chicago, 1975): 169–74.

5. In the edition by William Sladek, "Innana's Descent to the Nether World" (Ph.D. diss., Johns Hopkins University, 1974), this is 1.219f. See also 1.219–20 in Kramer's earlier and less complete edition in JCS 5.

6. See Green, *Eridu* (note 4 above): 174 for the references.

7. For citation and discussion of some of these passages, see Giovanni Pettinato, *Das altorientalische Menschenbild und die sumerischen und akkadischen Schöpfungsmythen* (*Abhandlungen der Heidelberger Akademie der Wissenschaften;* Heidelberg, 1971): 41–42.

8. Published by W. G. Lambert, "Fire Incantations," AfO 23 (1975): 39–45.

9. Creation from blood does not exist in Sumerian. Lambert has suggested that Enki mixed clay with his own blood in "Enki and Ninmah" (Lambert, "Creation of Man in Sumero-Babylonian Myth," CRRAI XI [1964]: 102). This rests on an erroneous translation of *mud mu-gar-ra-zu,* which should better be understood as "the creature you are creating/have created." Because of the nonexistence of this idea in Sumerian, and the mystic importance of blood in Israel, I have suggested elsewhere that perhaps this motif was introduced into Mesopotamia by the West Semites (Tikva Frymer-Kensky, "The

Atrahasis epic and Its Significance for Our Understanding of Genesis 1–9," BA 40 [1977]: 154).

10. One famous example is Rib Addi's letter EA 74:17 A. ŠÀ-*ia aššata ša la muta mašil aššum bali errèši,* "my field is like a wife without a husband because it is without a tiller": and similarly in other letters of Rib Addi. The relevant material has been collected by Marvin Pope, *Song of Songs* (AB 7c; Garden City, N.J.: 1977): 323–26.

11. Many cosmological perceptions are found throughout the ancient Near East (in its broadest sense) and should be considered part of a general religious heritage. This is true also of the idea of man growing as a plant. In Greek mythology we have the story of Jason's sowing of the dragon's teeth and the warriors who then arose. Persia also preserves a similar idea in the story of the first pair, Măsya and Mašyanag, who grew from a rhubarb plant which itself had sprung from the seed of Gayomard, the ancestor of man (*Greater Bundahišn* XIV 5–10; for discussion see Mary Boyce, *A History of Zoroastrianism: Vol. I, The Early Period* [*Handbuch der Orientalistik,* 1975]: 96–97 and 140). The concept is not confined to the Near East, however, and is referred to by Levi-Strauss as the *authochthonous origin* of mankind (C. Levi-Strauss, "The Structural Study of Myth," *Journal of American Folklore* [1955]: 428–44; reprinted in *The Structuralists: From Marx to Levi-Strauss* [Richard and Fernande de George, eds.; 1972]: 169–94; for authochthonous origin see p. 179). As can be seen from "the pickaxe," however, in Sumer the origin of man was premeditated rather than authochthonous.

12. This tradition was originally elucidated by Jacobsen, "Sumerian Mythology: A Review Article," JNES 5, 135 and n. 4. It was analyzed by van Dijk, "Le motif cosmique dans la pensée sumérienne," *Act. Or.* 28: 23–24, who named it creation by "emersion." For these passages see also Pettinato (note 7 above): 30–32.

13. So Jacobsen (note 12 above): 137. The alternative is to understand the term *uzu-è* as the "flesh-producer," i.e., Enlil (so van Dijk [notes 1, 12 above]: 24).

14. Quoted by Pettinato (note 7 above): 32.

15. The relevant passages have been catalogued by Abraham Even-Shoshan, *A New Concordance of the Bible,* vol. 1, p. 340.

16. The word for "sapling, shoot" is usually *yôneqet,* generally found in the plural *yônᵉqôt.* However, the parallelism of *yônēk //šōreš* in Isa 53:2 indicates the *yonēq* could also bear the sense of "shoot, sapling," or at least that Isaiah was consciously playing on the connection between *yônēk,* "nursling," and *yôneqet,* "sapling, shoot."

17. Reading *bilehi-ma,* "in (his) sap" or *bilehimō,* "in his sap" with possessive suffix following the enclitic *mem.* This last is chosen by Bright, *Jeremiah* 9ab 21 (Garden City, 1965): 84, following M. Dahood, *Gregorianum* 43, 66. The translation "in full sap" is Bright's.

18. I have omitted the many similes used in the Song of Songs. Considering the idyllic nature of the book, we would expect numerous nature similes even if they were not prevalent elsewhere in the Bible.

19. Reading *yirā'* with the *kᵉtib* and LXX. The *yir'eʰ* of the *qᵉre* is influenced by v. 6. See also Bright, *Jeremiah* (note 17 above): 115.

20. See note 16 above.

21. For the reading (*bᵉ*)*ᶜălêhû* "(to) its leaves" rather than *ᶜălêhă*, "to her" (with masculine referent) see Bright, *Jeremiah* (note 17 above): 82–83, n.e.e.

22. Reading *lī sōriyyah gepen nōkriyah*. Bright, *Jeremiah* (note 17 above): 11 reads *lᵉ soriyyah*, "what a foul-smelling thing you've become."

23. For comments on this passage and God as vintner see Pope, *Song of Songs* (note 10 above): 326.

24. Taking *bôqĕq* in the well-known sense of "be empty." The attempt of BDB (p. 132) to attribute this verse to another *bôqĕq* meaning "luxuriant" seems futile, for this other *bôqĕq* exists only in Arabic, and is otherwise unattested in the Bible.

25. Eichrodt takes the mother-vine to refer literally to Hamutal, the mother of the king (*Ezekiel*, Old Testament Library, p. 257). However, this interpretation means that he has to take vv. 13–14a "and now she is planted in the desert in a dry and thirsty land. And a fire has gone out from a limb of her branches and devoured her fruit, and she has no strong rod, a scepter to rule" as later additions. Eichrodt also believes that this spells the end of the Davidic dynasty, since no one can expect a vine that has been so brutally treated to grow again after being replanted. If we realize that the vine is Israel, however, vv. 13–14 fit integrally into the passage referring to exile. Moreover, the idea of replanting fits all the other passages which refer to the replanting of luxurious regrowth of the Israel-plant. Ezekiel uses similar imagery in his "parable of the vine and the eagles" (Ezek 17). The great eagle (Nebuchadnezzar/God) took a high branch of the cedar and set it in a city of merchants (Babylon/the Land of Canaan, v. 4), took seed of the land and put it into field and it grew and became a spreading vine (17:6). The vine then bent its roots toward another eagle (Egypt/Baal) that it might water it, and therefore God decrees that the vine should wither. The passage has immediate political import and is explained in vv. 11–18 as referring to the alliance made by Nebuchadnezzar with the seed of kingship which he brought to Babylon, but which then looked toward Egypt. However in v. 19 Ezekiel shifts gears from talking about breaking the covenant with Babylon to breaking Israel's covenant with God, and he continues with a promise of restoration (22–24) in which God will take the highest branch of the cedar and plant it on a high mountain of Israel, and it will grow and bear fruit. It seems likely that Ezekiel intends that his parable be read on two levels, and that this is what he means when he calls it a "riddle parable" (17:1). In both these passages in Ezekiel it is clear that he is alluding to the classic vine/vineyard image.

26. By comparison of this verse with the similar verse in Ps 80:9 it is clear that the referent "them" is to Israel rather than the nations.

27. Bright, following LXX, omits the phrase w^e ʾ*et kol há* ʾ*āreṣ lî hîʾ*, believing it to mean "that is, the whole land" and to be therefore a superfluous gloss (Bright, *Jeremiah* [note 17 above]: 184). However, the phrase is really a justification of God's destruction of the land (for, after all, the whole land is his), and perhaps a reassurance to Baruch that God will after all not abandon his land.

28. For a review of some of the suggested emendations (and rejections of them) see Cassuto, "The Prophet Hosea and the Books of the Pentateuch," 1933; rpt. in *Biblical and Oriental Studies*, p. 87 and Wilhelm Rudolph, *Hosea, Kommentar zum alten Testament*, p. 57.

20. For the justification of this translation see Orlinsky, *Notes on the New Translation*, p. 19. Childs, however, rejects this new translation as philologically weak (Brevard Childs, *Exodus*, Old Testament Library, p. 5).

30. Cassuto, "The Second Chapter of the Book of Hosea," 1927; rpt. in *Biblical and Oriental Studies*, 101–3. Cassuto, however, does not realize the implication of our phrase because of his feeling, expressed elsewhere ("The Prophet Hosea" [note 28 above]: 87), that the phrase is intended to remind the audience of the Exodus story, and that it means "come up from Egypt" and therefore "come back from Exile."

31. The play on Jezreel was noted already by Rudolph, *Hosea* (note 28 above): 58, who translates "und sie werden aus dem Boden wachsen." This translation was noted but not accepted by Mays, *Hosea*, Old Testament Library, p. 33, but perhaps the material in this article will give ample background to these verses and make this translation more assured.

32. The concentration on numbers is a prominent feature in the story of Balak and his fear of Israel, a clear parallel to the story in Exodus. In Num 22:5 and 11, the parallel phrase to w^e ʿ*alāʰ min hāʾāreṣ* is *kissāʰ / wayʿkas* ʾ*et* ʿ*ēn hāʾāreṣ*, "covered the face of the ground," again an idiom for sheer numbers.

Flood Myths

3 / Israel and the Ancient Near East: New Perspectives on the Flood

1979

The publication of a Babylonian flood story (*Gilgamesh* tablet XI) in 1872 and of a creation story (*Enuma Elish*) several years later made it inevitable that attempts would be made to analyze the biblical tradition in the light of the new material coming from Babylon. The Bible could not be studied in isolation once material became available from the surrounding cultures with unmistakable similarities to biblical motifs and biblical stories. The initial discoveries therefore immediately focused the attention of biblical scholarship on these comparisons, and led to the great "Bible and Babel" debate begun by Friedrich Delitzsch. Delitzsch published three lectures on this topic in which he claimed that everything valuable in the Bible was derived from Babylon. His motivation seems to have been more theological than scholarly, and reaction to his ideas was prompt and severe.[1]

The emotional upheaval caused by the discoveries from Babylon has long since subsided. However, the ongoing Assyriological investigations continue to be a focus for biblical studies which provide new illumination of key biblical ideas and concepts. The approach of most biblicist-Assyriologists today is to assume an organic connection between the Babylonian and biblical material and to attempt to use the Near Eastern texts as a key to providing new insights into the meaning of the Bible. Today I wish to call your attention to this type of approach by studying a topic that has become a classic for this kind of comparison, the case of the flood. I will review the material that I have already published in biblical journals ("The *Atrahasis* epic and Its Significance for Our Understanding of Genesis 1–9," *Biblical Archeologist* 40 (1977): 147–55; "What the Babylonian Flood Stories Can and Cannot Teach Us about the Genesis Flood," *Biblical Archaeology Review* IV (1978):32–41) and then go beyond it to indicate some of the new avenues for investigation suggested by this study.

The Babylonian flood stories have been compared to Genesis since the publication of *Gilgamesh* tablet XI. Details in these stories such as the placing of animals in the ark, the landing of the ark on a mountain, and the episode of the birds indicate the intimate relationship of these stories to Genesis and suggest that the Babylonian and biblical stories are different retellings of an essentially identical flood tradition. The usefulness of these tales toward improving our understanding of Genesis was nevertheless limited until the recent recovery of the *Atrahasis* epic. The Sumerian flood story has survived in a very fragmentary state, and can only be understood with the aid of the other known flood stories.[2] The *Gilgamesh* version is far more complete and is most similar in details to the biblical account, but is presented in a radically different context from Genesis, and the difference in context has caused differences in content in the stories, and in addition has been the cause of many spurious comparisons and distortions in modern scholarship. In the *Gilgamesh* epic an obviously ancient story is told to *Gilgamesh* as part of the tale of *Gilgamesh's* quest for immortality. Utnapishtim, the survivor of the flood, tells his descendant *Gilgamesh* the story of the flood in order to tell him why he became immortal, and at the same time convince him that he cannot become immortal in the same way. The flood narrative is introduced by *Gilgamesh's* question, "As I look upon you, Utnapishtim, your features are not strange, you are just as I . . . how did you join the Assembly of the Gods in your quest for life?" (*Gilgamesh* IE:2–7); the recitation is concluded by Utnapishtim's tale: he tells only those parts of the story that he knows, and he may leave out those aspects that do not concern him or fit his purpose. The reason that the gods decided to bring the flood is irrelevant to the personal story of Utnapishtim, and may never have been revealed to him. He therefore omits the cause of the flood in his recitation to *Gilgamesh*. Similarly, he tells nothing about the events after the flood except that there was a convocation of the gods that granted him immortality. The story is "personalized": it is restricted to the adventures of one individual, and the deluge is thereby emptied of all cosmic or anthropological significance. The *Gilgamesh* tale of the flood has as a result a very different tone from the flood story in Genesis. The difference in tone, however, is not a result of different literary, ethical, or religious conceptions, but is a direct result of the difference in literary format. One cannot compare the ideas in the two versions of the flood without setting up spurious dichotomies, and many comparative studies on the topic have suffered from such misguided apprehensions.

Unlike *Gilgamesh*, the *Atrahasis* epic presents the flood story in a context comparable to that of Genesis. The flood episode of this epic has been known for a long time, but the literary structure of the epic, and therefore the context of the flood story, was first reconstructed by J. Laessøe in 1956.[3] In 1965 Lambert and Millard published many additional texts from the epic, including an Old Babylonian copy (written around 1650 B.C.E.) which is our most complete surviving recension.[4] These new texts served as the foundation for the edition of the epic by Lambert and Millard,[5] which has made the story accessible to non-Assyriologists.

Like Genesis 1–11, the *Atrahasis* epic is a primeval history. It begins with a depiction of the world as it existed before man was created: "when the gods worked like man." The universe was divided among the great gods. Seven gods (called the Anunnaki in this text) established themselves as the ruling class, while the rest of the gods provided the workforce. After digging the Tigris and Euphrates rivers these gods rebelled and refused to work. The gods were thereby in a quandary: the work had to be done, and there was no one to do it. On the advice of Enki, the wisest of the gods, they decided to create a substitute to do the work of the gods. Enki and the mother goddess then created a substitute from clay and the flesh and blood of a slain god, "We-ilu, a god who has sense." This substitute is man. The author of *Atrahasis* has used ancient themes and motifs[6] and united them into a coherent account of man's beginnings in which he presents a picture of man's *raison d'être* as doing the work of the gods and relieving them of the need to labor.

Even though the creation of man solves the problem of a workforce, it creates new problems. In the words of the epic (I 352f, restored from tablet II 1–8):

Twelve hundred years [had not yet passed]
[when the land extended] and the peoples multiplied.
The [land] was bellowing [like a bull].
The gods were disturbed with [their uproar].
[Enlil heard] their noise
[and addressed] the great gods.
"The noise of mankind [has become too intense for me]
[with their uproar] I am deprived of sleep.

The gods decide to bring a plague to solve this problem. The plague ends when Enki advises man to bring offerings to Namtar, the god of the plague, and thereby induce him to lift the plague. Twelve hundred years later the same problem arises again (tablet II 1–8) and the gods bring a drought, which ends when men (upon Enki's advice) bribe Adad to bring rain. Tablet II is unfortunately fragmentary, but it is clear that the gods bring famine and saline soil, but these measures also do not resolve the problem. At last Enlil persuades the gods to adopt a "final solution" (tablet II viii 34) to the human question, and they decide to bring a flood to destroy mankind. This plan is thwarted by Enki, who has *Atrahasis* build an ark and thus escape. After the flood, after the gods have had occasion to regret their actions and to realize (by their thirst and hunger) that they need man, *Atrahasis* brings a sacrifice and the gods come to eat. Enki then presents a permanent solution to the problem. The new world after the flood is to be different from the old. Enki summons Nintu, the birth goddess, and has her create new creatures, who will ensure that the old problem does not arise again. In the words of the epic (tablet III vii 1):

> In addition, let here be a third category among the peoples
> among the peoples women who bear and women who do not bear.
> Let there be among the peoples the Pašittu-demon
> to snatch the baby from the lap of her who bore it.
> Establish Ugbabtu-women, Entu-women and Igiṣitu-women
> and let them be taboo and so stop childbirth.

Other post-flood provisions may have followed, but the text now becomes too fragmentary to read.

The structure of the *Atrahasis* epic is clear: the creation of man is followed by problems; attempted remedies fail and the decision is made to destroy man; one man is saved and a new remedy is then instituted to ensure that the problem does not arise again. Several years ago, Anne Kilmer and William J. Moran, working independently, demonstrated that the problem that necessitated these remedies in *Atrahasis* was that of overpopulation.[7] The methods of population control that were first attempted (drought, pestilence, famine) only abated man's increase temporarily, and the overpopulation of the world led to destruction (the flood) until permanent countermeasures were introduced by Enki to keep the size of the population down. *Atrahasis* tells us that such social phenomena as nonmarrying women, and such personal tragedies as barrenness and stillbirth (and perhaps miscarriage and infant mortality) have the vital function of keeping the population in control and thereby helping to ensure the continuation of man's existence.

Like the Babylonians, we have a consciousness of a limited ecology and an appreciation of the need to control human population. The Babylonian tale, composed no later than 1700 B.C.E., therefore seems very relevant to us today and can almost be called a "myth for our times." This however, is not true of biblical Israel. Israel did not share the modern belief, nor the belief of *Atrahasis* and some other ancient texts, that overpopulation was a serious issue. Israel's world was different, and it may be that the different viewpoint of Israel resulted from different ecological conditions, that Israel (unlike the Babylonians) considered underpopulation the more immediate threat.[5] Whatever the cause, there is no hint of concern for overpopulation. Barrenness and stillbirth (or miscarriage) are not considered social necessities and are not justified as important for population control. On the contrary, when God promises the land to Israel he promises that "in your land women will neither miscarry nor be barren," לא תהיה משכלה ועקרה בארצך (Exodus 23:26). The continuation of this verse, "I will fill the number of your days," את מספר ימיך אמלא, seems to be a repudiation of yet another of the "natural" methods of population control, that of premature death. In the ideal world which is to be established in the land of Israel there will be no need for such methods, for overpopulation is not a concern. Israel's different perspective is reflected in the flood story, for the version in Genesis is emphatically not about overpopulation. On the contrary, God's first command to Noah and his sons after the flood was "be fruitful and multiply and fill the earth," פרו ורבו ומלאו את הארץ (Genesis 9:1). This echoes the original command to Adam (Genesis 1:28) and is a rejection of the idea that the flood was brought as a result of attempts to decrease man's population. The repetition of this command in emphatic terms in Genesis 9:7, "and you be fruitful and multiply, swarm over the earth and multiply in it," ואתם פרו ורבו שרצו בארץ, makes it probable that this rejection was conscious, that the Bible was explicitly rejecting a central thesis of the *Atrahasis* epic, the idea that the fertility of man before the flood was the reason for his near destruction.

Despite this great difference between the *Atrahasis* epic and the story in Genesis, the *Atrahasis* epic has a crucial importance for biblical studies, for it reveals the structure of a primeval history and thereby focuses our attention away from the flood itself and onto the events immediately subsequent to it. It thus clarifies the reason for the flood. Genesis states that God decided to destroy the world because of the wickedness of man

(Genesis 6:5), וירא אלהים כי רבה רעת האדם בארץ. Although this has been understood to mean that God brought the flood as a punishment, such an understanding of the passage entails serious theological problems, such as the propriety of God's destroying the world because of the sins of man.[9] Such an understanding also makes the text seem somewhat paradoxical, for the "wickedness of man" is also given as the reason that God later decides never again to bring a flood (Genesis 8:21).[10] Since the evil nature of man has not been changed by the flood, and is presented as the reason for God's vow never again to bring a flood, we should not infer that the flood was brought as a punishment for evil. The importance of the *Atrahasis* epic to biblical studies is that it demonstrates that (in Genesis as well as in *Atrahasis*) the flood was brought in response to a serious problem in creation, and that this problem was rectified after the waters subsided. The changes that God made in the world can indicate the reason that he brought the flood. What was so wrong with the world that necessitated the flood and almost brought an end to the history of man, and what is it about the world after the flood that prevents it from having to be destroyed?

The events immediately after the flood are found in Genesis 9. In this chapter God offers Noah and his sons a covenant in which he promises never again to bring a flood to destroy the world and gives the rainbow as the token of this promise. At this time God gives Noah and his sons laws, and the difference between the worlds before and after the flood can be found in these laws. They are the structural equivalent of Enki's provisions in the *Atrahasis* epic. In *Atrahasis* the problem was overpopulation and Enki's solutions were designed to limit man's population. In the Bible the problem was "since the devisings of man's heart are evil from his youth" (Genesis 8:21) and God must do something if he does not want to destroy the earth repeatedly. His solution is to create laws to ensure that matters do not again reach such a state that the world must be destroyed. Genesis has a rather Hobbesian view of mankind[11]: it perceives an inherently evil aspect of man's nature, one naturally prone to violent and unrighteous acts, and this entails the recognition that man cannot be allowed to live by his instincts alone, that he must be directed and controlled by laws. Laws are the *sine qua non* of human existence, and it is for this reason that God's first act after the flood is to grant laws.

There remains the problem of why a flood had to be brought before mankind could be given laws. In *Atrahasis* this presents no problem, because one god—Enlil—decided to bring the flood, while another god—Enki—saves man and then provides the new solutions. In the Bible, however, it is God alone who both brings the flood and then brings laws so that he will never again have to bring a flood. The flood cannot simply have been a "punishment," for if man has evil instincts, and these have not been checked and directed by laws, how can he be punished for simply following his instincts? The cause of the flood must lie in the particular nature of the evil which filled the world before the flood, and the laws given immediately after the flood are a good indication of the nature of this evil.

Rabbinic tradition developed and expanded the laws given to Noah and his sons into a somewhat elaborate system of "the seven Noahide commandments": the prohibition of idolatry, blasphemy, bloodshed, sexual sins, and eating from a living animal, and the commandment to establish legal systems. Additional laws are sometimes included in these commandments, and the concept is best understood as a type of universal ethics, a "Natural Law" system in which the laws are given by God. In Genesis, however, there are only three commandments listed: (1) God commanded man to be fruitful, to increase, multiply and swarm over the earth; (2) He announced that although man may eat meat he must not eat animals alive (or eat the blood, which is tantamount to the same thing—Genesis 9:4); and (3) He declared that no one, neither beast nor man, can kill a human being without forfeiting his own life and He provided for the execution of all killers, "whoever sheds the blood of man, by man shall his blood be shed." The significance of the first commandment is clear; it is an explicit and probably conscious rejection of the Babylonian idea that overpopulation was the cause of the flood. Together the other two commandments introduce a clear differentiation between man and the animal kingdom. Man may kill animals for food (while observing certain restrictions), but no one, man or beast, can kill man, "for man is created in God's image" (Genesis 9:6). Taken independently, these two commandments embody two of the basic principles of Israelite law.

The Bible views blood as a very special substance.[12] Israel is seriously enjoined against eating the blood of animals, and this prohibition is repeated six times in the Pentateuch (Genesis 9:4; Leviticus 3:17, 7:26, 17:10–14; Deuteronomy 12:16 and 12:23–24). This prohibition is called an eternal ordinance (Leviticus 3:17) and the penalty for eating blood (at least in the Priestly tradition) is *karet* (Leviticus 7:27; 17:10,14). The reason for this strict prohibition is explicit: the spirit (נפש) of the animal is in the blood (Leviticus 17:11,14; Deuteronomy 12:23). The greatest care had to be exercised in the eating of meat. According to the Priestly tradition (Leviticus 17:4), animals (other than hunting game) had to be slaughtered at an altar, and failure to bring animals to the altar was tantamount to the shedding of blood. The sprinkling of the animal's blood upon the altar served as a redemption or purgation of the slaughter of the animal (Leviticus 17:11). In Deuteronomy, where the cult has been centralized, there are no local altars to which one can bring the animals. Permission is therefore given to slaughter animals anywhere, but (as with hunting game in Leviticus) the blood may not be eaten and must be poured upon the ground and covered (Deuteronomy 12:24).

The third commandment in Genesis 9, the inviolability of human life, is a fundamental axiom of Israelite philosophy, and the ramifications of this principle pervade every aspect of Israelite law and distinguish it dramatically from the other Near Eastern legal systems with which it otherwise had so much in common. Capital punishment is reserved for offenses against God and is never invoked for offenses against property (such as habitual theft) and, conversely, homicide is the prime offense in Israel, an offense that cannot be compensated or ransomed with money, an offense which demands the execution of the murderer. Despite the crucial importance of this principle, however, the demand for the execution of murderers is new and did not operate before the flood. Of the three stories transmitted from the ten generations between the expulsion from the garden and the flood, two deal with murder. In the first, the Cain and Abel story (Genesis 4:1–15), Cain becomes an outcast and must lose his home. However, he is not killed. On the contrary, he becomes one of "God's protected" and is marked with a sign on his forehead to indicate that Cain's punishment (if any) is the Lord's and that whoever kills him will be subject to sevenfold retribution. In the next story preserved, the tale of Lemech (Genesis 4:19–24), Lemech kills "a man because of my wounding, a young man because of my hurt" (Genesis 4:23) and he thereupon claims protection, declaring that as Cain was protected with sevenfold retribution, he, Lemech, will be avenged with seventy-sevenfold (Genesis 4:24). Murderers were treated differently before the flood, and this difference ultimately created the conditions that necessitated the flood.

Murder has catastrophic consequences, not only for the people involved but also for the earth itself, which has the blood of innocent victims spilled on it. The blood spilled on the earth makes the ground barren for Cain, who must therefore leave and become a wanderer (Genesis 4:10–12):

Your brother's blood cries out to Me from the soil. And now you are cursed by the earth which opened her mouth to receive the blood of your brother from your Hand. When you till the ground it shall no longer yield its strength to you; a wanderer and a vagabond you will be on the earth.

The cursing and resultant barrenness does not stop with Cain, but on the contrary continues to spread in the generations after Cain. By the time that Noah is born this has become a major problem, and we are told that he was named Noah because זה ינחמנו ממעשינו ומעצבון ידינו מן האדמה אשר אררה ה (Genesis 5:29). There is a problem in the transmission of this verse. The masoretic text says: "This one will comfort us from our acts and the toil of our hands." The Septuagint, however, reads, "This one will cause us to rest," which indicates an original Hebrew יניחמנו from the root *nwh* with enclitic *mem*. The Septuagint version fits better with the name Noah, but for us the difference is not crucial. Noah will alleviate the toil that is caused "because of the ground which God has cursed." By the generation of the flood the whole earth has become polluted and is filled with *ḥamas* (Genesis 6:11), הארץ לפני האלהים ותמלא הארץ חמס ותשחת . This is not the place for a technical discussion of the word *ḥamas*,[13] but it is clear that this is a general term for evil. The term *ḥamas* may be used in a physical way, for *ḥamas* can cover clothes (Malachi 2:16) and hands (Job 16:17; 1 Chronicles 12:17). In this it is like the term *damim* (blood, bloodguilt), and the close connection between *ḥamas* and *damim* can be seen from Ezekiel 9:9 where the masoretic text has ותמלא הארץ דמים, "and the land was filled with blood," but with a footnote that there is a variant version (נ"א) ותמלא הארץ חמס "and the land was filled with *ḥamas*." It is the filling of the earth with *ḥamas* and the resultant pollution that prompts God to bring a flood to physically erase everything from the earth and start anew. The flood is not primarily an agency of punishment (although to be drowned is hardly a pleasant reward), but a means of getting rid of a thoroughly polluted world and starting again with a clean well-washed one.[14] Then, when everything has been washed away, God resolves (Genesis 8:21):

I will no longer curse the ground because of man, for the devisings of man's heart are evil from his youth, and I will no longer strike all the living creatures that I have created

and then goes on to give Noah and his sons the basic laws that will direct man and thus prevent the earth's becoming so polluted again.

This, then, is the biblical story of the flood. The composer of Genesis 1–9 has taken a framework at least as old as the epic of *Atrahasis*, the framework of the primeval history of Creation-Problem-Flood-Solution, and has used this framework and the ancient tradition of the flood to illuminate some of the most fundamental Israelite ideas about evil, pollution, and purgation. In Israel, what we might consider "moral pollution" is a physical contaminant that represents a danger to humanity. Moral wrongdoings defile physically, and they defile the person who commits them, his family, the nation, and the earth.[15] This is a recurrent problem in the Bible, because Israel is supposed to be a pure and holy people, and because it has been brought into a pure and beautiful land. Israel has a responsibility to preserve the land of Israel from contamination, and the theme of the pollution of the land is a major element in biblical historiography. Israel was granted the land only after the land "had vomited out" the previous inhabitants who had defiled it with their sexual abominations; Israel is therefore warned not to defile the land in this way lest it vomit them out also (Leviticus 18:24–30). The prime contaminant of the land is the blood of the murdered, and the execution of murderers is a national concern. Israel is forbidden to allow compensation for murder, and even to allow an accidental murderer to leave a city of refuge (in which he is quarantined until the death of the priest releases him), for if Israel allows such compensation it would contaminate the land (Numbers 35:31f):

> You shall not pollute the land that you are in, for the blood will pollute the land, and the land may not be redeemed for blood spilled on it except by the blood of the spiller. You shall not contaminate the land in which you are living, in which I the Lord am dwelling among the children of Israel (Numbers 35:33–34).

When a corpse was found and the murderer was unknown, this represented a real problem for the people and a danger to the land. Recourse was therefore transferred to the procedure of the *eglah ʿarufah*, "(the breaking of the heifer's neck)," a ritual meant to cleanse the land and the people of the pollution caused by the murder. The elders of the nearest town were to bring a heifer to an uninhabited wadi, strike off its head, wash their hands over it, and state: "Our hands have not shed this blood, nor have our eyes seen (the deed). Be merciful, O Lord, to Your people Israel whom you have redeemed and lay not innocent blood into the midst of the people" (Deuteronomy 21:7–8). Even the proper and required execution of those deserving death was not without danger to the land, and the corpses of the executed had to be buried promptly so that "you should not contaminate your land" ולא תטמא את אדמתך (Deuteronomy 21:22–23).

Not only murder contaminates the land but also sexual abominations such as those enumerated in Leviticus 18, and even such less obvious sexual misconduct as the remarriage (by the original husband) of a divorced wife (Deuteronomy 24:1–4, Jeremiah 3:1). The third major contaminant of the land that is explicitly mentioned is idolatry (Ezekiel 36:18). And together these three—murder, idolatry, and sexual abomination—are given as the explanation of the flood story's *ḥamas* by R. Levi in *Bereshit Rabbah* 31:6. These, of course, are the three cardinal sins for which a Jew must suffer martyrdom rather than commit (B. *Sanhedrin* 74a); they are mentioned in Acts as offenses from which all nations must refrain (Acts 15:20), they (together with the nonobservance of the Sabbatical year) are given in the Mishnah as the reasons that exile enters the world (M. *Avot* 5:8), and they (together with the public promise and nondelivery of charity) are given in the Jerusalem Talmud as the reason that the rains stop (*Ta'anit* 66C).

The pollution caused by "moral" contamination causes the land itself to suffer. The "cursing" of the earth and its resultant lessening of fertility begins already with Adam (Genesis 3:17–19). The earth upon which Abel is killed then becomes barren (Genesis 4:11–12), infertility is a widespread problem by the time Noah is born (5:29), and ultimately God purges the world with man at the time of the flood (Genesis 6:13). After the flood God gives laws so that he will never again have to curse the ground because of man (Genesis 8:21), but this does not mean that the earth is immune to such "cursing" should the laws be disobeyed, and the land of Israel in particular is depicted as sensitive to the sins of man. Thus in Leviticus 18 we read that God curses the land because of the Canaanites, and that this is the reason that the land ultimately vomits them out. When Israel in its turn sins, and the land becomes polluted (חנפה) by their misdeeds, "a curse consumes the land," אלה אכלה ארץ (Isaiah 24:5–6). One of the ways that the earth suffers is by drought, and drought and famine are understood in Israel as the classic reprisal for wrongdoing.[16] The ultimate result of polluting the land, however, is destruction and exile, with the land lying desolate and the people exiled. Both Israel (Hosea 5:3) and Judah (Jeremiah 2:7 and cf. Jeremiah 3) are told that they have polluted the land, and the idea of the pollution of the land becomes a way for Israel to understand and to survive the cataclysm of the destruction. Not only does God pour His fury upon them because they defiled the land with their idols and because of the blood

which they spilled upon the land (Ezekiel 36:18), but also the desolation
is seen as a way in which the land could "fulfill" its "Sabbaths" and thus
recuperate from the misdeeds of Israel (2 Chronicles 36:21).

According to this understanding of the exile, the flood and the
destruction are two parallel events, one relating to the world as a whole,
the other to the microcosm of Israel. Both are necessitated by the pollution caused by human misdeeds, and it should be noted that both
are followed not only by the restoration of the remnant but also by the
inauguration of a new order. The flood inaugurates the Rule of Law,
a system to restrain and educate man that is further developed by the
covenant of Sinai. This covenant is broken, the land is polluted and ultimately desolated. At the restoration, after God has purified the people
(Jeremiah 33:8, Ezekiel 36:33), He is to reestablish relations with them
(Hosea 2:21, Jeremiah 31:33, Ezekiel 36:28) with a covenant (Hosea
2:20) which is called a "new covenant" (Jeremiah 31:31), an "eternal covenant" (Jeremiah 32:40) and a "covenant of peace" (Ezekiel 34:25). The
world of the restoration will be different from the world before it. There
is a stress on individual retribution (Jeremiah 31:29–30; Ezekiel 11:21;
14:12–23; 18; 33:12–20), which is a removal of the stress on the national
responsibility of Israel for the sins of its members,[17] and we should note
that Ezekiel's formulation of this change refers to the proverb which is
spoken "about the land/ground of Israel," על אדמת ישראל (Ezekiel 18:2).
The new covenant is to be fundamentally different from the Sinai covenant (Jeremiah 31:31) because the law of God is to be engraved on
the heart (Jeremiah 31:32); no one will have to study the laws anymore,
because everyone will know it (Jeremiah 31:33); they will all have a "new
heart and a new spirit" (Ezekiel 36:26). In other words, the Rule of Law
is to be superceded by a fundamental change in man in which it seems
that even his evil impulses are to be eradicated.

This association of the exile and the flood is not simply modern
midrash, for it is clear that Ezekiel, at least, understood the exile in this
light, and the early chapters of Ezekiel are replete with flood imagery,
particularly with the depiction of the land as full of *hamas* (Ezekiel 7:23,
8:17, 9:9, end of 12:19), with the use of the term *qeṣ* (Ezekiel 7:2–7, spoken to the land/ground of Israel לאדמת ישראל cf. Genesis 6:13) and perhaps the marking on the forehead of those who are to be saved (Ezekiel
9:4–5). We do not know when the flood story in Genesis attained its
present form, and it may be that the anticipation and experience of the
destructions of Israel and Judah influenced the way that Israel understood the flood. Whether this is true or not, however, it is clear that the

flood story in Genesis is a product of serious reflection on the mechanisms of sin, and that it is an integral part of the philosophy of Israel.

NOTES

1. Delitzsch's lectures, entitled *"Babel und Bible,"* began in 1902. An English translation of them was published in 1906 (Open Court Publishing Co., Chicago). For a review of the controversy and some reflections on the relationship between the Bible and Babylonian culture, see J. J. Finkelstein, "Bible and Babel," *Commentary* (November 1958): 431–44.

2. For the most recent edition of the Sumerian flood story see Miguel Civil in Lambert and Millard, *Atrahasis: The Babylonian Story of the Flood* (Oxford: Clarendon Press; 1969).

3. J. Laessøe, "The *Atrahasis* epic, a Babylonian History of Mankind," *Bibliotheca Orientalis* 13 (1956): 90–102.

4. Lambert and Millard, *Cuneiform Texts from Babylonian Tablets in the British Museum* (London, 1965).

5. Lambert and Millard, *Atrahasis: The Babylonian Story of the Flood* (Oxford: Clarendon Press; 1969).

6. See the short discussion by Tikva Frymer-Kensky, *Biblical Archeologist* 40 (1977): 155.

7. Anne Kilmer, "The Mesopotamian Concept of Overpopulation and Its Solution as Represented in the Mythology," *Orientalia* 41 (1972): 160–77; William J. Moran, "The Babylonian Story of the Flood (review article)," *Biblica* 40 (1971): 51–61.

8. For a consideration of the possibility of underpopulation and its causes, see Carol Meyers, "The Roots of Restriction: Women in Early Israel," *Biblical Archeologist* 41 (1978): 91–102.

9. For a study of the idea, commonly attributed to P, that all flesh had corrupted itself, see A. R. Hulst, "Kol Basar in der Priesterlichen Fluterzählung," *Oudtestamentische Studien* XII (1958): 28–68.

10. This contradiction was recognized by D. L. Peterson, "The Yahwist on the Flood," *Vetus Testamentum* 26 (1976): 438–46. Since Peterson assumes that the J account of the flood ended at Genesis 8:22, he is forced to conclude that the author understood God's plan (which he believed was either to rid the universe of man or to create a sinless man) was unrealistic, that he believed therefore that the flood was an "ineffective ploy" and that therefore the J version of the flood was a lifeless narrative. We have, of course, no way of knowing whether the earliest Israelite versions of the flood culminated in the giving of laws.

11. This, of course, has not always been the philosophy of Israel. The Bible also affords support for the idea that man is good, and even Genesis 8:21 can be reinterpreted to agree with this idea, as in the Midrash Tanhuma, where this verse is interpreted to mean that the evil inclination does not come to a

man until he becomes a youth, i.e., ten years old, and that it is man who raises himself to be evil (*Tanhuma Bereshit* 1.7).

12. The question of blood is very complex. For the most recent discussion see Bergman and Kedar-Kopfstein, דם, in *Theologisches Worterbuch zum alten Testament* (ed. Botterweck and Ringgren), vol. 2: 247–66; and the literature cited here.

13. For some preliminary remarks see T. Frymer-Kensky, *Biblical Archeologist* 40 (1977): 153.

14. This understanding of the flood is still preserved in Enoch 10:20–22, where the Earth is to be cleansed "from all defilement, and from all sin, and from all punishment, and from all torment (Enoch 10:22, translation by B. S. Charles, *The Apocrypha and Pseudepigrapha of the Old Testament*, vol. 2 (Oxford, 1913) 195.

15. The ideas of pollution and purity have been the subject of considerable thought in recent years. For nonbiblical studies of the subject, see Mary Douglas, *Purity and Danger*, London, 1966; Paul Ricoeur, *The Symbolism of Evil* (Boston, 1967); and *Proceedings of the XIth International Association for the History of Religions*, II, *Guilt or Pollution and Rites of Purification* (Leiden, 1968). For an introduction to ancient Jewish ideas on the subject, see Jacob Neusner, *The Idea of Purity in Ancient Judaism* (Leiden, 1973). For more specialized studies of pollution and purity, particularly as they relate to the temple, see Baruch Levine, *In the Presence of the Lord* (Leiden, 1974); and the many studies by Jacob Milgrom, particularly "Kipper," *Encyclopaedia Judaica* 10, 1039–43; "Sin-Offering or Purification Offering," *Vetus Testamentum* 21 (1971): 237–39; "A Prolegomenon to Leviticus 17:11," *Journal of Biblical Literature* 90 (1971): 149–56; and "Israel's Sanctuary: The Priestly 'Picture of Dorian Gray,'" *Revue Biblique* 83 (1976): 390–99.

16. This is stated clearly in terms of promise-threat in Deuteronomy 11:13–21, the second paragraph of the *Sh'ma*. In 1 Kings 8:35–36, 2 Chronicles 6:26–27 and 2 Chronicles 7:13 ("Solomon's Prayer") a major purpose of the temple is to provide a place and a way for the people to appease God's anger in time of drought and thereby induce him to bring rain. The drought in the time of Ahab is the classic example of such a punishment, but other droughts were understood in the same way (cf. Amos 4:7, Jeremiah 14). For the connection of pollution and drought see Ezekiel 22:24 where the land is called impure and unrained upon. For some observation on the question see R. Patai, "The Control of Rain in Ancient Palestine," Hebrew Union College Annual 214 (1939): 251–86; and for an explanation of the reason drought is such a major chastisement see T. Frymer-Kensky, "Biblical Water Cosmography and Its Near Eastern Analogues," paper presented to the national meeting of the Society for Biblical Literature, Fall 1977.

17. For the most recent discussion of the question of individual retribution see M. Weinfeld, "Jeremiah and the Spiritual Metamorphosis of Israel," *Zeitschrift fur alttestamentliches Wissenschaft* 88 (1976): 17–56.

4 / The *Atrahasis* Epic and Its Significance for Our Understanding of Genesis 1–9

2004

THE BABYLONIAN FLOOD STORIES

Three different Babylonian stories of the flood have survived: the Sumerian flood story, the ninth tablet of the *Gilgamesh* epic, and the *Atrahasis* epic. Details in these stories, such as the placing of animals in the ark, the landing of the ark on a mountain, and the sending forth of birds to see whether the waters had receded, indicate clearly that these stories are intimately related to the biblical flood story and, indeed, that the Babylonian and biblical accounts of the flood represent different retellings of an essentially identical flood tradition. Until the recovery of the *Atrahasis* epic, however, the usefulness of these tales toward an understanding of Genesis was limited by the lack of a cohesive context for the flood story comparable to that of Genesis. The Sumerian flood story has survived in a very fragmentary state, and even its most recent edition (by Miguel Civil in Lambert and Millard, *Atrahasis: The Babylonian Story of the Flood* (Oxford, Clarendon Press, 1969) can only be understood with the aid of the other known flood stories. The *Gilgamesh* epic presents a different problem for comparative analysis. Here the flood story is clearly in a secondary context, and, more important, this context is so different from the biblical as to cause serious differences in content. In the *Gilgamesh* epic the story of the flood is related as part of the tale of Gilgamesh's quest for immortality. Utnapishtim tells his descendant Gilgamesh the story of the flood in order to tell him why he became immortal and, in so doing, to show Gilgamesh that he cannot become immortal in the same way. This purpose is explicitly stated, for the story is introduced by Gilgamesh's question, "As I look upon you, Utnapishtim, your features are not strange; you are just as I . . . how did you join the Assembly of the gods in your quest for life?" (*Gilgamesh* XI: 2–7). Utnapishtim concludes his recitation with the admonition, "But now who will call the gods to Assembly for your sake so that you may find the life that you are seeking?" (*Gilgamesh* XI: 197–98).

The nature of the story as "Utnapishtim's tale" colors the recitation of the flood episode and makes it fundamentally different from the biblical flood story. The "first person narrative" format means that Utnapishtim can tell only those parts of the story that he knows, and that he may leave out those aspects that do not concern him or fit his purpose. For example, even though Babylonian gods are not portrayed as capricious and are considered as having reasons for their actions, Utnapishtim tells us nothing about the reasons that the gods brought the flood. This lapse is dictated by the literary format: Utnapishtim may not know the reason for the flood, or he may not record it because it is irrelevant to his purpose, which is to recount how he became immortal. Similarly, the only event after the flood that Utnapishtim relates to Gilgamesh is the subsequent convocation of the gods that granted him immortality. The result of the "personalization" of the flood story in the *Gilgamesh* epic is that the scope of the story is restricted to the adventures of one individual and its significance to its effects upon him, with the flood itself emptied of any cosmic or anthropological significance. The flood stories in Genesis and in *Gilgamesh* are so far removed from each other in focus and intent that one cannot compare the ideas in the two versions of the flood without setting up spurious dichotomies.

THE *ATRAHASIS* EPIC

The recovery of the *Atrahasis* epic provides new perspectives on Genesis because, unlike the other two Babylonian versions of the flood, the *Atrahasis* epic presents the flood story in a context comparable to that of Genesis, that of a primeval history. The flood episode of the *Atrahasis* epic has been known for a long time, but the literary structure of the epic, and therefore the context of the flood story, was not understood until Laessøe reconstructed the work (J. Laessøe, "The *Atrahasis* epic, a Babylonian History of Mankind," *Biblioteca Orientalis* 13 [1956]: 90–102). In 1965, Lambert and Millard (*Cuneiform Texts from Babylonian Tablets in the British Museum,* London) published many additional texts from the epic, including an Old Babylonian copy (written around 1650 B.C.E.) which is our most complete surviving recension of the tale. These new texts greatly increased our knowledge of the epic and served as the foundation for the English edition of the epic by Lambert and Millard (*Atrahasis: The Babylonian Story of the Flood* (Oxford, Clarendon Press, 1969).

The *Atrahasis* epic starts with a depiction of the world as it existed before man was created: "When the gods worked like man" (the first line and ancient title of the composition). At this time the universe was divided among the great gods, with An taking the heavens, Enlil the earth and Enki the great deep. Seven gods (called the Anunnaki in this text) established themselves as the ruling class, while the rest of the gods provided the workforce. These gods, whose "work was heavy, (whose) distress was much," dug the Tigris and Euphrates rivers and then rebelled, refusing to continue their labors. On the advice of Enki, the gods decided to create a substitute to do the work of the gods, and Enki and the mother goddess created man from clay and from the flesh and blood of a slain god, "We-ilu, a god who has sense," from whom man was to gain rationality. The various themes and motifs out of which this part of the epic is composed can all be documented elsewhere and do not seem to have originated with this text.

This epic, ancient though it is, is already the product of considerable development, and the author of the composition has utilized old motifs and has united them into a coherent account of man's beginnings in which he presents a picture of the purpose of man's creation, his *raison d'être*, as doing the work of the gods and thus relieving them of the need to labor. In the same way, he seems to have taken the previously known story of the flood and juxtaposed it to his creation story to continue the tale of primeval man and indicate the prerequisites of human life upon earth.

In the *Atrahasis* epic the creation of man causes new problems. In the words of the epic (1 352f., restored from Tablet II 108):

Twelve hundred years [had not yet passed]
[when the land extended] and the peoples multiplied.
The [land] was bellowing [like a bull].
The gods were disturbed with [their uproar].
[Enlil heard] their noise
[and addressed] the great gods,
"The noise of mankind [has become too intense for me]
[with their uproar] I am deprived of sleep."

To solve this problem, the gods decided to bring a plague, which ends when Enki advises man to bring offerings to Namtar, god of the plague, and thus induce him to lift the plague. This plague does not solve the problem permanently, for twelve hundred years later the same problem arises again (Tablet II 1–8) and the gods bring a drought, which ends when men (upon Enki's advice) bribe Adad to bring rain. Despite the fragmentary state of Tablet II, it is easy to see that the same problem recurs, and the gods bring famine (and saline soil), which again do not end the difficulties. At last Enlil persuades the gods to adopt a "final solution" (Tablet II viii 34) to the human problem, and they resolve to bring a flood to destroy mankind. Their plan is thwarted by Enki, who has Atrahasis build an ark and so escape the flood. After the rest of mankind have been destroyed, and after the gods have had occasion to regret their actions and to realize (by their thirst and hunger) that they need man, Atrahasis brings a sacrifice and the gods come to eat. Enki then presents a permanent solution to the problem. The new world after the flood is to be different from the old, for Enki summons Nintu, the birth goddess, and has her create new creatures, who will ensure that the old problem does not arise again. In the words of the epic (Tablet III vii 1):

> In addition, let there be a third category among the peoples,
> Among the peoples women who bear and women who do not bear.
> Let there be among the peoples the Pašittu-demon
> To snatch the baby from the lap of her who bore it.
> Establish Ugbabtu-women, Entu-women, and Igiṣitu-women
> and let them be taboo and so stop childbirth.

Other post-flood provisions may have followed, but the text now becomes too fragmentary to read.

Despite the lacunae, the structure presented by the *Atrahasis* epic is clear. Man is created . . . there is a problem in creation . . . remedies are attempted but the problem remains . . . the decision is made to destroy man . . . this attempt is thwarted by the wisdom of Enki . . . a new remedy is instituted to ensure that the problem does not arise again. Several years ago Anne Kilmer ("The Mesopotamian Concept of Overpopulation and Its Solution as Represented in the Mythology," *Orientalia* 41 [1972]: 160–77) and William J. Moran ("The Babylonian Story of the Flood" [review article], *Biblica* 40 [1971]: 51–61), working independently, demonstrated that the problem that arose and that necessitated these various remedies was that of overpopulation. Mankind increased uncontrollably, and the methods of population control that were first attempted (drought, pestilence, famine) only solved the problem temporarily. This overpopulation led to destruction (the flood), and permanent countermeasures were introduced by Enki to keep the size of the population down. The myth tells us that such social phenomena as nonmarrying women, and such personal tragedies as barrenness and stillbirth (and perhaps miscarriage and infant mortality) are in fact essential to the very continuation of man's existence, for humanity was almost destroyed once when the population got out of control.

GENESIS AND *ATRAHASIS*

The Babylonian tale, composed no later than 1700 B.C.E., is very attractive to us today and can almost be called a "myth for our times," for we share with the Babylonians a consciousness of a limited ecology and a concern about controlling the human population. In addition to this inherent relevance, however, it is very important for biblical studies, for it points out what (by the clear logic of hindsight) should have been obvious to us all along: there is an organic unity to the first section of Genesis. The importance of the *Atrahasis* epic is that it focuses our attention away from the deluge itself and onto the events immediately after the rains subside. In Genesis, as in *Atrahasis*, the flood came in response to a serious problem in creation, a problem which was rectified immediately after the flood. A study of the changes that God made in the world after the flood gives a clearer picture of the conditions prevailing in the world before the flood, of the ultimate reason that necessitated the flood which almost caused the destruction of man, of the essential differences between the world before the flood and the world after it, and thus of the essential prerequisites for the continued existence of man on the earth.

Unlike *Atrahasis*, the flood story in Genesis is emphatically not about overpopulation. On the contrary, God's first action after the flood was to command Noah and his sons to "be fruitful and multiply and fill the earth" (Gen 9:1). This echoes the original command to Adam (1:28) and seems to be an explicit rejection of the idea that the flood came as a result of attempts to decrease man's population. The repetition of this commandment in emphatic terms in Genesis 9:7, "and you be fruitful and multiply, swarm over the earth and multiply in it," makes it probable that the Bible consciously rejected the underlying theme of the *Atrahasis* epic, that the fertility of man before the flood was the reason for his near destruction.

It is not surprising that Genesis rejects the idea of overpopulation as the reason for the flood, for the Bible does not share the belief of *Atrahasis* and some other ancient texts that overpopulation is a serious issue. Barrenness and stillbirth (or miscarriage) are not considered social necessities, nor are they justified as important for population control. On the contrary, when God promises the land to Israel he promises that "in your land women will neither miscarry nor be barren" (Exod 23:26). The continuation of this verse, "I will fill the number of your days," seems to be a repudiation of yet another of the "natural" methods of population control, that of premature death. In the ideal world which is to be established in the land of Israel there will be no need for such methods, for overpopulation is not a major concern.

Genesis states explicitly that God decided to destroy the world because of the wickedness of man (Gen 6:5). Although this traditionally has been understood to mean that God destroyed the world as a punishment for man's sins, this understanding of the passage entails serious theological problems, such as the propriety of God's destroying all life on earth because of the sins of man. Such an interpretation also causes great problems in understanding the text of Genesis itself and creates what seems to be a paradox, for the "wickedness of man" is also given as the reason that God decides never again to bring a flood (Gen 8:21). Since the evil nature of man is presented after the flood as the reason for God's vow never again to bring a flood, we should not infer that God brought the flood as a punishment because man was evil. Genesis also states that God brought the flood because the world was full of *ḥāmās.* The term *ḥāmās* is very complex, and a semantic analysis is presented below. The wide range of meanings for the term *ḥāmās* means that a lexical analysis of the word is not sufficient to allow us to determine what particular evil is here called *ḥāmās* and what it was about this particular evil that necessitated a flood. The nature of the evil and the cause of the flood must be found in the story of Genesis.

The *Atrahasis* epic is so important to biblical studies because it enables us to determine the cause of the flood by focusing our attention away from the deluge itself and onto the events immediately after the flood, i.e., to Genesis 9. In this chapter God offers Noah and his sons a covenant, in which he promises never again to bring a flood to destroy the world, and gives the rainbow as the token of this promise. At this time God gives Noah and his sons several laws, and the difference between the antediluvium and postdiluvium worlds can be found in these laws. These laws are thus the structural equivalent of the new solutions proposed by Enki in the *Atrahasis* epic. In *Atrahasis* the problem in man's creation was overpopulation, and the solutions proposed by Enki are designed to rectify this problem by controlling and limiting the population. In the Bible the problem is not overpopulation, but "since the devisings of man's heart are evil from his youth" (Gen 8:21), God must do something if he does not want to destroy the earth repeatedly. This something is to create laws for mankind, laws to ensure that matters do not again reach such a state that the world must be destroyed.

The idea that man's nature is basically evil and that laws are therefore necessary to control his evil is a rather Hobbesian view of mankind, and it should be mentioned that this was not always the philosophy of Israel. The Bible also affords support for the idea that man is intrinsically good, and even Genesis 8:21 can be reinterpreted to agree with this philosophy, as in the Midrash Tanhuma, where this verse is interpreted to mean that the evil inclination does not come to a man until he becomes a youth, i.e., 10 years old, and that it is man who raises himself to be evil (Midrash Tanhuma Bereshit 1.7). The simple meaning of the statement in Genesis 8:21, "the imagination of man's heart is evil from his youth," however, indicates clearly that Genesis comes down on the *Leviathan* side of what is obviously a very old controversy about the nature of man. Such perceptions of an inherently evil aspect of man's nature, one which is naturally prone to violent and unrighteous acts, logically entails a recognition that man cannot be allowed to live by his instincts alone, that he must be directed and controlled by laws, that in fact, laws are the *sine qua non* of human existence. It is for this reason that God's first act after the flood is to give man laws.

THE FLOOD IN GENESIS

The realization that the granting of laws after the flood was a direct response by God to the problem posed by man's evil nature resolves the apparent paradox between the statement that the wickedness of man somehow caused the flood and the statement that the wickedness of man caused God to take steps to ensure that he will never again have to bring a flood. However, it does not answer the question of why the flood was necessary, why God could not simply have announced a new order and introduced laws to mankind without first destroying almost all of humanity. This problem does not arise in the Babylonian flood stories, where there is a clear distinction between the gods who decide to bring a flood (Enlil and the council of the gods) and the god who realized the

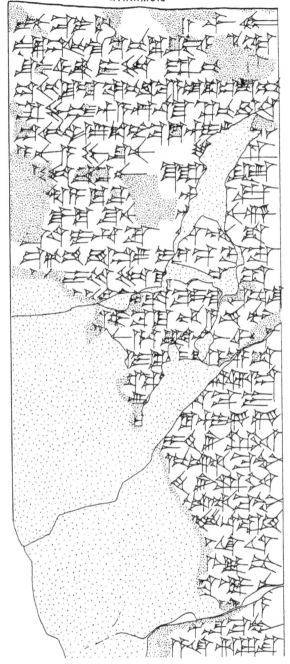

Copy of Tablet 1, column i (BM 78941 + 78943) of the *Atrahasis*
epic, which begins:
When the god like men
Bore the work and suffered the toil—

error of this decision, saved man, and introduced the new order (Enki). The problem, however, is quite serious in the monotheistic conception of the flood in which the same God decides to bring the flood, saves man, and resolves never to bring a flood again. If God is rational and consistent in his actions, there must have been a compelling reason that necessitated the flood. "Punishment" is not enough of a reason, for it not only raises the question of God's right to punish all the animals for the sins of man but also raises the serious issue of God's right to punish man in this instance at all: If man has evil tendencies, and if he has not been checked and directed by laws, how can he be punished for simply following his own instincts? The flood cannot simply have been brought as a punishment, and its necessitating cause must lie in the particular nature of the evil which filled the world before the flood. Our best way to find out the nature of the evil is to look at the solution given to control the evil, i.e., to the laws given immediately after the flood.

The oral tradition of Israel (as reflected in the Rabbinic writings) has developed and expanded the laws given to Noah and his sons after the flood into a somewhat elaborate system of "the seven Noahide commandments." The traditional enumeration of these is the prohibition of idolatry, blasphemy, bloodshed, sexual sins, theft, and eating from a living animal, and the commandment to establish legal systems. Additional laws are sometimes included among the commandments to Noah and his sons, and the system of Noahide commandments can best be understood as a system of universal ethics, a "Natural Law" system in which the laws are given by God. Genesis itself, however, does not contain a list of all seven of these commandments. According to Genesis 9, God issued three commandments to Noah and his sons immediately after the flood: (1) he commanded man to be fruitful, to increase, multiply and swarm over the earth; (2) he announced that although man may eat meat he must not eat animals alive (or eat the blood, which is tantamount to the same thing—Gen 9:4); and (3) he declared that no one, neither beast nor man, can kill a human being without forfeiting his own life, providing for the execution of all killers, "whoever sheds the blood of man, by man shall his blood be shed."

The significance of the first commandment (that of fertility) has already been mentioned: it is an explicit and probably conscious rejection of the idea that the cause of the flood was overpopulation and that overpopulation is a serious problem. Together the other two commandments introduce a very clear differentiation between man and the animal kingdom: man may kill animals for food (while observing certain restrictions in so doing), but no one, whether man or beast, can kill man. The reason for this "absolute sanctity of human life" (as it is usually called) is given in the text: "for man is created in God's image" (Gen 9:6). Taken independently, these two commandments—the prohibition against eating blood (and the living animal) and the declaration of the principle of the inviolability of human life with the provision of capital punishment for murder—embody two of the basic principles of Israelite law.

The Bible views blood as a very special substance. Israel is seriously enjoined against eating the blood of animals, and this prohibition is repeated six times in the Pentateuch (Gen 9:4; Lev 3:17; 7:26; 17:10–14; Deut 12:16 and 12:23–24). This prohibition is called an eternal ordinance (Lev 3:17), and the penalty for eating blood (at least in the Priestly tradition) is *karet*, which is some form of outlawry, whether banishment or ostracism (Lev 7:27; 17:11,14; Deut 12:23). The greatest care must be exercised in the eating of meat. According to the Priestly tradition, slaughtering of animals (other than creatures of the hunt) can only be done at an altar. Failure to bring the animal to the altar was considered tantamount to the shedding of blood (Lev 17:4). The sprinkling of the animal's blood upon the altar served as a redemption (Lev 17:11). In Deuteronomy, where the cult is centralized and it is no longer feasible to bring the animals to an altar, permission is given to eat and slaughter animals anywhere. However (as with the animals of the hunt in Leviticus), care must be taken not to eat the blood, which should be poured upon the ground and covered (Deut 12:24).

The idea expressed in the Third Commandment, that of the incomparability and inviolability of human life, is one of the fundamental axioms of Israelite philosophy, and the ramifications of this principle pervade every aspect of Israelite law and distinguish it dramatically from the other Near Eastern legal systems with which it otherwise has so much in common. In Israel, capital punishment is reserved for the direct offense against God and is never invoked for offenses against property. The inverse of this is also true; the prime offense in Israel is homicide, which can never be compensated by the payment of a monetary fine and can only be rectified by the execution of the murderer.

Despite the importance of this principle, if we look at the world before the flood, it is immediately apparent that this demand for the execution of murderers is new. Only three stories are preserved in Genesis from the ten generations between the expulsion from the Garden and the bringing of the flood. Two of these, the Cain and Abel story (Gen 4:1–15) and the tale of Lemech (Gen 4:19–24), concern the shedding of human blood. In the first tale Cain, having murdered his brother Abel, becomes an outcast and must lose his home. However, he is not killed. In fact, he becomes one of "God's protected" and is marked with a special sign on his forehead to indicate that Cain's punishment (if any) is the Lord's and that whoever kills him will be subject to sevenfold retribution. The next story preserved—that of Lemech five generations later—also concerns murder, for Lemech kills "a man because of my wounding, a young man because of my hurt" (Gen 4:23). Lemech, too, is not killed and claims the same protection that Cain had, declaring that as Cain was protected with sevenfold retribution he, Lemech, will be avenged with seventy-sevenfold (Gen 4:24). The main difference between the world before the flood and the new order established immediately after it is the different treatment of murderers, and the cause of the flood should therefore be sought in this crucial difference.

Murder has catastrophic consequences, not only for the individuals involved but also for the earth itself, which has the blood of innocent victims spilled upon it. As God says to Cain after Abel's murder (Gen 4:10–12):

> Your brother's blood cries out to me from the soil. And now you are cursed by the earth which opened her mouth to receive the blood of your brother from your hand. When you till the ground it shall no longer yield its strength to you; a wanderer and a vagabond you will be on the earth.

The innocent blood which was spilled on it has made the ground barren for Cain, who must therefore leave his land and become a wanderer. This process of the cursing and concomitant barrenness of the ground had become widespread. The explanation of the name given to Noah makes this point. The masoretic text reads: "This one will comfort us from our acts and the toil of our hands." Alternatively, if we follow the Septuagint (old Greek translation), the text would read: "This one will give us rest from our acts and the toil of our hands." Either way, the latter part of the verse, "because of the ground which God has cursed" is clear: Noah's name is explained by Genesis as related to the conditions which caused the flood, the "cursing" of the ground, and Noah's role somehow alleviates that condition.

By the generation of the flood the whole earth has become polluted, (KJV, "the earth also was corrupt") and is filled with *ḥāmās* (Gen 6:11). The wide range of meanings of the word *ḥāmās* in the Bible encompasses almost the entire spectrum of evil. The term can stand for evil of any sort (Ps 11:5; Prov 13:2); it may simply stand for falsehood, as in ʿēd *ḥāmās,* "false witness" (Exod 23:1; Deut 19:15; Ps 35:1) and its occurrence with *mirma* (Isa 60:18; Jer 6:7, 20:8), with the two together meaning something like "plunder and pillage." *Ḥāmās* has a very close connection to *dāmîm,* "bloodshed," as can be seen from Ezekiel 9:9. Like *dāmîm,* the term *ḥāmās* can be used in a physical way, for *ḥāmās* (or the pollution from it) can cover clothes (Mal 2:16) and hands (Job 16:17; 1 Chr 12:17). In Genesis, the earth is filled with *ḥāmās* and has itself become polluted because all flesh had polluted its way upon the earth (Gen 6:11–12). It is the filling of the earth with *ḥāmās,* and its resultant pollution that prompts God to bring a flood to physically erase everything from the earth and start anew. The flood is not primarily an agency of punishment (although to be drowned is hardly a pleasant reward), but a means of getting rid of a thoroughly polluted world and starting again with a clean, well-washed one. Then, when everything has been washed away, God resolves (Gen 8:21):

> I will no longer curse the ground because of man, for the devisings of man's heart are evil from his youth, and I will no longer strike all the living creatures that I have created

and goes on to give Noah and his sons the basic laws, specifically the strict instructions about the shedding of blood, to prevent the earth's becoming so polluted again.

POLLUTION IN THE BIBLE

The idea of the pollution of the earth is not a vague metaphor to indicate moral wrongdoing. On the contrary, in the biblical worldview, the murders before the flood contaminated the land and created a state of physical pollution which had to be eradicated by physical means (the flood). Although this concept may seem strange to us, it is not surprising to find it here in the cosmology of Israel, for Israel clearly believed that moral wrongdoings defile physically. This is explicitly stated with three sins—murder, idolatry, and sexual abominations—and it is interesting to note that these are the three cardinal sins for which a Jew must suffer martyrdom rather than commit them (*b. Sanhedrin* 74a). These are mentioned in Acts as offenses from which all the nations must refrain (Acts 15:20); these three offenses are given as the explanation of *ḥāmās* in the flood story by Rabbi Levy in Genesis Rabbah (31:16); and these (together with the nonobservance of the sabbatical year) are given in the Mishnah as the reasons that exile enters the world (Nezigin 5:8). According to the biblical tradition, the

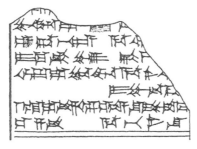

Copy of the fragment of Tablet II, column viii (Ni 2552), which translates:

> The Assembly . . [. . .
> Do not obey . . . [. . .
> The gods commanded total destruction,
> Enlil did an evil deed on the peoples.
> Atrahasis opened his mouth
> And addressed his lord.

pre-Israelite inhabitants of Canaan had defiled the land with the sexual abominations enumerated in Leviticus 18. As a result God had punished the land (Lev 18:25), and the land had therefore vomited up the inhabitants which had defiled it. For this reason, Israel is admonished not to commit these abominations and defile the land lest it vomit them out in the same way (Lev 18:24–28). Later, Israel was told that it had defiled the land (Jer 2:7) and that because Israel defiled the land with their idols and because of the blood which they spilled upon the land, God poured his fury upon them (Ezek 36:18).

The most serious contaminant of the land is the blood of those who have been murdered; the concept of "bloodguilt" is well known in Israelite law. Because of the seriousness of the crime of murder, and perhaps also because of the mystical conception of blood in Israelite thought, the blood of the slain physically pollutes the land. For this reason, the discovery of a corpse posed a real problem for the people. When such an unsolved murder occurred, recourse was had to the procedure of the ʿeglā ʿarûpā, "the breaking of the heifer's neck," a ritual meant to cleanse the land of the pollution of the murder; the elders of the nearest town were to bring a heifer to an uninhabited wadi, strike off its head, wash their hands over it, and offer the following prayer:

> Our hands have not shed this blood, nor have our eyes seen (the deed). Be merciful O Lord, to your people Israel whom you have redeemed and lay not innocent blood into the midst of the people (Deut 21:7–8).

The shedding of human blood was of concern to the whole nation, for it involved an actual pollution of the land. Israel was enjoined against this bloodguilt pollution and was admonished neither to allow compensation for murder, nor even to allow an accidental murderer to leave a city of refuge, for by so doing they would cause the land of Israel to become contaminated:

> You shall take no ransom for the life of a murderer who is deserving of death. He shall be executed. You shall take no ransom to (allow someone to) flee a city of refuge or to (allow someone to) return to live in the land that you are in, for the blood will pollute the land, and the land may not be redeemed for blood spilled on it except by the blood of the spiller. You shall not contaminate the land in which you are living, in which I the Lord am dwelling among the children of Israel (Num 35:31–34).

The idea of the pollution of the earth by murder, of the physical pollution caused by "moral" wrongs such as sexual abominations and idolatry, underlies much of Israelite law. The composer of Genesis 1–9 had reinterpreted the cosmology and the early history of man in the light of these very strong concepts. He has used a framework that is at least as old as the epic of *Atrahasis*, the framework of the primeval history of Creation-Problem-Flood-Solution, and has retold the story in such a way as to reinterpret an ancient tradition to illuminate fundamental Israelite ideas, i.e., the biblical ideals that law and the "sanctity of human life" are the prerequisites of human existence upon the earth.

EXCURSUS: THE *ATRAHASIS* ACCOUNT IN CUNEIFORM LITERATURE

Like Genesis, *Atrahasis* is the product of a long process of development, and many of the ideas and motifs contained in it can be traced elsewhere in Sumero-Babylonian literature. The idea of the division of the universe among the great gods can be found in the introduction to "*Gilgamesh*, Enkidu and the Netherworld," in which An takes the heavens; Enlil ,the earth; Ereshkigal receives the netherworld; and Enki sets sail for the Apsu. The working gods are found in UET VI 118: 20, and in "Enki and Ninmah" (11–12), in which the lesser gods work and dig the Tigris and Euphrates. The conception of the creation of man to relieve the gods from labor is found in "Enki and Ninmah" (25), as is creation from clay, for man is created there from the "heart of clay over the *abzu* (33). Clay as the material out of which man is created is quite common in Mesopotamian literature. In the creation of Enkidu in the *Gilgamesh* epic, long recognized as a doublet to the creation of man, Aruru washes her hands, takes the clay, and either casts it upon the steppe or draws a design upon it. Similarly, in the Babylonian Theodicy, Ea nips off the clay and Aruru fashions it. In the "ritual for the restoration of temples" Ea nips off the clay in the *abzu* and fashions both man and a whole host of lesser deities. In the Sumerian myth of the descent of Inanna to the netherworld Enki creates the Kalatur and the Kurgarra from the "dirt under one of his fingernails" (JCS 5:219–20).

The question of the killing of a god to create man presents a different picture. This motif is found in *Enuma Elish*, where Kingu, the head of Tiamat's forces, is killed after the defeat of Tiamat, and his blood is used in the creation of man. The only "Sumerian" text in which this motif is found, however, is the bilingual KAR 4, in which the Lamga gods are slain and mankind is created from their blood. This text has many ancient elements: the dividing of the universe, the digging of the Tigris and Euphrates, the giving to man of the hoe and the corvée basket. This text, however, seems to be a late reflex of these traditions, and the Sumerian seems to be very late. There would, therefore, seem to be no Sumerian tradition in the use of blood in the creation of man, and Lambert's attempt to find it in "Enki and Ninmah" ("Creation of Man in Sumero-Babylonian Myth," CRAAI 11 [1964]: 103) has now been given up (oral communication). Considering the special notion of blood that we find in the Bible, it seems likely that the blood motif in *Atrahasis* and in *Enuma Elish* may be a West Semitic idea, and may have entered Mesopotamian mythology with the coming of the West Semites.

Most of the motifs in the *Atrahasis* account of man's beginning are paralleled in the Sumerian myth of "Enki and Ninmah," and it is natural to assume that the Sumerian composition came first and that *Atrahasis* was based on this account of the creation of man. This may be, but the precedence of the Sumerian tale cannot be pre-supposed, and the whole matter deserves serious study. There are several puzzling phenomena in the Sumerian story which might indicate that "Enki and Ninmah" is an adaptation of an Akkadian tale. One of these is the use of the word *zub-sig* for that which is bound on man at his creation. In context this is almost certainly the (corvée) basket and must be a loan from Akkadian *šupšikku*, the form of the more common Akkadian *tupšikku* that occurs in *Atrahasis*. Although both *šupšikku/tupšikku* and *zub-sig* may be ultimately derived from a third (substrate?) language, the Akkadian word is fairly common in Akkadian, while *zub-sig* in this sense may be confined to this story. Similarly, the other word for corvée basket that is used in

"Enki and Ninmah" seems to be an Akkadian word (*terḫum*, line 12). In the light of such anomalies we should not assume that the Akkadian epic is derivative from the Sumerian, for "Enki and Ninmah" may have been written with *Atrahasis* in mind.

Dedicated to the memory of J. J. Finkelstein,
whose unique genius is sorely missed.

Goddess Myths

5 / Goddesses: Biblical Echoes

1994

The current interest in women in the Bible is partly theological. The wave of feminism has raised fundamental questions about the nature of monotheism, the sexuality of monotheism, and the gender messages it conveys. In the last twenty-five years or so, a new mythology has grown, the mythology of *the* Goddess, the Great Goddess, who was peaceful, earth-loving, women-loving, everything of perfection that can be imagined, and who was displaced by patriarchy.

This is a myth that is growing into a new religion. It has no relationship to historical fact, but it has become a foundational document and an orientational theology for many women struggling with the issues of how to maintain a religious consciousness when that consciousness has, for so long, been accompanied by cultural messages of unequal gender relationships and male domination in a hierarchy.

When we look at history, we realize that the myth of the Great Goddess is less history than psychology because, to some extent, it represents the wish of all of us to go back to the absolute peace and bliss we felt at our mother's breast and even before that in our mother's womb. The real world is not that peaceful; the real world is certainly not that blissful.

The last hundreed and fifty years have witnessed not only the development of many historical techniques for studying the Bible but also the development of the great disciplines of history and archaeology. We have discovered the ancient civilizations that surrounded and accompanied Israel, sometimes with animosity and sometimes with cultural interchange, on Israel's quest for a religious conception of the world. These are the cultures of ancient Mesopotamia, Egypt, Canaan, the Hittites, the Edomites, the Moabites, and, to a lesser extent, the Greeks.

We know those languages now, more or less—our Edomite is a bit shaky, our Sumerian is still a little primitive—but we have their documents, particularly those of the Mesopotamians, because they had no wood, so they wrote on clay, which is not biodegradable. These documents present us with a picture of living polytheism. What does a priest believe when he stands up and sings a hymn? What does the hymn say, not as recollected hundreds of years later by antiquarians, but in the lived experiences of, at least, elite worshipers?

When we read these documents, we realize that some of our precious new myths of this halcyon antiquity are not borne out by the facts. I'll mention just one, the one that is repeated so often in biblical studies—that the Canaanites had a female-centered, earth-friendly religion. When we read the texts, we find that the three female figures in Canaanite texts are extremely marginal and that the world is seen as a competition between the male forces of El, Baal, Mut, and Yam.

I like to focus on Sumer because there we have the most texts—a third-millennium assemblage of texts, extending into the first several hundred years of the second millennium. The second millennium—actually the years between 1800 and 1000 B.C.E.—was a time of tremendous transformation. Political institutions became more and more broad scaled. Religion was transformed in a way that continually and constantly diminished the role of goddesses.

The Sumerians invented writing. Their texts show us the most balanced position of female and male deities in the ancient world. But even in Sumerian culture, where our documents start around 2800 B.C.E. with the rudimentary beginnings of writing and end around 1700 B.C.E. with religious texts, we see tremendous changes. We can, in fact, detect a pattern. Female deities are more important early in the Sumerian period and less important later. Female deities that had control over certain cultural events and activities in the early period, let's say in 2300 B.C.E., become sidekicks by the later period.

Nevertheless, let me give you a picture of the role of goddesses in the classic flowering of Sumerian civilization, which is reflected in the literature composed during the periods we call Ur III and the early Old Babylonian period, from about 2200 to 1700 B.C.E. In these texts, goddesses fulfill certain specific functions. They are women in the sky, but they play the same roles in the family as women on earth. Their position and their nature are frequently discussed through stories about family relations.

We have the mother, the sister, the mother-in-law, the daughter (less important) and the wife. The mother is wonderful. There is no dark side to the mother in Mesopotamian mythology. This is long before Sigmund Freud and Melanie Klein. The mother is a pasteboard figure who is selfless, devoted, and loyal to her child. She does "what's good for you." The sister is her shadow, the most loyal person a man can expect, faithful unto, and even beyond, death. To have a sister is to be the most fortunate of all heroes. Even the mother-in-law is a lovely figure. She is particularly the friend of the daughter-in-law. If you can imagine such a thing. She is her key ally in the house. So that's all the good parts.

What a wife is like we do not know. We do have wives—we have the prototype of all wives, a goddess named Uttu, the goddess of weaving and spinning. In the magic literature, you call upon Uttu when you want to weave a web around someone. You would want to do that because one of the most dramatic kinds of magic ritual involves tying a person up, spinning a spell, and then cutting the threads. As the threads are cut, so are the evil forces that hold this person in their thrall. So Uttu appears fairly regularly in magic literature.

She also appears in several myths, and that's where we realize she is the archetypical wife, just as spinning and weaving are the archetypical wifely duties. Uttu appears first in a tale about the birth of the gods. At first, there are only two divine beings worth mentioning—Enki, a male figure, and Ninhursag, Mother Earth. And they copulate. From this union is born a goddess. Then Enki, who is male water (the subterranean waters and the river waters), copulates with his daughter, and another goddess is born. Enki looks at the new goddess and sees she's beautiful and sleeps with her, too. In each case, he seduces the goddess very easily, and she gives birth very easily, in nine days rather than nine months. And the baby comes out slick as juniper oil.

The fifth or sixth generation is Uttu. When she is born, Ninhursag, the grandmother of all, says to her, "When Enki comes to lie with you, do not say yes. Tell him if he wants you, he must bring you presents." Uttu is a comely female, and Enki desires her. At her request, he performs the Sumerian marriage ceremony—he brings a basket of fruit and knocks on her door. They are married, and they have sex. But Uttu's nine months are not nine days. She has become a wife and has such difficulty giving birth that the mother of all has to turn into the birth goddess—and that is why women always need help.

Uttu appears in another myth important for biblical studies, the story of the ewe lamb and the stalk of wheat. As one kind of entertainment in pre-MTV days, the Mesopotamian elite held banquets where they staged debates between winter and summer—which is more beneficial for humankind?—or between the palm and the tamarisk—which is a more important cultural element.

We have some twenty-odd debates like this, among which is a debate between a ewe lamb and a stalk of wheat or grain. It begins, as they all do, with how these elements came to be, going back to the beginning. It tells the story of how the gods, when they created humanity, which, as everybody knows, was done for the purpose of providing servants, gave humans the task of feeding them.

But in the beginning humans didn't have very much. When we were first created, we walked around naked like the animals, we ate fruits and grasses, and we drank water. And that's what we gave the gods—because that's what we had. But the gods got sick and tired of drinking water and eating grasses, so they held a council meeting and decided to elevate the condition of humankind so we would have better gifts to give them. In order to do that, they created the ewe lamb, the source of wool; and the stalk of grain, the source of bread and beer. They created Uttu, the goddess of spinning and weaving, to teach humans how to make cloth from the ewe lamb. The debate about the ewe lamb and the stalk of grain then goes off in areas that don't particularly interest us about which is more essential to civilization.

In this myth, Uttu is the foundational, transformative agent that moves us from the realm of natural existence—nakedness, water and grasses—to the beginnings of culture—wearing clothes and bringing meat and bread for the gods. Beyond this we know nothing about Uttu, and that is very significant, not because the texts are haphazardly silent about her, but because what a woman is *supposed* to do, what a wife is *supposed* to do, once she is married, is make cloth, bake bread and make beer. And that's a full-time occupation. Beyond that, she has no persona, no characteristics, no desires, no influence, no life. So the literature tells us nothing about her.

There are two more goddesses I would like to tell you about. Although Uttu, the standard middle-class and poorer-class wife, is not heard from again, upper-class women who are courted by rich men are promised a share of power. In fact, Sumerian royal women exercised considerable administrative duties and diplomatic functions and had a good deal of economic impact.

The image of the upper-class woman is the goddess Ninlil, who is raised like a proper daughter and to whom the god Enlil speaks. Enlil is the chief god of the capital city; he is the essence of the young, macho male who goes to war and then organizes things to his desires.

There are two tales about the meeting of Enlil and Ninlil. In one, he rapes her, is brought to trial, and is banished. She, having been thoroughly seduced by the rape (that's a very old myth), follows him to the depths of the netherworld. Enough said about that myth.

In the other myth, he sees her playing in front of her mother's house. He speaks to her mother and offers his hand in marriage. He promises her that her daughter will become, by marrying him, the chief administrator in Nippur, that she, second only to him, will make decisions and, along with him, decide the fates—kind of like Rosalynn and Hillary. In both the rape version and the marriage version of the tale, Ninlil becomes the mother of a vast array of important gods, all of whom are related to Enlil. She is the queen and queen mother who shares her husband's reflected glory and position.

The most enduring goddess, Inanna, starts out the same way as Ninlil. She comes from a middle-class family. We know this because she doesn't work as a child; she's playing on the steps in front of her house when she is seen by the god Dumuzi, who falls madly in love with her and tries to seduce her. He asks her to come away with him: "We will tarry in the moonlight, we will dally in the moonshine." And she says, "But what will I tell my mother?" He responds, "I will teach you the lies that women say."

But she doesn't buy any of this, and after a long courtship he has to come and ask for her hand. I mention the long courtship because the courtship of Dumuzi and Inanna was celebrated cultically—and probably also in the bars. We have lots of their love songs. If you were Sumerian and wanted to write a love song, you wrote it as Dumuzi speaking to Inanna or Inanna speaking to Dumuzi. These love songs are not going to become big hits. They don't translate very well: "Your hair is lettuce, your hair is cucumbers falling." They don't have much modern appeal. But they meant a great deal to the Sumerians.

Ultimately, Inanna and Dumuzi get married. Their marriage is the most consequential event that ever happened for humans. Every year in Sumer, the wedding was celebrated. As far as we can tell, it was always celebrated the same way in the royal period. The male figure, who was the king and who was also Dumuzi, was brought, presumably by the men of the town, in a procession with appropriate singing to the door of the palace or the temple where Inanna dwelt. There she, played by an anonymous woman, ornamented, adorned, washed and oiled like a bride, opened the door. The two of them then disappeared into the bedroom, where they spent the night. In the morning, there was a wedding feast to which all the nobles were invited, and Inanna blessed the king and the land.

The love songs and the marriage songs reveal a great deal about the nature of this marriage and what makes Inanna different from Ninlil. One text called "Preparing the Linen Garments" is a dialogue between Inanna and her brother. He says it's time to make the wedding sheets. And she says, "Who will grow the flax for me?" He says, "I'll grow it." "Who will dry the flax for me?" "I'll dry it." "Who will stretch the flax for me? Who will beat the flax for me? Who will ret the flax for me? Who will weave the linen for me? Who will cut the cloth?" At each point her brother Utu (not Uttu, but Utu) says, "I will do it for you. I will do it for you." The last line is, "Who will sleep with me there?" And he says, "Not I, that will be your bridegroom, Dumuzi."

Everybody gets a laugh. I'm sure that was true in ancient times, too. But, from all that we know from anthropology and from ancient documents, there is something wrong here. Flax making was a woman's job. Anything connected to making clothing, basically, was a woman's job. Women laid out flax even when they were old. Inanna basically says, "I'm going to get married, but don't expect me to do any of that stuff."

We have another dialogue, a wedding dialogue, between Dumuzi and Inanna in which he says to her, "I am not marrying you to be my servant. Bread you will not bake for me. Clothes you will not make for me. Food you will not cook for me. But you will sit with me at the table." Inanna is relieved of all the economic duties of a woman. Of course, wealthy women had servants to do the work, but it was their responsibility; they oversaw it. Inanna doesn't have any of those concerns, however. She has only one concern. In this same text, Dumuzi brings her before *his* gods, introduces her to the tutelary deity and prays that she will be the mother of many sons.

But she isn't! The epic literature contains references to just two minor children. And if Inanna had them, she must have had full-time nannies for them because she never turns into a mother figure. She never changes shape from the nubile young model of sexual attractiveness. She is called the "mistress of sexual attractiveness." She never turns into the antique woman with pendulous breasts and large thighs. She is eternally young and nubile—the Playboy bunny—the object of love and the personification of lust.

Not having to cook or weave or even take care of children from morning to night, she is the most incongruous of all creatures—a woman who is not kept barefoot, pregnant and in the kitchen. But she is rest-less. She comes to Enki, the administrator who's divvying out cosmic tasks, and says, "What have you got for me to do? You gave midwifery to Ninhursag. You gave sewing and weaving to Uttu. Why don't I have a job?" And he says, "But you are joy and lust and desire, and you are every place." And she says, in effect, "But what does that do for me?"

Inanna is portrayed as always trying to get more power. She man-ages, through her charm (and "hollow leg"), to become a co-administra-tor of the orders of the universe. She is known by the epithet of "the one who walks about." Only demons and Inanna walk about. Inanna is ferocious, the personification of bloodlust, whether it is sexual bloodlust or aggressive, warrior blood lust. So we have this strange creature, the undomesticated woman. She is basically unconfined. She sets out to conquer the netherworld but is trapped there and is finally rescued by the wise god Enki.

She is allowed to leave only if she delivers to the netherworld a sub-stitute because nobody can leave the netherworld once they've been there. When Inanna leaves the realm of the dead, a retinue of sheriffs (which becomes the word for demon)—two in front, two behind, and one on each side—accompanies her. She stalks the land looking for a substitute who will be doomed to the netherworld. She comes to where her husband lives and sees that he has been playing around with every girl in the palace; she gets very mad—and sends him to the netherworld.

Imagine this. It's the night of Halloween, the night of the long knives or the night of Passover. Everybody trembles in their houses while Inanna stalks the land looking for somebody to doom. And this is the goddess of joy, delight and sexuality! Somehow Freud was born a little earlier than we thought.

Inanna's husband would have been doomed to the netherworld for-ever, except that he has a sister who laments for him. She misses him beyond death, and she sings song after song for him. She makes such a big pest of herself that no one can stand it any more. So they decree, "Okay, *you* can take his place. Half of every year he will live here and you will go down there; the other half he will be dead." Suddenly we recognize this as an agricultural cycle of a dying and resurrected god. In fact, every year the Sumerians celebrated the birth of Dumuzi and the death of Dumuzi in the month of Tammuz (named for him). And every year they celebrated his meeting Inanna and the love songs and the sacred marriage.

Despite her powers, Inanna has no real place in the hierarchy. She's restless because women are supposed to be confined to their homes and their home duties, and she is not even occupied there. She is like a free radical—she is approachable, she floats around, and she's ready to bond. And she bonds with the highest of all humans, the King of Sumer.

From earliest recorded history, the kings of Sumer called themselves the spouse of Inanna and celebrated a sacred marriage to her. By so doing, they accomplished several things. They go back to the ritual, in which we don't know who the female is. She could be Mrs. King, but it's not said. She could be a prostitute or a priestess. Whoever she is, she is just Inanna, while the king is specifically said to be the king, and also Dumuzi.

Through the ritual, the male and female principles of the world are brought together. Culture, in the sense of urban life, represented by Inanna, and the forces within nature, represented by Dumuzi, are brought together. And the human world is related to the divine. The king is semidivine by virtue of his being the spouse of Inanna and also born of a goddess. From Inanna, who is on the periphery of the divine hierarchy, come divine blessings, including the cultural arts and agricultural fertility.

Every year this marriage is celebrated. At the wedding breakfast, the goddess Inanna announces a year of peace and abundance upon the land and security for the king. Inanna, with all her strangeness, is vital to the Sumerian understanding of the world. She is the goddess of agricultural fertility.

One of the major functions of goddesses is to be fertile. But there is no Great Goddess despite some recent claims to the contrary. Inanna is agricultural fertility; Ninhursag is the great mother and midwife, the mistress of animal and human fertility. We are so accustomed to the Bible putting together the fruits of the belly and the fruits of the land that we think of fertility as one. But the Sumerians didn't. They kept them separate. Basically, through the vagina the female force of the universe was considered determinative for the continuation of the universe—through birth by the mother goddess and through sexual encounter by the sex goddess, the Madonna and the whore, if you wish.

This all changed when Sumerian civilization was overwhelmed by the Semites. Babylonian civilization brought a new synthesis. Despite what you might hear about the sexiness of paganism, the Babylonians were prudes. They stopped celebrating the sacred marriage. Henceforth, they celebrate the marriage of a god and his or her spouse by taking two statues into a garden, singing a couple of songs and leaving the statues in the garden overnight.

They also perceive the rejuvenation of the world in nonsexual terms. Instead of celebrating the sacred marriage each year, they develop a completely different type of mythology. Written in Akkadian, this mythology began to have an impact during the second half of the second millennium. In the new Babylonian story, the *Enuma Elish*, formless waters commingle in the beginning and ultimately evolve into gods. There are two kinds of Babylonian gods—active gods who move around in the air and sky, creating winds; and static gods, denizens of the watery depths. When the winds move, they disturb the depths. So the male water figure attacks them to try to keep them quiet, but he is defeated by Enki. Then the mother water of us all pays heed to her children, the gods of stasis, who complain that they cannot sleep. So she threatens the newly emergent creativity.

Suddenly the gods who were able to defeat Apsu cannot defeat the mother water Tiamat. They are afraid even to approach her—except for Mr. Macho—Marduk—a young god who does not yet have a place on the divine council. Marduk is very strong and has twice as much godliness as anybody else. His father Enki tells him, "Come to the council. Do not bow down. Do not show respect. March in like a warrior, and they will listen to you." Marduk does this, and says, "I can fight for you, you divinities of the air and sky, you with your creative energy. After all, it's only a woman who's attacking you." A new spirit is in the air. "If you make me king of the gods," he says, "I will defeat her."

At this point, young Mr. Macho doesn't even have status as a fate-determining god. He can't do anything. But the others agree to his terms. To show him that he has moved into the realm of the mighty and powerful, they give him the power of the creative word. They say, "Speak." He speaks and a constellation comes into being. They say, "Speak again." He speaks and the constellation disappears.

So, armed with weapons of the storm and the wind, Marduk goes to fight the mother goddess Tiamat. They meet in single combat—and he defeats her. When she opens her mouth to swallow him, he blows her up with his winds. She becomes big as a balloon. He then takes his arrow of lightning and pierces her. A very ignoble ending. Then he takes her body and creates the universe, providing a permanent place for the gods so that each one knows his place, and there will be order in the universe, a differentiated world.

He then establishes a hierarchical state, where everybody knows *his* function, everybody has *his* place. I say "his" because there are no goddesses in this tale, just gods. They are the state and the governors. In order to support this system, so the male gods won't have to work, he conceives of the brilliant idea of creating an underclass, which is us, to do all the work. And every year his victory over disorder is celebrated as the governing principle of the world. As long as hierarchy, domination and order subdue the rash natural elements of the cosmos, the world is safe for another year.

This is not monotheism. This is classically developed polytheism. The same story, with some variations, is found in Canaan, among the Hittites and among the Greeks. The mythology of the last half of the second millennium tells of a world of power, hierarchy, status and the orderly control of things. And women have no place in this hierarchy.

Goddesses have no place in it. Goddesses are either trivialized into "consorts," Mrs. Gods, "first ladies," or domesticated, called upon in private situations, like the mother goddess at childbirth. The only goddess who escapes this eclipse is Inanna, who is called Ishtar by the Babylonians. Unable to be domesticated by her very nature, she becomes a major warrior goddess. At the same time, she makes men look beyond their roles in the cosmos to the messy stuff of home and procreation, something they wouldn't do if they really were orderly creatures.

What we find in developed paganism, in other words, in the religion of all the cultures that surrounded Israel, is *not* feminist religion but models of patriarchy and the patriarchal state. The divine image of patriarchy is of a king of the gods who sits on his throne, uses his power and collects his tribute.

Does this have anything to do with Israel? Yes and no. Israel has a fundamentally different system, in which the gender line is totally ignored or obscured. Rather than presenting a model of how women should be controlled, Israelite theology doesn't talk about women at all. We can argue *ad infinitum* about which is worse for women—to be dominated explicitly or to be ignored and rendered invisible. But without female principles, the nature of God undergoes a major transformation. God ceases to be phallic. You do not see God below the waist. There is no mention of God's fertility as coming from his loins. On the contrary, everything is cerebralized into the divine word, and God becomes a talking torso.

This change has major implications. On the one hand, it removes the warrant for male domination. But, as you know, history and culture rushed in to project male domination onto the religious base anyway and to imagine God with a phallus. But the ordering of the world, the essential running of the world, is desexualized, as it already was in Babylonian mythology of the late second millennium. God now has all the powers, even the domestic power of the birth goddess. As those of you who read Scripture know, the Bible tells us over and over that God controls birth—he stops up wombs, he opens wombs, he forms the baby in the womb, he determines the destiny of the baby, he sees the baby in the womb. God does everything.

But if God does everything and God has all the power, why does anything ever happen? In paganism, the world is always in flux—god against god, god cooperating with god, gods merging with each other, fighting with each other. You can see why things happen. In monotheism, why should God ever do anything? It could be a static world. What happens in the Bible is that the role of humanity expands beyond anything imagined in paganism.

In the Bible, the creature is created as a creature. So far, we could be in Mesopotamia. But the creature is restless and determined to grow. The creature grabs for wisdom. The goddess Uttu taught humans how to make clothes; Eve discovers it on her own. The first couple eats the apple, their eyes are opened, and they sew themselves garments. Through eating they learn how to sew, they change from natural beings into cultural beings. The next step is agriculture. They leave the Garden and become farmers.

In the genealogies of the first eleven chapters of Genesis, all the arts of civilization are developed by humankind. They are all born with us, including kingship. In Mesopotamia, kingship is a gift of the gods, as are smithing and artwork and song. Not in Genesis. There a formidable creature is developing. By the end of Genesis 11, the creature is so powerful that nothing can hinder it. It goes forth, is scattered over the whole world and builds a universe.

This creature is God's counterpart, God's *tselem,* the very image of God. In Mesopotamia, this term applies only to the king, who is a god's foil. In the Bible, it applies to all humans. Humanity, in the persona of Israel, determines the fate of the world by how human beings order their *own* culture. If human beings are good to each other, there will be abundant rain. If they do not lead ethical lives, the prophets tell us, the earth will dry up and mourn, and the heavens will cease to rain. First, Israel will be lost, and, second, humanity will disappear from the cosmos. The issue—the difference between paganism and Israelite monotheism—is stark. We are no longer sitting in the bleachers rooting for our favorite gods in the divine soccer game. We are the players.

Is there room for goddesses here? Is there room for women? It depends on whom you ask, and when. For as long as they could, human beings tried to escape the radical monotheism of Deuteronomy, in which human beings determine whether or not there will be births. Only in the last ten or fifteen years, with holes in the ozone and increasing pollution and nuclear threats and biological mutations and new viruses, has it become hard to escape the idea that humans determine the fate of the universe. And we had better do so consciously, because we do so unconsciously anyway.

But before we became so powerful that the results of our actions stared us in the face, we ran from our responsibility partly by developing a theology of repentance. We could come to God and say, "Gee, I'm sorry, I broke it." And God would fix it. Repentance became very important in the development of the image of God the Father, God who chastises but also accepts repentance. We developed the parable of the Prodigal Son who returns and other patterns of redemption through sacrifice, atonement and repentance. We find this idea both in temple theology and later in early Christianity and Judaism.

The search for ways to influence the Father to forgive us and, therefore, correct our mistakes also encompassed a search for anyone who could influence the Father on our behalf—for example, the prophet, whose job was to pray for Israel; the priest, whose job was to offer sacrifices. But why stop there? The dead, too, could intercede, especially mother Rachel. In Jeremiah's famous vision, mother Rachel, the mother of the northern tribes, has been mourning loudly, without stopping, for one hundred and fifty years. She cannot be comforted. Finally God says, "Okay, I'm going to reward your labor, your children will come back." So we look for a mother in Zion, the city herself, who opens her arms in the books of Lamentation and begins an incessant noisemaking and crying to soften God's heart, to bring the people back.

Our search for anyone who can intervene with God becomes the search for a beloved intermediary, Lady Wisdom, who unites us with God in our joint love for her, or Lady Jerusalem, who marries both God and Israel in the perfect eschaton and thereby conjoins them. Are these echoes of goddesses, who survived in some subterranean fashion? Or are these new manifestations of the same psychological and sociological phenomenon that gave rise to the goddesses in the first place?

Goddesses are mediators. Women are always mediators. Miriam is a mediator. You pray to your mother to help you with your father. You may pray to your father to help you with your mother, but if the father has the power, then you pray to your mother to help you. The development of female intercessors reaches a peak in the glorification of Mary; the Jewish counterpart is the devotion and pilgrimages to the tomb of Rachel.

It's hard to say if Lady Wisdom is a survival of the great goddesses of wisdom of the third and early second millennium or if she and the goddesses of wisdom are the result of our experiences in the first few years of life, when the wise one, who brings us into civilization and teaches us to eat food and wear clothes and go to the potty, is our mother, who, at some point, is all-wise in our eyes. Or is Lady Wisdom a cultural memory that in earlier times, when forests had to be cleared and trenches had to be dug and oxen had to be guided and horses had to be tamed, the upper-body strength of men dictated that they would do the physical activity, which meant that everything else—cooking, sewing, pottery making, beer making—would be done by women? Of course, this "everything else" seems a little bit magical and more sophisticated, and women developed the reputation of having access to secret knowledge. We don't know whether these are echoes or resonances.

In the time that remains, I want to focus on another aspect of this potential echoing. Goddesses are patrons of certain arts. In every pagan religion, humanity learns civilization from the gods. Everything is a gift from the gods, who oversee what you do and give you the skill to do it. If you look at what is associated with female gods and what is associated with male gods, you find an interesting pattern. The immediate transformational activities—making clothes, food, beer—are associated with goddesses because those are the things mothers do.

But goddesses are also mistresses of the obscure, the mantic arts, divination, riddle solving. Perhaps this reflects the role of the mother in early childhood and the role of women in early economic systems. You want a dream interpreted? Speak to your goddess. Even *Gilgamesh*, when he needs a dream interpreted, asks his mother, Ninsun. You want to send a sage to a foreign army? If you live in the third millennium, the sage may very well be a woman.

So the cultural arts, the mantic arts, singing and dancing are all associated with females (although, to some extent, also with males). In

Sumerian paganism, one particular god grows and grows and finally absorbs all of the cultural arts and the wisdom of the female deities. He is the god Enki.

But when we look at the Bible, we find something very interesting. In a patriarchal world where men were the major actors, in a world where women were not so much shackled as they were limited by the felt need to control their sexuality, despite all of the androcentric focus in the Bible, women keep cropping up as figures from the margin who know what should happen and who do whatever is necessary to make sure it happens.

Eve is just the first of many women who transform the human situation. She reaches for the fruit because she is fascinated by its ability to make one wise. But she isn't very different from mother Rebecca, who is privy to an oracle (which, apparently, wasn't given to Isaac) that Jacob, rather than Esau, is to be the inheritor, and who uses every means in her power to affect that outcome. Sarah also uses her power to insure that Isaac will be the heir. In her case we're not told if she knows this is in accord with the divine will, but with Rebecca we are told quite clearly that she knows. During the period of the Exodus, we find women acting independently. Miriam supervises and knows what's going to happen. Zipporah, Moses' wife, knows what to do when God attacks.

When we look at the historical books of the Bible, this pattern becomes regularized and clear. The first story in the historical books, in Joshua 2, is the story of Rahab, the prostitute of Jericho. Rahab, the marginal of the marginal, a prostitute of a foreign people, proclaims the divine decree; she is the one who tells Israel God will give them the land. At the end of the historical books, another woman, Hulda the prophetess, proclaims that Israel's occupation of the land will soon come to an end, at least temporarily. She is also the one who proclaims the validity or authoritativeness of the book of the Law we call Deuteronomy. In between, a female medium makes the pronouncement that Saul's reign is about to end and David's about to begin.

Whether these are echoes of the mantic rites of the goddesses or reflections of the psychological attachment to mother, we cannot say. But we should note that the Bible is consistently bracketed and punctuated by the wise words of women.

6 / Lolita-Inanna

2000

Inanna, as we all know, is the most changeable and mercurial of goddesses, a mistress of opposites and paradoxes, a god with radically
changeable personality and functions, a god who not only bends gender
but may also change sex in herself, and at least cultically, in her worshipers. Is there a rational order to these changes? To what degree can they
be plotted according to the place in which she is worshiped, the time
when the texts were written, or the type of texts we read?

In order to unravel the complex evidence about Inanna, it may be
valuable to pick a genre of texts and approach them with radical ignorance, putting out of our mind everything we know about Inanna in
order to see what these texts say in isolation. I chose to begin with the
Dumuzi-Inanna songs, because this is a fairly large corpus and because
of their inherent interest to us as sacred marriage texts. The study of
these songs has been greatly facilitated by the critical edition prepared
by Yitschak Sefati, *"Love Songs in Sumerian Literature: Critical Edition
of the Dumuzi-Inanna Songs."*[1]

First, having just read through all these poems, I have to bear witness to the fact that, to this woman at least, they are not very interesting
literature, and certainly not very erotic. These songs speak in two modes:
in one, the inner meaning of the texts and ritual is apparent: Dumuzi
is the king and Inanna bestows fertility on him. In this mode, Inanna is
praised as the fertile and fructifying goddess, a vine and a furrow, the
true plant who mates with the shepherd. She is the goddess who blesses
Ama-usum-gal-anna[2] and rewards him with abundance,[3] giving him life
and long days[4] as he stands before her in prayer, blesses him on the
wedding bed.[5]

In the other mode of the Dumuzi-Inanna texts, the pair speak as
lovers, and the goddess/king aspect recedes into the distance. Mostly
we hear Inanna's voice, describing Dumuzi, her love for him, and her

expectations from him. The Dumuzi who appears in these texts is resplendent and noble, friend of An, and much beloved of Inanna. Inanna in these stories is another story. As the object of love, she is, above all, sweet. When Dumuzi speaks, he speaks of the great joy in her kisses and her lips. She is ka-làl ama-na-mu, "my one who is the honey-mouth one of her mother"[6] and the làl ama-ugu-zu/na, "the honey of the mother who bore her."[7] The mention of her mother is appropriate, for she is a "young maiden," ki-sikil, "a child," lu-túr, and "sister" nin_9. The beloved is yet a child.

Dumuzi-Inanna C[8] reveals that Inanna is a child of privilege and leisure. It is a commonplace among historians that childhood is a modern invention, that in the premodern era children were expected to work. The privileged, of course, might have their work done by others. Dumuzi-Inanna C begins with a male addressing Inanna. Since he calls her "my sister," it is possibly Utu, but it is more probably Dumuzi, who calls Inanna "my sister" in these texts. In fact, since Inanna calls both Dumuzi and Utu "brother" and Dumuzi calls both Inanna and Amageštinanna "sister" in these texts, it is sometimes hard to tell who the characters are. In Dumuzi-Inanna C, the male asks a question: "my sister, what have you done while you were in the house? O child, what have you done while you were in the house?" Inanna has neither worked nor studied. She has spent the day washing, anointing, putting on fine garments, washing and dressing her hair and adorning herself with jewelry. Possibly this text presents a scene in which Inanna has been preparing herself as a bride, as she does in the Iddin-Dagan Sacred Marriage text. But perhaps the texts present a more common scene in the life of Inanna. Inanna may spend many days in such total self-preoccupation. Like many a teenage girl off from school, Inanna has spent her day primping. Unlike modern teenagers, however, Inanna has no expectations of either school or work. When Inanna does not spend the day adorning herself, she spends her day in play e-ne-di and song èn-du du_{11}-ga-mu-dè.[9]

Not even the anticipation of her wedding makes Inanna plan to work. In the better known "Dialogue between Utu and Inanna," Utu offers to perform all the steps to make her bridal sheet.[10] When he offers to bring her the green flax, she refuses to work it and gets him to agree to ret, spin, dye, weave, and bleach it. Even in marriage, Inanna will not have to perform domestic tasks. In the wedding text Dumuzi-Inanna C_1[11], Inanna tells Dumuzi that she cannot use a loom, and Dumuzi promises her that she will not have to work in this marriage, "I have not carried you off into servitude . . . O, my bride, cloth you will not weave for me; O Inanna, yarn you will not spin for me; O my bride, fleece you will not ravel for me!" Inanna will not make clothes, weave flax, or spin wool. She can continue to spend her days as she has before.

A child of privilege, Inanna is also a child of luxury. Like Isaiah's daughters of Zion, with their adornments and their jewelry (Isa 3:16–24), Inanna is the adorned daughter of luxury who spends her day on make-up and jewelry. "She puts kohl on her eyes, lapis lazuli on her neck."[12] In Dumuzi-Inanna C[13] the young girl Inanna has adorned herself, wearing a gold necklace and beads. She eagerly awaits the husband who will bring her gifts. Possibly the poem is set on the night before the wedding banquet, and her washing and adorning has been for the wedding. But the timing is not clear, and she may be anticipating an as-yet-unset wedding. Dumuzi promises to bring everything he has to her: ᵈInanna-zu téš mu-ra-an-sum (line 21). And Inanna is eager for these gifts: ḫé-túm-túm ḫé-túm-túm dig-dig-ga-bi ga-na ḫé-túm-túm (line 32). When Dumuzi will bring food, Inanna will make him happy, and they will go to dance. Another song has her expecting butter and milk from the shepherd.[14] But as a girl of privilege, she can also expect wondrous presents from her suitor: crystals[15] and lapis, gold and jewels.[16]

Dumuzi-Inanna C reveals that Inanna is a very young girl. She is just entering puberty, first sprouting breasts and pubic hair, and looks forward to sporting with her beloved: i-da-lam gaba-me ba-gub-gub, i-da-lam gal₄-la-me síg ba-an-mú úr-mu-ti-in-na-šè di-di-dè ba-ba ga-ba-ḫúl-ḫúl-le-en-dè-en.[17] "Now my breasts stand out, now my mons grows hair. To the breast of my bridegroom; as we go, Baba, let us rejoice!" Inanna's ardor is also the ardor of a very young girl: she talks about him incessantly, she spends her day in yearning,[18] she gushes about her "honey-man," all of whom is delightful honey.[19] Anticipating her wedding, she prays that sex with him will be sweet[20] and declares him her destiny: "My [mother] who bore me gave birth to me for you."[21]

Inanna is not a wild girl. She is not Dinah, seduced as she went out to see the girls of the land. When Dumuzi meets her, falls in love with her, and tries to induce her to come away with him, she obeys all the rules of propriety, demanding that he come to her mother's house ká ama-me-da nam-mi-gub, so that he can properly become her husband.[22] In the midst of dancing with her beloved, she sends to her father to arrange a wedding.[23] Even in her erotic daydreams, she pictures Dumuzi coming to her father's house.[24] She may have erotic fantasies and yearnings, but she does not give in to them. On the contrary, she is docile and obedient, protecting her family's honor and "holding out for the ring." In other literature, Inanna can represent the power of eros that ignores and transcends convention. In these love songs of Inanna and Dumuzi, there is nothing defiant about her, nothing angry, nothing dangerous, nothing wild. She is the conventional well-brought-up daughter.

The image of Inanna that emerges from these texts is of a beautiful young girl in first bloom, self-absorbed and materialistic, preening and primping and prone to daydreaming and infatuated love. She is, in short, the archetypical preteen and in our culture, this quintessential object of love would be in sixth or seventh grade.

This love for the young as-yet-unformed woman is partly understandable as a reflection of the marriage age at a time when women could expect to die young. But there is more to it than that. Shakespeare's Juliet was thirteen, but Dante's real-life love Beatrice was only nine when he met her and fell in love with her. Petrarch's Laura was twelve, and Salome was eleven when she danced for Herod and enticed him to give her the head of John the Baptist. In our culture, Nabokov gave us two words for such women, "nymphet" and "Lolita," the young girl whom Humbolt Humbolt loved so passionately. The movie star equivalent of the Inanna of these texts is not Sharon Stone or Demi Moore, but Brooke Shields as she appeared in *Pretty Baby* when she was eleven. It is probably significant that Brooke Shields has not had a movie hit since she became a woman. In a way, this love for the very young girl is the heterosexual equivalent of the boy-love of Greek society. It is love for the eternal almost, the one who already holds the promise of sexual delight, and yet is still "on the verge" of limitless potential; the one who is still sweet and innocent, still malleable, still docile, still untouched by the experiences and sorrows the more mature lover has already endured, and still unformed by these experiences and sorrows into the person she will someday be. There is no hint in this girl-child of the complex Inanna that she will later become.

One might add a note about the much discussed connection between love and tragedy, eros and thanatos. Those who insist on loving an unformed and self-absorbed child cannot be prepared for the inevitable changes that this love object will undergo. Disillusionment and disaster are sure to follow if not, indeed, death in Venice, or, in our case, in Uruk. Love for ephemeral girl-children may bring disaster, love for mature self-realized women probably will not. When we

celebrate the marriage of Lolita-Inanna to Dumuzi, we must anticipate seeing the struggles of the woman to emerge from this cocoon,
struggles that may lead to her tragedy, as, in our case, to the death
of Dumuzi.

NOTES

1. "Love Songs in Sumerian Literature: Critical Edition of the Dumuzi-
Inanna Songs." Ph.D. thesis, Bar-Ilan University, 1985. Sefati's book was published in English after I wrote this article. I have changed all the references
to page numbers of the published version, but have otherwise not changed
the article.

2. Dumuzi-Inanna F: Sefati text 6, pp. 171–176.

3. Dumuzi-Inanna O : (ISET I p. 60, SLTN 141 1–11, SLTN 90 rev 1–12).
Sefati text 12, pp. 210–217.

4. Dumuzi-Inanna P: (PAPS 107, p. 519f + TIM 9, 10) Sefati text 13, pp.
218–235.

5. Dumuzi-Inanna D1, Sefati text 21, pp. 301–311.

6. Dumuzi-Inanna B: (SRT 31); lines 3, 5, 7, 9, 11; Sefati, p. 128.

7. Dumuzi-Inanna B: lie 2; Sefati, p. 128; Dumuzi-Inanna C (SRT5); line
22; Sefati, p. 134.

8. Dumuzi-Inanna C: was first translated by Kramer, 1969: 97f. See Sefati,
text 3, 132–150.

9. I Dumuzi-Inanna H (TMH NF III 25); lines 3, 4; Sefati, p. 185; cf.
Jacobsen, 1976: 28–30.

10. Dumuzi-Inanna A: see Sefati text 1, pp. 120–127.

11. Sefati text 20, pp. 286–300. Cf. Jacobsen, 1987: 19–23.

12. Dumuzi-Inanna E1: Sefati text 22, pp. 312–319.

13. Sefati text 3, pp. 132–150.

14. Dumuzi-Inanna R: Sefati text 14, pp. 236–246.

15. Dumuzi-Inanna I: Sefati text 9, pp. 194–205.

16. Dumuzi-Inanna T: Sefati text 15, pp. 247–256.

17. Dumuzi-Inanna C: lines 39–41; Sefati, p. 135.

18. Dumuzi-Inanna D: Sefati text 4, pp. 151–164; see Jacobsen, 1976:
27–28.

19. Dumuzi-Inanna E; Sefati text 5, pp. 165–170.

20. Dumuzi-Inanna T; Sefati text 15, pp. 247–256.

21. Dumuzi-Inanna Z: line 1; Sefati, pp. 281–282.

22. Dumuzi-Inanna H: reverse 4; Sefati, p. 186; see Jacobsen, 1976: 28–30
and 1987: 10–12.

23. Dumuzi-Inanna T; Sefati text 15, pp. 247–256; Cf. Jacobsen, 1976:
35–36.

24. Dumuzi-Inanna Z; Sefati text 19, pp. 281–285.

BIBLIOGRAPHY

Jacobsen, Thorkild. *The Treasures of Darkness: A History of Mesopotamian Religion.* New Haven: 1976.

———. *The Harp That Once . . . Sumerian Poetry in Translation.* New Haven: 1987.

Kramer, Samuel N. *The Sacred Marriage Rite, Aspects of Faith, Myth, and Ritual in Ancient Sumer.* Bloomington and London: 1969.

Sefati, Yitschak. *Love Songs in Sumerian Literature: Critical Edition of the Dumuzi-Inanna Songs.* Bar-Ilan Studies in Near Eastern Languages and Culture. Ramat Gan, 1998.

COMPARATIVE CULTURE II: JUDAISM AND CHRISTIANITY

7 / The Image: Religious Anthropology in Judaism and Christianity

2000

When Jews think about Christianity, they are often struck by ideas and images fundamentally different from Jewish traditions. Icons, statues, incense, crucifixes, and even crosses create a physical environment radically different from Jewish worship; notions of trinity and incarnation form a mental universe equally bizarre to traditional Jewish concepts. It is with some degree of relief that Jews often turn to Christian ideas of humanity and society, finding common ground with Christianity precisely on the common ground of earth and human beings. The nature of human beings and of the human relationship with God affords at least a common theological language with which to think about the issues of human existence, the language of *tselem elohim* and *imago dei:* the image of God.

THE "IMAGE" IN THE HEBREW BIBLE

This language of the "image of God" has its source in the Hebrew Bible, in the first chapter of Genesis: "God created humanity in his own image; in the image of God he created him" (1:27). Genesis does not spell out the implications of the "image"; possibly there is a connection here with God's blessing, with fertility, and with "dominion" over the earth. In Mesopotamia and Egypt, kings erected statues of themselves at the farthest reaches of their empires to represent their dominion. In Akkadian, the word for statue is *tsalmu,* the same as Hebrew *tselem* (image). Furthermore, Assyrian texts describe the king himself as *tsalam ili,* "image of the god," the representative of God on earth. In the same way, says Genesis, humans are to act for God on this earth, administrating and performing other acts of "dominion."

Genesis 5:1–3 develops the concept of "image" further as it begins the genealogies with a recapitulation that God created humanity in God's likeness *(demut elohim); the* passage then specifies that "God created them male and female, blessed them and called them 'Adam.'" The next verse makes the meaning of the term "likeness" clear, for Adam "begat in his image as his likeness" and called his name "Seth." God created us to be like God, and even though God is beyond gender, it is the nexus of male and female that is the likeness and creates the likeness. As we create children, we take on the God-like role of creator. Moreover, we create children who look like us, and we, and they, look like God. The use of the word *demut* in these two sentences makes the physicality of our likeness to God apparent.

A completely different aspect of the concept of "image of God" emerges in the more legally oriented passage of Genesis 9:1–8, the re-institution of humanity after the flood. Here a fundamental difference between humanity and the animals is reinforced: human beings can kill and eat animals (with some restrictions), but no one, not even an animal, can kill a human. Whoever kills a human being forfeits his life, because "in the image of God He made humanity." Here, the concept of "image" determines not how we should act, but how others should act toward us. Each human is to be treated as the representative of God. In this way, the concept of "image of God" creates a sense of the inviolability and sacredness of human life.

These Genesis passages form the basis for a religious anthropology that concentrates on the divine aspects of human form and function. Both the New Testament and early Jewish sources found this concept of *tselem* very attractive, maybe because the Greco-Roman world knew images and statues, surrounded as it was by rules concerning the treatment of the statues of Roman emperors. In this cultural milieu, it was perhaps inevitable that the relationship of humanity and God, described already in the Hebrew Bible as one of image to source, should be explored in terms of the image of God.

THE RABBINIC AND NEW TESTAMENT "IMAGE"

The Rabbis of this period emphasize the connection between humanity and God. To them, our physical resemblance is a sign of a connection so deep that injury to a human being injures God. They understand the deep paradox underlying Genesis 9, which proclaims the sanctity of human life even as it announces that this sanctity will be safeguarded by the death of a human being. Rabbi Meir tells a parable about a king whose twin brother was an outlaw. The king crucified him, but as he was hanging on the cross the passersby saw (they thought) that the king had been hung.[1] The implication is clear: what is done to human beings reflects on God. In the same spirit, Rabbi Akiba declared that "whoever sheds blood cancels the image,"[2] a sentiment expressed also by the Mekhilta, which relates a parable about a king who enters a state, puts up statues and impresses coins, only to have the statues broken and the coins invalidated: "so too, one who spills blood is one who lessens the king's image."[3] This way of thinking about human beings had great legal implications; as Rabbi Akiba and Rabbi Tarphon declared, "if we were in the Sanhedrin, no one would ever be killed" (M. Mak. 1:10).

The Rabbinic notion of image is concrete: it relates to people's looks, to their face and form, which are like God's, and not to some concept of mind, soul, spirit, or intellect. The bodily resemblance leads Hillel to declare that we have an obligation to care for our body as the image of God.[4] Moreover, since each individual person is the image of God, we have an obligation to maximize the image of God both by creating more people and by not killing people: "whoever does not engage in procreation has diminished the divine image;" and those that harm the image have a major impact on God in the world and, in a more mystical sense, on the very self of God.[6]

The physical resemblance between humans and God is also a factor in New Testament teaching, particularly in relationship to the appearance of Jesus, who was a perfect representation of God. John reports Jesus' response to Philip's request to see the father: "Anyone who has seen me has seen the father" (Jn 14:8–9). Similarly, some of the Epistles stress that Christ is the "image of the invisible God" (Col 1:15; cf. 2 Cor 4:4), "the radiance of God's glory and the exact representation of his being" (Heb 1:3). Jesus may be the most perfect image (a position that some Jewish sources ascribe to Jacob),[7] but all of the rest of us are also in the image of God. Like the Jewish sources, James, asking how we can praise God and also curse men who have been made in God's likeness, understands that the "image" concept should determine how we treat each other (Jas 3:9). This practical consequence of seeing people in God's image is also expressed by "Pseudo-Clementine," an author writing in the first half of the second century who was possibly Jewish-Christian. Clementine picks up Genesis' idea of dominion, declaring that the purpose for which humans are "impressed as with the greatest seal in his form" is so that he will "rule over all and all will serve him." Moreover, declares Clementine, "whoever wants to worship Him will honor His image."[8]

Paul introduces a new element into the concept of the image, a dynamic and relative sense: "we are being transformed into his likeness with ever-increasing glory" (2 Cor 3:18). The new self of the faithful is being renewed in the image. When the Rabbis talk about "lessening the image," they are referring to the quantity of humans in the world, for all of us are the image. Paul, on the other hand, speaks about quality, for each of us can be more the image.

ORIGINAL SIN AND THE FALL OF THE "IMAGE"

Becoming more of the image can also mean that we can be less of the image. Christian sources speak often about "the Fall" of Adam and Eve, a fall that damaged the very nature of humanity. There are some similar Jewish traditions, clustered around the idea of *adam ha-rishon*, the first Adam,[9] but these traditions are nowhere near as common as the Christian discussion of "the Fall" or "original sin." The second-century theologian Irenaeus distinguished between the "image" and the "likeness." The likeness was lost in the Fall, but the image remained, and the likeness was restored when God became his image at the incarnation. For a long time, Christian writers incorporated the notion of the Fall of humanity into their concept of humans as an essential part of the idea of the image of God. Humanity was born in the full image and likeness. After the Fall, in some way this image was lessened, disfigured, or destroyed, and humans could no longer be full images of God. God's redemption, which began with the incarnation, served to remedy this flaw in humanity, and it is belief in this redemption, expressed concretely through baptism, that enables people to be restored in God's eyes.

"The Fall" and "original sin" are difficult concepts for Jews. Even though Jewish tradition speaks of Adam's sin and punishment, the idea that we are still somehow involved in this very ancient sin and punishment offends basic Jewish ideas of justice. One of the stories basic to Jewish spiritual formation, Abraham's argument with God over the fate of Sodom, rejects the notion of collective punishment: "God forbid that you should do such a thing, to kill the righteous with the wicked, that the righteous should be like the wicked" (Gen 18:25).

Punishing anybody but the perpetrator offends Abraham's (and our) sense of justice: "God forbid, should the judge of the world not do justice?" (Gen 18:25). Jews also find the "verticality," the transgenerational nature, of the punishment problematic. It is true that the Ten Commandments contain God's promise to "visit the sins of the fathers upon the sons," but this punishment does not carry past the third or fourth generation; only the good deeds are to resonate to thousands of generations. The Hebrew Bible ultimately rejects even the idea that God can punish to the fourth generation, as the prophet Ezekiel proclaims a new moral order after the Babylonian exile in which God would not punish any child for the sin of the parents (Ezek 18). Given this clear teaching of individual responsibility, it is hard for Jews to follow language that speaks of a sin or punishment inherited from Adam.

Jewish eyes also have problems with the remedy for this sin. Rabbinic tradition concentrates on commandments that have to be performed, actions of both moral and ritual valence. These commandments describe the life that one is to live in order to please God. One of the earliest Jewish traditions, attributed to Antiochos of Socho, declares, "Do not be like servants who serve their master expecting to receive a reward; be rather like servants who serve their master unconditionally, with no thought of reward" (M. *Avot* 1:3). Despite this ideal, the Rabbis developed an elaborate conception of reward and punishment and, in fact, declared belief in reward and punishment to be one of the core essential beliefs. A doctrine that considers human beings to be incapable of right action and makes salvation dependent upon a specific belief in the salvific life and death of Jesus seems to go against the very basis of the Jewish system of *mitzvot.*

On closer examination, of course, the difference between the Christian and Jewish notions of salvation is not that enormous. A recurrent motif of the High Holiday liturgy proclaims the importance of remembering the virtues of the patriarchs, and above all Abraham's willingness to sacrifice Isaac. The merit of this act accrues to all future Jews, and is a "trump card" that they play in the drama of sin, repentance, and atonement. If Abraham's act can reverberate throughout the eons, one can understand that Jesus' sacrifice can have a transformative impact. Nor is the requirement of belief entirely unknown in Judaism. The Mishnah speaks of those who "have no share in the world to come": those who do not believe that the resurrection is a biblical doctrine, and those who say that the Torah was not revealed (M. Sanh. 11:1). The legend of Elisha ben Abuya underscores the importance of such beliefs for Rabbinic Judaism.

Elisha was one of the four great sages who took a mystical voyage to heaven. While he was there, he saw the angel Metatron sitting and writing the merits of Israel in a book. Elisha was surprised to see Metatron sitting, since he knew that angels do not get tired and therefore should not need to sit. As a result, Elisha deduced that *perhaps* there might be two powers in heaven. This momentary loss of total faith in the absolute unity of God was enough to remove him entirely from the Jewish system. He became "the other" *(aher)*, and even God, when calling for his "wandering children" to return, adds, "except for *aher.*"[10]

The Jerusalem Talmud's version of the "otherizing" of Elisha ben Abuya also indicates the extreme importance of certain essentials of Rabbinic belief. The Jerusalem Talmud relates two stories in which Elisha lost faith that God rewards actions with their just rewards or punishments. In one story, Elisha saw a boy fall out of a tree as he was in the act of performing the mitzvah of returning a fallen egg to its nest. If God rewarded good and punished evil, certainly the boy would not have died while performing a righteous act! In the other story, Elisha saw the tongue of a great martyred Torah sage and no longer believed that the great righteous act of Torah study had just rewards.

Once Elisha lost his faith he stepped outside the Jewish system. And even though he remained physically in the Jewish community and continued to teach Rabbi Meir,[11] he was no longer part of the community in his own eyes, in the eyes of the community, or (according to the stories) in the eyes of God. Belief, then, at least in certain key precepts, was as crucial as the performance of the commandments. The Christian idea that belief in the savior is necessary for salvation should not seem so strange in the light of these Jewish traditions.[12] On the other hand, the notion of the advent and pervasiveness of original sin, so important in Paul and classical Christianity, finds little counterpart in Jewish thought.

THE PHILOSOPHICAL "IMAGE"

Another key difference between Christian and Jewish ideas developed as Christianity adopted the language of Greek philosophy. The New Testament, like the Hebrew Bible, considered the human being indivisible: a person was an indissoluble mix of body, mind, soul, and spirit. The image and likeness of God, therefore, referred to the whole package.

The use of the metaphor of the impressions on a coin to express the idea of the image underscores the physical likeness of humans to God, and it is the body that bears this physical likeness. A tradition about Hillel makes the bodily nature of the image explicit. Hillel declared that he performed God's commandment in the act of going to the bathroom or bathhouse, for he was rendering his obligation to the body in the image (*Avot de-Rabbi Natan* B 30). As Christianity became more Hellenized, it began to adopt the Greek mind/body dichotomy, distinguishing between the "lower" and "higher" aspects of a human being. In this vein, Irenaeus locates the image of God in human rationality and freedom of will.[13] The "likeness" of God was the "robe of sanctity" the Holy Spirit gave Adam. This spirit was lost in the Fall and restored in redemption. In effect, Irenaeus sees the human being as triune, made up of body, soul, and spirit. The image is the rational soul, possessed by all; the likeness, possessed only by believers, is the spirit, a kind of added gift. The body does not figure into this mode of thought at all.

The body undergoes an even greater fall in Gregory of Nyssa, who holds that only when one has ridded oneself of creaturely passions can one behold the image of the divine nature "in their own inner beauty." Rather than use the metaphor of impressing coins, he chooses the sculptor's technique of "lost wax," *cire perdu:* "For God has stamped the image of the good properties of his own essence in your makeup as when a sculptor carves in wax the image of a sculpture he intends to cast."[14] Sin, which is congenital, overlays this image, and since our lives are permeated with passion, the image is permeated with evil. To Gregory, the cure lies in the precepts that the Lord taught, as in the Sermon on the Mount. The divine image is stamped on a virtuous life, the demonic on the sinful one, and one must strive to become pure by virtuous life so that the divine image can be formed in us by pure conduct. The divine image is thus an inner potential that we must attain.

The concern with governing the passions that was so prevalent in the Greco-Roman world is part of the reason that the body was eclipsed in classical Christian conceptions of the image of God. A quintessentially Greek notion, this concern also takes root in Judaism—for instance in the classic formulation "who is a hero: the one who conquers his urges"[15] and in the valorization of Joseph "the righteous" *(ha-tsadik)* for his resistance to the temptation of Potiphar's wife (Gen 39). The worries about temptation, particularly sexual temptation, permeate Hellenistic Judaism and play their role in the elimination of women from Jewish public life.

THE ANTHROPOMORPHIC DILEMMA

In Judaism, there is even a further reason for the interiorization and decorporalization of the "image and likeness of God." A physical understanding of "the image" limits God to the human form. The many powerful metaphors of God in human form—as a young warrior, an old sage, a loving mother—can create a mental "graven image" that can easily become idolatrous in its restriction of God to the human body. Religious unease with the depictions of God as human (what we call "anthropomorphisms") develops early in Jewish tradition, and the targums (the various Aramaic translations of the Bible) employ numerous circumlocutions to eradicate the human language with which God is depicted in the Hebrew Bible.

In Christianity, the presence of God on earth, incarnate in human flesh and form, would seem to finesse the anthropomorphic dilemma, for the incarnate God, who is the exact representation of God, provides a template in whose image the rest of humanity can be described. But the problem is only deflected, not eliminated. A corporeal sense of "image" could be understood to mean that this human-form existence constitutes the totality of the divine essence. Moreover, the historical Jesus was a male. Even more specifically, Jesus was a young, circumcised male. Might one deduce that humans of different ages, skin tones, gender, or foreskin are somehow less in the image of God? Christianity quickly made it clear that the age, skin tone, and foreskin of Jesus were historical circumstances, not essential parts of the image of God. Christianity, however, has had a harder time ridding itself of the notion that gender is more significant than age, and that women are somewhat less the divine image than men.

Perhaps because of this inherent problem of anthropomorphism and limitation in image language, the divine-like aspect of humanity has sometimes been expressed in other language, in terms, for instance, of the presence of sparks of divinity or of the Spirit (the *Shekhinah*) within human beings. Another solution has been to interiorize the meaning of "image," as Gregory does, or to intellectualize it, to define the image of God in humanity as the human intellect. This interpretation ultimately derives fom Greek philosophers, notably Plato and Aristotle, whose idea of God was intellect and who believed that the human intellect was the divine element in humans. Such conceptions came into both Judaism and Christianity with the growth of the philosophical traditions, espoused in Judaism by Maimonides (1135–1204) and in Christianity by Thomas

Aquinas (ca. 1225–1274). To Aquinas, the image was the intellect. All humans have a natural aptitude for understanding and knowing God; those who know God and love God perfectly ("the blessed") have the image "by likeness of glory." In these different manifestations, the image can be faint, dim, or disfigured—or bright and beautiful. Maimonides shares both the identification of the image as intellect and its limitation to a few individuals, for only those people whose intellect is in its most perfect state are really the image of God.

A less philosophically driven but no less noncorporeal seat of the image is the "soul." Perhaps in reaction to the changing sense of "intellect" from the Renaissance on, John Calvin (1509–1564) speaks of the image in the soul, although the body still has some sparks, and at the final restoration the image will be restored to the body. More recent Christian thinkers have gotten away from ontological descriptions of the image. Karl Barth (1886–1968) defines humanity's relational quality, which he calls its "existence in confrontation," as the image of God. An individual's ability to have an I-thou relationship with others and with God is the essential meaning of "image of God." Furthermore, the creation of humanity as "male and female" allows for an I-thou confrontation between man and woman, and for the same kind of confrontation between man and God. Emil Brunner (1889–1966) argues on similar grounds that the "image" resides in relationship and responsibility and expresses the notion of a creature who can respond to a call of love with responsive love.[16]

Alongside these different interpretations of the image of God have come different understandings of the Christian concepts of "the Fall" and "original sin," so important to Paul and early Christian thinkers, so essential to Augustine, and so strange to Jewish ways of thinking. Aquinas places far less emphasis on the loss of the image in a fall than many earlier writers. Nevertheless, he, too, believes that human beings were deprived of something at the Fall: "the gift of supernatural grace" that helps us control our passions. To Irenaeus, it was the likeness-bearing spirit that was lost.[17] By contrast, the Fall was far more significant to John Calvin, who considered fallen humanity to be depraved and afflicted with a perverted nature, a pessimistic view of humanity also held by Martin Luther. Calvin held that there are some remaining traces (*notas*) of the image of God, but it is frightfully deformed, and both reason and will have been weakened.

"Fall" language has become far less pervasive in modern Christian discourse. For more modern thinkers like Barth and Brunner, the Fall has ceased to be a historic fact. Human beings are the image of God, it is their nature. The image is essentially fixed, inherent, and cannot be lost.

THE IMAGE OF GOD: AN EVALUATION

The image of God means many things to different Christians, as it does to different Jews. In more metaphysical circles, it depicts the relationship of the persons of the Trinity. In more mystical circles, it can point to an essential connection between humanity and God. In Jewish tradition it has sometimes been used to support the imperative for procreation to make more images. Today it is most often used to say something about human beings, though what exactly the image is used to say varies widely. At rock bottom, however, the notion that humans are created in the image of God forms the basis of a religious anthropology that stresses the God-like aspects of human existence. Even in the past, when the concept of "the image" was invoked in connection with the Fall in order to state that the image had been obscured, deprived, or depraved, it nevertheless expressed a belief that beyond all that, humans still have something special, that before matters deteriorated, humanity was God-like, and what we had once, we can have again.

We can no more pin down the exact nature of this God-like quality than we can pin down the nature of God. Often, the two depend on each other. Those who would define God as the World Intellect define the "image" as intellect; those who would define God as "love" locate the image in the human capacity to love; those who would define God as process or relationship define the image in the same way. Whatever God is, as God's image, humans share in the divine.

THREE IMPORTANT ASPECTS OF THE "IMAGE"

The first appearance of image talk, in Genesis, has three key features that demonstrate the value of the concept of "image" despite its elusiveness and indeterminacy. First, humans are created through joint activity, as God interrupts the pattern of the creative word to state "we will make in our image." The use of the plural "we" indicates intentionality and cooperation in the creation of humanity, regardless of whether the "we" implies cooperation between the persons of the Trinity (as many Christians have suggested), among all the elements of the divine world (as some Jewish thinkers have said), or between God and the world (as other Jewish thinkers have offered). Whatever the precise interpretation, the plural nature of the creation of humanity applies both to the creator ("we") and to the creature ("he created them male and female"). Social relationship is an indispensable part of both human nature and human purpose, and there can be no utterly single human being.

The second aspect of the image that emerges from Genesis is that humans are given dominion over the rest of creation. Dominion is also part of human nature and purpose, for as the representative, or avatar, of God on earth, humanity cannot *not* be in charge. Whether we define our "dominion" as the right of conquest or the demand of stewardship, whether we embrace control or run from it, humans have power in and over the world. Everything we have done, from the day we invented our first tool, has modified and changed our environment. Humans have a major impact on the world. Deuteronomy expresses some of this human impact as it declares the dependence of fertility on God's reaction to human action (Deut 11:13–17). Genesis 1 expresses our impact on the world by noting our God-like agency and dominion. Human dominion is part of the created order; we cannot escape it and should not ignore it or try to deny it. The language of the "image of God" can enable us to embrace the responsibility. It is not hubris to acknowledge that we have such power. On the contrary, admitting it and accepting it as our nature can help us assume responsibility and accountability for this undeniable facet of human existence.

A third aspect of the "image of God" emerges from the socially and legally oriented passage of Genesis 9, which expresses some of the fundamental aspects of humans living in society. This passage extends the God-like nature of human action depicted in Genesis 1. Genesis 1 alluded to the human impact on the earth; Genesis 9 speaks explicitly of human control of animals. This text grants humanity the right of life-or-death over animals. The primacy of human over animal life was already implicit in God's clothing Adam and Eve in animal skins, but Genesis 9 gives a stamp of approval to humanity's right to kill animals and also acknowledges humanity's carnivorous nature. It permits humanity's violence towards animals even as it sets controls by declaring blood inviolate. Genesis 9 also makes it clear that nobody, animals or humans, can kill a human being. Turning from the subject to the object of action (from what the image does to how the image should be treated), this command extends the implications of the concept of "image." Humans may be God-like in their right to kill animals, but not in their right to kill each other.

THE UNIVERSALITY OF THE "IMAGE"

An essential part of the "image of God" is that it is shared among all humans. Each human being lives among other humans, who are also the "image of God." Each human being has the right to be treated as a stand-in for God in all circumstances. Legal formulations, from Genesis 9 through Rabbinic writings, have concerned themselves with the necessity of making this right concrete in a way that assures that human beings, God's representatives, are treated in a godly fashion. Human beings should not be murdered, says Genesis 9; they should not be executed, say Rabbi Akiba and Rabbi Tarphon; they should not be cursed, says James. Even Calvin, who emphasized the depraved and deformed nature of the fallen human being, nevertheless admonished people to look at the image of God in all humans, to look beyond their worthlessness and to see the image of God.

The essential importance of "image of God" is that it stands alone and eternal, independent of any qualities a human being might possess. Nobody can be more of the image of God than anyone else. There can be no moral qualification: no matter what kind of a life someone has led, no matter how much evil that person may manifest, he or she is no less an image of God than the greatest saint, and cannot be treated as any less God's image. There can also be no qualification or distinction among individual human beings according to class, race, gender, or age, and there can be no distinction between people on the basis of personal merit. The "image of God" is a universal quality of human beings, not limited to a few just or wise people.

There can also be no distinction among nations or other organizations. No group or nation is more the "image of God" than any other. It doesn't matter whether people are believers or nonbelievers in Christ and Christianity, whether people are part of Israel or the nations, whether people consider themselves the image of God or even deny that there is God or that there is any special worth to humanity. Nobody is "other" to the image of God, and no one can be treated in ways that do not recognize this divine quality. The "image of God" is an essential aspect of human nature, shared by all, and the treatment of all human beings must be mindful of this "imagehood." All people, without fail, are equally to be treated as one would treat God.

In practical terms, "imagehood" means that human beings can have dominion only over the earth and over animals. No person can have full dominion over another human being. This imperative has often been ignored in the past, as the subordination of individuals and of nations was claimed as the right of the powerful. But the idea of humanity as "image of God" makes no sense if it does not limit the ability of one human or one group of humans to exert their will over another. This is a bedrock concept in Judaism and Christianity.

Today, in an age of increasing respect for a diversity of cultures and social organization, this "image of God" view of human beings should set limits to how much we embrace and respect other mores. All human life is sacred. The genuine need for all of us to respect each other's culture should not induce us to accept the right of men to murder their wives, sisters, or daughters, as is done with horrifying frequency in Jordan, Saudi Arabia, Iran, and Afghanistan, to name only a few of the places in which such murders are culturally approved and even applauded. No amount of pluralism and tolerance should stop us from protesting the killing of widows or the more frequent burning of brides for dowries (as is happening in India) or the exposure of infant daughters (as in China). No ideas of social diversity and no euphemisms of "female circumcision" should make us ignore the suffering of women because of genital mutilation in parts of Africa. No belief in cultural autonomy should let us close our eyes to the use of genocide and mass rape as instruments of war or to the ongoing traffic in and possession of slaves. It is not cultural imperialism or Eurocentrism to protest such behaviors. Our concept of humanity as the image of God demands that we consider the worth of individual humans and act accordingly. There can be no distinctions between "lesser" or "greater" images of God, autonomous or subordinate, for if we begin to make such distinctions, then the notion of image becomes a meaningless bit of self-congratulation. It is our duty to recognize and respect the image of God in all people, whether they themselves accept such a concept or not.

FROM IMAGE TO IMITATION

Acknowledging human dominion and its limits is not by itself adequate for a full religious anthropology. The concept of the "image of God" does not refer only to God's power and dominion. There are other aspects of God that the image of God should share. Human "images" have a responsibility to behave in God-like ways, to walk in God's path and imitate God's action. *Imitatio dei*, the "imitation of God," is an integral part of *imago dei*, God's image; imitation enables the image actively to "image" God. Paul states this bluntly, exhorting the people to be imitators of God (Eph 5:1) and to "be imitators of me as I am of Christ" (1 Cor 11:1). He also has a specific example of what form such imitation should take: "forgive one another as God forgave and live a life of love as Christ loves us" (Eph 5:2). This idea of *imitatio dei* is formulated just as bluntly by Abba Saul in the Mekhilta: "Resemble Him! Just as He is gracious and merciful, so you should be gracious and merciful" (*Mekhilta Shirata* 3 on Exod 15:2b). The Sifre to Deuteronomy also elaborates on this idea in a comment on the injunction "to go in his ways":

> As God is merciful, so you too be merciful. The Holy Blessed One is called "gracious," so you too be gracious . . . and give freely. God is called "righteous," so you too be righteous, God is called "devoted," you too be devoted, for thus it is written "all you call by my name will escape" (Joel 3:5) and "all who are called by my name, I have created for my glory" (Isa 43:7).[18]

It is noteworthy that the idea of "imitation of God" always refers to those qualities of God that human beings most fervently desire. No one in either Jewish or Christian tradition has ever used the concept of "imitation of God" to counsel people to get angry and punish others, or to counsel people to insist that their commands be obeyed. "Imitation of God" never prescribes behavior that takes advantage of power and dominion. On the contrary, "imitation of God" always involves self-control, self-abnegation, and love of others. "Imitation of God" enumerates as God's behaviors those behaviors that we hold morally superior and beneficial to humanity, like love, forgiveness, and compassion.

In Genesis Rabbah, Rabbi Simlai finds textual proof that God performs many of the key "acts of loving-kindness" that Rabbinic Judaism recommends:

> We have found that the Holy Blessed One blesses bridegrooms and adorns brides and visits the sick and buries the dead. Blesses bridegrooms, from "God blessed them" (Gen 1:28), adorns brides ("God built upon his side," Gen 2:22), visits the sick ("God appeared to him by the terebinth of Mamreh," Gen 18:1), and buries the dead ("God buried him in the ravine," Deut 32:6). R. Shmuel bar Nahman said, "even consoles the dead, for it is written 'God appeared to Jacob when he came from Padan-Aram and blessed him'" (Gen 35:9).[19]

As historically conscious contemporary thinkers, we recognize that the Rabbis project onto God the human traits that they consider most desirable, so that these traits can be reflected back as divine exemplars, as warrants and mandates for humans to act in this way. By projecting these traits onto God, Rabbi Simlai provides a divine template to encourage humans to behave in this way. The most elaborate Jewish expression of this concept of *imitatio dei* is by Moses Cordovero (1522–1570) in *Tomer Devorah*, in which he derives the requirements for compassion, tolerance, kindness, and right action from the attributes of God listed in Micah 7:18–20.

The notion of imitation of God seems circular, for our description of the Godly nature and behaviors that we are to imitate conforms to the pattern of behavior that we wish to encourage. Nevertheless, ascribing these patterns to God has great persuasive power, enabling those doing the describing to convince others that they should follow these patterns of behavior. We are imagining the God we are trying to image, and we seek to be the image of the God we imagine. Possibly, this circular rhetoric has far less persuasive impact upon those who understand the mechanism of projection involved here. Nevertheless, the concept of "imitating" or "imaging" God retains its importance, for believing that one is following in God's way enriches the experience of performing ethical actions. To the sense of rightness that the deed itself inspires, the notion of "imitation of God" adds a dimension of sacredness to the ethical act. Being mindful of the divine precedent makes one aware of acting as God's representative or image, increases one's awareness of the presence of God, and (traditional language would add), increases God's presence. Even after we become aware that we have no incontrovertible way of knowing that God acts in these ways, a philosophy of "the image of God actively imaging God" creates an awareness and presence of God. *Tomer Devorah* suggests that such active imaging has an even greater impact, for the performance of the actions has a theurgic effect, that is, it brings forth these behaviors in God.

Jews can appreciate the fact that the actions of the historical Jesus provide Christians with an accessible role model. From a Jewish perspective, the imitation of Christ, *imitatio Christi*, is understandable, and Paul could be sure that his audience would understand him when he told them to imitate him as he imitated Christ. The somewhat controversial Christian question about right action—What would Jesus do? (WWJD)—brings the imitation of God down to earth in the simplest, most dramatically visible way, presenting an unadulterated role model whose behavior is wholly good (unlike the behavior of the characters of the Hebrew Bible). For many, WWJD is a two-edged sword, both simplifying matters for pedagogical and dramatic purposes and oversimplifying them, and in doing the latter, forgetting the transcendent qualities of Jesus and the special purpose of his life. Of course, not even the most literal proponents of WWJD would not want the imitators of Christ to publicly humiliate their mothers or to call down the punitive power of the state against them, both things that Jesus did.

Much of the Christian discourse on these topics seems quite familiar to Jews, especially those Christian discussions that have moved beyond the concept of original sin and its impact. Even notions of the Fall can be appreciated when they are taken as a metaphor for the deficiencies of the "fallen universe." The concepts of "image of God" and "imitation of God," particularly in their modern manifestations, present a sense of human nature, purpose, and destiny that can provide common ground for mutual understanding and mission. They provide a basis for understanding and appreciating the closeness of Judaism and Christianity, a basis that does not at the same time serve to "otherize" nonmonotheist religions. Unfortunately, this shared philosophy of the "image of God" is not often recognized. Christians speak of the image of God and the imitation of God as if these were uniquely Christian developments that derived directly from Genesis 1; Jews often speak of *tselem elohim* as an exclusively Jewish way of appreciating the dignity and sacredness of human life. It is important to realize the significance of these concepts in both Judaism and Christianity and the fact that the development of these concepts often took place with mutual cross-fertilization. Embracing a joint religious humanism should enable us to continue to enrich each other in an increasingly open and mutually inclusive way.

NOTES

1. T. Sanh. 9:7 and cf. B. Sanh. 46b. Many of the Rabbinic sources have been collected and analyzed by Yair Loberbaum in his 1997 Hebrew University Ph.D. dissertation, "Imago Dei: Rabbinic Literature, Maimonides and Nahmanides."

2. T. Yev 8 (end).

3. Mek. Bahodesh 8.

4. ARN B 30.

5. Gen. R. 34,20 (see also B. Yev 64a); T. Yev 8 (end).

6. M. Sanh. 6:5.

7. Gen. R. 68:2.

8. Pseudo-Clementine, homily 17 22,6.

9. See Gen. R. 11:2, 12:6.

10. This is the version in B. Hag. 15a-b. The legend of Elisha ben Abuya is first found in the Tosefta and has a long development in Jewish sources.

11. Elisha's relationship with R. Meir is mentioned in a number of sources, including B. Hag. 15a.

12. TJ Hag. 2:1 77b-c.

13. Irenaeus, *Against Heresies*. See the discussion in Anthony A. Hoekema, *Created in God's Image* (Grand Rapids, Mich.: Eerdmans, 1986), 33–42.

14. Gregory of Nyssa, *Sermon on the Sixth Beatitude*, trans. Joseph E. Trigg, in J. Patout Burns, *Theological Anthropology* (Philadelphia: Fortress Press, 1981), 29–38.

15. Ben Zoma in M. *Avot* 4:1.

16. For a discussion of Calvin, Barth, and Brunner, see Hoekema, *Created in God's Image*, 44–49, 49–52, and 52–58, respectively.

17. See Hoekema, *Created in God's Image*, 36–42.

18. Sifrei Deut. Ekev 49.

19. Gen. R. 8, 13.

8 / Biblical Voices on Chosenness

2001

When people think of the Bible on questions of election and covenant, it is the voice of Deuteronomy that comes through loud and clear, for Deuteronomy emphasizes the special relationship between God and Israel, God's "chosen people." As Deuteronomy states,

> You are a people holy to the Lord your god; the Lord your God chose you from all the peoples on the earth to be his treasure-people. It is not because you are the most numerous of peoples that the Lord set his heart on you and chose you—indeed, you are the smallest of peoples. It was because the Lord desired you and kept the oath he made to your fathers that the Lord freed you with a mighty hand and rescued you from the house of bondage, from the power of Pharaoh king of Egypt. Know therefore that only the Lord your God is God, the steadfast God who keeps his covenant faithfully to the thousandth generation of those who love him and keep his commandments, but who instantly requites with destruction those who reject him (Deut. 7:6–10).

These verses contain most of the components of Israel's ideas about its special relationship with God. God considers Israel God's particular treasure, God's *segulah,* a term that appears elsewhere in Deuteronomy (Deut. 14:2, 26:18) and is celebrated in song (Ps. 135:4). This special relationship was promised to Israel's ancestors, and is founded on love. God desired Israel's fathers (Deut. 10:15), and God has chosen Israel out of desire and love (Deut. 7:7–8). Like "treasure," God's love for Israel is also celebrated in song (Ps. 47:4). And the love must be reciprocated: Israel must "love your God with all your heart and with all your soul and with all your might" (Deut. 6:5). The reciprocal nature of this mutual love can be expressed by a formula of bilateralism: Israel is YHWH's people, and YHWH is Israel's God (Deut. 29:12). This bilateral formula, reminiscent of a wedding formula, appears in Exodus (Exod.6:10) and Leviticus (Lev. 26:12), and is important to Israel's Priestly prophets, Jeremiah (Jer. 7:23; 11:4;

24:7; 30:22, 25; 31:22; 32:38) and Ezekiel (Ezek. 14:11; 36:28; 37:23, 27; see also Zech. 8:8).

As our Deuteronomic passage indicates, the relationship with God formally began with God's taking the people out of Egypt. This exodus set up an intimate relationship with God in which God's presence stayed within Israel (Exod. 29:46). Israel thus became holy and was required to be holy (here and Lev. 11:45, and throughout Lev. 16). The ongoing relationship is expressed, on Israel's part, by performing the acts that God requires of it. God demonstrates the divine interest in this relationship by the great acts of the past and the ongoing presence of prophets and Nazarites: "I brought you up from the land of Egypt and led you through the wilderness forty years to possess the land of the Amorite. And I raised up prophets from among your sons and Nazarites from among your young men" (Amos 1:10–11).

Two concepts from the world of law do not appear in this passage from Deuteronomy 7:6–10. Leviticus uses the concept of "servant": "For the children of Israel are mine as servants. They are my servants that I took out of the Land of Egypt; I am the Lord their God" (Lev. 25:55 and throughout the chapter). This concept of servant, applied to the whole people of Israel, is important language for the exilic prophet Isaiah (Isa. 41:8–9; 42:1, 19; 44:1–2, 21; 48:4; 49:3; 65:9). Also from the world of law is the legal concept of *nahalah*, literally, "a patrimony, heritage," property that belongs to someone in perpetuity. God chose Israel as God's own *nahalah* (Deut. 4:20–22) and God gave the land to Israel as her *nahalah* (Deut. 4:37; 15:4; 10:10; 20:16; 24:3; 25:19; 26:1).

God's gifts of love, freedom, and land come with strings attached. Israel is not a free agent. It is bound to God in a close relationship that must be expressed in specific actions. These acts are Israel's obligations and duties, and, at the same time, Israel's expression of her love for God. Deuteronomy spells out these obligations carefully by use of the form and language of international treaties. Israel has a covenant with God; Deuteronomy spells out the terms of the treaty, Israel's exact obligations and the results to Israel of her not fulfilling them. But obligation is explicitly required by the love-language as well as by the legal conceptualization of the relationship. Leviticus declares that the Exodus from Egypt demands fair business practices (Lev. 19:26) in addition to exclusive loyalty to God; and that Israel's position as God's servants demands special attention to social justice (Lev. 25–27); Deuteronomy declares that a *segulah*-people must be careful what it eats (Deut. 14:2). The gift of land as *nahalah* entails obligation both not to defile it and to respect life and treat people well (Deut. 15:4; 19:10; 21:23; 24:4; 25:19).

All the interrelated concepts of covenant, choice, servitude, possession, treasure, and love demand special devotion of Israel to God and both cultic and social actions that demonstrate such devotion. The Priestly writings place great emphasis on the special nature of the land of Israel. Like Deuteronomy, the Priestly writings hold that God gave this land to Israel as its patrimony, its *naḥalah*, and this gift entails an obligation not to defile it and to respect life and treat people well. The Priestly writings see God's concern for the land as the prime explanation of Israel's history. The land cannot continue to be occupied by those who are unworthy and defile her. Leviticus 18 discusses the abominations that the aboriginal inhabitants performed in the land. As a result, the land became polluted, God cursed the land, and the land vomited out its inhabitants. This cleared the way for Israel to inherit the land. Israel must be careful not to pollute the land as her predecessors did.

Another Priestly passage, Numbers 35, gives us an indication why God is concerned to ensure the purity of the land. For example, murder causes the pollution of the land. Such pollution can be removed by the execution of the murderer, but if the homicide was accidental, the killer ought not to be killed. In the case of an accidental homicide, the killer should run to a city of refuge. There they hold a trial. If the killer is judged a murderer, he or she must be delivered to the blood-avenger for execution. If the death is ruled accidental, the killer stays in the city of refuge until the death of the chief priest offers some symbolic atonement. The text warns:

> Do not take ransom to [let someone] flee to the city of refuge or to [let someone] return to live in the land until the death of the priest. Do not contaminate the land where you are, for blood will contaminate the land, and the land cannot be absolved from blood spilled on it except by the blood of the one who spilled it. You must not pollute the land in which you are dwelling, in whose midst I am living, for I YHWH am living in the midst of the children of Israel (Numbers 35:33–35).

The land of Israel is the earthly site of God's presence. Leviticus spells out what will happen if Israel does pollute the land: "do not do these abominations . . . and the land will not vomit you out as you pollute her as it vomited out the nation before you" (Lev. 18:25). Israel's special status with God will not enable her to stay in the land if she pollutes it. Rather than allow the land to be contaminated, God will remove Israel from the land.

This obligation to keep the patrimony pristine and unpolluted is a dramatic expression of the fact that Israel's position is not secure. Both the priestly paradigm of pollution and the more family crime-and-punishment paradigm of Deuteronomy show the dark side of having an intimate relationship with God: there are dire consequences to not following God's dictates. "Rejecting" *(ma'as)* God's word can lead to disaster. The Priestly writings remember the near-end of Israel's relationship to God at the beginning of its history. According to the Book of Numbers, Israel actually rejected God when it was in the desert, asking why it had come out of Egypt (Num. 11:20; 14:30). In reaction, God was prepared to destroy Israel and begin again with the progeny of Moses. Moses interceded and convinced God that God's reputation would be destroyed if God destroyed Israel, and God settled for holding back the gift of the land until the generation that rejected God died out. God stayed with the people, but only a new generation could inherit the land.

Things do not always go smoothly after the conquest of the land, and things begin to go very wrong in Israel's history as Israel begins to encounter serious ecological and politico-military difficulties. These hardships impel biblical thinkers to reflect on Israel's relationship with God. To the eighth-century prophets, these hardships are a sign that Israel's relationship with God has gone awry. God loves Israel, says Hosea, but Israel wants other gods (Hos. 3:1). Israel has rejected God's word, God's Torah, say Amos (Amos 2:4) and Isaiah (Isa. 5:24; 8:6; 30:12), as, much later, Jeremiah (Jer. 8:9). The evil Israel endures is a result of this rejection. It is not that Israel is any different from the other nations. Or rather, Israel's lack of difference from the other nations is precisely the problem. As Amos declares, "You alone have I singled out of all the families of the earth; that is why I will call you to account for all your iniquities" (Amos 3:2).

THE IRREVOCABLE RELATIONSHIP

It is clear that God punishes Israel. But the punishment can be seen as chastisement, or even as a fulfillment of convenantal sanctions. Will God go beyond sanctions to reject Israel or abrogate *(hefer)* the covenant? Leviticus promises that even if God exiles Israel, God would still keep the covenant; God would not abrogate it or reject Israel in exile (Lev. 24:40–45). In similar fashion, Samuel promises that whatever happens, God will never abandon God's people (1 Sam. 12:22). But the weight of history impels first Isaiah and later Jeremiah to announce that God has broken the covenant and abandoned Israel (Jer. 7:29). The destruction of Jerusalem is proof to the writer of the Book of Kings that God has rejected both the city (2 Kgs 23:27) and the seed of Israel (2 Kgs 17:20). In this spirit, the Book of Lamentations mourns that God has abandoned king and prophet (Lam. 2:6) and all of Israel (Lam. 5:22).

But the spirit of despair does not hold sway in Israel. The eighth-century prophets prophesied restoration even while they prophesied destruction (Hos. 2:16–25, Mic. 7:14–15, Isa. 11:11–16) and the later prophets predict a new Exodus that would redeem Israel in such a way as to eclipse the Exodus from Egypt (Jer.16:14–15; 23:2–7; 31:31–37; Ezek. 20:33–42). Most of all, the exilic prophet Deutero-Isaiah becomes the harbinger of the grand new redemption. Isaiah declares that God chose Israel and does not reject her (Isa. 41:9). Israel likes the language of servant and of choice, for Israel is God's *behiri*, "my chosen one, my choice one" (Isa. 42:1; 43:20; 48:4; 65:9, 22); he also reiterates the theme of God's love for the ancestors: "Israel, my servant Jacob, whom I have chosen, Seed of Abraham, my lover" (Isa. 41:8). Even after it became clear that the exodus from Babylon was not the glorious new Exodus the prophets had envisioned, Israel maintained faith in its ongoing irrevocable relationship with God. It is this permanence that lies at the heart of Israel's covenant with God—it is indissoluble, will never end, and therefore always demands Israel's survival. Indeed, this is a major purpose of the whole idea of covenant: it copes with the overwhelming power of a universal creative deity (an attribute of God that Amos also stresses) by harnessing the dragon. God becomes a little more predictable, and the upheavals God creates a little less arbitrary. The "radical freedom of God," so important to early modern theologians, is curtailed by God's covenantal relationships, and the people can understand a little more about what happens to them.

GOD, ISRAEL, AND THE NATIONS

The other question embedded in the idea of a chosen relation with God is the relationship of God with other nations of the world. On this question, the Bible's many voices present a complicated, multifaceted picture of the relationship of Israel, God, and the other nations. The Book of Genesis is concerned with the various nations that descend from Abraham. God gave these other nations their land in the same way that God gave Israel hers. The Moabites and Ammonites are descended from Lot, who chose the eastern part of the promised territory, and the

Edomites are descended from Esau, to whom God gave Edom, or Mt. Seir. Deuteronomy respects the divine right of their descendants to their respective lands. As Israel is on its way to Canaan it is told, "you are to pass through the border of your brethren the children of Esau . . . contend not with them, for I will not give you of their land . . . because I have given Mount Seir to Esau for a possession" (Deut. 2:4–5). They receive the same instruction about the lands of the Moabites and Ammonites (Deut. 2:8–23).

The appearance of these nations in Amos gives a more complete picture of the mechanism by which people got their lands and entered into special relationships with God. They appear in the "for three transgressions of . . . for four I will not restore him" litany against the nations in the first two chapters of the Book of Amos. This prophecy is often considered an example of Amos's universalism, but in truth, the nations are very carefully chosen. The list begins with Damascus, the northernmost country being formed, and then proceeds to Gaza, the most southern of the territory. The third country is Tyre, then Edom, Ammon, and Moab, and then Judah and Israel. Edom, Ammon, and Moab are Abrahamic nations that descend from Lot and Esau. Moreover, as Deuteronomy explains, they did not inherit their lands until after they had acquired them from other peoples. As for the Arameans (Damascus) and the Philistines (Gaza), Amos reveals God's relationship to them in an important statement: "Are you not like Ethiopians to me, O Israelites," says the Lord, "whom I brought up out of the land of Egypt and the Philistines from Caphtor and from Kir?" (Amos 9:7). By bringing them into the land they could inherit, God has established rights over these peoples. They have become obligated to God, and the obligation demands a certain standard of behavior. If they violate this standard, God will react to their misdeeds by exile or destruction. The other nations share with Israel their origin in a different land, their upheaval from those lands, and their arrival in the present territory because of divine intervention.

This view of world history is not a logical necessity. Indeed it differs dramatically from the type of scenario presented by some indigenous people that stresses the intimate connection of the people with the land from which they sprang. The Bible's picture is, however, an accurate reflection of the history of the Eastern Mediterranean area. By the middle of the second millennium B.C.E., a series of natural disasters paved the way for a game of musical nations in which the great peoples of the inhabited world were on the march. The volcanic explosion of the island of Santorini (Thera) and the earthquakes that seem to have preceded it effectively ended the Minoan civilization and sent the Minoan Greeks to Troy (as in the Trojan Wars), to Egypt as the Sea Peoples, and to Israel as the Philistines. This migration, referred to by Amos (Amos 9:7), has been demonstrated archaeologically, for the earliest levels of the Philistine city of Ashdod, for example, show Cypriot pottery, Cypriot not only in form but also in the clay from which it was made. These countries were, of course, inhabited: the Egyptians had to struggle against the Philistine invaders for quite a while, and in Israel the Philistines established a network of five cities that lasted until they were defeated by David around 1000 B.C.E. In Turkey, the defeated Trojans moved eastward to central Turkey (and, according to Virgil's *Aeneid,* eventually also westward to the Italian peninsula). But this meant that the Hittites also migrated, out of Asia Minor and into Syria. There they displaced the Hurrians, who moved northeast to the area around Lake Van, where they became in the first millennium the powerful kingdom of Urartu. In Syria, the Hittites also met up with the Arameans, a pastoral people who were moving northwesterly out of land that was turning into desert because of the droughts of that period, a climatic change probably also related to the massive volcanic explosion in the Mediterranean. The union between the Arameans and the Hittites is called the Arameo-Hittite symbiosis by historians, and is known to the Bible as Aram. The world scene that Israel knew was a stage of massive dislocation and resettlement, and to Israel, of course, all this activity must be at the will of YHWH, who brought them from their homelands and could return them there.

Amos's statement that Israel has the same standing before God is somewhat hyperbolic, for he himself declares that Israel's relationship to God is more intense than those of these nations and the standard to which Israel is held is appreciably higher: "You alone have I known from all the nations of the earth and therefore I visit upon you the reckoning of all your misdeeds" (Amos 3:2). This is a quantum difference, for God "knows" Israel, has an intimate relationship with it. Elsewhere, Amos gives us an example of this "knowing": God had sent prophets and Nazirites to Israel (Amos 2:11). The prophets have explained God's desires; the Nazirites have perhaps mediated God's presence. This attention by God has increased Israel's obligations, and therefore raised the stakes so that *all* Israel's misdeeds—not only gross atrocities—call for divine punishment. The one advantage Israel has is that even when God will destroy Israel, God will never effect a *kallah,* a total destruction, and destruction will be followed by restoration (Amos 9:9–12).

Amos concentrates on "greater Canaan" and the nations with whom God has already established this pattern of selection-importation-obligation-judgment-punishment. Isaiah, writing not long after, turns his attention to the future, to a time after God has completed this particular cycle. Isaiah considers the case of Egypt, which will receive her own punishment and be oppressed. But then, in a surprising turnaround, Isaiah predicts,

> It shall be for a sign and a witness unto the Lord of hosts in the land of Egypt; for they shall cry unto the Lord because of the oppressors, and he will send a savior and a defender who will deliver them. The Lord will make himself known to Egypt, and the Egyptians will know the Lord on that day and they will worship him with sacrifices and offerings and vow vows and pay them (Isa. 19:20–23).

By this future time, Assyria will also worship God (we don't have Isaiah's vision of how) and the three will be a triple blessing in the midst of the earth, for God will say, "Blessed be Egypt my people and Assyria the work of my hands, and Israel mine inheritance" (Isa. 19:25). The election of Israel has been joined by God's arrangement with the two major powers of Isaiah's time. We are far from the exclusiveness with which ideas of chosenness and covenant are so often joined.

The tension between Israel's monotheist vision of a universal God and Israel's self-identification as God's people continues after the destruction. The exilic prophet Deutero-Isaiah prophesies about the redemption of the people, in which the whole cosmos will sing as God transforms the world to redeem Israel (Isa. 44:23; 49:13). "I have given Egypt as your ransom, Ethiopia and Sabea for you. For you are precious in my sight and I love you" (Isa. 43:3). The Egyptians, Ethiopians, and Sabeans—indeed, all the nations—will come to Israel, bringing her exiled children and great tribute (Isa. 45:4; 49:22–23; 60:4; 66:18). Israel will have a covenant of peace that is everlasting: "mountains may depart, hills be removed, but my *hesed* will not depart from you, nor my covenant of peace to be removed" (Isa. 54:10). To Deutero-Isaiah, God's embrace of Israel is one of the basic elements of the cosmos: "And I have put My words in your mouth, and have covered you in the shadow of My hand, that I may plant the heavens, and lay the foundations of the earth, and say to Zion, you are My people" (Isa. 51:16).

All of this sounds terribly ethnocentric and triumphalist, even chauvinist. And yet at the same time, Deutero-Isaiah makes it clear that anyone can enter the special covenanted relationship with God, and that whoever wants to enter God's people by keeping the Sabbath and the moral order is accepted as a member of Israel (Isa. 56:2–3). Isaiah's vision is very different from that of Ezra: Ezra wanted to define Israel as tightly as possible, restricting the term to those who returned from the Babylonian exile and reading the Israelites who had never gone to Babylon out of the people. Isaiah, on the contrary, maximalizes his definition to include all those who want to join the covenant. Moreover, all those who join themselves to God and the covenant are part of the temple community, "for my house will be called a house of prayer for all people" and will gather others to God along with the ingathered exiles (Isa. 56:6–8). Like Zechariah after him, and like the eighth-century Isaiah and Micah before him, Deutero-Isaiah sees the temple as the center of a world community of separate nations who come to worship. But if all the peoples become part of God's realm, what role does Israel play? Isaiah has two mutually exclusive visions. In one, the Israelites benefit from the universal kingdom: the nations bring them their wealth, and the Israelites serve as the priests of God (Isa. 61). But in another prophecy, Isaiah declares that God will gather all the nations and tongues, and once the nations bring their exiled Israelites back as their offerings to God, God will take priests and Levites from these other nations (Isa. 66:18). Then what of Israel? Isaiah never spells it out, and can only affirm that Israel will also remain in the new period of peace and harmony: "As the new heavens and the new earth which I shall make shall remain before me," says the Lord, "so will your seed and your name remain" (Isa. 66:22). The exact role of Israel is not specified, but the covenant assures that it will no more disappear in harmony than it did in adversity.

The tension between Israel's belief in its special identity and its sense that its role as God's people is destined to extend to all other peoples has never been resolved. Earlier triumphalist visions of a universal religion that looks just like Judaism have given way in some Jewish minds to a more pluralist notion that someday people will realize that there is a universal presence among us, and that they will act on that realization. This universalist eschatological vision includes a basic sense that Israel's covenant is everlasting and that somehow in some way Israel will survive to continue its mutual "knowing" and "loving" with God. In the words of the prophet Micah, "All peoples will walk in the name of their gods and we will walk in the name of the Lord our God forever and ever" (Mic. 4:5).

9 / Jesus and the Law

1986

Writing about Jesus and the law[1] is a little like trying to solve an algebra problem when all that is known is that, perhaps, X has some sort of relationship to Y. As should be clear from the preceding selections, we have trouble knowing exactly what we mean when we talk about "Jesus"; furthermore, it is very difficult to know what the law was to which Jesus stood in some relationship. For this reason, as one reads the literature, one can choose at will from conclusions that Jesus was a revolutionary eschatological figure, an antinomian messianic figure, a pietist, a Pharisee, a Sadducee, a Dead Sea covenanter, a Hillelite, a Shammaite, a proto-rabbi, and a forerunner of "Liberal Judaism." Nevertheless, despite these difficulties, we persist in trying to understand Jesus' attitude toward the law, for the law was a matter of great acrimony and dispute for the early church. Christians disagreed on whether the whole Israelite law should be considered in force; whether only circumcision should be abrogated (as necessary for the conversion of the gentiles); whether dietary and Sabbath laws should be considered of the past; whether there should be a distinction between Jewish Christian and gentile Christian so that only the born Jews should observe the law; whether all should abandon the law.[2] The disputes were quite bitter, and ultimately resulted in any observance of the Hebrew law being considered heretical for Christians. In our modern era, which seeks authenticity in the earliest "pristine" time of Christianity, it seems imperative to understand what Jesus may have taught, or what he may have been understood to have taught, before the church fathers, before Paul, and before the Hellenization of the church.

Focusing on Jesus and the law almost seems to do violence to our general impression of Jesus, for law does not appear to have been at the center of Jesus' activity. Although Jesus preached in the synagogues, and gave popular lectures (al fresco), the traditions portray him as having spent much of his time healing. He seems to have felt that the presence of God, or the kingdom of God, was manifested through his own ministry, and particularly through his miracles and his healings. In this way, Jesus can be seen as a charismatic figure and compared to such other prominent charismatics as Honi the Circle Drawer and Hanina ben Dosa.[3] Like him they were from Galilee; like him they were considered particularly close to God; like him they effected healings, although usually by the efficacy of their prayer rather than by their personal power. There were, however, significant differences between Jesus and these Galilean charismatics. Unlike them, Jesus did not make rain, which was their most significant achievement. And unlike him, as far as they were remembered, they did not preach, nor did they travel with a coterie of student-disciples. In this, Jesus was like the rabbis, the interpreters and expounders of Torah, and it is legitimate to ask, what was the relationship of the teaching of Jesus to the Torah of Israel?

It is wrong to translate Torah by "law." Torah, literally "divine instruction," included all the teachings of Israelite tradition—all the books of Scripture and, in fact, in Rabbinic theology, all the teachings about the books of Scripture, and all the teachings derived from Scripture. It included ethics and prophecies as well as legal prescriptions. One can and should study the ideas of Torah as ideas. In addition, in more practical terms, the urgent task of teachers of Torah was the *Halakhah*, the transformation of legal pronouncements, ethical statements, and prophecies into practical guidelines for action—in other words, into laws. When we speak of Torah or *Halakhah* or even of "the Law," we mean the whole system of individual legal prescriptions, the ideology from which they derive, the mechanisms by which this ideology is translated into statutes, and the mechanism by which changing circumstances and changing ideology can be incorporated in the system.

The centuries before and after Jesus were times of great flux in the *Halakhah*. Changing economic and political fortunes and the impact of Hellenistic ideas and foreign governments had created great changes in the understanding and application of Torah. Arguments raged among various factions about how (or even whether) to adapt the law of the Hebrew Bible to changing times; new concepts were incorporated and various ideas of law underwent extensive development. Much practical *Halakhah* had been transformed by the "great assembly" (whether or not it existed) during the Hellenistic period, and even greater changes were effected by the Rabbis after the destruction of the temple in Roman times. At the time of Jesus there was no unanimously accepted monolithic, immutable law toward which he had to take a stance. There may already have been a conscious ideology (known to us from later Rabbinic sources) that the Torah was indeed unchangeable, but even this theology held that the unchangeable Torah encompassed the written Scripture, its interpretations, and its methods of continued reinterpretation. In practice there were many alternative ways of living within the law in times and circumstances not envisioned by the written Torah. In trying to understand the relationship of Jesus and the law we have to understand his relationship to the laws he inherited, to the interpretations with which he was familiar, and to the processes of its transformation.

What evidence do we have at our disposal to try to answer these questions? We have an organized presentation of pronouncements about the law presented in the Sermon on the Mount, and we have individual statements of Jesus presented in the form of controversies with the Pharisees and the Scribes. And we have a curious bit of negative evidence: nowhere in the Gospels do we find a statement by Jesus that the law should be abolished, or even that the law belonged to the past; nowhere do we find Jesus even revoking the commandment of circumcision, the first of the commandments to be vitiated by the church. In the world of Jesus, Torah was a given, questioned as to meaning but not as to existence. There is no tale of Jesus actually breaking one of Israel's laws, and despite the concerns of the early church, despite its need to justify abandoning many of the laws, and despite its later desire to declare the law null and void, no one puts the revocation of the law into the mouth of Jesus. Moreover, the synoptics present a rather harmonious picture of Jesus' actions and attitudes vis-à-vis the law, even though the evangelists themselves (we think) were addressing different needs in the developing church and held differing attitudes towards Judaism and toward the law. The Matthean Jesus is a better legal scholar: he is more careful in his debates, he uses more sophisticated legal reasoning, but there are really no major differences between the Matthean and the Marcan Jesus. Despite our necessary skepticism toward our sources, these facts make us more ready to accept these pronouncements of Jesus preserved in the synoptics as at least received tradition (Jesus of history if not Jesus of biography) rather than as tendentious invention.

THE DEBATES WITH THE PHARISEES[4]

Before we can turn to the traditions in which Jesus engages in controversy with the *pharisaio*, we have to state our hesitation and reservations. In the first place, we don't really know who the *pharisaio* are.[5] If they are Pharisees, is the Pharisaic movement the same as the later Rabbinic? If so, why are their positions so strangely at variance with later Rabbinic tradition, so that if we did not know history we would swear that Jesus, and not these "Pharisees," was the precursor of Rabbinic Judaism? The agenda that is so important to these Pharisees is the same agenda reflected in the traditions that we have about the great Pharisees (or proto-rabbis) before 70 C.E.: tithing, purity laws, Sabbath laws, although here too we cannot be absolutely certain that this was truly a pre-70 agenda.[6] Yet the positions held by the Gospels' Pharisees do not follow Rabbinic lines, not even those of the stricter Shammaite school, and they seem more like the very strict constructions of the sectarians of the Dead Sea Scrolls and the Book of Jubilees. For this reason, some have attempted to divorce these New Testament characters from the Pharisees of Rabbinic tradition, and to identify them with the *perushim*, "sectarians," of whom we occasionally hear in Rabbinic sources. But were there really so many Dead Sea-type sectarians in the Galilee,[7] or even table-fellowship Pharisees? As far as we can tell, the Pharisees held no political power until 70, when they became part of the Rabbinic movement at Yavneh, and even then they were not the sole voice, and perhaps not even the dominant voice, at Yavneh.[8] Yohanan ben Zakkai, the leader of the Rabbinic group at Yavneh, spent (according to legend) eighteen years in the Galilee, during which time he was only asked to decide upon two questions of law (as recorded in JT *Shabbat* 16:715d); is it possible that Pharisees were so involved in Galilean practice that Jesus kept encountering them? Or were they sectarians from whom he had broken away, who were trying to prevent him from attracting more disciples?

We also have to ask questions about the controversy form. Did Pharisees really come so often to question Jesus? Did the heathen really come to inquire about the essentials of the law from first Shammai and then Hillel (BT Shabbat 31a, ARN A15, 61)? Did a heathen really come to argue with Yohanan ben Zakkai about the rules of the red calf (*Be-midbar Rabbah* 19:8; *Pesikta de-Rav Kahana* 4 and parallels)? On the one hand, this kind of controversy form is characteristically Rabbinic: Jews studied in pairs and in groups and studied (then as now) "dialectically," which means by arguing with each other, sometimes passionately and heatedly. On the other hand, the individual controversy tales about both Jesus and the early rabbis often simply seem to form the background for some pithy and pregnant utterances. It may be that the presentation of a controversy narrative sets the scene for this statement by quickly defining the parameters of the debate. If this be so, the Pharisees of these stories may be a literary foil, and we need not ask if Jesus really encountered them at every turn. One further comment about dialectical tradition: whether the controversies were real or literary, the *pharisaio* of the New Testament, as presented by the evangelists, do not follow one of the basic rules of the convention. If one is bested in an argument, if one's opponent has discovered either a new answer or a new question, the proper response is not anger or plotting revenge (as do Mark's Pharisees), but delight, astonishment, and/or reward. According to the Hillel legend, when Hillel won his disputations with the sons of Bathyra, he was appointed *nasi* (Pes 66a, TJ Pes 6:1). Even though this story may not be historical, it illustrates how the dialogic learning process was understood.

Despite these caveats, we cannot simply dismiss everything in these controversy stories as having arisen in this post-Yavneh period and as totally unhistorical. We should pay attention to the statements of Jesus that form the focus of these stories, and therefore to the lines of his thought on some of the legal issues of his day.

The dispute between Jesus and the Pharisees centers on several important issues: in the straight polemic of Matthew 23, Jesus attacks them on tithing, the preoccupation with which he declares insignificant compared to the weightier matters of the law (Matt. 23:23). In the same place, he attacks them on purity regulations, for he declares that they purify the outside of the cup (Matt. 23:25). In the actual dialogues Jesus attacks them for allowing a son to abandon his financial obligations to his parents by means of a vow (Matt. 15:1–6); they attack him for eating with sinners, they question him about allowing his disciples to eat without washing their hands (Mark 7:14–23, Matt. 15:10–20), and about divorce; they attack him for letting his disciples pluck and eat grain on the Sabbath, and for healing on the Sabbath. The issues in these disputes ring true, for the Pharisees were a group determined to observe a fully holy life in all aspects of life, and not only in the temple. As such, they were scrupulous about tithing, so that they would not be eating food that had not been properly tithed, and they were scrupulous about purity regulations, which they extended to all dietary laws so that they

"ate secular food in purity." Like all Jews at the time they were interested in the observance of the Sabbath. In order to maintain this they
formed, it appears, a table fellowship, eating only with those whom they
could trust to have tithed and observed purity laws. (It should be noted
that the Pharisees were willing to eat with Jesus.)

To turn first to the hand-washing stories of Mark 7:14–23 and
Matthew 15:10–20. The Pharisees ask him "why do your disciples break
the tradition of the elders?" in that they do not wash hands before eating. Here the question of the Pharisees (who thereafter say nothing)
seems to point to a real disagreement in practice: Jesus does not demand
this aspect of purity regulations. We should of course note that there
were many Jews, non-fellows in the Pharisaic fellowship, called *Am
ha-Aretz*, who were not observing the purity rules. (Later one of the five
major rabbis at Yavneh, Simeon ben Nathaniel, ate food in an unclean
state [Tosef. Av. Zar. 3:10]. There are also pietists, Hasidim, who obey
purity rules that are defined differently from those of the Pharisees.)[9]
However, Jesus is not said to have mentioned this. Instead, in the form
of the dispute that we have, he first goes on the attack, condemning
Pharisees on the question of filial vows (about which more later), and
then gets to the crux of the story, a pithy statement to the crowd, "What
goes into a man's mouth does not make him 'unclean,' but what comes
out of his mouth, that is what makes him unclean." Later, the disciples
ask him to explain what is obviously a radical statement, and he explains
that all that enters the body ultimately exists, but the true uncleannesses
are the evil thoughts in a person's heart. It is clear that Jesus is taking
the opportunity to deliver a moral lesson about the true purity, that of
right action, and the true object of concern, the purification of one's
thoughts and utterances. This is also his use of purity regulations in
Matthew 23:25, where he accuses the Pharisees of declaring the outside
of a cup clean while the inside is unclean: there he uses the language of
a real debate about whether cups can transfer uncleanness from outside
to inside in order to again illustrate his concern with the interiority of
cleanliness. But what about the externals? Does Jesus really mean to
abandon all concern about purity regulations? If he does, he is clearly
at variance with Pharisees and Qumran, though perhaps not with the
ordinary people and not even with the Sadducees, who limited purity
considerations to the temple. But does this statement really throw out
all purity regulations? A somewhat analogous story is told about Yohanan
ben Zakkai (Numbers Rabbah 19:8 and parallels), for an idolater came to
him claiming that the laws of the red cow were sorcery-type regulations.

He drew an analogy to exorcism and the idolater left, but the disciples demanded a better explanation of the question. Yohanan said, "In truth, the dead do not defile and the water does not purify." Yohanan (who incidentally was not a Pharisee, for the traditions about him do not concern purity or tithing),[10] abandons the whole theory underlying the categories of purity and defilement. In this case, however, Yohanan demanded that the law be followed because it is a commandment of the Torah itself. Like Yohanan, Jesus denies the principle of purity; in the case of hand washing, which is not prescribed in the Torah, he feels under no obligation to follow it, or at least to demand that his disciples follow it. What he would have said about those purity regulations that are found in the Torah, we do not know. It has been argued that the fact that Jesus does not object to being touched by the women with a bloody discharge shows that he was not concerned with purity laws of any type, but this is an irrelevant argument. Not all blood, even genital, was considered menstrual; and, more important, despite, or perhaps in agreement with the parable of the good Samaritan, Israelite law did not demand that one actively avoid impurity, which would mean not caring for one's sick and dying, not burying the dead, not having sexual intercourse, and not procreating. Israelites were to perform all of these positive commandments and then remove impurity; they were not to avoid them in order to avoid impurity.

THE SABBATH CONTROVERSIES

Keeping the Sabbath holy is one of the ten commandments, but the exact definition of keeping the Sabbath is not mentioned there. From at least the time of Isaiah and Jeremiah there was an increasing tendency to specify the prohibition of things not to be done on the Sabbath. From the intertestamental and later books we know that the prescription of Sabbath laws was an increasing concern, that ultimately there was an attempt to codify all possible activity into permissible and prohibited. Opinion was not unanimous as to what was and was not permissible, and debates occurred, particularly between the Sadducees, who held to the strictest possible interpretation of Sabbath regulations, and Pharisees, who attempted to work within the law to make the Sabbath enjoyable. During the early Rabbinic period there was a concern not only with lenient interpretation of inherited rules, but also with the formulation of principles for which the Sabbath should be set aside. The primary—but not the sole—reason was the saving of life. Although this would have seemed self-evident to us, there is some evidence that Qumran did not even consider this cause to set aside the Sabbath. The temple cult certainly set aside the Sabbath. The Pharisee Eliezer ben Hyrcanus of Yavneh is known to have ruled that circumcision set aside the Sabbath, as did the Passover, and as in fact did the Omer (for, according to Pharisees, one could harvest the Omer on the second day of Passover, even if it fell on Sabbath). Ultimately, Rabbinic Judaism allows the Sabbath to be overridden for the needs of a mitzvah for any possibility of danger, and even, it seems, in order to make the sick comfortable.

Jesus was confronted with having allowed his apostles to pluck and eat grain on the Sabbath. Although plucking for agricultural purpose is forbidden, we don't know whether stripping an ear would have been considered plucking the fruit, nor whether plucking for the sake of eating would have been considered agriculture at this time. When Jesus was questioned, however, he did not use these arguments, nor the argument that the needs of a mitzvah to save life set aside the Sabbath, which had possibly not been enunciated yet. Nor did he argue from danger to life, for presumably the apostles were not starving. On the other hand, he also did not say that the Sabbath was irrelevant to him, despite the attitude of the later church. Jesus counters with two arguments, both of which state the same thing. He relates that David had eaten holy food on his journey, even though he was neither a priest nor even in a state of impurity. If, therefore, David had eaten something set aside for God, how is it wrong that the disciples set aside the Sabbath for their purposes? Matthew adds another argument, that in the temple the priests profane the Sabbath, and that something greater than the temple is here. Therefore, if the Pharisees had known the true meaning of "I wish for mercy and not sacrifice" they would not have condemned the disciples. He then concludes with a pithy statement of which the Marcan form is "the son of Man is lord even of the Sabbath" and the Matthean form, "Man is lord of the Sabbath." The two forms of the logion mean much the same, for Mark seems to be reflecting a literal translation of Aramaic *barnash*, i.e., everyman. This pericope has often been misunderstood to mean that Jesus considered himself greater than the Temple, and that as the "son of man" (taken as an eschatological term) he could supersede the Sabbath. However, if this were the case, what would be the purpose of quoting Hosea's "I desire *hesed* and not sacrifice"? That which is greater than the Sabbath, holier than the Temple, is precisely *hesed* (see Sigal). In a sense, this is a more radical statement than the eschatological, for Jesus is saying that the well-being of humans is more important than literal interpretation of Sabbath restrictions. He repeats this theme when asked why he healed the bent-double woman on Sabbath when she could have been healed on the other six days of the week, having already been crippled for eighteen years (Luke 13:10–17). He again brings up the theme when he asked (Mark 3:1–6, Luke 6:6–11) whether it is lawful to do good or to do evil on the Sabbath, or when he was asked whether it is lawful to heal on Sabbath (so Matt. 12:9–13). In Matthew's version Jesus again used a *kal va-homer*, this time by claiming that people would pull a sheep out of a pit on Sabbath (which, incidentally, seems to have been forbidden at Qumran) and that humans are more valuable than sheep, thus proving that "it is lawful to do good on Sabbath."

Jesus' prime principle is that doing good, i.e., *hesed*, must supersede the Sabbath, and in support of this he attests Hosea, "I desire mercy and not sacrifice," an attestation that he also uses to justify eating with sinners. Each time he prefaces the prooftext with a statement about his special exegesis of it—in the Sabbath episode, "if you had known . . . you would not condemn the guiltless"; in the case of the sinners, "go and learn what this means" (Matt. 9:13). This passage from Hosea does not have to imply that *hesed* should become the prime motivating factor in the law. Nevertheless, this interpretation of the passage is not unique to Jesus. In *Avot de-Rabbi Natan*, the story is told about Rabbi Yohanan ben Zakkai that, when asked about what could take the place of the Temple for the expiation of sins, he responded that the mechanism for this was already known, that it was doing good, *gemilut hasadim*, i.e., *hesed*. As support for his opinion he used the same verse from Hosea, "I desire *hesed* and not sacrifices" (ARN A4 B8). Was Jesus the first to enunciate this principle, which was transmitted and adopted before the parting of the ways between Judaism and Christianity? Or did Matthew learn this tradition from the rabbi of Yavneh and then put it into the mouth of the earlier Jesus? Or are Jesus and Yohanan both part of a contemporary tradition that, rather than being concerned with purity and tithing, concerns itself more with *hesed* and with the love commandment of Leviticus 19:18? We, of course, cannot answer this question, but it should be clear that Jesus has no intention to abolish or even to violate the Sabbath, but rather to set it aside if necessary in favor of the holy principle of *hesed,* just as the earlier law had set it aside in favor of the holy principle of sacrifices.

The fourth issue on which the Pharisees question Jesus is the issue of divorce. And here, for the first time, we find a substantive difference in the evangelical accounts. In Mark, the Pharisees ask the question.

Jesus points out that Moses permitted but did not command divorce, then follows with a *binyan ab* from the fact that God created male and female (Gen. 1:27) and man is to cleave to his wife (Gen. 2:24), declaring that they are therefore no longer two but one, and therefore "what God has joined together, let not man separate." Jesus further explains to his disciples that if anyone divorces his wife and marries another woman he commits adultery, and if she divorces (some say deserts) her husband and marries another, she commits adultery. This would seem to be an absolute prohibition on divorce. Matthew however (19:2–8) says that divorce is forbidden except in cases of *porneia* (horrendous sexual practice, such as adultery or incest); furthermore, he states the more Judaic view that if anyone divorces his wife (except for adultery) he causes her to commit adultery. The implication in Matthew seems to be that adultery destroys the marital bond, so divorce can follow (and in the view of the Hebrew Bible, it seems must follow). We do not know which position was Jesus,' but we know that both positions stand along a continuum in the contemporary debate over divorce.[11] The Hillelites permit divorce for any wrongful act of the wife, sexual or not; Akiba ultimately allowed divorce on demand (of the male, of course). The Shammaites allowed divorce if the wife committed sexual indecency, which included public bathing or wearing loose hair or sleeveless clothes. At Qumran it appears that they never allowed remarriage, whatever the opinion on separation and divorce. In Rabbinic Judaism there were two tendencies; a desire to find divorce lawful, and a desire to find it wrongful. Although the Rabbis could not find reason to forbid it, they made it difficult by establishing stiff financial penalties in the *ketubah*. Jesus, it seems, was content to prohibit it not on the basis of exegesis of law, but by arguing legally from the Genesis narrative, something that Christianity continues to do and that Judaism has always been reluctant to do. We should note that in this case also, although Jesus certainly innovated over biblical statute, he did this within the frame of law as an ongoing reinterpretive process.

There is one controversy in which Jesus attacks the Pharisees. In the hand-washing debate, he accuses them of violating the law themselves. According to Jesus, they violate the fifth commandment, the command to honor one's father and mother, in that they allow a son to vow his goods as a *korban*, thus making his goods inaccessible for the support of his parents. This statement may reflect a discussion of that time, for the problem is addressed by the Yavnean Pharisee Eliezer ben Hyrcanus, who declared that the honoring of one's parents would be sufficient reason to annul such a vow of *korban*.

A serious question arises with this charge against the Pharisees. Is Jesus the pot calling the kettle black? Jesus, after all, is not portrayed in the Gospels as very kind to his own parents. He was impatient with his mother (as we all are) at Cana (John 21:1–4). Furthermore, when told that his mother and brothers were outside and wished to speak to him, he embarrassed them in public by saying that his disciples were his real mother and brethren (Mark 3:31–35, Matt. 12:46, Luke 8:19). When an anonymous woman who heard him speak proclaimed, "Blessed be the womb that bore you and the breasts that gave you suck," Jesus answered, "No, say rather 'blessed be he who hears the word of the Lord and follows.'" Jesus is depicted as calling for the division of families (Luke 12:52–53) and as requiring people to hate their families in order to follow him (Luke 14:26). We must ask what is going on here. Is it possible that Jesus (or the early church) is abrogating one of the six commandments of the Decalogue that he is elsewhere held to have proclaimed (Mark 10:17–19)?

The answer to this question lies in the nature of the Decalogue, which was always treated as charter ideology, rather than as statute. It was therefore frequently reinterpreted. Deuteronomy uses laws to interpret the Decalogue; Jeremiah and Ezekiel changed the principle of divine retribution to the third and fourth generation. So here too we have a particular interpretation of the commandment to honor one's parents. This interpretation is reflected in the *Mekhiltah* to Exodus 20:2, which states, in a form somewhat reminiscent of the Sermon on the Mount, that one might think that the commandment means to honor with words, and therefore Exodus 20:2 teaches that it means honor with substance by providing for food, drink and clean garments. If one construes the commandment to mean only material provision, then Jesus fulfilled it by commending his mother to another's care at his death.

There is a reason that Jesus (and the early church) chose to follow such a narrow interpretation of the commandment. The demands of their situation as creators of a new way demanded that children sometimes reject the ways of their parents and go against the wishes and demands of their parents in order to follow Jesus. Similarly, at the time of the Babylonian exile, Jeremiah and Ezekiel declared an end to divine cross-generational retribution in order to meet the need of the exilic generation to know that they would not continue to be punished for the sins of preexilic Israel.

This brings us to the Sermon on the Mount, with its statement of fidelity to the "least of the commandments" and its statement of intent to fulfill the law, followed by the six antitheses in which Jesus "fulfills" the law. The general scholarly opinion is that the completed Sermon on the Mount is a Matthean construction in which he presents his image of a new Moses and a new Sinai. However, the components of this sermon, the individual pronouncements of Jesus, may have been part of the tradition that Matthew received.

To turn to the antithesis, Jesus deals with six topics: murder, adultery, divorce, oaths, talion, and love of neighbor. In the first two, Jesus extends the prohibitions to include emotions that might lead to them. He forbade divorce (except in cases of adultery) and oaths, he counseled against using the legal revenge of talion, and he extended love of neighbor to include love of enemy.

Is any of this radical? Certainly, Jesus went beyond the literal interpretation of the prohibitions of the Ten Commandments to call for inner purity. He went beyond the call of the law to forbid things that had not been previously permitted. To find out how a Pharisaic rabbi would have handled some of the same topics that Jesus considered, we can look at Eliezer ben Hyrcanus, who held that Sabbath could be put aside for circumcision and for Passover, who pronounced on the tithing of dill, who held to the purity of the outside of the vessel, and who annulled the vow children might make to the detriment of parents. He also dealt with oaths and vows, not forbidding them, but addressing himself to the question of how to declare such oaths null and void. Similarly, neither the Pharisees nor the Rabbis had a practical task; they were concerned to set forth parameters and guidelines to action. In other words, they acted to establish laws that people could live by. They established the laws *(din)* and the parameters of the law *(shurat hadin)*, even while they exhorted people to go beyond the parameters of the law *(lifnim mishurat hadin)* into the realm of the counsels of perfection.[12] In the collection of pronouncements presented as the Sermon on the Mount, Jesus offers only counsels of perfection. Counsels of perfection are not practical law, and demanding that people be perfect beyond the requirements of the law does not abrogate the law.

Even if Jesus had intended to abolish one of the laws of Israel which he mentioned, this would not mean that he intended to abrogate the Law. There is a fundamental misconception in attempts to find an antinomian Jesus here: you can abolish a given law without revoking or abrogating the whole system of Torah. Yohanan ben Zakkai, who was so instrumental in both preserving the Torah after the destruction of the Temple and in placing the study and observance of Torah at the center of the Jewish faith, did not hesitate to do away with large portions of the law. He abolished the trial of the suspected adulteresses (Num. 5:11–31), and he presided over the dissolution of the entire sacrificial system after the destruction of the Temple. Yet he is regarded as the savior rather than the destroyer of the law. As far as we can tell, Jesus not only had no wish to destroy the law, he did not even go as far as Yohanan ben Zakkai.

But if Jesus was law-abiding and law accepting, we must ask, "what happened here?" How could Christianity have moved so quickly to abrogate the laws? Although we know the many reasons that it was advantageous to the church to abolish the law in order to attract the gentiles, how could it have taken the license to do so? There is an inherent domino effect in any counsels of perfection, for if perfection cannot be reached, there is little to guide one as to where the practical person should make a stand. An emphasis on interiority also gives no guide to action. *Hesed* is a dangerous principle of law, for how can *hesed* be legislated? As Jesus became the center of Paul's faith, the way was open for Paul and others to abolish the law, or at least any laws detrimental to the spreading of Jesus' teaching to the gentiles, i.e., circumcision, Sabbath, and dietary rules. Rabbinic Judaism took a different path, for although the Rabbis also adopted *hesed* as a major principle, they used the rest of the same verse of Hosea 6:6 to show that knowledge and study of the law were required by God. In Judaism, then, the study of the law and its doing became the operative center of religion.

NOTES

1. For some of the more important works, see Robert J. Banks, *Jesus and the Law in the Synoptic Tradition* (Cambridge University Press, 1975); Donald Hagner, *The Jewish Reclamation of Jesus: An Analysis and Critique of Modern Jewish Study of Jesus* (Zondervan, 1984), 87–132; John P. Meier, "Law and History in Matthew's Gospel: A Redactional Study of Mt. 5:17–18," *Analecta Biblica* 71 (1976); Geza Vermes, *Jesus and the Jew: A Historian's Reading of the Gospels* (Macmillan, 1973), and *The Gospel of Jesus the Jew* (Fortress, 1983); and Stephen Westerholm, *Jesus and Scribal Authority*, Coniectanea Biblica New Testament Series 10 (Lund, 1978). Other suggested readings are Joseph Baumgarten, *Studies in Qumran Law* (Leiden, 1977); Bruce Martin, "Matthew on Christ and the Law," *Theological Studies* (1984): 53–70; and Benedict

Thomas Viviano, *Study as Worship: Aboth and the New Testament* (Leiden, 1978).

2. On the different groups, see Raymond Brown, "Types of Jewish/Gentile Christianity," CBQ 45 (1983).

3. See particularly the works of Geza Vermes: "Hanina ben Dosa," *Journal of Jewish Studies* 23 (1972): 28–50; 24 (1973): 51–64; and *Jesus the Jew* and *Gospel of Jesus* in note 1.

4. For general information about the Pharisees, see Louis Finkelstein, *The Pharisees*, 2 vols., 3d ed. (Philadelphia, 1962); and Jacob Neusner, *The Traditions about the Pharisees*, 3 vols. (Leiden, 1971), and *Early Rabbinic Judaism* (Leiden, 1975). For discussion about the relationship between Jesus and the Pharisees, see John Bowker, *Jesus and the Pharisees* (Cambridge, 1973); Michael J. Cook, "Jesus and the Pharisees—The Problem as It Stands Today," *Journal of Ecumenical Studies* 15 (1978): 441–60; Asher Finkel, *The Pharisees and the Teacher of Nazareth* (Leiden, 1964); and Phillip Sigal, "The Halakha of Jesus of Nazareth According to the Gospel of Matthew" (Ph.D. diss., University of Pittsburgh, 1979).

5. See Sigal, "Halakha."

6. See in particular Neusner, *Traditions.*

7. So, particularly, Sigal, "Halakha." Note that "Pharisees" itself means "Separatists," as far as we can tell.

8. This is stressed by Neusner, *Eliezer ben Hyrcanus: The Tradition and the Man*, 2 vols. (Leiden, 1973). He points out that Eliezer ben Hyrcanus seems to represent the Pharisee tradition, but that Yohanan does not.

9. For the *'amme ha'aretz*, see Aharon Oppenheimer, *The 'Amme Ha-retz* (Leiden, 1977).

10. See Jacob Neusner, *Development of a Legend: Studies on the Traditions Concerning Yohanan ben Zakkai* (Leiden, 1970).

11. For a discussion on this continuum, see Sigal, "Halakha."

12. For an excellent discussion of *lifnim mishurat hadin*, see Sigal, "Halakha."

10 / Covenant: A Jewish Biblical Perspective

2005

"Covenant" is in the air again. The concept had enormous popularity in the early and mid-twentieth century,[1] when it was hailed as the key to biblical theology. But its popularity among modern thinkers waned as biblical theologians abandoned their attempt to find the one central principle of the Bible and began to concentrate instead on discovering the multiplicity of biblical voices and their complexity. Now, however, the idea of "covenant" is reemerging as an important paradigm for our contemporary understanding of the intricate interrelationships between humanity, Israel, and God.

"Covenant" is a richer, more varied, and more complex idea in the Hebrew Bible than in later Judaism or Christianity. In Christianity, covenant was explicitly abandoned as "fulfilled" or mutated into the eschatological "new covenant," somewhat foreseen by Jeremiah and Ezekiel. The old covenant, with its laws and conditions, was associated with the concept of "chosenness" or "election" and was dismissed as Jewish and Jewish alone. At the same time, the term "new covenant," which in Jeremiah and Ezekiel meant nothing short of a change in human nature, became a term for Christian faith with no real separate referent. The biblical covenants did not fare much better under Judaism. The regulations of the Sinai of covenant evolved into the *halakhah* and remained as a core element of Judaism. But the Rabbis did not picture the *halakhah* and its commandments as a covenant. To them it was a "yoke" of submission to the commandments (*'ol mitzvot*) or the "yoke of the Kingdom" (*'ol malkhut*), submission to God. The idea of "covenant" receded and the very term *brit*, "covenant," was limited in Mishnah and Talmud to *brit milah*, the covenant of circumcision.

The *brit milah* is a very important aspect of Judaism,[2] for it is the sign of Jewish loyalty to its special relationship with God. Rabbinic Judaism limits the term "covenant" to circumcision, but circumcision is not a trivial matter, and the act of circumcising one's sons remained both a preliminary and an ultimate declaration of faithfulness to the bond between Israel and God. Circumcision can be a very dangerous act. In addition to its inherent physical dangers as an operation on a very young boy, historical factors made circumcision even more dangerous, for it is the physical sign of being Jewish, and marking the boy as Jewish opened him to all the dangers that have beset the Jews. But these dangers only increased the ability of circumcision to signify the importance of the divine-Israel relationship. The decision of parents to circumcision their infant sons in the face of such dangers has been a major act of parental loyalty to God and a demonstration of their determination to keep themselves and their children in a special relationship to God. Indeed, the loyalty demonstrated by circumcision lies behind one of the most important liturgical poems of the Day of Atonement, "Like Clay in the Hands of the Potter, So We Are in Your Hands." As Jews acknowledge their utter vulnerability to God, we ask God not to look only to our evil urges (and their consequences), but to look at the covenant. Circumcision, the act of loyalty and steadfastness by which we maintain our intimate relationship with God, is our ace as we petition God to demonstrate compassion and benevolence towards us and all Israel.

Despite its intense importance, the Rabbinic notion of covenant is very narrowly conceived. Covenant in the Hebrew Bible, by contrast, is a rich and diverse concept, and its many nuances give it potential importance for contemporary thinking about God and humanity. When we examine the biblical passages relating to covenant without the interpretations they have attracted through their traditional rabbinic, patristic, dogmatic or modern receptions, we can perceive the many facets of this multidimensional concept, and it may then provide a conceptual framework with which to understand how we relate to God. Covenant has been studied before; it is a much studied, possibly even over-determined subject, but most analyses are interested in imposing modern categories on the ancient material, dividing it analytically into "conditional" or "unconditional," "political" or "ritual," or other somewhat arbitrary subdivisions. Instead of such structural analyses, it is worth looking at the material as it begins to appear in the text, and letting these appearances teach us what they will.

In the first section of the Bible, the primordial history of Genesis 1–11, "covenant" plays a major role. The world had to be almost totally destroyed, after which God set up a new world order to prevent such destruction from becoming necessary again. This new order entails a covenant between God and Noah and his sons. Much has been made recently of the Rabbinic notion of the Noahide covenant or "Noahide laws,"[3] the rules by which all nations can be adjudged worthy. To me, this concept is condescending, possibly even triumphalist. Such a concept is understandable as the words of a people almost destroyed and held captive by Rome, the great city of law. In its time it provided self-assurance that in this one area (on which Rome prided herself) Jews were not inferior. Today the words ring very differently, and even though some contemporary Jewish thinkers have embraced them, others, like me, find them offensive. But that is the Rabbinic notion of the Noahide commandments. The biblical concept of God's covenant with Noah is very different from this Rabbinic notion, and it may offer a contribution to our own thinking.

The covenant with Noah in Genesis 9 comes after the flood purged an earth that had become too polluted. God has concluded that human beings do wrong as part of our very formation and God does not want to continue to smite the earth or its inhabitants because human misdeeds pollute the earth. God therefore first sets up an automatic procession of nature which God will no longer interrupt in reaction to human actions (Gen 8:21–22):

כ"א: וירח יהוה את ריח הניחח ויאמר יהוה אל לבו לא אסף לקלל עוד
את-האדמה בעבור האדם כי יצר לב האדם רע מנעריו ולא-אסף עוד
להכות את-כל-חי כאשר עשיתי:
כ"ב: עד כל-ימי הארץ זרע וקציר וקר
וחם וקיץ וחרף ויום ולילה לא ישבתו:

YHWH smelled the savory smell and thought
I will not continue to curse the earth
because of humanity anymore,
for the formation of the human heart is evil from childhood.
And I will not continue to strike all living beings as I did.
As long as the days of the earth:
seed-time and harvest, cold and heat,
summer and winter, day and night
will not cease.

As God calls Noah and his sons together, God promises never again to bring a flood to destroy the world. Since God has realized that an evil impulse is built in, or "hardwired" into human beings, God also presents provisions to control the violence that could result. These new laws begin by giving humans the right to kill animals. This right is not unrestricted, for humans cannot eat animals alive, and cannot eat their blood, which is tantamount to life. Nevertheless, the killing of animals is not a breach of natural order: it is part of the new cultural order that God constitutes after the flood. This new world order marks a clear division between humans and animals; it establishes the dread of human rule upon the animals. At the same time, the new rules make it very clear that the right to kill is not mutual: nobody—human or animal—has the right to kill a human being without forfeiting one's own life. This important principle is expressed by means of a legal maxim:

שפך דם האדם באדם דמו ישפך כי בצלם אלהים עשה את-האדם:

(As for) the one who spills the blood of a human being, by a human being his blood is to be spilled, for He (God) made the human being in the image of God (Gen 9:6).[4]

The provision of capital punishment for murderers entailed in this maxim is often noted as "the sacrosanct nature of human life" or "the inviolability of human life," and is considered a lynchpin of biblical law. But it is not the key element of this new provision, which is often mistranslated, or passes unnoticed altogether. The second half of the legal maxim, "by a human being his life is to be spilled," establishes the demand that human beings themselves have the responsibility to guarantee the sacrosanct character of human life. The reason for this responsibility is "for He made the human being in the image of God," an allusion to the purpose of the creation of humanity in Genesis 1:26–28. Texts from Mesopotamia and from Egypt proclaim the king to be the image of God, by which they mean that the king was an avatar of his god, able to channel the god's presence when the god was not there and commanding the reverence due to the god. In Genesis, this function, like ruling, the other royal function, is expanded to apply to all humanity. God created humanity to administer the cosmos and to channel divine presence. God now "fine-tunes" humanity's role, making it clear that God will no longer take the responsibility for the punishment of murderers and, by extension, other miscreants. God's attempt at personal micromanagement of human behavior, which began with God's treatment of Cain, had resulted in disaster as the pollution caused by human misbehavior built up to the critical stage of destruction. Now, having acknowledged that humanity's very formation will result in misbehavior, God gives human beings the task to police themselves. These new provisions are the covenant that God made with Noah, his sons, and all humans after the flood.

The chapter that began with this new covenant and its sign, the rainbow (Genesis 9), continues with a story that illustrates how the new order works. Noah has drunk himself into a stupor, as we might expect from the survivor of such a massive destruction, and was lying exposed in his tent when his son Ham saw him and, instead of either rectifying the situation or ignoring it, "tattled" to his brothers. His action may seem trivial, but it was actually extremely serious because by neglecting the honor due to the father, Ham threatened the hierarchy by which the fragile new world was ordered. When Noah heard about Ham's misbehavior, he reacted severely, cursing Ham's son Canaan with eternal servitude. Readers long have been bothered by the fact that Noah cursed Canaan instead of Ham.[5] However, this act is not as unfair to Canaan as we might suppose. Since the curse was upon all the descendants of the one cursed, the impact on Canaan was the same whether he was cursed directly or through his father Ham. It was not necessary to mention Canaan by name in order to curse him.

But the specific mention of Canaan had two other effects. First, it mentioned Israel's hated enemy by name, providing an opportunity to relish a primeval curse on the one people who represented everything abominable to biblical Israel. Second, and more important, singling out Canaan and cursing him rather than Ham eliminated the other sons of Ham from the curse. The mighty imperial Assyrians and Babylonians were all descendants of Ham, even though contemporary classification systems would consider them "Semites." An Israelite audience would have laughed to think that their conquerors were under some primeval curse to be their servants. Limiting the curse to Canaan eliminates the obvious discrepancy between Noah's curse and Israel's reality.

There is another problem with the curse of Canaan: it was fundamentally wrongheaded, as it invited ideas about national subordination and servitude into the newly ordered world. Noah's curse of Canaan was not his shining moment. Even more than his drunkenness, even lower than his humiliation in front of his sons, the curse was the absolute nadir of Noah's existence. It presents a sharp contrast to the destiny of the flood survivor in Mesopotamian myth. In the *Gilgamesh* epic, the gods acclaimed Utnapishtim as the savior of humanity and granted him immortality. The curse story shows that even Noah, righteous in his generations, was hardwired with the capacity to do wrong, and that human wrongdoing was certain to continue after the flood. But the greatest significance of the curse story is neither its object (Canaan) nor its content (slavery), but its subject: Noah is the one who pronounced the curse. Before the flood, God did the cursing, cursing the serpent and the land, and whoever would murder Cain. Now it is the human leader who pronounces the curse, and, wrongheaded though his curse may have been, God neither corrects nor rebukes him. Now that God has set up this new order and established it as a covenant, God cannot go back. God is out of the day-to-day picture of managing the world, and human beings have to manage (or mismanage) their own affairs.

COVENANTS BETWEEN GOD AND ISRAEL

The Ancestor Covenant: The Covenant of the Land

The Bible then turns from the universal to the "particularistic" or national scene. God reenters human affairs as God forms a special relationship with one man, Abraham, and his descendants. God promises to give Abraham and his descendants the land of Canaan, a promise God calls a covenant. This promise is offered first to Abraham, then to his son Isaac but not to Ishmael, then to Isaac's son Jacob and not to Isaac's son Esau, and thereafter to all the children of Jacob. God provides Ishmael and Esau with their own destinies and territories, but the covenant of the land of Canaan goes in one straight line to Isaac and Jacob, and then afterward it goes to all Jacob's children. The exclusive inheritance of this covenant is underscored by the fact that in both these cases the younger son inherits the promise despite the fact that the customary norm was for the oldest son to be chief heir to his father's patrimony.[6]

This odd and apparently unfair pattern of the covenant of the land finds its explanation in the striking analogies of this covenant to Mesopotamian grants of land recorded on the inscribed boundary stones (*kudurru*) that stand on the boundary of the land they discuss. The *kudurru* records the history of the land. When the family's possession of the land begins as a royal grant, the history has the following stages:

1. The king gave the grant to a man (first generation).

2. The land returned to the throne upon the death of the one to whom the land was given.

3. The king repeated the grant, giving the land to one chosen heir of the original recipient (second generation).

4. The land returned to the throne upon the death of this second recipient.

5. The king repeated the grant again, giving it to one chosen heir of this second recipient (third generation).

6. Upon the death of this third generation recipient, the land no longer returned to the throne. It has now become part of the patrimony of the recipient family and was automatically inherited by the heirs. The land now belongs to the family as an eternal possession.

The ancestral promise of the land follows the same stages:

1–2. The original promise to Abraham is given in Genesis 12, repeated to Abraham after his separation from Lot in Genesis 13, and solemnized by ritual in Genesis 15. It contains three parts: a) multiple progeny, b) other nations will bless themselves or be blessed by the ancestor, and c) the land will be given to Abraham and his descendants. This last part, the promise of the land, is solemnized as a covenant in a solemn ritual in Genesis 15, the "covenant among the carcasses": "On that day God cut a covenant to give the land to Abraham's descendants" (Gen 15:18).

3–4. After the death of Abraham, God repeated the promise to Isaac (Gen 26:3–4):

ג:גור בארץ הזאת ואהיה עמך ואברכך
כי לך ולזרעך אתן את כל-הארצות האל
והקמתי את-השבעה אשר נשבעתי לאברהם אביך:
ד:והרביתי את-זרעך ככוכבי השמים והתברכו בזרעך כל גויי הארץ
ונתתי לזרעך את כל-הארצות האל:

Reside in this land and I will be with you and I will bless you
for I will give all these lands to you and your progeny.
I establish the oath which I swore to your father Abraham
And I will multiply your progeny like the stars of the sky
And all the nations of the earth will bless themselves by your progeny
And I will give you and your progeny all these lands

Only Isaac received the renewed land-grant covenant that God had made with Abraham. Abraham's other son, Ishmael, received a separate promise, a prediction that his descendants would be a wild untamable people, subservient to no one and subordinate to no state.

5. As Isaac's death approached, he chose to designate Esau as his favored son before God (Gen 27:7):

ואכלה ואברככה לפני יהוה לפני מותי:

"I will eat and bless you before YHWH before I die."

Jacob, however, took Isaac's blessing and left the home. At Bethel, God confronted him and granted him the land and the other parts of the promise (Gen 28:13–4):

י"ג:אני יהוה אלהי אברהם אביך ואלהי יצחק
הארץ ארש אתה שכב עליה לך אתננה ולזרעך:
י"ד:והיה זרעך כעפר הארץ ופרצת ימה וקדמה צפנה ונגבה
ונברכו בך כל-משפחת האדמה ובזרעך:

I am YHWH, the god of your father Abraham and the father of Isaac.
The land upon which you lie—I will give it to you and your descendants.
Your descendants will be like the dust of the earth
and you will burst forth West and East and North and South.

God repeated the promise when Jacob returned to Bethel after his adventures in Mesopotamia (Gen 35:11–12):

ואת-הארץ אשר נתתי לאברהם וליצחק לך אתננה
ולזרעך אחריך אתן את-הארץ:

The land that I gave to Abraham and to Isaac I will give to you;
and to your progeny after you I give this land.

6. As the death of Jacob approaches, he tells Joseph that God's grant to him is an eternal possession (Gen 49:3–4):

ד: ויאמר אלי הנני מפרך
ונתתי את-הארץ הזאת לזרעך אחריך
אחזת עולם:

(El-Shaddai appeared to me at Luz and blessed me)
And He said to me, Look, I will make you fertile
and I will give this Land to you and to your progeny after you
as an eternal possession.

The great-grandson, Joseph, is the transitional figure in the land covenant. He inherits the promise of the land from Jacob, and Jacob makes him the *de facto* chief heir by giving each of his two sons, Ephraim and Manasseh, a portion equal to that of each of their uncles, thus giving Joseph the traditional "double portion" of the chief heir. The "double portion" ultimately includes a double portion of the land, for Ephraim and Manasseh are each tribes of Israel with their own geographical tribal area. All the "children of Israel" inherit the land by virtue of being sons of Jacob, rather than by special renewed covenantal promise from God. The land, now being an "eternal possession," is part of the patrimony that they inherit along with any other goods that their father might have possessed, and which they in turn pass on to their children. Then, when the "children of Israel" come into possession of the land, Ephraim and Manasseh each take their own geographical area.

Jacob's twelve sons are also the beginning of the fulfillment of God's other promise to Abraham, Isaac, and Jacob, that of great fertility and many progeny. Population estimates of ancient Israel project that each family had on average two and a half living children;[7] the twelve sons of Jacob (and of Esau) begin the fulfillment of the promise of great fertility given to Abraham and Isaac. Joseph almost lives to see the fulfillment of the grant of the land in his time, but not quite, and his bones are carried back by the returning Israelites. The gratification of this covenant of the land is delayed both in the time in which it was set, the time of the ancestral characters, and in the time of the readers, who anticipate and then experience the loss of the land to the Assyrians and to the Babylonians, and who await its future reclamation by the descendants of Jacob, renamed Israel.

The covenant of the land is often called an "unconditional" covenant, but it entailed definite expectations.[8] When God goes to investigate and ultimately destroy Sodom, he turns back to tell Abraham (Gen 18:19):

כי ידעתיו למען אשר יצוה את-בניו ואת-ביתו אחריו ושמרו דרך יהוה
לעשות צדקה ומשפט למען הביא יהוה על-אברהם את אשר-דבר עליו:

For I have known him
so that he can give commands to his sons and their households
and they can keep the way of YHWH
to do social justice
so that God will bring for Abraham that about which He spoke to him.

The sentence spells out God's purpose: God has entered an intimate relationship with Abraham in order to reveal to him how to do social justice so that he can instruct his household. The commands will come from Abraham; the knowledge of what social justice is and how to achieve it is knowledge that Abraham acquires by virtue of God's "knowing" him.

The execution of social justice is the purpose for God's intimacy with Abraham, and it is also the reason that God "knows Moses by name," as Moses argues with God on behalf of Israel (Exod 33:13):

ועתה אם-נא מצאתי חן בעיניך הודעני נא את-דרכך ואדעך
למען אמצא-חן בעיניך וראה כי עמך הגוי הזה:

> And now if I have found favor in your eyes,
> show me your way and I will know you
> so that I will find favor in your eyes,
> and see that this nation is your people.

By knowing God's way, Moses will know God, and this knowledge of God is both the result and the purpose of God's knowing him intimately. This is the reason for the prophet Amos' frustration with Israel. As Amos states, "for you alone have I known . . ." (Amos 3:2). God has an intimate relationship with Israel so that they will know what God wants. But instead, complains Amos, their heaping up of the fruits of violence in their sumptuous houses is a sign that they do not know how to do right (Amos 3:10). Even though God has sent God's intimates, the prophets, to explain things to them, the people have not listened, and therefore God will take note of each of their wrongdoings.

We are not told why God made this grant to Abraham, whether it was as a reward for Abraham's past actions or simply a step in God's plan; or why he chose Moses. But from the time of the choosing, Moses wants to know God so that God will (continue to) like him. And when it comes to renewing the plan in the next generation, God tells Isaac (and the readers) that the covenant is being renewed because Abraham hearkened to God and observed God's instructions (Gen 26:5):

עקב אשר-שמע אברהם בקלי וישמר משמרתי מצותי חקותי ותורתי:

> *Because of the fact that Abraham hearkened to my voice*
> *and observed my tradition, my commandments, my rules and my instruction.*

Once the covenant became an "eternal possession" of the children of Israel, God would no longer revoke it. In the same way, Moses tells God that in order to know Moses and have Moses know God, God must see that Israel is now God's people. They have entered into a covenant of peoplehood, and God cannot revoke it. But God could make Israel wait for its fulfillment. This was true at its inception, the time of the ancestors, and it was true in the desert; it was also true at the time of the canonical recording of both covenants, when Israel sat in exile. As the history of the children of Israel continued, the possession of the land became ever more delayed. The promise of the land remained a cherished eternal possession of Israel, but the land could not serve as the sole basis for the ongoing relationship between God and Israel, and another ancestor covenant received more attention, the covenant of circumcision.

The Ancestor Covenant: The Covenant of the Flesh

In Genesis 18:19 God describes God's relationship with Abraham as "I have known him." Elsewhere, God tells Abraham to "walk before me" (Gen 17:1):

התהלך לפני והיה תמים:

Walk before me and be perfect.

With this, Abraham joins the company of the antediluvian Enoch (Gen 5:22) and Noah (6:9), who are said to have "walked with God."

God offers Abraham a new covenant, a covenant of great fertility, which emphasizes his status as ancestor to many nations and kings, a status marked by a change of his name from Abram (exalted father) to Abraham (father of multitudes) (Gen 17:2–6). This new covenant is an eternal covenant to be Abraham's God and God of his descendants after him (Gen 17:7):

ז: והקמתי את-בריתי ביני ובינך ובין זרעך אחריך לדרתם לברית עולם
להיות לך לאלהים ולזרעך אחריך:
ח: ונתתי לך ולזרעך אחריך את ארץ מגריך
והייתי להם לאלהים

And I will keep my covenant with you
and with your descendants after you
for their generations, an eternal covenant,
to be your god and god of your descendants after you
and I give you and to your descendants after you
the land in which you live
the whole land of Canaan
as an eternal possession
and I will be your god.

At first glance, this seems to be the same promise, of fertility, of important descendants and of the land that God made with Abraham at the covenant among the carcasses (Gen 15). But this covenant establishes an eternal relationship: to be your God. Jacob's children, Israel, will not only inherit the land, they will inherit this special relationship with God.

Unlike the land grant, this covenant is immediately granted forever as an "eternal covenant." The covenant is stunning in its simplicity: God promises to be the god of Abraham's seed forever. Moreover, the name change to Abraham, which recognizes that he will be the ancestor of many nations, opens the possibility that all the nations descended from Abraham have the possibility of this special relationship with God, and the covenant is established for all his generations forever. This is an unbreakable bond and nothing will make God break it.

In return, Abraham's descendants are expected to accord God whatever service is appropriate for a people to accord its god. The only action that is spelled out is circumcision, which is at one and the same time a condition of the covenant and its sign (Gen 17:9–11):

ט:ואתה אתה את-בריתי תשמר אתה וזרעך אחריך לדרתם:
י:זאת בריתי אשר תשמרו ביני וביניכם ובין זרעך אחריך המול לכם כל זכר:
י"א:ונמלתם את בשר ערלתכם והיה לאות ברית ביני וביניכם:

And you should observe my covenant,
you and your seed after you for their generations.
This is my covenant which you should observe
between me and you and your seed after you: circumcise all the males.
You should circumcise the flesh of your foreskins
and it will be the sign of the covenant between me and you.

Abraham's descendants are to circumcise on the eighth day of life. In this way, it reveals the organ of generation at the earliest possible age. It demystifies the phallus, for the circumcised penis looks like the erect phallus in miniature. It also provides a nonerotic place for sex in human-divine relations: sex is the means for continuing this special relationship with God, and the penis is the instrument for perpetuating it. The covenanted people who circumcise are in a special relationship with God. Groups or individuals who stop circumcising their children have by that act rejected God as their god. Circumcising one's household and especially one's son is an affirmation of willingness to stay bound to God despite the vagaries and travails of history.

The two covenants of Abraham probably originated in two different groups in Israel, with the covenant among the carcasses being preserved and told by the government and other teachers, and the covenant of the flesh, like so many matters of the flesh, being the concern of the Priests. They may also have been conceived at different times, for the covenant among the carcasses bears striking similarities, including verbal, to Near Eastern covenants from as early as the Mari correspondence (ca. 1700–1600 BCS)[9] and as late as the time of Jeremiah (sixth century BCS). The emphasis of the covenant of circumcision on the relationship between the people and God, rather than on the land, may have become increasingly popular as Israel faced, and then experienced, the loss of the land during the period from the eighth to the sixth centuries. But the early prehistory of the covenants is almost irrelevant, for in the Torah, Genesis presents an ideal picture of Abraham's relationship to God, and in this presentation both covenants are included. Together, they also surround the story of Abraham's relationship to Hagar, an account of the origin of Abraham's role as "father of many nations."

COVENANTS BETWEEN ISRAEL AND GOD

The Covenant of Intimacy

The Exodus from Egypt was a watershed in Israel's self-portrait. A special insert at the covenant among the carcasses announced the centuries-long delay before the land would actually be given to Abraham's descendants. Centuries later, when God heard the suffering of the slaves in Egypt, God took note of this promise to Abraham and sent Moses to announce that YHWH would deliver them from Egypt (Exod 6:5–6), and would establish an intimate covenant with them (Exod 6:5–7):

ז:ולקחתי אתכם לי לעם והייתי לכם לאלאהים
וידעתם כי אני יהוה אלהיכם המוציא אתכם מתחת סבלות מצרים:

I will take you to me as a people and I will be your god.
You will know that I YHWH am your god
who took you out of the sufferings of Egypt.

The symmetrical statement, "I will take you to me as a people and I will be your god" announces God's intention to form a close relation between God and this new people (*'am*) that God forms as God takes the people out of Egypt.[10] Indeed, the impetus for the delivery of the people was the promise to the ancestors, but Moses does not only speak to their descendants. As the plagues increasingly show God's mastery over the whole cosmos, Moses addresses his words to the whole people of Egypt, too. The people who left Egypt to form God's ʿ*am* were those who listened to Moses and placed blood on their doorposts on the night of the slaying of the Egyptian first-born. The Torah tells us that a mixed multitude left Egypt and followed God, however imperfectly. This is the ʿ*am* with which God forms his covenant.

God's statement of intent to Moses is normally attributed to P, which records the traditions in the Torah that were preserved by Israel's priests. The covenantal formula "You will be/I will take you as my people and I will be your god" is also the core of the Priestly record of God's covenant with Israel in Leviticus (Lev 26:12). But not only Israel's priests used this formula. The teachers of the Deuteronomic school remember it as the central core of the revitalization of the covenant in the plains of Moab (Deut 29:13), and it may have been recited at covenantal renewal ceremonies throughout Israel's history. The prophets remember this intensely personal covenant made in the desert, and Jeremiah recalls the divine invitation to follow God, "hearken to me," in this new relationship (Jer 7:22–23 and cf. 11:4):

כי לא דברתי את-אבותיכם ולא צויתים
ביום הוציא [הוצאתי] אותם מארץ מצרים לע-דברי עולה וזבח:
כי אם-את-הדבר הזה צויתי אותם לאמר
שמעו בקולי והייתי לכם לאלהים ואתם תהיו-לי לעם
והלכתם בכל-הדרך אשר אצוה אתכם
למען יטב לכם:

> For I did not speak to your ancestors or command them
> about offerings and holocausts on the day that I took them out of Egypt.
> But rather this is the thing that I commanded them:
> "Listen to my voice and I will be your God and you will be my people,
> and you will go in all the ways that I show you
> so that it will go well with you."

It makes sense that this covenantal formula serves as the key expression of the intimate relationship between God and God's people. The balanced syntax, "I will be your x and you will be my 1/x" is well known from the ancient world, where it is used in contracts that create new intimate relationships between people. It is used in marriage contracts, and its application to the relationship between God and Israel may have contributed to Israel's understanding of itself as wife of God. It is also used for adoptions, even adult adoptions, as when a boy will say to a

man, "You will be my father and I will be your son." The negative of
these formula—"you are not my wife," or "you are not my husband"—is
a key statement in divorce; for this reason Hosea's children are named
lo-ruḥama and *lo-ami* because, God says, "You are not my people and I
will not be yours" (Hos 1:9).[11]

The prophets have no recollection of a covenant at Sinai, with its
stipulations and laws. To them, Israel's covenant with God creates a
close personal relationship akin to the relationships known from family life: Israel is God's son or God's wife, and within these metaphorical
understandings, the covenant and its formula have their place. After the
ravages of history, Jeremiah looks forward to Israel's restoration when a
transformed Israel will once again be God's people and God will be their
god (Jer 30:22,25; 31:20; 32:27). Ezekiel also adopts this hope for a new
covenant with a new Israel (Ezek 11:20; 14:11; 36:28; 37:23). But now
the law engraved on stone has no place in this new covenant—just as the
laws were not the essence of the covenant of intimacy that God formed
with Israel in the desert. Now, God will transform Israel by imprinting
the divine rules on Israel's heart.

Sinai and the Corporate Covenant

The Torah's great sacred narrative brings this new people through the
desert to Sinai. There, God offers them a covenant. The people are composed of more than the descendants of Abraham, Isaac, and Jacob, and
God's credentials are not restricted to God's covenant with the ancestors
(Exod 19:4–6):

ד:אתם ראיתם אשר עשיתי למצרים ואשא אתכם על-כנפי נשרים ואביא אתכם אלי:
ה:ועתה אם שמוע תשמעו בקולי ושמרתם את-בריתי והייתם לי סגולה מכל-העמים
כי-לי כל-הארץ:
ו:ואתם תהיו-לי ממלכת כהנים וגוי קדוש
אלה הדברים אשר תדבר אל-בני ישראל:

> You have seen what I did to Egypt
> and how I carried you on eagle's wings and brought you to me.
> Now, if you really listen to my voice and observe my covenant
> you will be a treasure above all the peoples, for the whole earth is mine.
> You will be a kingdom of priests and a holy nation.

God's credentials are the deeds that he did to Egypt and his trans-
portation of the people to Sinai "on eagles' wings." As God invites the
people to be a "kingdom of priests and a holy nation," God reminds
them of what they have just seen, that the whole cosmos belongs to God.

The group signals their readiness to enter into this covenant with the formulaic, "Everything that YHWH spoke, we will do" (Exod 19:8):

ח:ויענו כל-העם יחדיו ויאמרו כל אשר-דבר יהוה נעשה

The people answered all together, "Everything that YHWH spoke we will do."

Newly published tablets from Mari (seventeenth century B.C.E.) show us that God's invitation and the people's answer are the classic preliminaries to making a political treaty in the West Semitic world of the second millennium. The chapters that follow are a complex and somewhat chaotic account of the formation of this new covenant,[12] complete with the role of Moses as the envoy of the great king. As often occurs in the Bible, ritual and legal texts are presented in story form, not "You shall do X . . . " but "and then they did X." Exodus 12 presents the celebration of the Passover sacrifice as a narrative account of the first night of Passover; Leviticus 16 presents the ritual of Yom Kippur as the story of the inauguration of the Tabernacle service. And Exodus 19–24 presents in linear form a dramatic narratization of Israel's memory or imagination of the events at Sinai, along with a presentation in story form of the essence of covenant. The story begins with three days of purification and abstention, which culminate with the arrival of God to the mountain accompanied by lightning, thunder, the loud blowing of the shofar, and the trembling and shaking of the mountain itself. In some form, God then announces the Ten Commandments to and through Moses, beginning with the first essential demand for exclusive fidelity, and a sharp declaration that God is zealous in defense of God's prerogatives. The passage ends with the people's unanimous resumption of their original acceptance, "all the things that YHWH spoke, we will do" (Exod 24:3). Moses then seals the covenant with a blood ritual (Exod 24:5–8):

ה:וישלח את-נערי בני ישראל ויעלי עלות ויזבחו זבחים שלמים ליהוה פרים:
ו:ויקח משה חצי הדם וישם באגנות וחצי הדם זרק על-המזבח:
ז:ויקח ספר הברית ויקרא באזני העם ויאמרו
כל אשר-דבר יהוה נעשהו נשמע:
ח:ויקח משה את-הדם יוזרק על-העם ויאמר הנה דם-הברית
אשר כרת יהוה עמכם על כך-הדברים האלה:

He sent the lads of the Israelites and they offered sacrifices to YHWH in cows.
Moses took half the blood and placed it in basins
and half the blood he threw on the altar.
He took the book of the covenant and read it out in the ears of the people.
They said, "All that YHWH spoke, we will do and listen."

> Moses took the blood and threw it on the people.
> He said, "Here is the blood of the covenant
> that YHWH has cut with you about these matters."

Moses took the "scroll of the covenant," which he or a secretary had written, and read it before the people, who once again proclaimed, "everything which YHWH has spoken we will do," and then added, "and we will listen" (Exod 24:7). This "book of the covenant" is analogous to the tablet written up at the cutting of a political treaty; reading the record of this covenant becomes one of the ways that the people are expected to observe the covenant. In the Bible, this literary document becomes a way into and an experience of the special relationship with God, part of that which makes Israel "holy." The covenant is then sealed with the sprinkling of the "blood of the covenant" on the people, and Moses goes back up the mountain to commune with God.

In the middle of this section, either as its original core or as a later insertion, sits Israel's most ancient collection of laws. In this way, the canonical Torah incorporates the principles of law and justice as an essential ingredient in "observing" the covenant.

Deuteronomy's Corporate Covenant

The covenant between the people and God is reenvisioned in the Book of Deuteronomy, which represents itself as Moses' recollection of the experience and of the laws. The structure of the covenant, here, is more "modern"—it conforms to the Assyrian political covenants of the eighth and seventh centuries instead of the Western political covenants of the seventeenth century B.C.E.[13] In this way, the covenant could seem contemporary and immediate to its readers rather than sounding like an archaic remnant from premonarchic times. Written in times of trouble for Israel, the Book of Deuteronomy seems the product of a revival movement, an attempt to make the pristine and perfect past new again and to replace the miserable state that the movement intends to rectify. The laws are now seen as essential to the covenant, for the lack of social justice is the cause of Israel's troubles, and God is bringing Israel's troubles upon her—not in violation of God's obligation as her God, but rather in fulfillment of the terms to which Israel agreed. Many of the laws show a deep suspicion of the monarchy, which the Deuteronomy-influenced Book of Kings blames for Judah's exile. The laws of Deuteronomy, now stipulations of Israel's treaty with God, include many family rules, conspicuously absent from the Exodus collection (usually called the Book of the Covenant by contemporary scholars). This, too, fits with the historical books, which see the mistreatment of subordinate family members to be a major cause of Israel's defeats. Deuteronomy does not trust monarchs; at the same time, the Book of Judges presents abuse by fathers to be the reason that the old rule by Judges imploded and monarchy was introduced. Both the premonarchic and monarchic systems of government failed in their need to make Israel "a kingdom of priests and a holy nation." And the search goes on.

Personal Covenants with God: David and Pinhas (Phineas)

This is not the place to examine the covenants of David and Pinhas closely. Briefly put, the former establishes the descendants of David as monarchs forever, and the latter establishes the descendants of Pinhas as priests forever. The covenant of Pinhas is called "an eternal covenant of peace" because he stepped forward to protect Israel from God's wrath after the sin at Ba'al Pe'or.[14] In Numbers 25, Pinhas was "zealous" for God in that he killed the miscreant prince Zimri and the Midianite princess Kozbi; elsewhere he stopped the plague through successful intercessory prayer (Ps 106:30). Like Israel's corporate covenant, these personal covenants will not be broken—at least as long as Throne and Temple stand. Individual misdeeds will be punished, and wicked descendants may be removed from their position. But the position will immediately be given to another descendent of David or Pinhas.

Moses and Elijah are not rewarded with such covenants even though they are loyal and zealous beyond normal expectations. But Moses and Elijah are prophets, and no one could inherit the position of a prophet, who was personally appointed by God.

Personal Covenants between People: David and Jonathan, Ruth and Naomi

Personal covenants mark the creation of new relationships, a formation of a kin based on friendship rather than blood. They center upon an oath in which God is expected to guarantee that the covenantal partners will act toward each other with all the devotion and benevolence that could be expected. They parallel the treaties between nations in which nations swear fealty to one another. These covenants may also ultimately be based on family patterns, for nations of equal status adopt each other as brothers, and smaller nations seek a treaty with their "father," the great king. David and Jonathan become like brothers, and Ruth and Naomi like mother and daughter, or more accurately, like father and son.

These personal covenants highlight an essential feature of Israel's covenants with God. In both the covenants of intimacy and the corporate covenants, God is both party to the covenant and its guarantor. To enter into such a relationship requires enormous trust that God is trustworthy, that God will abide by the covenant's stipulations. After all, covenants pose severe limitations on God's freedom. Why should God keep to terms that might seem distasteful to God at critical moments?

Covenants tame the dragon—but only if the dragon agrees to be tamed. To trust the dragon requires faith, and Israel has to keep reassuring herself that God is trustworthy. As with so many things, the prophet stands as interlocutor on such a matter. The prophet is God's envoy who announces God's displeasure. At the same time, the prophet is expected to turn around and remind God of the covenant God made with an imperfect Israel and all its foibles.[15]

The prophet will use his understanding that God wants all the other nations to think well of God, that Israel is expected to be the vanguard, and that ultimately God wants all the nations to come to acknowledge God—so that God can be the final arbiter between nations and there will be no reason for war.

COVENANTS TODAY

The notion of covenant fell on hard times in the Roman period. Christianity emphasized that it was the bearer of the new covenant to which Jeremiah and Ezekiel referred, but said little about what this would mean in imperial times. The Rabbis were not much kinder to the concept of covenant. In a time when Israel had no autonomy, the notion of covenant, with its relationship between entities that maintained their own integrity, was replaced by a sense of submission, of being under the yoke of the great king (*'ol malkhut)* and under the yoke of the commandments (*'ol mitzvot)*. The term "covenant" was limited to the covenant of circumcision, which was then the very definition of being Jewish. Since Israel's neighbors no longer circumcised their males, "submission," already in the wind in Deuteronomy, became the desideratum in both Judaism and Christianity.

Submission is not quite as popular today. The self has been gaining importance since the Renaissance, and a self that is entitled to the pursuit of happiness sometimes needs not to submit. A self endowed by its creator with the right to life and liberty ought to stand up for these rights even if that means not submitting to authority. Submission to God, which had involved as a codicil submission to the king, was sometimes interpreted as requiring submission to God instead of to the king or other political leader. The lack of ease with the whole concept of submission became magnified enormously in the second half of the twentieth century after the first half of the century showed into what atrocities people accustomed to submission can be led. And even submission to God came into disfavor when the latter half of the twentieth century witnessed how religious leaders could use violence to advance their views. The less confidence that people place in total submission, the more attractive "covenant" becomes.

"Covenant" places limits on God's radical freedom, allowing human beings to influence divine behavior. Of course, the only one who can limit God is God, but in coming to covenant, God voluntarily restricts divine freedom even as we limit our own. These limits depend on God's own word in promise, but so does our very existence on Earth. A covenant with God is a little like the famous bargain with the scorpion or, for that matter, a political treaty with a superpower: the binding force of the treaty, bargain, or covenant is only worth as much as the good will of the more powerful power. If God wants to ignore God's own covenant, nobody can stop God. The world depends on God's keeping God's covenant with Noah. There is no guarantee that God will not destroy everything except the fact that God is trustworthy. And if God is trustworthy in the divine promise not to destroy the world, then God must be presumed to be trustworthy in other covenants into which God enters voluntarily.

We no longer feel as powerless as everyone but the Romans did during the Roman period. We have been forced to acknowledge what God already foresaw at the tower of Babel, "now, nothing that they wish to do can be withheld from them" (Gen 11:6). As Robert Oppenheimer declared when he saw the first nuclear explosions, "we have become like God in our power to destroy," and every day we get closer to achieving god-like powers to create. With such power behind us, kneeling in submission is much like the ostrich placing its head in the sand. We have to look up and see reality, and covenantal thinking presents the best option for acknowledging that we are powerful beings who desire to control ourselves.

The intricate array of covenants that the Bible presents to us offers us some guidance in thinking through each matter. Clearly, fundamentally, the universal covenant of Noah (not the Rabbinic Noahide covenant) addressed our continued existence on Earth.

Our very existence on the earth is not guaranteed by any need of God, for we have never been told or figured out why God needs the earth at all. Should God decide some day either that God has no interest in the world, or in having humanity administer the cosmos, then there is absolutely no guarantee that we will continue to exist. Only God's promise not to destroy the world again—and God's trustworthiness to keep the divine word—stand between us and disaster. But although there may be no doubt that God keeps God's word—are we really sure that God has promised not to destroy the world? Like most oracles, this divine promise is fundamentally ambiguous, for God actually promises never again to bring a flood to destroy all of humankind. Perhaps God could destroy humanity and leave Earth intact, to be governed by superintelligent cockroaches (the only creature to be more or less unchanged since the time of the dinosaurs) or by some other highly evolved insect. And to provide even more ambiguity, God promises never again to bring a flood to destroy the world; God never says that God will not bring a fire next time!

Given the lack of external guarantees, it is clear that God has left the continued existence of humanity in our own hands. We are to manage the world: God will not intervene, and it should surprise nobody that God did not intervene at Auschwitz or in Rwanda. The world is ours—God has created it, but God then gave it to us to run it in God's image. We are God's image, which means that what we do is the way God acts in the world, and God will not act outside of this image.

In the Bible's portrayal, the first cycle of humankind began with our pre-Neolithic creation in southern Iraq and concluded with our urban civilization scattered from Iraq to the rest of the world. During this cycle, human beings created all of world civilization (apart from Law, which was God's gift). The second cycle began with Abraham leaving Iraq, and God once again actively participating in the world, forming a special relationship with one family and then with one people. God presents the features that distinguish Israelite civilization through revelation of cult, temple, monarchy, and individual laws, and seals these presentations with various covenants. But once again, God's attempts at micromanagement fail and Israel returns to Iraq.

Can the covenants from this cycle of civilization be of value to us today? The personal covenants of Throne and Temple, David and Pinhas, have no reality to us today, and we can argue whether a day will come when they will again be important. But the covenants of intimacy with God may serve as a bridge by which we can acknowledge God's special interest in our individual ethnic identities. God has a covenant with Abraham's family that endured far past the ancient biblical state, and by maintaining faith despite all hardships and difficulties and the constant delay of any benefit, it is, itself, a paradigm for our behavior. But Abraham's covenant belongs to Israel, and the covenant of the flesh belongs to the people who mystically belong to the flesh of Abraham, Isaac, and Jacob.

I would not presume to suggest what form covenants between other groups and God should take, but the Bible's vision of national covenant provides a way to feel the presence of God in a richer, more multifaceted way than the universal but generic channeling of God's presence by human beings. The covenants of intimacy, based on human relations, also open the door for individual ethnic covenants, for a father can have many children, though each child has one father, and a king can have many subjects. Acknowledging the ultimate unity of all reality does not mean that one has to ignore or ride roughshod over the benefits of having many cultures and civilizations. The key that we have to figure out is how to celebrate many separate nations, each with its own covenant with God, without descending into war. It was disagreement between nations and the stresses brought by war that ended the preexilic phase of biblical culture, and just as Abraham came out of Chaldean Ur, so too Israel was exiled by war back to Chaldean Ur.

We are now in the third stage that began with the restoration of Israel from Babylon. Learning to live without war is the task of this phase. If we succeed, we might have the vision of Isaiah in which war is no longer the final arbiter among nations. But God has not revealed the formula, has not suggested terms for a new covenant. I speak, of course, as a Jew, and Christians might claim that God has indeed revealed the formula, which is by faith in Jesus Christ. But this new Christian covenant has not ushered in a period of universal peace, though it once tried to bring it to pass by war. God will not fight on some side or another to bring peace. God should not be invoked to bless the weapons or curse the enemies. God stands for and manifests God's self in a universal peace achieved by peaceful means, in a unity without subordination, in a universality composed of particularities. The world of humanity, like the world of matter, must express the unity of God that was glimpsed by the Israelites so long ago. Traces of divine unity remain to be detected in nature, in the DNA of human beings and the mitochondria that we all share from our common mother, and in the multifaceted view of truth and of reality presented in the Bible.

NOTES

1. For an excellent presentation of our knowledge up until that point, see D. J. McCarthy, *Treaty and Covenant: A Study in Form in the Ancient Oriental Documents and in the Old Testament*, 2nd ed. (Rome: 1981). For further insight into the political treaty form underlying Deuteronomy, see H. Tadmor, "Treaty and Oath in the Ancient Near East," *Humanizing America's Iconic Book*, G. M. Tucker and D. A. Knight, eds. (Chico, Calif.: 1982). Much recent study has concentrated on the Priestly covenantal traditions, for which see Menahem Haran, "The *Berit* 'Covenant': Its Nature and Ceremonial Background," *Tehillah le-Moshe: Biblical and Judaic Studies in Honor of Moshe Greenberg*, Mordechai Cogan, Barry Eichler, and Jeffrey Tigay, eds. (Winona Lake, Ind.: Eisenbrauns, 1997): 202–20; Jacob Milgrom, "Covenants: The Sinaitic and Patriarchal Covenants in the Holiness Code (Leviticus 17–27)," *Sefer Moshe: The Moshe Weinfeld Jubilee Volume*, Chaim Cohen, Avi Hurwitz, and Shalom Paul, eds. (Winona Lake: Eisenbrauns, 2004): 91–102; in addition, the publication of new Mari letters (J. M. Durand, ed., *Les documents épistolaires du palais de Mari*, coll. Littératures anciennes du Proche-Orient 16–18, 3 vols. [Paris: Cerf, 1997–2000]), which have cast important new light on the form of treaties in the Old Babylonian period, and which in turn have led to an increase in our understanding of the presentation of the Sinai covenant in Exodus (see Frank H. Polak, "The Covenant at Mount Sinai in the Light of Texts from Mari," *Sefer Moshe: The Moshe Weinfeld Jubilee Volume*, 119–43.

2. See Lawrence Hoffman, *A Covenant of Blood* (Chicago: University of Chicago Press, 1995).

3. See David Novak, *The Image of the Non-Jew in Judaism: An Historical and Constructive Study of the Noahide Laws* (Toronto: Edwin Mellen Press, 1983).

4. For a discussion of these rules, see Tikva Frymer-Kensky, "The *Atrahasis* epic and Its Significance for Our Understanding of Genesis 1–9."

5. Most recently, the Nation of Islam published *The Secret Relationship of the Blacks and the Jews*, which identifies Hamites as African Blacks and says that the curse authorized the Jews (and ultimately Christians) to participate in the African slave trade. For an examination of this issue see David H. Aaron, "Early Rabbinic Exegesis on Noah's Son Ham and the So-Called 'Hamitic Myth,'" *JAAR* 63/4 (1996): 721–59.

6. See Tikva Frymer-Kensky, "Patriarchal Family Relationships and Near Eastern Law," *BA* 44 (Fall 1981): 209–14.

7. Lawrence Stager, "The Archaeology of the Family in Ancient Israel." *Bulletin of the American Schools of Oriental Research* 260 (Fall 1985): 1–35.

8. See Moshe Weinfeld, "The Covenant of Grant in the Old Testament and in the Ancient Near East" *JAOS* 90 (1970): 184–203; 92 (1972): 468–69.

9. For the Mari correspondence, see J. M. Durand, ed. *Les documents epistolaires de mari litteratures anciennes duProche-Orient* 16–18, 3 vols. Paris: Cerf, 1997–2000.

10. See Rolf, Rendtorff, *The Covenant Formula: An Exegetical and Theological Investigation* (Edinburgh: T & T Clark, 1998), and Seock-Tae Sohn, "I Will Be Your God and You Will Be My People": The Origin and Background of the Covenant Formula," in *Ki Baruch hu: Ancient Near Eastern, Biblical, and Judaic Studies in Honor of Baruch A. Levine.* Robert Chazan, William Hallo, and Lawrence Schiffman, eds. (Winona Lake. Ind.: Eisenbrauns, 1999): 355–72.

11. The verse ends: ואנכי לא-אהיה לכם. Possibly the word *le'elohim* has dropped out, but it is equally possible that Hosea intended to say "I will not be yours," meaning "I will not be anything to you," relying on the audience to remember the regular formula and playing on it.

12. See the article by Frank H. Polak, "The Covenant at Mount Sinai in the Light of Texts from Mari," in *Sefer Moshe: The Moshe Weinfeld Jubilee Volume,* Chaim Cohen, Avi Hurwitz, and Shalom Paul, eds. (Winona Lake, Ind.: Eisenbrauns, 2004): 119–43.

13. This covenant formula has been studied intensively since George Mendenhall, "Covenant Forms in Israelite Traditions," BA 17 (1954): 50–76. See D. J. McCarthy, *Treaty and Covenant: A Study in Form in the Ancient Oriental Documents and in the Old Testament,* 2nd ed. (Rome, 1981).

14. For this covenant see Tikva Frymer-Kensky, "Another View of Parashat Pinhas," *WRJ Women's Commentary on the Torah* (Women of Reform Judaism, 2003).

15. For this important function, see Yochanan Muffs, "Who Will Stand in the Breach? A Study in Prophetic Intercession," *Love and Joy: Law, Language and Religion in Ancient Israel* (New York: Jewish Theological Seminary of America, 1992): 9–48.

FEMINIST PERSPECTIVES I: GENDER AND THE BIBLE

11 / The Bible and Women's Studies

1994

In the past two decades there has been a tremendous change in biblical studies. The scientistic philosophy that prevailed for more than a century has given way, in biblical studies as in other humanities, to a more sophisticated understanding of the interaction between the now and the then, the reader and the text. Old ideas of history as "what actually happened" and text as having one correct and original meaning have yielded to a current view of the continual interaction of the viewer and what is seen, of the text and its reader. No longer do we believe that there is a truly "value-neutral" way of reading literature or reconstructing history.

Women's studies did not *cause* this paradigm shift, but they are part of an enormous change in our perception of reality. When only European middle-class Protestant men were doing the reading, they were able to see their consensual understandings as objective. When new voices entered the cultural dialogue—the voices of Catholics, Jews, Asians, Afro-Americans, Africans, people speaking from the perspective of poverty, and women—then the presuppositions that underlay the old objective readings increasingly came to the surface, and the context was understood as part of the reading of the text. This new understanding has made it possible to see beyond the traditional readings of biblical texts to reach newer interpretations and insights.

The impact of this paradigm shift in biblical studies can be seen in several ways. There are increasing numbers of new readings of biblical stories from the perspectives of liberation, the third world, womanism, and feminism. In addition, literary criticism of the Bible has grappled with the ways that stories have multiple codes that signify meanings and the way that reader responses can be shaped by the text as well as by the culture of the reader. This turmoil in biblical studies has brought a general openness in the field studies to women's studies—an expectation that women's studies can provide fresh perspectives on the texts—and an almost eager receptivity to solid feminist scholarship. There are relatively few people actively doing women-centered analyses of the Bible, but there is general awareness of their efforts and a willingness to learn from them.

RECOGNIZING PATRIARCHY

The first impact of women's studies on biblical studies has been the recognition that the Bible is a patriarchal document from a patriarchal society. Feminism and women's studies have enabled us to see the parameters of this patriarchy. Biblical society was patrilocal: women left their fathers' households and authority at marriage and physically moved to their husbands' domain. If the husband was still under the authority of his father, then the wife would also come under his authority. Women were subordinate to the men of the household, and men exerted control over women's sexuality.

Patriarchy has a strong economic component. In ancient Israel, women did not normally own land, which made them economically dependent on men, first on their fathers, then on their husbands, and ultimately on their sons. The Bible contains repeated injunctions to care for widows and the fatherless. This humanitarian command is nevertheless predicated on the assumption of patriarchy: the widow is dependent on the concern and goodwill of males only because she herself has no real property.

Women were not part of the great public hierarchies that developed. The central public organizations of court, temple, and army did not include them. They were not judges, courtiers, or diplomats; they were not military leaders; and they were not priests. To a very large extent, their activity was confined to the private sphere. Yet women were not secluded in their homes. They could be seen in public, they could sing and dance, and women of talent could compose and perform victory dances, love songs, and laments.

Surprisingly, women could be prophets. Miriam, the sister of Moses, and Deborah the Judge are both termed prophet in biblical text. Moreover, 2 Kings 22 relates an episode in which the High Priest Hilkiah and the scribe Shaphan go to the prophet Huldah, who confirms that the scroll they have found while repairing the temple is significant and, moreover, that God will carry out its predictions of disaster. The text does not comment on the fact that the prophet was a woman. The casual way she is mentioned indicates that her position was not anomalous; women could be expected to be prophets and to have the prophetic authority to declare something a vital part of sacred tradition. Yet women were not priests. The presence of women as prophets but not as priests may be attributed to the fact that prophecy is by its very nature nonbureaucratic. Prophets operate individually, without a hierarchy of command. As a result, their authority is based on personal charisma and believability rather than on an organizational power base. Although women's skill and charisma could help them attain prophetic authority (much as their skills could lead to considerable power in the household), the hierarchical structure of the priesthood was closed to them, as it was to all men not born into priestly families.

In biblical Israel, individual women could become powerful. This should not blind us to the fact that as a group women were not treated the same way as men, and society was structured along gender lines in a way that disadvantaged women. This structure, which we often call patriarchy, was characteristic of ancient Israel. Despite the charged atmosphere in which the Bible's treatment of women is sometimes discussed, however, Israel was neither the creator of patriarchy nor the worst perpetrator in the ancient world. Anthropology shows patriarchy to have been widespread, almost universal, and history shows that all the great historical civilizations were patriarchal, including the civilizations that preceded and surrounded ancient Israel. The patriarchy of Israel was part of an inherited social structure from the ancient world. A comparison of biblical laws with those of Assyria readily shows that the Bible did not rival Assyria in the extent to which it subordinated women.

Nevertheless, we make a profound statement when we acknowledge that the Bible is patriarchal. We are brought to the realization that the Bible contains a fundamental moral flaw: it does not treat all humans as equals. We in the modern world are learning that respect for the equality of all human beings and their common dignity is a moral imperative. Our perception of a moral imperative that does not derive from biblical teaching indicates that the Bible is no longer our only or even our *final* arbiter of morality. This has enormous religious implications. The authority of the Bible must be tempered with the authority of our experiences as human beings and our principles of morality. It is true that many of our moral ideas ultimately come from the Bible, but it is also true that they have been inspired by our continued reflection on the Bible during the millennia since it was written. The Bible did not eradicate slavery; it was up to people to do so. The Bible did not eradicate economic oppression, and we do not have a clue as to how to do so.

Because of their implications for our own time, feminist studies of the Bible (and I would argue, all biblical studies) cannot remain isolated from the political implications of their research, nor from their impact on the lives of people. There is no value-neutrality with regard to oppression: if one does not consciously address a problem, one becomes part of the problem. Therefore, there is no absolute cleavage between feminism, feminist theology, feminist hermeneutics, and the study of women in the Bible or in the biblical world.[1] Precisely because of the intersection between politics and biblical study, feminist scholars such as Elisabeth Schüssler-Fiorenza have urged all biblical scholars to take an active part in the moral and theological discussions of our time.[2]

THE WOMEN

The study of women in the Bible is hindered by the public nature and androcentricity of the text itself. The Bible concerns itself with the communal history of Israel. Women did not play a great role in the public institutions of the ancient world, and the Bible focuses on the movers and shakers. As a result, women are rarely the major actors in biblical stories, and the stories themselves never deal with the lives of women-among-women, to which men had little access. Finding out about the history of women in biblical times often means ferreting out information that the androcentric biblical authors were either not interested in or were not interested in communicating to their audiences.

Uncovering the lives of biblical women poses serious methodological problems that are shared by all attempts to reconstruct a biblical history. To fill in the gaps in the biblical record other than by mere speculation, we must turn to such disciplines as archaeology, ancient Near Eastern studies, anthropology, and sociology. Archaeology and ancient Near Eastern studies provide data, written and unwritten, that are independent of the Bible. They can provide details about the size of families, the nature of subsistence, the laws of the surrounding world, and other information. Anthropology and sociology shed light on cross-cultural patterns and provide models that can help reconstruct life in ancient Israel. The most successful attempt to use such social science data to understand women's history was made by Carol Meyers.[3] Basing her work on information and models from peasant societies to supplement our knowledge of Israel in the period of the judges (about 1200–1000 B.C.E.), Meyers points out that when the most important arena of life was the household, where women had an active role and an important economic function, they had greater access to power than in later state societies in which the public arena developed and women were excluded. For Meyers, as for others, the period of the judges was a high point in the prominence of women in Israel.[4]

The Bible is more than the record of ancient Israelite civilization, and the woman-centered study of the Bible is more than a reclamation of the history of women in ancient Israel. The Bible is also a work of art. It is a literary text that presents people and ideas in an artistic fashion. There has been a great renewed interest in studying the Bible's major female characters; stories of the Bible's great women and extensive bibliographies are developing on such characters as the matriarchs,[5] Hagar,[6] Tamar,[7] Miriam,[8] Rahab,[9] and Deborah and Yael.[10] From these and other studies it has become clear that the Bible often portrays women as heroines who possess the characteristics that Israel needs to emulate. Women were the saviors of Israel at the beginning and at the end of the biblical period. The savior figure at the beginning is Yael, a marginal woman, wife of the Kenite Heber. Yael took advantage of the fact that the Canaanite general Sisera fled from battle into her tent. She agreed to guard him, gave him warm milk, and lulled him to sleep; then she pounded a tent-peg into his temple to kill him and thus save Israel. The savior figure at the end of biblical history is Esther, another marginal figure. She was a Jew living in exile who became queen of Persia and used her royal connections to foil the villain Haman's plot to destroy Persia's Jews. These women, who conquered mighty enemies by their wits and daring, were symbolic representations of the people and pointed to the salvation of Israel.

HER STORY

The Bible has many stories in which women play secondary roles. One of the aims of women's studies and a technique of feminist literary criticism is to recover minor characters (and women were always minor) by ignoring the biblical narrators' concentration on heroes, focusing instead on *"her story."* The biblical scholar Burke Long has focused on the role of the "great woman" of Shunnem, who appears in the narratives about the prophet Elisha.

At the beginning of the story, the Shunnemite acknowledges the prophet Elisha's privileged position and shows her support by feeding and housing him. At the end of the story, she proclaims his holiness. Nevertheless, at the heart of the story, she is a determined mover and shaper of events who insists that Elisha come to the aid of her son. Long points out that our reading of this story as an Elisha tale is socially formed: the story was written to glorify Elisha as prophet and miracle worker; it was preserved as part of a cycle of tales about the prophets Elijah and Elisha and has been read by generations interested almost exclusively in the heroized prophet. When we read it this way, we may not notice that the story is also the story of a great woman.[11]

Focus on the women in such tales can also yield important insights into ancient social structures. In my own study of biblical gender,[12] the Shunnemite was noteworthy, first as an independent woman who extends patronage to Elisha and then as a determined petitioner willing to confront everyone—husband, prophet, and king—in her pursuit of the physical and economic well-being of her household.[13] Moreover, read closely, this story indicates how gender intersects with class. The Elijah and Elisha stories take place against a backdrop of great poverty among the rural poor. Most of the miracles that Elijah and Elisha perform involve providing food for a starving peasantry. In contrast to all the poor women found in these stories, the Shunnemite is wealthy. This factor gives her striking boldness in her dealings with the prophet; after all, she is his patron and benefactor, the one who provides food and hospitality on his journeys. Wealthy women have greater freedom of action than poor women do, and sometimes even more than poor men.[14]

It is possible to go deeper into the story. The Shunnemite stands out among the women of Israel in being independent of her husband. She does not ask his permission when she entertains Elisha, bringing him into the picture only when she wishes to make an addition to her house. Later, when she seeks Elisha, she does not inform her husband why she is leaving. Though she is wealthy, does her economic well-being not depend on her husband's goodwill? Is she not in danger of divorce? A clue to the answer lies in her puzzling reply to Elisha when the prophet wants to reward her for her beneficence: "I live among my own kin" (2 Kgs. 4:13). This odd statement seems to contradict what we know about ancient marriage. We expect her to be living among her husband's kinfolk, not among her own.

The puzzle deepens. When Elisha saves her son, he warns her of famine, and she and her family leave for seven years. When she comes back, she goes to the king to reclaim her property. The king gives instructions to "restore all her property and all the revenue from her farm from the time she left the country until now!" (2 Kgs. 8:6). The pronouns used are striking: *Her* property? *Her* farm? This is not the language we expect from the Bible, for the laws indicate that women did not own land. Surely, the land is her husband's, if he is still alive, or her son's. Either there is a greater gap between the laws and the narratives than we have assumed, or there is something special about the position of the Shunnemite. Her statement to the prophet, "I live among my own kin," suggests that the Shunnemite might have had the status of a daughter of Zelophehad. The five daughters of Zelophehad appear in the Book of Numbers; they petition to inherit the portion of their father, who died without sons. Their petition is granted and it is decreed that if a father dies without sons, the daughters are the rightful heirs.[15] Later a provision is added that the daughters who inherit are to marry their own tribesmen in order to keep the land in the family.[16] A daughter of Zelophehad *owns* her land for her lifetime. She is not as dependent for her livelihood on men as other women are. If her husband divorces her, she stays on her land. This is probably why the woman of Shunnem, singular among the barren women in the Bible, does not actively seek a child before Elisha announces that she will have one. Because she is economically secure, the Shunnemite has no need to ask her husband's permission either to seek or entertain Elisha. The same economic security makes it possible for her to enjoy both status and a secure old age even without ever having had a child. The story of the Shunnemite can be understood as a biblical example of how women act when the *economic* constraints of patriarchy are removed.

A similar study can be done of another minor character, Abigail.[17] Abigail appears as the wife of a wealthy landowner, Nabal ("the boor"), during the time when the future king David is an outlaw leader. David appears before Nabal to ask for payment for the protection that David has given Nabal's shepherds during the year. Nabal refuses to pay, reasoning that he has not hired David to protect him. David leaves angry and vows to bring his men back to destroy Nabal's household. The Book of Samuel is focused on how David became king, and the story of Abigail is told because she preserved David's chances to be king. When, however, we focus attention on Abigail rather than on David, we see interesting things. Like the Shunnemite, Abigail is both wealthy and noted for her bold initiative. She is not present at her husband Nabal's negotiations with David, perhaps indicating that she is less important and less active in her household than the Shunnemite is in hers; after all, we have no reason to suspect that she owns her own land. But she is no less decisive. Realizing that David must be angry at her husband because of his refusal to pay David, Abigail acts immediately. She deduces correctly that David might attack her household and quickly intercepts him while bearing him gifts. Her insight saves both Nabal and David from catastrophe, her brilliant rhetoric convinces David not to kill every male in Nabal's house, and David blesses her and God, who sent her to him. Once again, an intelligent, determined woman is influential far beyond the formal confines of patriarchy.[18] Just as anthropology has come to a more sophisticated understanding of the various types of power and the access of women to informal power, so too in biblical studies it has become apparent that biblical women had considerable influence on their world.[19]

By focusing on the women in biblical stories, feminist biblical scholarship has also illuminated the institutions of ancient Israel. In Israel there existed the position of *gevirah*, or queen mother.[20] That it was an actual position rather than an honorific title is indicated by the fact that Asa removed his mother from this position because she had made an *asherah* (a sacred grove, tree, or tree-sculpture) (1 Kgs. 15:13). The existence of the position of queen opens the possibility that the *gevirah* might have been well situated for harem intrigue, maneuvering to ensure the high status of her sons. In this way, the *gevirah* may have helped determine policy and succession. Bathsheba was certainly active on behalf of her son Solomon. The other queen mothers whose names are known to us (Maacah, mother of Asa; Hamutal, mother of Jehoiahaz and Zedekiah; and Nehushta, mother of Jehoiachin) were, like Bathsheba, the mothers of younger sons who helped put their sons into the kingship. As a result, these women influenced biblical history and attained a particular prominence during their sons' reigns.

THE BIBLE ON GENDER

The study of individual women in the Bible has led to several unexpected discoveries. A major example is that even though women were subordinate in the socioeconomic and legal systems, the Bible does not attempt to justify this subordination by portraying women as subhuman or as *other* in any way. The biblical stories portray women as having the same set of goals, the same abilities, and the same strategies as biblical men.[21] To use modern terminology, the Bible is not *essentialist* on gender; it does not consider differences between the sexes to be innate. The same is true of other social divisions in Israel: the Bible has no social Darwinism and does not depict either slaves or poor people as essentially different from "standard" Israelites. The Bible inherited its social structure from antiquity and did not radically transform it.[22] At the same time, the Bible did not justify social inequality by an ideology of superiority or otherness. On the contrary, the Bible's explicit ideology presents a unified vision of humankind wherein women and men were created in the image of God and no negative stereotypes are attached to women, the poor, slaves, or foreigners.

There is a strange dissonance here. The social structure, with its cleavages and oppressions, is not in harmony with the Bible's ideology of equality. Only the Garden of Eden story (Gen. 3–4) seems to note this contradiction, announcing simply that gender inequality is the norm of the imperfect universe. The rest of the Bible does not consider the relation of hierarchical structures to equal worth at all. Of course, the tension between the Bible's ideology and social structure could not endure forever.[23] Postexilic writings pay more attention to gender, and ultimately Israel is greatly influenced by Hellenistic thinking, which treats women as categorically "other." Nevertheless, this later development should not obscure the fact that preexilic Israel had no ideology of gender differences. In the first Temple period, the dualist axes along which the cosmos was perceptually divided were divine-human, holy-profane, pure-*tame* and Israel-nations. Male-female was not such a category. One of the intriguing questions remaining in biblical scholarship is the place of *woman,* both foreign and Israelite, at the two intersections of Israel-nations and divine-human.

READING WITH NONPATRIARCHAL EYES

The gender blindness of the Bible's view of humanity prevents the Bible from being a completely patriarchal text, and, indeed, one of the significant results of feminist studies in the Bible has been the realization that the biblical text itself, read with nonpatriarchal eyes, is much less injurious to women than the traditional readings of Western civilization. There is much to recover in the Bible that is not patriarchal, even beyond hitherto neglected stories of strong heroines. The enterprise of liberating biblical text from its patriarchal overlay, called *depatriarchalizing* and first advocated by Phyllis Trible, has revealed important aspects of biblical literature.[24]

The most discussed example of depatriarchalization is the Adam-and-Eve story, long notorious for its denigration of women. A new reading was provided by Trible, who pointed out that the creation of Eve implied no inferiority; the word *ezer* (helpmate), used to describe Eve, connotes a mentor-superior in the Bible rather than an assistant and is used frequently for the relation of God to Israel (and not for the relation of Israel to God). Moreover, in mythology the creation order traditionally indicates that the last-created is the culmination of creation, which is certainly the implication of the structure of Genesis 1, in which humans are created after the rest of creation. In Genesis 2, one might argue that the use of *ezer* for Eve and her last-created position was intended to suggest the woman's superiority over the man. At the very least, the text indicates that humans were destined to be equal partners. Eve shows no inferiority to Adam anywhere in the Garden story, and the subordination of women after the expulsion from the Garden is part of the consequences of sin.[25]

Trible's explanation has had widespread acceptance. Some later readings of the story, however, most notably that of Susan Lanser, have pointed out that biblical authors could have expected their readers to respond in certain culturally conditioned ways and that therefore the story relies on patriarchal attitudes to form an indictment of Eve.[26] The truth is that the meaning of the story depends precisely on the assumptions that readers make while reading it. The Adam-and-Eve story is extremely laconic and cannot be retold without the reteller or reader adding additional information. This is true of many other tales in the Bible; they are constructed so that much is left to the reader to fill in and interpret. What one adds to the story determines whether the stories will be liberating or oppressive. In a way, biblical stories may be considered a moral challenge, and it is for the reading community to read them for a blessing rather than a curse.

Biblical stories are often ambiguous. One way, used in the Garden story, is by *gapping;* leaving out important details of the story. An additional way is by self-contradiction: the Bible sometimes gives two different readings in the text itself. Judith Plaskow has made the passage in Exodus 19:15 infamous on this point.[27] Moses is preparing the people for the Revelation when he says, "Make ready for the third day—do not go near a woman." Moses looks at the people and sees only men.[28] A similar blindness appears in the Tenth Commandment with the injunction against coveting your neighbor's wife. Is it all right to covet your neighbor's husband? Women are clearly included in the other commandments and are always considered bound by the covenant of Sinai. Their sudden transformation from subjects of the law ("Do not") to the objects of coveting is startling. The answer may be that women are normally thought of as full persons and legal agents, but the thought of sexual relations transforms women into objects upon whom one acts, or rather, in these cases, into objects upon whom one avoids acting.

A closer look at Exodus 19 reveals that Moses is supposed to be the intermediator between God and Israel, relaying God's words to the people. Yet the narrative has God tell Moses to go to the people and tell them to sanctify themselves for two days, wash their clothes, and be prepared for the third day, when God will come (Exod. 19:10–12). The narrator, who quotes God, does not quote God as saying, "Do not go near a woman." God is not blind; God sees that the people are male and female.[29] It is Moses, with the shortsightedness of a human male, who suddenly addresses only the males. The narrated text contains complex layers of voices. Is there a critique of Moses implied here? Is the text implying that the patriarchal blindness toward women is certainly *not* from God? This is not the only instance in which we hear the voice of patriarchy and the voice of patriarchy's critic in the same story. In the dialogue between God and Abraham in Genesis 17:18–19, there are also two voices, and, once more, the less patriarchal voice, which I call a countervoice, is divine. In this scene, God reiterates the promise to provide Abraham with children, and Abraham remarks that this promise has been fulfilled with the birth of Ishmael. At that point, it is *God* who replies that Ishmael will have his own covenant, but that the promise to Abraham must be fulfilled through Sarah, and announces that Isaac will be born to Abraham and Sarah the following season. By relating this interchange, the narrator of the story warns both ancient and modern readers that we should not be too quick to accept Abraham's androcentric view of the nature of the covenant.

The Bible that subtly warns its readers not to focus solely on the men in its text does not sound like the same Bible that has been quoted throughout history as a way of keeping women in their place. Much of the patriarchy that we associate with the Bible and all of its misogyny has been introduced into the Bible by later generations of readers. One of the impacts of women's studies has been to focus attention on this phenomenon and on the question, "How did we get from there to here?" Once we divorce the text from its patriarchal message we must attempt to delineate some of the influences that began to transform, or rather deform, the Bible into a more patriarchal text. Many of these first become visible in the Hellenistic period and grow more intense as Western history continues.[30]

THE TEXTS OF TERROR

Another goal of women-centered Bible studies is to focus on the stories in the Bible that look patriarchal, seem to have no possibility of
reinterpretation, and clearly read like *texts of terror*.[31] These are the
tales of victims, of women abused beyond the structural norm of patriarchy, of women who are physically and emotionally destroyed by others. One such story, the story of Hagar, is well known. Hagar, Sarah's
personal slave and Abraham's concubine-wife, has no protectors. The
text states that Sarah abused Hagar—that she treated her improperly.
Hagar runs away, but God tells her to return and submit, and she does
so until Sarah finally sends her and her child away.[32] This story starkly
illuminates the relations between women in a patriarchy. Relative to
Hagar, Sarah has all the power. Gender intersects with class: Sarah
is of the dominant class and therefore in a far better position than
Hagar. Moreover, Sarah's actions are perfectly legal. She acts entirely
according to customary law when she makes Hagar the surrogate birthgiver. When she feels threatened, she abuses Hagar and finally sends
her away. Sarah has a perfect right to do so;[33] she is, after all, only
freeing her slave and allowing her to take her son with her. Yet, no
one would say that Sarah (or Abraham) has acted with compassion.
Sarah's motives are clear: she herself is vulnerable and dependent on
Abraham's goodwill toward her. Ultimately, Sarah lacks both economic
security and autonomy, and this makes her incapable of acting well
toward her social inferior. The modern reader may be horrified by her
actions and yet sympathetic to both her and Hagar.

There is no reason to think that an ancient reader would have reacted
differently than the modern reader. As is usual in these biblical stories,
the narrator seems neutral and shows no sympathy for Hagar, nor, for
that matter, for Sarah. Where would the sympathies of the reader be
expected to lie? On the one hand, Sarah is the ancestress of the people
reading the story; Hagar is not. There is the matter of race involved
here, or at least ethnic consciousness: Hagar starts as a foreigner (an
Egyptian) and ends as a foreigner (the mother of the Ishmaelite peoples). Sarah enables Isaac, Israel's ancestor, to be his father's successor.
Would not the ancient reader root for the home team? Still, such treatment of foreigners is not supposed to happen in Israel. Over and over
again the Israelites are told to be kind to the foreigner, for they too
were once foreigners. Israel is also admonished always to be sympathetic to slaves, for they too were once slaves. Sarah and Abraham did

not go through the slavery experience of Egypt, but their readers have and should remember these injunctions. The story continues to sound stranger: after Hagar runs away, God tells her to return; Israel's law demands that Israelites *help* fugitive slaves; why does God not help? Furthermore, Sarah mistreats Hagar *before* she herself becomes a captive concubine in the court of Egypt.[34] Afterward (perhaps because she understands what slavery is), Sarah sets her free and allows her to keep her son, and at that point Hagar becomes a freed slave—the very model of what Israel will later become. Hagar, the newly emancipated Egyptian slave, then goes into the wilderness, whereupon she receives a revelation from God and a promise of nationhood. An ancient Israelite audience could not have missed the many allusions to their own salvation history. Hagar is the prototype of Israel, whose people will be slaves in Egypt, mistreated, and later freed; who will escape to the wilderness and receive God's revelation on Mount Sinai; and who will become the people of Israel. In this story, Sarah who is the progenitress of Israel, and Hagar, the prototype of Israel, are compelled by their situation to be at odds. Israelite readers not only recognize the tragedy of the two women in patriarchy but they also understand how much this tragedy is magnified by the fact that the future Israel is here at odds with itself. The story thereby stands as testimony to the serious problems of a present-day social situation rather than to the personal characteristics of the biblical characters.

Such considerations reveal the great complexity of the tales of terror. They assail the reader's emotions from all directions and make readers distinctly uncomfortable with what is going on. The same play of negative factors is prominent in the tale of Jephthah's daughter (Judg. 11).[35] The narrator is ostensibly telling the tale of one of the judges of Israel, Jephthah. The story begins with Jephthah's birth; immediately the reader's sympathies are with him. He is the son of a prostitute whose half-brothers turned him out when their father died. A disinherited fugitive, he (like David after him) forms a private army and becomes known as a warrior. When his town, Gilead, is in trouble, the elders ask him to save them. He agrees to rescue them if afterward they will make him their head.[36] So far, so good: the underdog has made good, the low has become high, the biblical dream has come true. But something terrible happens. The pious Jephthah makes an oath to sacrifice to God whatever comes to greet him first after his victory. Did he expect an animal? Why not specify? In the tragic event, it is Jephthah's daughter who comes rejoicing. She is his only child;

besides her, according to the text, he has neither son nor daughter. The problem is clear. If he sacrifices his daughter, he will have no progeny; his name will die. In Israel, this fate, called *karet,* is considered the worst fate that can happen to a man, and the threat of it is reserved as a sanction for serious offenses against divinity.[37] The daughters of Zelophehad use this Israelite attitude to acquire the right to inherit their father's estate, arguing that otherwise he would lose his future name without having done anything to deserve that penalty. The wise woman of Tekoa uses this Israelite attitude to manipulate David.[38] The narrator knows that the audience will react with great horror at the prospect of his killing his only child, and that this horror will be *on behalf of Jephthah.*

But what about Jephthah's daughter? Although nameless (at least to us), she too is known to ancient Israel, for as the narrator reminds us, every year the Israelite daughters go to the hills to lament her passing. Furthermore, the narrator makes the audience respect and admire her, for it is she who declares that vows must be honored and that God must be our primary consideration. Jephthah's daughter is a pious and faithful woman who is remembered in cult and story: surely nobody in Israel viewed her death lightly. Moreover, the Bible does not condone child sacrifice. The idea of a great savior of Israel offering his daughter in sacrifice would have been as horrible to the ancient Israelite as it is to the modern reader.

One again, the reader is left disquieted: something is very wrong. No character acts with malice, and yet the most vulnerable character is horribly abused. The reader waits for salvation. Why does somebody not stop the sacrifice? In the world of the reader (ancient and modern), such events do not pass. What reader could kill another with impunity? Fathers do not have the right to kill their children. The story of Jephthah and his daughter points to something seriously lacking in the days of the judges: no one can control the fathers. Abraham, too, had the right to sacrifice his son; no human court would have sought him. The family is its own world, and the father is its ultimate authority. Moreover, a careless vow in this instance compels the father to act against his own self-interest. There is no priesthood to help him undo his vow. There is no authority higher than the family. In the binding of Isaac (Gen. 22), God intervenes to save the son, but God does not intervene to save Jephthah's daughter. The story of Jephthah's daughter, like all the stories in the Book of Judges, tells us that God will no longer intervene to save people who are in danger or who are being abused.

The story of the concubine in Gibeah with which the Book of Judges ends brings these issues into focus.[39] The girl is vulnerable; she is a minor wife, a concubine. When she is unhappy, she runs home. But her father gives her back to her husband-master. The father has already given her to another; now he gives her away again. She is solely under the authority of this new man, a Levite. Levites are a dignified class in Israel, but this Levite is suddenly vulnerable. When they stop in a town of strangers, the strangers attack. A stranger is vulnerable, for he travels without his family to protect him. Since he is alone, there is no one to rescue him. His host offers his daughter to assuage the mob; the Levite sends out his concubine. We are shocked: surely, no one can be gracious to another man by sacrificing his daughter to a mob. The story makes us realize that, in those days, men had ultimate powers of disposal over their women. Abraham could give Sarah to Pharaoh; any man could give his daughter to another as a wife or concubine; Jephthah could sacrifice his daughter to God. The scene in Gibeah is parallel to the story of Sodom and Gomorrah in Genesis 18–19. There, Lot, the only righteous man in town, sent his virginal daughters to the mob that had assembled to abuse his visitors. There is a great difference between Genesis and Judges: when Lot sends out his daughters, the angels of God save them. In the Book of Judges, God no longer intervenes to save individuals and the concubine is raped to the point of death.

The terror of this story continues. The Levite takes revenge by butchering her body to muster the tribes against the tribe of Benjamin. The civil war that follows nearly wipes out a tripe of Israel; to resuscitate it, hundreds of women are captured into rape-marriages. Horror follows horror, and the narrator caps it with the message: in those days there was no king in Israel, and each man did as he wanted.

This story sets us up to await the kingship as an end to such abuse, and indeed the story has many parallels to the first stories about Saul, the first king of Israel. Nonetheless, kingship does not stop the problems that are caused by society's unequal power alignments. The king may act as a force of control over ordinary men, but who can control the king? King Saul tries to kill David; no one can stop him, and David has to flee. David himself is no guarantee of the end of dominance and oppression. After David becomes king, he sees Bathsheba bathing, covets her, and sleeps with her. Later, when Bathsheba tells David that she is pregnant, and Uriah will not sleep with her because he is engaged in battle, David arranges for Uriah to die in battle. David disposes of people as he wants; there is no one to stop him.[40] Yet, when David's daughter Tamar is raped by her half-brother Amnon, David does not protect her or avenge her by killing his son, Amnon the rapist. The reader of the story, who expects that the state will provide protection for the vulnerable,[41] now sees that the state cannot control itself.

These biblical tales of terror portray the horrible things that happen to women under patriarchy; they serve as a warning to us to prevent such happenings, and they were probably included in the Bible to show how things went wrong in Israel. Neither the lack of polity of the Genesis ancestors nor the localized sporadic government of the period of the judges could prevent such outrages. But neither could kingship, as the stories of Bathsheba and Tamar clearly show. The Bible, after all, was written as the sky was falling, in the shadow of the disastrous conquests by the Assyrians and the Babylonians.[42] The historical books maintain their faith in the ultimate justice of God and the cosmos by blaming Israel for its own destruction: because such things happened, Israel was destroyed. This is not misogynist storytelling but something far more complex, in which the treatment of women becomes the clue to the morality of the social order.

WOMAN AS SYMBOL

The literary treatment of women illuminates other symbolic uses of women and of the female. Just as women are relatively small and powerless in society, so is Israel small and powerless among the nations. Some of the heroines in the Bible symbolize Israel rising and subduing its enemies. This is particularly true of Yael, the Kenite woman who killed the Canaanite general Sisera at the beginning of the period of the judges, and Esther, the "diaspora Jew," who married the king of Persia and prevented the extermination of the Jews of Persia. *Woman* is also the personification of Israel in the marital metaphor of Israel as the wife of God. This well-known and much-beloved image is not as simple as it first appears. It captures well the intimacy between God and Israel, but it captures equally well the terror that such intimacy can hold with a more powerful force. This is not the equal love affair of the Song of Songs, interpreted either as human love or as the love of God and Israel. This is a patriarchal marriage: the husband has all the power. In today's view the marriage is also abusive, for the husband gets angry, punishes, and then proclaims his love and wants reconciliation.[43] The beloved wife is also a victim, and the woman symbol captures both love and vulnerability.

The marital metaphor has another problem: it codifies the gender of God as male. Monotheism has a potential advantage over polytheism, for it can create a divine world in which there is no gender division, no division of powers or attributes between male and female. This advantage, however, is only a potential advantage. In ancient Israel the gender of God was usually thought of as male because males were predominant in the social order. If the gender of God is *frozen* as male, then the danger is present that males will become the earthly representatives of divinity, and females will be frozen out of what is sacred. This does not fully happen in biblical Israel, which preserves images of God as mother. Nevertheless, the marital metaphor is one example of the dangers of this process.

In postexilic Israel another danger of using woman as symbol becomes clear. The images of Zion as daughter and Zion as mother become combined in an eschatological vision with the idea of the wife of God. In many ways this is a beautiful vision of wholeness: the Madonna (mother Zion) and the virgin (daughter Zion) are fused with the "whore." Moreover, Zion is seen as the wife of Israel as well as the wife of God (Isa. 62:5). She becomes a symbol and means of union for God and Israel—they both love her; and their love for her unites them. If Israel is the lover of the woman Zion, however, then there is a danger that Israel will be seen as totally *male* and the women of Israel will become invisible. This is the danger of all the female divine symbols that begin to multiply in the postexilic and Second Temple periods. In these periods, the portrayal of wisdom as a lover-woman develops into the depiction of the divine Sophia as the wife of her devotees, and the Torah as the beloved of her sages. Rabbinic writings also have an image of the Sabbath as a bride. In all these metaphors, the human is *male*, his partner is an unearthly female, and the flesh and blood women are not part of the image at all.[44] The use of the feminine as a symbol can serve highly patriarchal purposes when human women are left out.

There are many other questions raised by feminist scholarship. Some are questions about sexuality. When the Bible addresses the subject of sexuality and its control, men are seen as agents and women as objects. What does this say about biblical ideas of sexuality, and in turn, how does that interact with our current attempts to construct a nonpatriarchal theology of sexuality? The Bible is not antisex, but it does not develop a clear understanding of sexuality, and postbiblical religion, particularly Christianity, had developed a distinct antisex bias.

There are still other questions being addressed today. Some questions concern the ancient Israelite religion and the role of the Asherah: Was the Asherah the feminine part of God? Was it a case of idolatry? Why was it ultimately exorcised from biblical religion, and did this contribute to or reflect the emergence of God-as-husband?[45] Beyond these are two interlinked questions: Were women better served by polytheism, which created a symbolic straightjacket of what a female and a male can be, and which nevertheless afforded women an undeniable and unremovable part of the sacred, or were women better served by monotheism, which does not *necessarily* limit the roles and characters of women, but which was clearly used for patriarchal purposes? Can the Bible be the inspiration for a truly liberated monotheism, free of patriarchy and all other forms of oppression? In the past twenty years, as we have come increasingly to appreciate the intricacies, ambiguities, and multiple meanings of biblical texts, it has become ever more apparent that the answer is truly up to us.

NOTES

1. None of the notes in this article is meant to be exhaustive. A complete annotated bibliography of women in the Bible is being prepared by Mayer Gruber and should be published soon. For the many issues involved in feminist studies and the Bible, see the articles in two pioneering anthologies: Adela Yarbro Collins, ed., *Feminist Perspectives on Biblical Scholarship*, Society of Biblical Literature Centennial Publications (Chico, Calif.: Scholars Press, 1985); and Letty M. Russell, ed., *Feminist Interpretation of the Bible* (Philadelphia: Westminster, 1985); Nancy Fuchs-Kreimer, "Feminism and Scriptural Interpretation: A Contemporary Jewish Critique," *Journal of Ecumenical Studies* 20 (1983): 534–48; Katharine Doob Sakenfeld, "Feminist Perspectives on Bible and Theology: An Introduction to Selected Issues and Literature," *Interpretation* 42 (1988): 5–18; and Phyllis Trible, "Five Loaves and Two Fishes: Feminist Hermeneutics and Biblical Theology," *Theological Studies* 50 (1989): 279–95.

2. See Elisabeth Schüssler-Fiorenza, "The Ethics of Biblical Interpretation Decentering: Biblical Scholarship," presidential address to the Society of Biblical Literature, *Journal of Biblical Literature* 107 (88): 3–17.

3. Carol Meyers, *Discovering Eve: Ancient Israelite Women in Context* (New York: Oxford, 1988).

4. In addition to Meyers, see Jo Ann Hackett, "In the Days of Jael: Reclaiming the History of Women in Ancient Israel," in Clarissa W. Atkinson, Constance H. Buchanan, and Margaret R. Miles, eds., *Immaculate and Powerful: The Female in Sacred Image and Social Reality* (Boston: Beacon, 1985, 15–38); and Claudia

V. Camp, "The Wise Women of 2 Samuel: A Role Model for Women in Early Israel?" *Catholic Biblical Quarterly* 43 (1981): 14–29. My own, somewhat different, view is expressed later in this chapter.

5. See, among others, Christine G. Allen, "Who Was Rebekah: 'On Me Be the Curse, My Son,'" in Rita M. Gross, ed., *Beyond Androcentrism: New Essays on Women and Religion* (Missoula, Mont.: Scholars Press, 1977, 183–216); Kathleen M. Ashley, "Interrogating Biblical Deception and Trickster Theories: Narratives of Patriarchy or Possibility?" *Semeia* 42 (1988): 103–16; Samuel Dresner, "Rachel and Leah," *Judaism* 38: 151–50; Irmtraud Fischer, "Sara: Frauen unter der Verheißung," in Karin Walter, ed., *Zwischen Ohnmacht und Befreiung, Biblische Frauengestalten* (Freiburg: Herder, 1988, 23–31); Nelly Furman, "His Story versus Her Story: Male Genealogy and Female Strategy in the Jacob Cycle," in Collins, *Feminist Perspectives,* 107–16, Society of Biblical Literature, Biblical Scholarship in North America 10 (Chico, Calif.: Scholars Press, 1985; rep. in *Semeia* 46 [1989]: 141–49); Eva Renate Schmidt, "1 Mose 29–31: Vom Schwesternstreit zür Frauensolidarität," in Eva Renate Schmidt, Mieke Korenhof, and Renate Jost, eds., *Feministisch gelesen,* vol. 2 (Stuttgart: Kreuz, 1989, 29–39); Phyllis Trible, "Genesis 22: The Sacrifice of Sarah," Gross Memorial Lecture, Valparaiso University, 1989; Marie-Theres Wacher, "1. Mose 16 und 21: Hagar-die Befreite," in Schmidt, Korenhof, and Jost, *Feministisch gelesen,* vol. 1 (1988), 25–32; Mary K. Wakeman, "Feminist Revision of the Matriarchal Hypothesis," *Anima* 7 (1981): 83–96.

6. Phyllis Trible, "The Other Woman: A Literary and Theological Study of the Hagar Narratives," in James T. Butler, Edgar W. Conrad, and Ben C. Ollenburger, eds., *Understanding the Word: Essays in Honor of Bernhard W. Anderson (Journal for the Study of the Old Testament,* Sheffield: Almond, 1985, 221–46); and Phyllis Trible, "Hagar: The Desolation of Rejection," in idem, *Texts of Terror: Literary-Feminist Readings of Biblical Narratives* 9–35, *Overtures to Biblical Theology* 13 (Philadelphia: Fortress, 1984); and Jo Ann Hackett, "Rehabilitating Hagar: Fragments of an Epic Pattern," in Peggy L. Day, *Gender and Difference in Ancient Israel* (Minneapolis: Fortress, 1989, 12–27).

7. Johanna W. H. Bos, "Out of the Shadows: Genesis 38; Judges 4:17–22; Ruth 3," *Semeia* (1982): 37–67; Calum Carmichael, "Forbidden Mixtures," *Vetus Testamentum* 32 (1982): 394–415 (on Tamar and Judah); Fokkelien van Dijk-Hemmes, "Tamar and the Limits of Patriarchy: Between Rape and Seduction," in Mieke Bal, ed., *Anti-Covenant: Counter-Reading Women's Lives in the Hebrew Bible, Journal for the Study of the Old Testament* (SS) 81, Bible and Literature Series, 22 (Sheffield: Almond, 1989), 135–56; J. Emerton, "Some Problems in Genesis 38," *Vetus Testamentum* 25 (1975): 338–61; idem, "Judah and Tamar," *Vetus Testamentum* 29 (1979): 403–15; idem, "An Examination of a Recent Structuralist Interpretation of Genesis 38," *Vetus Testamentum* 26 (1976): 79–98; Angelika Engelmann, "2. Samuel 13, 1–22: Tamar, eine schöne und deshalb geschandete Frau," in Schmidt, Korenhof, and Jost, *Feministisch*

gelesen, vol. 2, 120–26; Barbara Georgi and Renate Jost, "1. Mose 38: Tamar, eine Frau kämpft für ihr Recht," in Schmidt, Korenhof, and Jost, *Feministisch gelesen,* vol. 2, 40–46; Randy L. Maddox, "Damned If You Do and Damned If You Don't: Tamar, a Feminist Foremother," *Daughters of Sarah* 13 (1987): 14–17; Susan Niditch, "The Wronged Woman Righted: An Analysis of Genesis 38," *Harvard Theological Review* 72 (1979): 143–49; Helen Schungel-Straumann, "Tamar: Eine Frau verschafft sich ihr Recht," BiKi 39 (1984): 148–57; Joan Goodnick Westenholz, "Tamar, *Qedesa, Qadistu,* and Sacred Prostitution in Mesopotamia," *Harvard Theological Review* 82 (1989).

8. Rita Burns, *Has the Lord Spoken Only through Moses? A Study of the Biblical Portrait of Miriam* (Atlanta: Scholars Press, 1987); Carol Meyers, "Of Drums and Damsels: Women's Performance in Ancient Israel," *Biblical Archaeologist* 54 (1991): 16–27; Annette Rembold, "Und Mirjam nahm die Pauke in die Hand, eine Frau prophezeit und tanzt einem anderen Leben voran: Das Alte Testament feministisch gelesen," in Cristine Schaumberger and Monika Maaßen, eds., *Handbuch Feministische Theologie* (Münster: Morgana, 1986), 285–98; Phyllis Trible, "Bringing Miriam out of the Shadows," *Bible Review* 5(1) (1989): 14–25, 34; idem, "Subversive Justice: Tracing the Miriamic Traditions," in Douglas A. Knight and Peter J. Paris, eds., *Justice and the Holy: Essays in Honor of Walter Harrelson* (Atlanta: Scholars Press, 1989), 99–109; Marie-Theres Wacker," Mirjam: Kritischer Mut einer Prophetin," in Karin Walter, ed., *Zwischen Ohnmacht und Befreiung, Biblische Frauengestalten,* (Freigurg: Herder, 1988), 44–52.

9. Elinor Artman, "Between Two Gods," *Journal of Women and Religion* 1 (1981): 8–12; Phyllis A. Bird, "The Harlot as a Heroine: Narrative Art and Social Presupposition in Three Old Testament Texts," *Semeia* 46 (1989): 119–39; Yair Zakovitch, "Humor and Theology or the Successful Failure of Israelite Intelligence: A Literary-Folkloric Approach to Joshua 2," in S. Niditch, ed., *Text and Tradition: The Hebrew Bible and Folklore,* Society of Biblical Literature Semeia Studies (Atlanta: Scholars Press, 1990), 75–98; and "Reply to Zakovitch," in Niditch, *Text and Tradition* (1990), 99–106.

10. For Deborah: Peter C. Craigie, "Deborah and Anat: A Study of Poetic Imagery (Judges 5)," *Zeitschrift für die alttestamentliche Wissenschaft* 90(3) (1978): 374–81; Stephen G. Dempster, "Mythology and History in the Song of Deborah," *Westminster Theological Journal* 41 (1978): 33–53; Katharina Elliger, "Debora: 'Mutter in Israel,'" in Karin Walter, ed., *Zwischen Ohnmacht und Befreiung, Biblische Frauengestalten* (Freiburg: Herder, 1988), 53–61; J. Cheryl Exum, "Mother in Israel": A Familiar Story Reconsidered," in Letty M. Russell, ed., *Feminist Interpretation of the Bible* (Philadelphia: Westminster, 1985), 73–85; Jürgen Kegler, "Debora: Erwagungen zür politischen Funktion einer Frau in einer patriarchalischen Gesellschaft," in Willy Schottroff and Wolfgang Stegemsn, *Traditionen der Befreiung 2: Frauen in der Bibel* (Munchen: Kaiser, 1980), 37–59; Barnabas Lindars, "Deborah's Song: Women in the Old

Testament," *Bulletin of the John Rylands University Library of Manchester* 65(2) (1983): 158–75; Rachel C. Rasmussen, "Deborah the Woman Warrior," in Bal, *Anti-Covenant,* 79–93; for Yael, see esp. Yair Zakovitch, "Sisseras Tod," *Zeitschrift für die alttestamentliche Wissenschaft* 93 (1981): 364–74; and Mieke Bal, *Murder and Difference: Gender, Genre, and Scholarship on Sisera's Death* (Bloomington: Indiana University Press, 1988).

11. Burke O. Long, "The Shunammite Woman: In the Shadow of the Prophet?" *Bible Review* 7 (1991): 12–19, 42.

12. Tikva Frymer-Kensky, *In the Wake of the Goddesses: Women, Culture, and the Biblical Transformation of Pagan Myth* (New York: Free Press, 1992), 118–43.

13. Ibid.

14. On the other hand, a parallel story about Elijah and a widow-woman indicates that even poor women could have considerable freedom of action. Elijah could live in the widow's house without causing a local scandal. Cf. 1 Kings 17:7–24.

15. 1 Kings 27: 1–11.

16. 1 Kings 36.

17. Jon Levenson, "I Samuel 25 as Literature and as History," *Catholic Biblical Quarterly* 40 (1978): 11–28; Moshe Garsiel, "Wit, Words, and a Woman: 1 Samuel 25," in Y. Radday and Athalya Brenner, eds., *On Humour and the Comic in the Hebrew Bible* (Sheffield, England: Almond Press, 1990), 161–68; and Frymer-Kensky, *In the Wake of the Goddesses,* 133–34.

18. Jon Levenson, "1 Samuel 25 as Literature and as History," *Catholic Biblical Quarterly* 40 (1978): 11–28; and Frymer-Kensky, op. cit.; Garsiel, "Wit, Words, and a Woman," 161–68.

19. For a discussion of some of the newer anthropological approaches to power, see the editor's introduction to Jill Dubisch, ed., *Gender and Power in Rural Greece* (Princeton: Princeton University Press, 1986), 3–41.

20. For recent studies of this role, see Niels Erik A. Andreason, "The Role of the Queen Mother in Israelite Society," *Catholic Biblical Quarterly* 35 (1983): 179–94; Zafrira Ben-Barak, "The Status and Right of the Gebira," *Journal of Biblical Literature* 110 (1991): 23–34, with an extensive bibliography; and Zafrira Ben-Barak, "The Queen Consort and the Struggle for Succession to the Throne," in Jean-Marie Durand, ed., *La Femme dans le Proche-Orient Antique, Comptes Rendu de la rêconte assyrologique* 33 Paris 1986 (Paris: Editions Recherche sur les Civilisations, 1987), 33–40.

21. For details see Frymer-Kensky, *In the Wake of the Goddesses,* 118–43.

22. Note that even the prophets sought to ameliorate the condition of the poor and blamed the wealthy for taking advantage of them. They did not advocate uprooting the social order and eliminating economic classes.

23. In our own time we have two major examples of societies whose social structure does not match their ideology. In the former Soviet Union, where

the proclaimed Marxist classlessness and economic equality were totally at variance with the reality of life, the ideology and the state that proclaimed it totally collapsed. In the United States we proclaim democratic classlessness and economic equality of opportunity but the rich are getting richer, the poor are multiplying, and there is a large underclass. How this tension will be resolved remains to be seen.

24. Phyllis Trible, "Depatriarchalizing in Biblical Interpretation," *Journal of the American Academy of Religion* 41 (1973): 30-48; and idem, *God and the Rhetoric of Sexuality, Overtures to Biblical Theology* 2 (Philadelphia: Fortress, 1978). More recently, see idem, "Feminist Hermeneutics and Biblical Studies," *Christian Century* (Feb. 1982): 116–18; and idem, "Five Loaves and Two Fishes: Feminist Hermeneutics and Biblical Theology," *Theological Studies* 50 (1989): 279–95. Other such approaches are by J. Cheryl Exum, "'You Shall Let Every Daughter Live': A Study of Exodus 1:8–2:10," *Semeia* 28 (1983): 63–82; idem, "'Mother in Israel': A Familiar Story Reconsidered," in Letty M. Russell, ed., *Feminist Interpretation of the Bible* (Philadelphia: Westminster, 1985), 73–85; and Toni Craven, "Women Who Lied for the Faith," in Douglas A. Knight and Peter J. Paris, ed., *Justice and the Holy: Essays in Honor of Walter Harrelson* (Atlanta: Scholars Press, 1989), 35–49. Some scholars are more interested in indicting the Bible, such as Esther Fuchs, "For I Have the Way of Women: Deception, Gender, and Ideology in Biblical Narrative," *Semeia* 42 (1988): 68–83; idem, "Marginalization, Ambiguity, Silencing: The Story of Jephthah's Daughter," *Journal of Feminist Studies in Religion* 5(1) (1989): 35–45; idem, "The Literary Characterization of Mothers and Sexual Politics in the Hebrew Bible," in Collins, *Feminist Perspectives,* 117–36. So, too, see Pamela Milne, "Eve and Adam: Is a Feminist Reading Possible?" *Bible Review* 43 (1988): 12–21, 39; and idem, "The Patriarchal Stamp of Scripture: The Implications of Structuralist Analysis for Feminist Hermeneutics," *Journal of Feminist Studies in Religion* 5(1) (1989): 17–34.

25. See Trible, *The Rhetoric of Sexuality.*

26. Susan S. Lanser, "(Feminist) Criticism in the Garden: Inferring Genesis 2–3," *Semeia* 41 (1988): 67–84. For an overview of the negative argument, see Milne, "Eve and Adam." For a newer depatriarchalizing reading of the actions of Eve, see Frymer-Kensky, *In the Wake of the Goddesses,* 108–17.

27. See Judith Plaskow, *Standing Again at Sinai* (San Francisco: Harper and Row, 1990), 25–27.

28. Note that later Rabbinic commentators were careful to read women back into this chapter, but Moses was not.

29. Rabbinic Judaism clearly put women back into the picture at Sinai. God's commanding Moses to speak to the "House of Jacob" and the "Sons of Israel" was understood to mean the women (the "house") and the men (the "sons"), and interpreters commented on the reasons that the women were mentioned before the men.

30. See Frymer-Kensky, *In the Wake of the Goddesses,* 203–12. There is a considerable body of literature emerging on the Bible in the Hellenistic period. See, e.g., Betsy Halpern Amaru, "Portraits of Biblical Women in Josephus' Antiquities," *Journal of Jewish Studies* 39 (1988): 143–70; Leonie Archer, "The 'Evil Women' in Apocryphal and Pseudepigraphical Writings," in R. Givenon, M. Anbar, et al., Proceedings of the Ninth World Congress of Jewish Studies, 1986, 239–45; James L. Bailey, "Josephus' Portrayal of the Matriarchs," in L. Feldman and G. Hata, eds., *Josephus, Judaism, and Christianity* (Detroit: Wayne State University Press, 1987), 154–79; Cynthia Baker, "Pseudo-Philo and the Transformation of Jephthah's Daughter," in Bal, *Anti-Covenant,* 195–209; Leila L. Bronner, "Biblical Prophetesses through Rabbinic Lenses," *Judaism: A Quarterly Journal of Jewish Life and Thought* 40 (1991): 171–83; Sharon Cohen, "Reclaiming the Hammer: Toward a Feminist Midrash," *Tikkun* 3:55–57, 93–95; Louis H. Feldman, "Josephus' Portrait of Deborah," in A. Caquot, M. Hadas-Lebel, and J. Riaud, *Hellenica et Judaica,* 1986, 115–28.

31. This felicitous term was coined by Phyllis Trible in *Texts of Terror.*

32. For readings on Hagar, see Cynthia Gordon, "Hagar: A Throw-Away Character among the Matriarchs," *Society of Biblical Literature Papers* 24 (1985): 271–77; Jo Ann Hackett, "Rehabilitating Hagar: Fragments of an Epic Pattern," in Peggy L. Day, ed., *Gender and Difference in Ancient Israel,* (Minneapolis: Fortress, 1989), 12–27; Sean E. McEvenue, "Comparison of Narrative Styles in the Hagar Stories," *Semeia: An Experimental Journal for Biblical Criticism* 3 (1975): 64–80; Trible, "Hagar: The Desolation of Rejection," 9–35.

33. Near Eastern contracts differ on whether the wife can *sell* the slave woman even after she has borne the master's children. For details see Tikva Frymer-Kensky, "Near Eastern Law and the Patriarchal Family," *Biblical Archeologist* 44 (1981).

34. The alternation of names may be confusing to someone not familiar with these biblical stories. When God announces that Sarai will give birth to Isaac, God also renames her Sarah, a name that means "princess." Similarly, Avraham (Abraham) is a renaming of Abram to indicate that he is the father (Av) of many.

35. Peggy L. Day, "From the Child Is Born the Woman: The Story of Jephthah's Daughter," in Peggy L. Day, ed., *Gender and Difference in Ancient Israel* (Minneapolis: Fortress, 1989), 58–74; J. Cheryl Exum, "The Tragic Vision and Biblical Narrative: The Case of Jephthah," in J. Cheryl Exum, ed., *Signs and Wonders: Biblical Texts in Literary Focus* (Society of Biblical Literature Semeia Studies, 1989), 59–83; Esther Fuchs, "Marginalization, Ambiguity, Silencing: The Story of Jephthah's Daughter," *Journal of Feminist Studies in Religion* 5(1) (1989): 35–45; Beth Gerstein, "A Ritual Processed: A Look at Judges 11:40," in *Anti-Covenant: Counter-Reading Women's Lives in the Hebrew Bible,* ed. Mieke Bal, *Journal for the Study of the Old Testament*

(SS): 81, Bible and Literature Series, 22 (Sheffield: Almond, 1989), 175–93; W. Lee Humphreys, "The Story of Jephthah and the Tragic Vision: A Response to J. Cheryl Exum," in *Signs and Wonders: Biblical Texts in Literary Focus*, ed. J. Cheryl Exum, Society of Biblical Literature Semeia Studies (1989), 85–96; Michael O'Connor, "The Women in the Book of Judges," *Hebrew Annual Review* 10 (1987): 277–93; Anne Michele Tapp, "An Ideology of Expendability: Virgin Daughter Sacrifice in Genesis 19:1–11, Judges 11:30–39 and 19:22–26," in *Anti-Covenant: Counter-Reading Women's Lives in the Hebrew Bible*, ed. Mieke Bal, *Journal for the Study of the Old Testament* (SS): 81, Bible and Literature Series, 22 (Sheffield: Almond, 1989), 157–74; Phyllis Trible, "A Meditation in Mourning: The Sacrifice of the Daughter of Jephthah," *Union Seminary Quarterly Review* 36 (1981): 59–73; idem, "The Daughter of Jephthah: An Inhuman Sacrifice," in *Texts of Terror: Literary-Feminist Readings of Biblical Narratives,* 93–116.

36. This pattern of the warrior becoming king is well known in both history and mythology. Marduk became king of the gods in this way, as did the Greek tyrants.

37. For the penalty, see Donald Wold, "The *Kareth* Penalty in P: Rationale and Cases," in P. J. Achtemeir, ed., *Society of Biblical Literature 1979 Seminar Papers* (Missoula, Mont.: Scholars Press, 1979), vol. 1, 1–46. For its uses, see Tikva Frymer-Kensky, "Pollution, Purification, and Purgation," in Carol Meyers, ed., *And the Word of the Lord Will Go Forth* (Winona Lake, Ind.: Eisenbrauns, 1983), 399–414.

38. See the story in 2 Samuel 14. The wise woman pretends to be a widow, one of whose two sons has killed the other in a fight. If she delivers the killer to the family for execution (as Israelite law demands), then, she declares, her husband, a good man, would be left without a name or remnant. David responds by placing the killer's son under his own protection, and the wise woman then makes David realize that it is his own son, Absalom, who needs pardon for having killed his brother.

39. For this story see Susan Niditch, "The 'Sodomite' Theme in Judges 19–20: Family, Community, and Social Disintegration," *Catholic Biblical Quarterly* 44 (1982): 365–78, and Trible, *Texts of Terror.* The conclusions expressed here, however, are my own.

40. For the story, see 2 Samuel 11.

41. Deuteronomy reflects the transfer of much power over the family from the father to the community. See Tikva Frymer-Kensky "Deuteronomy," in Carol A. Newsom and Sharon H. Ringe, *Women's Bible Commentary* (Louisville, Ky.: Westminster/John Knox Press, 1992), 52–62.

42. The Assyrian conquest of the Northern Kingdom of Israel and decimation of the Southern Kingdom of Judah was in 722 B.C.E.; Judah survived until it was conquered by the Babylonians in 589 B.C.E.

43. See Renita Weems, "Gomer: Victim of Violence or Victim of Metaphor," *Semeia* 47 (1989): 87–104; and Frymer-Kensky, *In the Wake of the Goddesses,* 144–52.

44. See Carol A. Newsom, "Woman and the Discourse of Patriarchal Wisdom: A Study of Proverbs 1–9," in Peggy L. Day, ed., *Gender and Difference in Ancient Israel,* (Minneapolis: Fortress, 1989), 142–60; and Frymer-Kensky, *In the Wake of the Goddesses,* 175–83.

45. See Frymer-Kensky, *In the Wake of the Goddesses,* for discussions of sex and of the asherah. The questions I am asking here, however, remain unanswered.

12 / The Ideology of Gender in the Bible and the Ancient Near East

1989

At first sight, Sumer and Israel seem separated by an overwhelming distance. Apart by at least a millennium, different in ecology and in language. Nevertheless, the two cultures had much in common, and show many facets of the same cultural continuum. The Sumerian texts have a compelling importance to the study of biblical literature and thought. They illuminate otherwise undetected nuances in biblical texts and help us understand, sometimes by contrast and sometimes in continuation, many of the Bible's (and frequently our own) important concepts and institutions. It is with great pleasure that I dedicate this small paper to Å. Sjöberg, whose important contributions to the study of Sumerian language and literature are incalculable, and who has nevertheless never lost his interest in, and love for, the Hebrew Bible.

Ever since the time of Hesiod, Western civilization has looked upon gender as an absolute distinction between men and women. The Greeks considered females to be inherently so different from males that they spoke of a *genes gynaikon,* a "race of women," in effect calling woman an entirely different species from man. The Greek philosophical systems viewed the male-female polarity as the major axis of their thinking. In this dichotomy, women were the reflex of men in all aspects: men were cultured, women natural; men civilized, women wild; men god-like, women bestial; men aggressive, women submissive; and so forth. Man embodied all those characteristics that the Greeks considered the highest achievements of their civilization, and woman, by contrast, had all the characteristics that the Greeks denigrated and discarded. The contest between men and women and, in particular, the replacement of women's modality by the superior male culture is the theme of many Greek myths, from Hesiod's Theogony and the Amazonomachia to Euripides' *Oresteia.*

This sense of the female as something other than the male has been a staple of Western culture. Often, the female was considered inferior to the male. Sometimes, as in early modern times, females have been "exalted" as purer, gentler, more noble, more sensitive, more tender, more compassionate, and less corrupt than men. This view, in fact, has been enforced by nineteenth-century psychoanalysis, which enshrined the difference between "masculine" and "feminine" and mythologized it with the Jungian view of the "anima" (the female hidden within each man) and the unobserved and totally hypothetical "animus" (the purely analogous male within each female). The exact view of the nature of females changes periodically: they have been considered more sensitive, artistic, and compassionate than men; more practical, levelheaded, and sensible; or more materialistic, overbearing, and whiny. Whatever the current cultural definition of female and male, the constant factor in such gender thinking is a division of the world into "masculine" and "feminine" attributes, in which the culture defines those characteristics that it considers the full achievement of humanity as the ideal characteristics of its men, and fills in the gaps by defining women as the embodiment of the flip side, that is, polar opposites of these characteristics.

Ever since the work of Simone de Beauvoir, modern social theory has considered this concept of woman as "other" to be a universal aspect of civilization. It is with some surprise, therefore, that one pursues a study of gender in the Bible. The Bible, of course, has no abstract formulations about the nature of women or men. But the Bible does have a surprisingly large corpus of stories, poems and statements about women. The biblical image of the female can be gleaned from these stories by asking several questions: what are the goals of these women, how do they proceed to achieve these goals, and what powers and strategies do they have to help them attain their goals? An understanding of gender-thinking then requires a further question: to what extent do the goals, powers and strategies of women differ from those of men? There is, of course, a caution necessary in assembling this information, for these women are found in many different genres of biblical literature: in poems, historical writings, ancestor-tales, wisdom literature, and prophetic books. Some of these women are historical personages, while others may be legendary or simply fictional inventions. The stories about them come from different circles and different periods in the millennium of biblical writing. It would not be proper to ignore this and proceed on the naïve assumption that the Bible speaks with one voice. In the final analysis, however, this difficulty turns out to be more apparent than real, for when the results of this inquiry into gender are controlled for genre, period and school, they do not change. The biblical record (until such late books as Ecclesiastes) is remarkably consistent in its view of the nature of women and gender.

When we survey the biblical depiction of the goals and strategies of women, a startling fact emerges. There is nothing distinctively "female" about the way that women are portrayed in the Bible; nothing particularly feminine about either their goals or strategies.[1] To turn first to goals: women are portrayed as more loyal to their husbands than to their birth families, desirous of having children and concerned with their well-being, and eager for the welfare and peace of Israel. These goals were not uniquely "female." On the contrary, Israel actively promoted the nuclear family, and was determinedly pronatalistic. Both the biblical male characters and the authors of the stories clearly believe in the necessity for close pair-bonding and the rearing of children. These beliefs are completely in accord with the needs of early Israelite society. On the other hand, those goals which might be considered female-specific, such as female solidarity and rage, are completely absent from the biblical record.

To turn next to the attainment of goals, it is clear that Western categories of aggressive/submissive and active/passive simply do not apply. Women in the Bible pursue their goals as actively as men. They have certain techniques and strategies at their disposal; they can use their access to food to set the mood and so influence people; they can use their powers of persuasion through reason, rhetoric and persistence (nagging); and they can trick and deceive when they cannot persuade. None of this is different from the strategies that men outside the power structure could be expected to use. They are all methods of indirect power, used by people who cannot take direct action: women, and subordinate men. Strategies and powers that are normally associated with women in our culture are conspicuously absent from the Bible. There is no sense of beauty as a woman's power. The beauty of Sarah and Bathsheba could set them up to be victims in that men of power might desire and take them. But beauty is not something that women consciously use to attract men; not, at any rate until the great change in Israel's gender thinking in the Hellenistic period, a change epitomized by Esther and Judith. Similarly, erotic attraction is also absent from the biblical tales of women's persuasion. There are no stories of sexual enticement, no femmes fatales, no figures like Mata Hari who use sex to seduce and then deceive men. There are women who actively seek sex in the Bible, either for enjoyment (like the "other woman" in proverbs and Potiphar's wife) or for children (like Tamar and possibly Ruth). But in these cases sex is the woman's goal; it is never a woman's strategy in order to gain power, influence, or information; never a woman's weapon by which she seeks to disarm or weaken men.

In sum, the Bible presents no characteristics of human behavior as "female" or "male," no division of attributes between the poles of "feminine" and "masculine." The metaphysics of gender unity that is revealed in this study is also expressed in the biblical creation stories. In Genesis 1, man and woman are created together, both literally in the form and figure of God. In Genesis 2, the first human is alone and God decides that Adam needs an *ʿezer kenegdo,* a suitable companion. God thereupon creates the animals; for early human is so simple that God could seriously entertain the notion that a cow could be "man's best friend." When, however, none of the animals turns out to be a suitable companion, God creates another human, a woman, thus creating the pair-bonding of man and woman. Lest the message be lost, the Bible then interrupts the narrative to inform us that for this reason man leaves his mother and father and cleaves unto his wife and they form one flesh.

This concept of gender unity is astonishing to us. Not only is it different from the cultural concepts that we have inherited but also it seems totally at odds with the socio-economic system of ancient Israel, one in which life was structured along gender lines, with women effectively frozen out of all public bureaucracies. It is easy to see why this concept was supplanted by the Greek dualistic polarities after the conquest of Alexander: the Greek system, distasteful as it might be to us, nevertheless offered a way to express and understand the differences between men's and women's lives and privileges. It is not as easy to understand how such a disjunction between life and metaphysics could have existed throughout the pre-Greek history of Israel.

The significance of the Adam and Eve story for the question of gender is clear when we compare it to two Mesopotamian literary creations, the epic of *Gilgamesh* and the Ṣaltu hymn. In the *Gilgamesh* story, the superiority of Gilgamesh leads him to oppress his people. When their outcry reaches the gods, they realize that Gilgamesh acts this way because he has no equal. They decide upon the special creation of a new being who will be as superior as Gilgamesh; the mother goddess takes clay and creates Enkidu—another male The true companion for Gilgamesh is not a woman to occupy his attention, but a male to be his close companion. After the epochal meeting of Gilgamesh and Enkidu, the next section of the *Gilgamesh* story is, indeed, a buddy adventure tale. This divine resolution of the problem of Gilgamesh's arrogance indicated a cultural sense that the truest bonding possible is between two members of the same gender. This is not to say that the attitude was "sexist" in our modern sense: the gods do not create a male because a female is inherently inferior. But it does indicate a gender-conscious sense that the true equality that leads to a great bonding is between male and male. At the same time, in the Old Babylonian Ṣaltu (*Aguŝaya*) hymn, the true equality and bonding for a female is another female. In this hymn, Ishtar is unlike the other goddesses: she is undomesticated, fierce, and wild, and her ferocity has begun to frighten and dismay the other gods. Here too, the resolution is not to bring a male to "tame" her, but rather to create a companion that will occupy her time, and so the god Enki creates a new goddess, another fierce female, Ṣaltu, and sends her to Ishtar. The motivation behind the creation of same-sex companions for Gilgamesh and Ishtar is a matter of difference, of distinctiveness, of a sense that man and woman can never be as like to each other as man to man or woman to woman.

It is not easy to get at Mesopotamian concepts of gender, particularly after the beginning of the Old Babylonian times. There are no general pronouncements aside from the late proverbial "woman is a sharp iron dagger that cuts the throat of a man."[2] There are also very few narratives about females. There are fewer myths in Akkadian than in Sumerian, and the role of goddesses in Akkadian-language myths that derive from the Old Babylonian period (*Atrahasis, Gilgamesh*) is very circumscribed: The mother goddess creates, other female figures interpret dreams, give advice, and lament; Ishtar is scorned and takes revenge. In later myths, the role of females is even smaller: in *Enuma Elish*, the only female figure is the mother who must be defeated before Marduk can become king and organizer. Ishtar does not get eclipsed after the Old Babylonian period to the same extent as other goddesses and her martial nature is well attested in Assyrian royal inscriptions. Nevertheless, she also plays no part in these later myths; not even to the extent of being shown fearful of Tiamat or impotent before Erra. The only clear evidence of gendered thinking we have from Akkadian language texts are the *Aguŝaya* hymn and the *Gilgamesh* epic. They show evidence of an ideology of gender differences, and the *Aguŝaya* hymn makes this explicit by calling Ishtar's ferocity her *zikrūtu*, her manliness.

The Sumerian material is at the same time more abundant and more problematic. In the many stories involving goddesses, goddesses appear in the various roles that women play in human society. Goddesses are shown as mothers, a role not limited to the mother goddesses: Nisaba is the matriarch mother-in-law *(buršuma)*; Amagištinanna the sister; Ninlil, the queen; Uttu, the domestic wife; and Inanna is the nondomesticated woman. In many of these roles the figure is a unidimensional stereotype: Nisaba is wise; mothers and sisters are loyal and devoted (even beyond death); Uttu's character traits are invisible. It is only in the figure of Inanna that we have a richly developed character.

In the cycle of poems about Inanna and Dumuzi,[3] young maiden Inanna sets out on the path of womanly domestication. In her courtship she behaves like a proper young lady, worrying about the niceties and legalities of the social interaction between the sexes. Despite her love for Dumuzi, Inanna does not violate social convention, and in Dumuzi-Inanna H, she refuses to dally in the moonlight with Dumuzi, unwilling to lie to her mother.[4] It seems strange to envision the goddess of sexual attractiveness and desire as reticent sexually, but in her aspect of the young, sexually desirable not-yet-bride she is a sexual innocent:

> I am one who knows not that which is womanly—copulating.
> I am one who knows not that which is womanly—kissing.
> I am one who knows not copulating, I am one who knows not kissing.[5]

In these songs, Inanna behaves like a typical young girl about to be a bride. She prepares for her wedding, adorning and dressing herself, and expressing her desire that her bridegroom provide the food for the wedding (Dumuzi-Inanna A and C). There is one drastic difference between Inanna and the rest. Inanna weds without assuming any of the economic duties of a wife. Before she agrees to marry, she and Utu (her brother) have a conversation about the making of linen sheets. When he offers to bring her the green flax, she declines to ret, spin, dye, weave, or bleach it (Dumuzi-Inanna A).[6] The treatment of flax and the creation of linen is one of the archetypical works of women, and Inanna's ignorance and refusal of it is a denial of the production role of women. Similarly, at her wedding, Inanna may tell Dumuzi (the text is broken) that she does not know how to use a loom, and he certainly replies to her with assurances that "I have not carried you off into servitude . . . O my bride, cloth you will not weave for me, O Inanna, yarn you will not spin for me, O my bride, fleece you will not ravel for my . . . bread you will not knead [for me]" (Dumuzi-Inanna C).[7]

There is another stipulation that Dumuzi makes to Inanna at their wedding that indicates a difference between her and other brides. She is to eat at the splendid table at which he himself eats. His own mother and sister do not have this privilege, but Inanna will do so, and will not have to perform any of the domestic duties of ordinary wives (Dumuzi-Inanna C iv 1 6–13). Dumuzi expects only one wifely role from Inanna: the bearing of children, and at his wedding he brings Inanna to the chapel of his personal god and prays that she give birth to a son. This, however, does not happen. Inanna does not turn into a maternal figure. In some texts Inanna is the mother of Šara and of Lulal, but they seem ancillary and irrelevant to her persona and identity. Inanna has neither maternal nor domestic economic duties. She thus remains without any of the usual roles and functions of the ordinary married woman. Released from all such duties, she is unencumbered. She has nothing to occupy her time, and, at the same time, nothing to make her conscious of her marital status. She is the unencumbered woman, the wife whose domestic status is so nebulous that it cannot be possible to domesticate her.

Because of this lack of attachment, Inanna has no true social niche. Inanna herself complains of this marginality in Enki and the World Order. She points out that the mother goddess has her functions, that Uttu the weaver, Ninmug the smith, and Nisaba the scribe all have clear roles in society, but that she herself does not. Enki's reply only emphasizes her anomalous nature, for he reminds her of her role in war, and of her ability to transcend and reverse boundaries. She, who has a great variety of powers and roles, nevertheless does not fit any of the niches that society has provided for its women. As a result, she is restless and seeks additional power and prominence, as in "Enki and Inanna," and "The Descent of Inanna." Inanna is frequently on the move, described as going or walking about. As evening and morning star, she can be observed in different parts of the heavens at different times of the year, and this may have contributed to her peripatetic image. But her freedom as the unencumbered woman is certainly a major part of it, for she is a woman "on the loose." At least by Old Babylonian times, this was not what one expected from properly married women, who were expected to leave their house only on legitimate errands. The one who goes out (*wāṣiat*) is equated in Proto-Diri with the kar.kid$_2$ "the prostitute" (with whom, as women without a domestic role, Inanna was identified). Society's lack of ease with roaming women is also indicated by the fact that Inanna shares her attribute as *sāḫirātu* (the one who roams about) with the dreaded Lamashtu demon.

Inanna shows what might happen to a wife who is not kept "barefoot and pregnant in the kitchen." In her search for a real role to play and a secure power base, she can serve as a fearsome admonition of the dangers of the unencumbered woman. In her lack of encumbrances, Inanna lives essentially the same existence as young men. Like them, she is called "hero."[8] Like them, and even more than them, she loves warfare and seeks lovers. She is a woman in a man's life, free to be the quintessential femme fatale.

What does this tell us about the nature of women and men? Is Inanna "alone of all her sex," a phrase originally coined of the Virgin Mary to indicate the lack of similarity between her and mortal women? Or does Inanna demonstrate a deep societal suspicion that without the social constraints that society places on women, they would indeed be very like men? This question is very interesting to us from the point of view of religious history, faced as we are with the alternative views of Greece (and the Western culture which inherited it) and the Bible. But it is irrelevant to the gender role of Inanna within Sumerian culture. Inanna stands at the boundary of differences between man and woman. She transcends gender polarities in herself, and is further said to overturn them in others, turning men into women and women into men. This boundary position is celebrated in her cult, for at her festivals men dress as women and women as men, and cultic dancers wear outfits that are men's clothes on the right and women's on the left. In this cultic and hymnal confusion or melding of genders, Ishtar ultimately protects and reinforces the gender line. As in all rituals and occasions of rebellion, the societally approved, scheduled, and regulated breaking of a norm actually serves to reinforce it. Male-female gender division is not the only polarity that Innana-Ishtar exemplifies, transcends, mediates and ultimately protects,[9] but it is one that she clearly lives out in her own mythic persona.

Inanna's freedom from domestic encumbrances and the restlessness that it engenders may also account in part for the ferocious energy with which she confronts gods and humans. She is the model of the nondomesticated woman. She represents a woman not occupied with social roles, like a man in many of her wants and capabilities, both threatening and assuring the social order. She is dangerous, fearsome, and threatening by her freedom, and yet appealing and attractive at the same time. Unpreoccupied by domestic pursuits, she is free to be the ultimate femme fatale. The image of Inanna as a woman in a man's lifestyle reinforces social patterns of how men and women are actually expected to behave.

As for the Bible, this leaves us with the intriguing question as to where the notion of gender unity came from and how it endured through the biblical period. It may have originally been plausible during the early, formative, peasant period of Israel's formation, when males and females had intermeshing and economically comparable roles in subsistence and household management. Unlike in other religious systems, however, the increasing complexity of life, with its accompanying expanding hierarchical structure of family and polity, did not bring on a philosophically gendered concept to account for the new social realities. I would speculate that the survival of a concept of gender equality in spite of the social mismatch is due to the theological thought-life of the Bible, for a concept of gender unity fits well with a religious system in which humans are the image and counterpart of God and there is only one God.

NOTES

1. For a full discussion of these issues, see my book *In the Wake of the Goddesses.*

2. "Dialogue of Pessimism," 1.52; Lambert BWL 146.

3. These poems have been collected and edited by Yitzhak Sefati, "Love Songs in Sumerian Literature: A Critical Edition of the Dumuzi-Inanna Songs" (unpub. Ph.D. diss., Bar-Ilan University, 1965) with complete bibliography and translation, and philological commentary in Hebrew. The most recent translation into English is by Thorkild Jacobsen, *The Harps That Once...Sumerian Poetry in Translation.* New Haven & London: Yale University Press, 1987.

4. Sefati, "Love Songs," 209–217. English translation by Jacobsen as "The Wiles of Women," *Harps,* 10–12.

5. Samuel Noah Kramer, "BM 23631: Bread for Enlil, Sex for Inanna," OrNS 54 (1985): 117–130, 11 138–140.

6. Sefati, "Love Songs," 115–124. Translated by Jacobsen as "The Bridal Sheets," *Harps,* 13–15.

7. Sefati, "Love Songs," 323–339 iv 5; 14–18. Translated into English by Jacobsen as "Dumuzi's Wedding," *Harps,* 19–23.

8. For *ur-sag* see Römer, OrNS 38 (1969); and Castellino, RSO 36.

9. On Inanna/Ishtar as the transgressor and preserver of boundaries, see the insightful paper of Rivkah Harris, "The Paradox of Ishtar, Destroyer of Boundaries" (forthcoming).

13 / Sanctifying Torah

1997

The story of the Garden of Eden in Genesis 2–3 is not really a story about sin and punishment. If we read the story from a perspective that cherishes human culture and that values moral agency over submission, the story relates humanity's first step toward knowledge. But with knowledge comes loss of innocence, and without innocence there is no bliss of paradise.

We all undergo this primordial experience when we leave the bliss of infancy and begin our first steps toward individual existence. Whole cultures relive this experience as they discover that "the emperor has no clothes" or that a tulip is, after all, just a flower. They now are wiser, but they have lost the trust that let them imagine great value and beauty. As individuals and as societies, every advance in knowledge or maturity entails a loss of the innocent pleasures we enjoyed before. Women, of course, share in the common experiences of all humankind, but women also may experience a form of knowledge and loss peculiar to women of our culture. At some point, many of us begin to sense that our experiences as women do not quite harmonize with our religious traditions. Sometimes our experiences complement what we are being taught, and sometimes they absolutely contradict it. In either event, our experiences never have been incorporated into the teachings of our tradition.

With that first glimpse, our eyes were opened, and we saw that we were naked, for the tradition never provided clothes for us. For many of us, this destroyed forever our trust in the absolute wholeness and goodness of our religious traditions. This is the first moment of feminist consciousness. It is the end of our innocence, and we have left the Garden of Eden forever. We no longer can accept Scripture naïvely, uncritically, and submissively.

For some, this excursion into the real world has been a profoundly alienating experience; many women in our time have left Judaism (as many have left Christianity) in anger at the blindness of our religious texts and of their interpreters throughout the millennia. Many others have maintained their loyalty to a Jewish status quo, despite feelings of dis-ease and suspicion. And still others have determined to revise Judaism to incorporate spiritual experiences and teachings that bring into the *center* the previously *marginalized* women and their experiences. The past thirty years have witnessed an explosion in women's participation in traditional education and ritual, as well as the creation of special "womenspaces" for women's education and women-centered ritual.

But this is only the beginning. All around us we are witnessing a great desire for spirituality and God-centering. While the myriad of new forms being developed satisfy many, they only create a greater need in others. Rituals, prayers, and practices which develop only from women's experiences seem like flowers suspended by gossamer threads from somewhere above and within—they are lovely but delicate, and they do not grow. They need to sink their roots into the densely textured soil of traditional religious language and teaching. We who have been alienated want to go back; we who have stayed, by drawing from our personal wells, want access to the source of living waters. But the way seems blocked by the fiery swords of suspicion and alienation.

Some women manage to "unlearn" their knowledge of the truth in order to find their way back to the tree of life in the garden of naïve trust. These are "masters of return" *(ba'a lot teshuvah)* whose desire for the garden can suppress their knowledge. But most of us do not want to unlearn the precious lessons we have been teaching each other. We want to find the life-giving tree somewhere else, not in the safe, innocent space of suppression and submission. We want to find the tree of life whose fruits can be eaten with eyes opened by our hard-won feminist awareness. And this tree is the Torah: "A tree of life to those who hold fast to her." Jewish women want a positive relationship with the Bible; alienation from it denies us its life-sustaining gifts.

Of this living Torah we say, "All her paths are pleasant." But can we who are aware of our absence in much of the Torah say this? Does our attraction to the gifts of the Torah demand that we suppress our ever-growing awareness that it presents problems for women? We who cannot unlearn (and do not want to try) seem to be caught on the horns of a great dilemma: On the one hand, we need to point out that the Bible assumes social structures, such as patriarchy, that appear to us to be morally flawed. On the other hand, we long for the assurance of having the Bible as sacred Scripture. The dilemma resolves itself, though, when we realize that submission is not the only way to read the Bible. The opposite of submission *is not* alienation, but informed engagement, a dialogue, and wrestling. This, too, is a biblical path, and "All her paths are pleasant."

"The Torah is a tree of life." The Torah lives in the real world, and we need to read the Bible as it exists in the real world, not in some garden of an idealized past. This means paying attention to all the resonances and ramifications of the Bible in the experiences of women in Jewish life and community, both yesterday and today. Which passages are empowering to women, and which passages create difficulties? Are the problems in these passages inherent in the text, or have they arisen because the text has been given patriarchal interpretations? Which passages can be redeemed by new readings?

The study of such passages is a sacred enterprise, for a holy Scripture cannot intend injury to anyone. The Torah is a tree of life only when "All her paths are pleasant." Hurtful, unredeemable passages are not pleasant paths—they can destroy the holy Torah. To submit to such passages would be to endanger the very life of Torah, all of whose paths are and must be pleasant. Therefore, a teaching which is not pleasant, not life-giving to those who hold to Torah, should not continue to be Torah.

The loss of innocence brings hard labor. We who have our eyes open no longer can live in oblivious bliss; we have to be a partner to God, both in our activities in the world and in our interpreting of Torah. "The Torah is a tree of life to those who hold on to her." In our labors, we are to wrestle, struggle, and above all, hold on, saying to the Torah, as Jacob to the angel, "We will not let you go till you bless us."

Below we consider some questions raised by the Book of Exodus, which contains within it a whole spectrum of passages that impact women, both positively and negatively.

ON THE STAGE OF HISTORY: EXODUS AND WOMEN

Part One: Enter Women

The beginning of Exodus sets up the world of men's affairs. The family of Jacob comes down to Egypt and the tale unfolds: A new Pharaoh arises who, not remembering Joseph, is frightened at the ever-multiplying alien group in his land. He enslaves them and then orders the male children killed at birth, a strange injunction, for to kill a population surely one should kill the future birth-givers. But Pharaoh is only worried about the men, as they might fight against him. The girls are insignificant. Without men, they are not even Israel; married to Egyptians, they will produce Egyptian children.

In this story, told from an intensely male-oriented perspective, the women begin to act. First come the midwives, Shifrah and Puah. Are they actually Israelite women? Should we read the text as *ha-meyaldôt ha-ivriyot*, the Hebrew midwives, or as *meyaldôt haʿivriyot*, the midwives who serve the Israelites? Perhaps they were Israelite, for midwives usually come from the community they serve. Or perhaps they came from another people. Now, however, they cast their lot with Israel, defying Pharaoh's orders to kill the Israelite baby boys. Called on the carpet, the midwives trick Pharaoh by belittling the Israelite women as "animals" (too often softened in translation as "lively") who give birth so quickly they need no midwives. Falling for the trick, and not seeing the power of these women to defy him, Pharaoh repeats his mistake, this time commanding everyone to throw the boy children into the Nile and let the daughters live.

Immediately we meet a *daughter*, the daughter of Levi, who gives birth to a boy child. Just as the midwives had done, she defies Pharaoh's orders, hides the child for three months, and then sets the baby adrift in an ark on the river. Another daughter—her daughter—follows to observe, and yet another daughter—Pharaoh's daughter—saves the child, knowing that it is a Hebrew baby. Thus, Moses was born and saved, and the redemption of Israel was begun.

The women in this story are not named. It is from elsewhere in the Bible that we learn the mother of Moses was called Yochebed and his sister's name was Miriam. It is only from much later midrash that we know the daughter of Pharaoh as Bithya. In this story they are nameless, and by their anonymity they are archetypical: they are *daughters* . . . women . . . the very ones overlooked by both Pharaoh and the tradition that counted and remembered only the men who came from Egypt. Three daughters—Israelite and Egyptian—have foiled the plans of men and shaped the destiny of the Jewish people.

The story of "savior women" has not yet ended: Moses has not yet become the deliverer. First, he must grow up, nursed by his birth mother and tended by his adoptive mother. Then he leaves his mothers and Egypt to return when the time is right for deliverance. But his appearance as savior comes in a traumatic crisis in which God, the One mightier than Pharaoh, attacks him. Once again, he is saved by a woman, his wife, Zipporah, who acts quickly to avert doom by circumcising their son.

The midrash adds to these tales of bravery and loyalty of the women in Egypt. Moses' father, Amram, seeks to prevent the slaughter of sons by divorcing his wife: where there are no boys, there will be no murders. But his daughter, Miriam (then five years old), shows him that his decree is worse than Pharaoh's, for he will deny life to everyone, girls as well as boys. The Talmud relates how the nameless women of Israel kept Israel alive in Egypt. When their husbands were beaten down, despairing, and exhausted, the women took pains with their appearance, packed reviving lunches, reassured their husbands that slavery would not last forever, and seduced their husbands under the apple trees, thus keeping the people alive. And when it came time for the women to give birth, they went out once more to the trees to give birth there, so that no one could hear their cries and kill their babies.

Furthermore, these stories continue. After the Exodus, when the men of Israel almost destroyed the people by making a golden calf to worship, the women of Israel refused to participate, and their earrings had to be ripped from their ears. It is because of such stories that the tradition states: "As a reward for the righteous women of that generation, Israel was redeemed from Egypt" (see *Shemot Rabbah* 1,12), a phrase that certainly applies to all the steadfast women of the Exodus.

One might attribute women's strength during this time of oppression to the fact that women always have had at least a taste of oppression. In their personal lives, they never had much autonomy, so their lives were not changed all that much by eternal oppression. Perhaps because oppression did not come as a shock to these women, they didn't fall into a slough of despondency into which the men may have descended. Never having had much autonomy or authority, women may have developed the coping and survival skills for a life of subordination. They may have been accustomed to ignoring outside events and regulations, accustomed to maneuvering through the system to follow their own imperatives of helping their husbands, protecting their children, and being loyal to their God. When people who are accustomed to having authority are denied it, they may be stymied or even collapse. But those who possess skill at wit and deception always can use these methods to attain their goals.

The actions of the women of the Exodus story, the "righteous women of that generation," are memorable and praiseworthy, but they are not extraordinary, not limited merely to a few heroines of the past. We all have seen the strength of women in adversity. Women fight to keep their families together in times of war, economic deprivation, and epidemics. Reticent, dependent women "who never balanced a checkbook" turn into superwomen when they have to nurse ailing husbands or raise their families alone because of widowhood or divorce. All the strengths and talents that have been invisible—even to the woman herself—start coming to the fore. It is as if women are turned inside out by trouble: when the going gets tough, it seems, women get going.

And our need for the actions of such "righteous women" recurs eternally. They are needed not only in times of disaster, war, disease, and tragedy; such heroic actions are needed continually, for the time of the redemption is eternally at hand. The *haggadah* reads, "In every generation we must look at ourselves as if we had been redeemed from Egypt." In every generation, contemporary Jewish women must look at themselves as if they were the women of the ancient slavery and redemption. These women are a challenge to our beliefs and actions, and as with any challenge, they demand action on our parts.

Our first imperative is to *remember* these women—to tell their stories. They have been neglected and ignored for too long. However, we cannot blame the Rabbis for this. On the contrary, the Rabbis remembered and celebrated these women. The story of the women and the apple tree is recorded more than once in Rabbinic literature and had important consequences in Jewish practice. Women are full participants in the Passover seder and are expected to drink the four cups of wine because, says Rabbi Joshua ben Levi, "they had a part in this miracle" (BT *Pesachim* 108a). To Rabbi ben Levi, drinking the four cups at Passover—as with hearing the *Megillah* at Purim and lighting Hanukkah candles—is incumbent on women as a type of reward for their part in the redemption. The medieval commentators Rashi and Rashbam,explain this dictum, telling the story of the women and the apple trees. This story also plays a role in the seder, determining the recipe for *haroset*. *Haroset* is *required* at the seder, *not optional.* Why? Rabbi ben Levi says, "in memory of the apple"; Rabbi Yohanan says, "in memory of the mortar"; and Abbaye explains that we make the *haroset pungent* to remember the *apple* and *thick* to remember the *mortar.* Later the commentators connect the apple to the verse in Song of Songs, "I awaken you under the apple tree."

The Rabbis of the Talmud and midrash, as well as medieval commentators, all told and retold the stories of the women of the Exodus. In this century, they have been forgotten. Most Americans know their extrabiblical stories through Louis Ginzberg's monumental *Legends of the Jews.* In this seven-volume compendium of midrash, the apple tree is still there, but only in the legend that the women of Israel gave birth under the tree and left the children there, so that God preserved them by planting them in the earth. The story of the women who revived their husbands no longer appears. In remembering the women of the Exodus, women today *restore* a venerable part of the tradition that sustained Israel through the dark days, but subsequently was jettisoned in this century.

The second imperative is *to look clearly at the world in which we live*. "In every generation we [women] must look upon ourselves as if we [were the women who] came out of Egypt." This is not a redeemed world, and Israel and the world are still in need of repair. The Exodus from Egypt *began* the process of redemption; it *did not complete it*. The liberation from bondage must be present and ongoing. But, if we are to complete this redemption, we cannot wait for others to act. We must repeat the actions of the heroic women in preserving Israel. And we must go one step further, not waiting to act until others have collapsed. Bringing on the redemption requires that we be strong, even when others are not strong.

There is a third imperative. We must *expand the horizons* in which they acted. The women of the Exodus knew that bearing children was necessary to ensure survival. They acted to bear children (the women of the apple trees) and to rescue and protect children (midwives and the women of Moses' family). To bear a child is an act of bravery and love. To protect a child is an act of heroism and self-sacrifice. But to protect life and bring on redemption means more than to save a child from death. To preserve life, we must protect the conditions in which babies can flourish; the family, the home, the city, the world. To preserve the life of Israel, we must protect *all* children. Furthermore, to preserve life requires that we preserve ourselves. Hard as it is for women to realize, the care of ourselves is the beginning of redemption. Without us, children do not flourish and the world cannot be redeemed.

If we remember and continue the actions of the women of the Exodus and continue to expand their scope, then perhaps one day Jewish tradition will remember that "as a reward for the righteous women of *our* generation, Israel and the world were relieved from sorrow."

Part Two: Exit Women

As soon as Moses is ready to become "the savior," women disappear from the scene. The foreground is filled by the men—Moses, Aaron, and Pharaoh; the increasingly visible background is completely occupied by

God. The heroines of the first stage—the midwives, Moses' mother and sister, and Pharaoh's daughter—are nowhere to be seen. In the grand drama of redemption, women appear only once, when Miriam leads the women in dance and song to celebrate the victory at the Red Sea. When the battles have been won, the women can be seen rejoicing; during the struggle they are invisible.

Zipporah, Moses' wife, is not even present at the celebration. When her father, Jethro, comes to see Moses after the redemption, he brings Zipporah and the children. This is our first record that Moses had sent her away at some point. Was it because she was not a slave and the redemption from Egypt was not her fight? Or was it to keep her safe? Did Moses, out of some benevolent "chivalrous" instinct, prevent Zipporah—the very woman who had saved him from God's attack—from being exposed to danger? Perhaps their children were the reason: concern to protect his sons might have made Moses relegate their mother, Zipporah, to taking care of them. And perhaps the same concern for children that made the women of Israel defy the edicts of Pharaoh also could make them stand back and protect the children, as the men concentrated on danger and battle. Whatever the reasons, in this text women have disappeared from the action.

But Moses does not rush to reintegrate Zipporah into his life. He immediately takes Jethro into the tent for a long meeting (Exod. 18:6–8). If he even notices Zipporah and his sons, he does not acknowledge them. Moses, the leader, is a "man of vision," and like many men of vision through the ages, he follows his vision and pays no attention to his own children or his wife. Moses has his eyes fixed on the world of men and God.

This lack of attention that Moses pays to women resurfaces in the following chapter in a devastating fashion. There it is no longer a private family matter, but becomes national in its scope and historic in its effect. As the people are encamped at Sinai, Moses goes up to God and brings back word of the divine intent to make the people God's own treasured possession. After the people agree, Moses ascends a second time. He is told that God will come in a cloud so that all the people will see. God instructs Moses to go to the people and tell them to purify themselves for two days, wash their clothes, and be prepared for the third day, when God will come down to the mountain in the sight of the whole people. Moses brings back this word and the people purify themselves and wash their clothes. And then Moses says: "Be prepared these three days: go not near a woman." Moses looks at the people and sees only the men. It is to them that he speaks: "Go not near a woman." The leader of men speaks to men—the women become objects of men's actions, rather than subjects in their own right! Moses' tunnel vision gets the better of him. Perhaps (to psychologize a bit) his past dependence on women and his massive obligation to them blinds and blocks him. If he actually were to see women, he constantly would be reminded of their crucial place in his life. Whatever the reason for this myopia, it gets the better of him.

GO NOT NEAR A WOMAN!

This is a pivotal moment. When Moses looks at the people and sees only the men, he excludes women from the congregation of Israel. At this moment, the women reenter bondage. They lose their status as full members of the community. They are no longer the redeemed, but ones that the redeemed should not approach.

This pronouncement by Moses is the exact mirror of Pharaoh's command to kill the boys, which occurred at the beginning of the Exodus. Yet the women of Israel who defied the Pharaoh are silent here. When the men of Israel were weak and the oppressive authority external, the women were strong and defiant. Now, when a man of Israel becomes the oppressive authority, nobody speaks.

Zipporah, who spoke sharply to God and Moses before, now is silent; perhaps having been sent away once, she doesn't want to risk it again.

The midwives, who defied Pharaoh, are silent, too. When the choice was clear, they feared God more than they feared Pharaoh. Now, however, the choice is not so clear. Perhaps they believe that in order to fear God, one must show allegiance to God's designated leader.

The women of Israel, who (in the midrash) spoke up and encouraged their husbands to have faith, are also silent. Perhaps they do not perceive a threat to children and survival and cannot recognize that their exclusion at this minute is a threat to all the girl-children of Israel.

Miriam, who (in the midrash) confronted and rebuked her own father, Amram, is silent as well. The moment, after all, is one of great danger and great piety: God is coming. Is it not a moment for solidarity rather than confrontation? Love of God and Israel might dictate swallowing one's anger and keeping silent, a time to be as invisible in one's own eyes as one is in the eyes of Moses.

In this moment of piety and anticipation, the women may have had their thoughts on God and their eagerness to revere God. After all,

Moses—as the leader God sent to redeem them from bondage—is supposed to speak for God!

GO NOT NEAR A WOMAN!

But the narrator makes it clear that Moses does not speak for God in this critical moment. He is, on the contrary, acting out of his own psyche, out of the same male-centered blindness to women that he demonstrated when he paid attention to Jethro more than to his wife or children. The narrator gives us an important lesson here: the voice of God is mediated by the words of human beings. Even divine revelation is filtered through the eyes, the experiences, and the idiosyncrasies of human religious leaders. In this case, the leader is Moses who, despite his early history of being saved by women—or perhaps because of it—just does not see women. And so to God's command to prepare, Moses adds his own interpretive words, "Go not near a woman," words that turn the women of Israel into objects of the (male) congregation's actions.

GO NOT NEAR A WOMAN!

The ramifications of this treatment of women can be seen in the Ten Commandments that follow in the next chapter. The Fourth Commandment, the Sabbath Commandment, states: "The seventh day is a Sabbath to the Lord your God; you should not do any work, you, your son and your daughter, your manservant and your maidservant, and your beasts and the stranger within your gates" (Exod. 20:10). The "you" here includes both husband and wife, for it makes no sense that the daughter and maidservant would rest while the wife works. The women are included as the subject of the laws—but they are totally invisible and must be teased out by logic. This is the best the law has to offer. The worst comes in the Tenth Commandment, which reads: "You shall not covet your neighbor's house, you shall not covet your neighbor's wife or his manservant or maidservant or ox or ass or any of his possessions." "You" and "your neighbor" are both men; they must respect each other's property and prerogatives. The women? They are *objects* of the law, the ones who must not be coveted, rather than the ones who must not covet that which is their neighbor's.

The laws that follow continue the uneven treatment of women and men. Occasionally, women are not simply the property of men, and in some ways, women and men have equal status—i.e., fathers and mothers cannot be hit or cursed (generation takes precedence over gender); human life is sacred (the same stoning awaits the ox that gores to death a man, a woman, or a child). But in other cases, the treatment clearly is not equal: A Hebrew manservant is set free in the seventh year; a Hebrew woman-servant is not, she becomes the property of her owner. A girl must stay chaste in her father's house and is not entitled to choose her partner. If she takes a lover, her father collects the virgin's bride-price from him and still may refuse to give consent to a marriage. No such provision exists for a son. Israel is enjoined not to allow a witch—a woman with occult power—to live; nothing is said about a man with such powers. And even the humanitarian rule that commands Israel to take care of the widow or orphan assumes that women are dependent and need caretaking. It is a reflection of a patriarchal system in which women do not have access to economic resources, such as land.

Biblical Israel did not invent patriarchy; it characterizes the social system of all ancient cultures. However, neither did Israel seize the opportunity to dismantle patriarchy (or slavery) and become a truly liberated people. The condition of women in Israel after the Exodus from Egypt is not quite slavery, but it is far from liberation. The women of Israel have not been fully redeemed.

GO NOT NEAR A WOMAN!

Jewish tradition attempts to restore women as participants of the revelation at Sinai. For example, Rashi and later commentators note that in the critical scene in Exodus 19, God commanded Moses to "speak to the house of Jacob and tell the children of Israel." They explain that the "house of Jacob" means the women and the "children of Israel" are the men. But their very attempt to undo Moses' exclusion of women reflects exclusion. Understanding the term "the house" for women has a good philological basis: the word "house" means "wife" in Aramaic, including the Aramaic of the Talmud. However, the "house of Jacob" is *not* an *autonomous* entity; it is a *dependent part* of Jacob's orbit, an appendage that (similar to the physical house) should not be coveted. Even though tradition may explain that this "house" is mentioned first because it often is responsible for the behavior of the household, the "house" is considered separate from the "children of Israel," and traditional Jewish law preserves and intensifies the unequal treatment of women.

GO NOT NEAR A WOMAN!

Jewish tradition is represented not only by Moses, the commandments, and the laws; it also includes the narrator of the Book of Exodus, who stands outside the action and alerts us to what is happening. This narrative voice is an independent voice; not the voice of God, and certainly not the voice of Moses. This narrative observer sees and relates the heroism of the women of Exodus 1–4, the disappearance of women in Exodus 19, and their continued faithfulness and piety in Exodus 35, as they bring their jewelry and offer their labor for the building of the Tabernacle. This narrator, whose identity we do not know, is not a "nobody." This narrator is the voice of Torah, and hearkening to it is as important as hearkening to Moses or the laws.

GO NOT NEAR A WOMAN!

The moment at Sinai, even as the redemption from Egypt, is an eternal, ever-present moment. All Jews—men and women—stood at Sinai, and all stand there still. The women of today, still faced with exclusion and uneven treatment, must decide whether or not to be silent. The temptations to acquiesce are great—piety, tradition, inertia, the call for group solidarity in the face of anti-Semitism and assimilation, the demand for harmony for the sake of Jewish continuity—all seem to argue for a continuation of the silence. But history speaks, revealing to us the results of acquiescence to the suppression of women's voices and to the subordination of their wills to the authority of men. And the Torah's voice also speaks, showing us that the exclusion of women was not demanded by God. This is the voice that can empower women to speak in the name of God's will. In each generation—in this generation—women must speak out.

Breaking the silence is a transformative act that examines the regulations and prescriptions of the Jewish social order. Breaking the silence is an obligatory act that pays heed to the command *la'asok bedivrei Torah* (to engage in the affairs of Torah) and strives to maintain the unity of Israel, Torah, and the Holy. There is, of course, danger when we seek to scrutinize the Torah in the name of the very values that Torah teaches us. The danger is that we will be as myopic as Moses, seeing only ourselves and not others whom we may not notice. We must pay attention to *all* who may be disadvantaged by the cultural and social system, not merely to the marginalization and objectification that we, ourselves, have experienced. In our fervent engagement with Torah, women and men must study and speak as agents for our own good, for the good of all Israel, and for all the world's inhabitants. Then we will turn breaking the silence into a holy act that restores to the Torah the "pleasantness" of its ways, when those ways have become oppressive because of human imperfection. In our efforts to liberate the Torah from oppression, we will keep the Torah holy, and we will emerge from the continually recurring critical moment of Sinai as a truly liberated and holy people.

14 / Reading Rahab
1997

As we study a biblical story that is often simple on its surface, it opens like a rose to reveal complexities and significance unhinted at on the surface. I am delighted to dedicate this reading to Moshe Greenberg, who taught us to lift our eyes from the word and the verse and to look at biblical texts as coherent literary units.

The historical books of the Bible open with the story of Rahab, the prostitute who saved the Israelite spies trapped in Jericho. On the surface, this is a charming story of a familiar antitype in folklore, the prostitute-with-the-heart-of-gold. This biblical Suzie Wong is helpful to the spies, has close ties with her family, and has faith in God's might. But the charm does not explain its prominence as the first of the conquest stories, strongly associated with the triumphal entry into the land. Its importance begins to become clearer as we take a careful look at the way the story is constructed. It begins and ends with a frame: the charge that Joshua gives the two men that he is sending on a reconnaissance mission and their report to him. He tells them to "go and see the land and Jericho" (Josh 2:1), and they return to declare, "God has given the land into our hands; all the inhabitants are melting away before us" (Josh 2:24).[1] Neither we nor the spies are given more information. Joshua doesn't charge the men to discover the defenses, and they do not gather any military information. In the next "spy story," when Joshua sends men to Ai (Josh 7:2–4), he makes it clear that the men are to 'spy,' using the key word °*rgl*, a technical term also used in the later story of the Danite spies at Laish (Judg 18:2–11). Yet another "spy story" in the Deuteronomistic History uses a separate technical term °*tûr*, 'to scout,' the term used in one of the biblical stories that is a direct "intertext" to our story: Moses' sending of the spies to scout the land in Numbers 13.

The Rahab story is a masterpiece of allusive writing. It is set in the first five chapters of the Book of Joshua, which contain numerous pentateuchal allusions designed to have readers keep in mind the activities of Moses as they read Joshua. The beginning of the book introduces Joshua as the second Moses when God announces to Joshua that he will be with him as he was with Moses (Josh 1:5). Events of these chapters then recapitulate events at the beginning of Moses' mission. An angel appears to Joshua with sword extended and tells him to remove his shoes because the ground on which he stands is holy ground (Josh 1:5); Moses at the burning bush (Exod 3:5) is the only other person told this. The burning bush theophany in Exodus is followed by a frightening scene: when Moses first heads to Egypt to begin the process of redemption, God attacks him and is only assuaged when Zipporah circumcises their son with a flint knife (Exod 4); similarly, Joshua circumcises the Israelites with flint knives (Josh 5).[2] The most striking parallel is the Israelites' miraculous crossing of the Jordan; Israel passes through the Red Sea on the way to the desert and through the Jordan on its way out of the desert. Both crossings are miraculous, and mention of them has major frightening impact on foreign nations. In this context, it is not surprising that the Rahab story, the first of the tales of the conquest, should contain a parallel to the story of Moses and the spies.

When Moses sends the twelve spies, one to a tribe, he gives them a specific charge: "you shall see what this land is and whether the people living there are weak or strong, few or numerous; whether this land is good or not good and whether the cities are open or fortified; whether the land is fat or thin, is wooded or not, and you shall be strong and bring back fruit" (Num 13:18–20). The spies are all choice men, great men of Israel, whose names are recorded. Nevertheless, despite their pedigree, these great men conclude that the land cannot be conquered. The nations are strong; the land can be lethal, and there are giants in the land, compared to whom the Israelites look and feel like grasshoppers (Num 13:30–33). Only two men, Joshua and Caleb, trust Israel can conquer the land. As a result, the entire generation stays in the wilderness until death overtakes them.

Now, in the Book of Joshua, it is forty years later, and a new generation is poised to enter the land. This time, Joshua sends only two men.[3] They are not said to be prominent; on the contrary, the story gives the impression that Joshua picked any two men. The men are sent with no clear charge and not told what they should report. They are not special men and never give any impression of initiative or daring throughout the story.[4] However, this time, these two ordinary men come back with the report that only the exceptional Joshua and Caleb could give before: that God has given the land to Israel.

Within this framework of charge and response, the story of Rahab unfolds. In the next act, the men go directly to the house of Rahab the prostitute where they are almost caught, but she hides them, lies to the king's men, and then helps them escape. Hiding and lying is the way biblical women demonstrate their loyalty. For example, when Absalom is alerted that the sons of Zadok have gone to warn David, the women quickly lower themselves into a well on the property of a man in Bahurim. The woman of the house spreads a cover over the well and then declares that the men have already returned to Jerusalem (2 Sam 17:17–22). The Canaanite general Sisera expects Yael to give him exactly this kind of protective deception, saying that he was not there (Judg 4:18–20).[5]

There is yet another subtle allusion to a biblical woman who hides: when Rahab hides the spies, the author uses the relatively rare word **spn: watispĕnô*, 'and she hid him.' The knowledgeable reader will think immediately of the story of Moses' birth, when Moses' mother saved him by hiding him: *watispĕnēhû*, 'and she hid him.' This phrase occurs only twice in the whole Bible, and the reader, alerted by the manifold allusions to Moses in Joshua 1–5, may catch the resonance: as the "hiding" of the infant Moses started the Exodus events, so Rahab's "hiding" of the representatives of the infant Israel begins the process of the conquest.

Rahab asks that she and her family be spared in the destruction, as a compassionate service *hesed* in return for the *hesed* she has shown them. The spies duly promise, and in Joshua 6 we hear that she was indeed saved. Once again, this story has a very close "narrative analogy." In the story of the conquest of Bethel in the first chapter of the Book of Judges, the Josephites who are scouting Bethel see a man coming out of the city. They offer him *hesed* if he will reveal the entrance to his city (by sparing him when they defeat the city).[6] But the story of the man who revealed the entrance to this important city is told in four verses. In contrast, Rahab's story takes up a whole chapter and then still has to be finished in chapter 6.

The Rahab story is not longer because it contains details. On the contrary, the story is so sparse that scholars have speculated that chapter 2 is a vestige of an originally longer tale.[7] Only the important narrative sequences are related, and the story is full of "gaps" that the readers must fill in by considering analogous texts and by imagination and speculation. Why did Joshua send the spies? There are clues in Numbers 13, but the narrators say nothing explicitly. Why did the spies go to Rahab's house? Is it because a prostitute's establishment is a good place to blend in unobserved and listen to people,[8] or is it because men who have been out in the wilderness all their lives immediately head to the bordello for soft beds and soft women? The narrator doesn't say; the reader can decide.[9] How did the king find out? Some suspicious readers have suggested that Rahab herself sent word so that she could demand *hesed*.[10] The story attains its length not by narrative detail, but by the inclusion of three dialogues, each of which is vitally important in understanding the significance of this story to Israel.

The first dialogue is an interchange between Rahab and the king of Jericho. He assumes that the men are spies who have come "to investigate" the land,[11] and demands that she bring them out. This is Rahab's moment of truth, and she chooses Israel, declaring, "the men came to me, but I didn't know from whence; and when the gate was about to close at dark, the men went out I know not whither" (Josh 2:4–5). Rahab is smart, proactive, tricky, and unafraid to disobey and deceive the king.[12] She reminds us of two other women who are portrayed in this way, the two midwives in Egypt who defy the Pharaoh's orders to slay the Hebrew children. Once again, the beginning of the conquest echoes the beginning of the Exodus.

Rahab is also dominant in the third dialogue, between herself and the spies (2:16–21). When Rahab lowers them outside her window, she tells them to flee to the hills. This seemingly extraneous suggestion is a clue to yet another intertext, the story of Lot and the angels in Genesis 19, in which the angels tell Lot to "flee to the hills." The stories first seem very unlike each other, but they share a similar vocabulary[13] and similar plot sequence: two men enter and lodge in a city that is about to be destroyed; their host defies a demand to "bring out the men," the city is destroyed, the inhabitant who lodged them is saved and told to "flee to the hills," and the story ends with an etiological notice about the descendants of the host. A lexical allusion further reinforces the reference, for Rahab is said to have saved the 'envoys,' *malʾākîm*, the same Hebrew word that is also translated 'angels' (Josh 6:25)[14] and is used for the angels in Sodom. There are further parallels: both stories take place in the Jordan plain and may have originally been preserved as local legends, and in both cases the men lodge in the house of a character who is marginal to the city's social structure: Lot as an outsider, Rahab as a prostitute. However, Lot is hesitant and tentative as the angels save him; in Joshua, the visitors are saved by the assertive, proactive Rahab.[15]

The men adjure Rahab to gather her family into her house and to tie a scarlet cord in the window. The family must stay inside during the destruction; whoever ventures outside may be killed. Only those who stay inside the house marked with the scarlet cord will be safe from devastation. Once again, the alert reader, ancient and modern, catches the reference: on the night of the slaying of the firstborn of Egypt, the Israelites were to mark their doors with lamb's blood and stay inside in order to be safe from destruction.[16] Once again, the saved are to stay inside the house marked in red; Rahab's family is to be rescued from Jericho, as the Israelites were from Egypt.[17] This resourceful outsider, Rahab the trickster, is a new Israel.

The second discourse is the heart of the story. Rahab begins by acknowledging God's intentions: "I know that God has given you this land and that dread of you has fallen upon us, and all the inhabitants of the land are melting before you" (2:9). This is clearly an exaggeration: if no one has the spirit to stand against Israel, what are the king of Jericho and his soldiers doing chasing these envoys? But it is an important message, and Rahab is the oracle who declares that God has given Israel the land. She is the first of the prophets who appear in the historical books to announce to Israel the paths of their history and the first of the women who declare and pronounce the will of God. The lines of women and prophets begin with Rahab and converge again at the end of 2 Kings and 2 Chronicles in the figure of Huldah the prophetess, who announces the destruction of Judah.

Rahab's speech is couched in language familiar to the readers in ancient Israel. The use of the special terms *eima*, 'dread,' and *namog*, 'melt,' introduce us to the vocabulary of the Holy War of the conquest of Canaan;[18] these particular phrases allude to the great song of Israel's sacred history, the Song of the Sea, preserved in Exodus 15: "All the dwellers of Canaan are aghast, terror and dread descend upon them."[19] The prediction made by the song is indeed coming true—the process of conquest has truly started.

Rahab acknowledges God with the words "I know," the very words with which Jethro pronounces his faith in God: "Now I know that the Lord is greater than all gods" (Exod 18:11) and with which the Syrian general Naaman declares God's greatness: "for I know that there is no such God in all the land" (2 Kgs 5:15). This phrase, *I know,* is a formula by which people from foreign nations come to acknowledge God. This literary use may have its origin in a rite of passage, a kind of proto-conversion that may have been practiced in ancient Israel. In the historical books, Rahab is presented as the first of the inhabitants of the land to join God and Israel.[20]

In return for her demonstration of loyalty in saving the spies, Rahab asks for *hesed* from Israel. Her request for *hesed* is reminiscent of the request that Abimelech made of Abraham: "Do with me according to the *hesed* that I did to you" (Gen 21:23).[21] Abimelech sought a treaty with Abraham; Rahab seeks an arrangement with Israel. This doesn't mean that the finished text of the Genesis story was in the possession of the author of the Rahab story. On the contrary, the verbal correspondence between them comes from the fact that both use legal language, reflecting the juridical importance of this treaty transaction. Rahab's speech contains all the essential elements of the classic Deuteronomic form of covenants. The *preamble* and the *prologue,* in which Rahab confesses the greatness of God, are in verses 9–11; Rahab's *stipulations* (salvation for family and sign of assurance) are in verses 12–13, and the Israelites' *stipulations* (silence and staying within the house) and the *sanctions* (salvation/death) are in verses 18–20; the *oath* is in verses 14 and 17; and the *sign* (the scarlet cord) is in verses 18–21.[22] This request for *hesed* is a formal arrangement by which Rahab seeks to join Israel, and the oath and sign that the Israelites give is their acceptance of her and her family into this arrangement.

The denouement of the story comes in Joshua 6. When the Israelites conquer Jericho, Joshua sends the two men to Rahab's house, they bring out Rahab and her family, and she lives 'in the midst of Israel,' *beqereb yisra'el*, "until this very day" (Josh 6:25). All has ended happily, Israel has been enriched by the family of a heroine, and the conquest has begun.

But is this the way the conquest is to proceed? Deuteronomy has very different ideas about how to treat the inhabitants of the land: "You must doom them to destruction, make no pacts with them, grant them no quarter."[23] The idea of *herem,* total war, is an essential cornerstone of Deuteronomy's philosophy of history: the slaughter is necessary so that the inhabitants do not then introduce foreign ideas and foreign ways into Israel. The story of the conquest of Jericho in chap. 6 uses eleven variations of the verb *herem.* Just before Joshua sends the spies to get Rahab, the narrator tells us, "They destroyed everything in the city, man and woman, youth and aged." In this context, it seems strange to see Rahab and her family joining Israel, and one might conclude that the first thing that the Israelites did on entering Canaan was to break the rule of the *ḥerem*.[24]

This saving of Rahab from the *ḥerem* seems even more problematic as we proceed to the next chapter in Joshua, which relates the Israelite defeat at Ai and its cause: Achan's violation of the *ḥerem* at Jericho. The two situations seem parallel, with parallel phrases: as Rahab is in the midst of Israel, Israel is warned that it must take away the *ḥerem* in its midst, the *ḥerem* being the Sumerian cloak that Achan took from Jericho. Achan and all that is his are killed just as Rahab and all that is hers are saved; the mound of stones that marked the spot stands in Israel "to this very day." Given the Deuteronomic explanation that the *ḥerem* is to prevent contamination by foreign ideas, it would seem that saving *people* from the *ḥerem* is a more serious violation than saving a cloak, and we might begin to suspect that there is a dark side to the Rahab story. And yet—Achan's "liberation" of the cloak is punished by a defeat at Ai, whereas the men's promise to liberate Rahab is followed by a glorious victory. In fact, the conquest of Jericho is clearly a conquest by God, who intervenes to perform a miracle of felling the walls, a clear mark that Israel has *not* angered God by agreeing to save Rahab. The juxtaposition of the Rahab and Achan stories presents a discourse on the nature of the *ḥerem* and obedience to it. When Achan ignored the *ḥerem* for selfish reasons, all of Israel was punished until he was found and executed; when the men of Israel ignored the *ḥerem* as an act of *ḥesed* to repay *ḥesed*, then God reacted by miraculously conquering Jericho. The *ḥerem*, this story would seem to imply, is not an absolute and should be superseded by issues of justice and mercy.[25]

The next group of stories in the Book of Joshua also revolves around this issue of the *ḥerem* and its application. After Ai, the book turns to the Gibeonites. Rahab states, "For we have heard how God dried up the Reed Sea before you as you went out of Egypt and (we have heard) what you did to the two Amorite kings of Transjordan, Sihon and Og, whom you utterly destroyed" (2:10). With the same words, "for we have heard," the Gibeonites describe their coming to believe in God: "for we have heard the reports of Him and all that He did in Egypt and all that He did to Sihon king of Heshbon and to Og king of the Bashan" (Josh 9:9–10). The name of God has grown great, the report has gone out. The kings of the Amorites gather to fight, but the Gibeonites are moved by this report to try to ally themselves with Israel. Knowing that Israel is not to sign pacts with the local people,[26] they trick Israel into believing that they come from far away.[27] They remain in Israel as hewers of wood and drawers of water for both the community and for the altar of God. Once again, a tricky outsider has escaped *herem* and joined Israel. And once again, when the Gibeonites are attacked and Israel comes to their rescue, Israel wins by a miracle. As the sun stands still, God has come visibly and directly to the aid of Israel.

The Rahab and Gibeon stories in Joshua may indicate that Israel had a tradition that told the story of the conquest as a process during which many inhabitants of the land stayed and became aligned with and ultimately joined Israel. This tradition understood the *herem* to have applied only to those nations or kings who actively opposed Israel. The "Amorites" do not fight in Joshua 5:1, and no battle is related; the Canaanite kings in 9:1–2 resolve to fight and are defeated; the alliance under King Jabin fought, and Hazor was destroyed as a result (Josh 11). In this view of the settlement of Canaan, the battles of conquest were "defensive," fought against those who sought to resist Israel. However, those who were convinced by the stories of God's might were assimilated rather than destroyed.[28] This view of the conquest as a process that included the amalgamation and incorporation of local inhabitants is strikingly like the account of the settlement of Israel that is currently accepted by archaeologists and historians.

Rahab and the Gibeonites refer to Egypt and to Sihon and Og; significantly, God "hardened Pharaoh's heart" and later did the same to Sihon and Og. In these cases, the stubbornness of the people served as the justification for conquering them, and their conquest followed a pattern of demoralization, hardening, and annihilation. One might ask why God "hardened" some people's hearts and not others.[29] In the case of Pharaoh, Exodus tells us he hardened his own heart before God hardened it. This may also have been true of Sihon and Og. Since Sihon and Og wanted to fight Israel, God made their resolve even firmer. Rahab and the Gibeonites show that there was an alternative to fighting the Israelites and that those whose heart was moved to fear God did avoid destruction. On the other hand, Joshua 11:19–20 declares that God hardened everyone's heart (except Gibeon) to fight so that they would be destroyed. In any event, God must have had God's own reasons for sparing these people.

The Book of Joshua is part of the Deuteronomistic history, a reflection on Israel's history written at the time of the destruction, when the sky was falling, that attempts to make sense out of the fact that God has caused (or at least allowed) Israel to be destroyed. Deuteronomy does not trust foreign alliances or foreign women and couples its demand for the *ḥerem* with a prohibition of intermarriage with the local inhabitants.[30] To Deuteronomy the very purpose of the *ḥerem* is to prevent intermingling and intermarriage and the subsequent introduction of "foreign" ideas into Israel.[31] Joshua 23:13 and Judges 2:3 (both Deuteronomic passages) explain why many inhabitants of the land are not eradicated: they are to be "a snare and a trap" for Israel, "a scourge to your sides and thorns in your eyes" that will ultimately lead to Israel's loss of the land. From this perspective, the nations that remain are the source of evil danger, and Rahab, saved as an act of reciprocated *ḥesed,* is ultimately a stumbling block to Israel's survival. The rescue of Rahab is Israel's first act of apostasy, committed immediately after Israel's entry into the land. The Deuteronomist does not make any directly negative statements: the repeated use of the verb *ḥerem* in Joshua 6 reminds the reader of Deuteronomy and insinuates that the saving of Rahab contains the first seeds of the nation's destruction.

The very first words of the Rahab story inform us that Joshua was at Shittim when he sent out the spies. Whether this detail was original or added by a later hand, Shittim subtly cues us (the biblically sophisticated readers) to the wider ramifications of the story in the underlying discourse about the permeability of Israel's boundaries. Shittim is the place where Israel angered God by going astray with the Moabite women in the incident of Ba'al Peor in Numbers 25. During this incident, moreover, an Israelite man called Zimri brought a Midianite princess, Kozbi, into the Israelite camp and his chambers. Immediately, Phineas the priest stabbed them both. For this act, Numbers 25 records, Phineas was rewarded with a *brît shālôm* 'a pact of peace.' As we juxtapose these two Shittim stories, Rahab's position, profession, and name take on new significance. There is no hint of sex in the Rahab story, but Rahab is a professional prostitute, a *zōnâ,* the same word (*zānâ*) with which Israel is described as going astray at Shittim. Rahab's very name means 'wide, broad.' She is the 'broad of Jericho'—the wide-open woman who is the wide-open door to Canaan and maybe the open door to apostasy.[32] Kozbi, on the other hand, was a princess of Midian, and marriage with her might have facilitated alliances and peace with Midian. But Kozbi's name means 'deception,' and she is killed immediately. She is not given any chance to profess her loyalty to God or Israel. To Phineas (and to the narrator of the story), the sight of a foreign woman being brought into Israel is such a danger that she must be eradicated immediately, she and the man who brought her to him. Had this same[33] Phineas been at Jericho, Rahab would have been killed rather than spared. The Kozbi story is clearly and unequivocally against intermerging; the Rahab story presents both voices to this long-standing Israelite dispute. Rahab the trickster-foreigner is a type of Israel, who survives by her wits and comes to God by her faith. Rahab the whore is the outsider's outsider; the most marginal of the marginal. She is the quintessential downtrodden from whom Israel comes and with whom Israel identifies.[34] Just as her pious behavior reverses expectations of how prostitutes act, so her elevation is a reversal of the normal expectations for a prostitute's future. Once again, as in choosing the younger sons and freeing the slaves, YHWH interrupts normative societal expectations by calling the poor and the downtrodden and raising them over others. The saving of Rahab the good Canaanite prostitute is part of and an example of God's nature and Israel's mission. Her name, Rahab "the broad," is emblematic of God's inclusion of the many and of the permeable boundaries of the people of Israel. Phineas and Deuteronomy see the open boundaries as danger; another reader may see them as opportunity.

In the end, it is the reader—both singly and in community—who must decide how to read Rahab. After the exile, some of Israel's prophets view the early remnant nations as signs of hope that Israel will survive;[35] they no longer share the Deuteronomic view. Despite the fact that Ezra and Nehemiah demanded that the Israelites divorce their foreign wives and that intermarriage was prohibited in the Maccabean period, Christian and Jewish tradition both remember Rahab as an exemplary positive figure.[36] She is cited in the Second Testament as a model of faith[37] and as a second Abraham, justified by her deeds.[38] In Jewish tradition she is remembered as one of the great righteous proselytes.[39] In one major midrashic tradition, she marries Joshua[40] and becomes the ancestress of priests and prophets, including Jeremiah and Ezekiel.[41]

This righteous proselyte-prophet is listed in Matthew as the ancestor of Boaz and thus the ancestor of David. Jewish midrash also preserves such a tradition, pointing out the similarity between the "scarlet threaded cord" with which Rahab's house is marked and the "scarlet thread" that marked the first-born son of Tamar, ancestress of David, and the many parallels between Rahab and Ruth.[42] Thus in both religious traditions, Rahab takes her place in the extraordinary genealogy of the Messiah.[43] These traditions have taken the choice offered by the story and have read Rahab, her contribution and her inclusion, in the most positive light possible.

NOTES

1. *Gam* does not always mean 'and'; more often it means 'in return, in consequence of.'

2. These parallels are seen by Robert Alter, who points out that the word *baderek*, 'on the way,' is used in both stories. In Exodus they are on the way to Egypt; in Joshua they were not circumcised on the way from Egypt (*The World of Biblical Literature* [New York: Basic Books, 1992], 117–21).

3. See Robert Culley, "Stories of the Conquest: Joshua 2, 6, 7, and 8," HAR 8 (1984) 25–44. See also Yair Zakovitch, who overplays the ordinariness of the women ("Humor and Theology or the Successful Failure of Israelite Intelligence: A Literary-Folkloric Approach to Joshua 2," in *Text and Tradition: The Hebrew Bible and Folklore*, ed. Susan Niditch (Atlanta: Scholars Press, 1990), 75–98.

4. Zakovitch, "Humor and Theology." This should be read with Frank M. Cross, "Reply to Zakovitch," in *Text and Tradition*, 99–106.

5. She, of course, has other ideas; see the discussion below. Even Rahab's act of lowering the men out her window has a biblical parallel, for Saul's daughter Michal saves David by lowering him out the window and then lying about her reasons (1 Sam 19:9–106).

6. Judg 1:22–26. The importance of this analogy is noted by Robert G. Boling, *Joshua: A New Translation with Notes and Commentary* (Garden City, N.J.: Doubleday, 1982).

7. J. Alberto Soggin, *Judges: A Commentary* (Philadelphia: Westminster, 1981) and Robert Culley, "Stories of the Conquest."

8. So Ann Engar, "Old Testament Women as Tricksters," *Mapping of the Biblical Terrain: The Bible as Text*, ed. Vincent Tollers and John Maier (Lewisburg, Pa.: Bucknell University Press, 1990), 143–57.

9. Josephus, *Ant*. 6.2, fills in at this juncture by explaining that the spies first surveyed the city; only then did they go to Rahab's. In modern times, Ottosson suggests that the fact that the men went to Rahab's house suggests that she was associated with them either because she was originally a nomadic woman or because she belonged to asocial circles (Magnus Ottosson, "Rahab and the Spies," in *Dumu-é-dub-ba-a: Studies in Honor of Ake W. Sjöberg*, ed. Hermann Behrens, Darlene Loding, and Martha T. Roth (Philadelphia: Babylonian Section, University Museum, 1989). On the other hand, Zakovitch is extremely negative in his judgment of the men, whom he considers "first-class bunglers" (Zakovitch, "Humor and Theology").

10. Rahab has suffered greatly at the hands of some modern scholars. Once again, it is Zakovitch who is most extreme and suggests that it was Rahab herself who informed the king in order to make the men obligated to her (ibid., p. 85).

11. The king uses the word °*hpr*, the very word that Deut 1 uses in referring to the spies that Moses sent.

12. The "trickery" of Rahab, like the trickery of other women in the Bible, has occasioned much disapproval and defense. See my *In the Wake of the Goddesses* (New York: Macmillan, 1992), 136–39, especially the discussion on Rivkah.

13. F. Langlamet, "Josue, II, et les traditions de l'Hexateuque," RB 78 (1971): 5–17, 161–83, 321–54. Langlamet finds seventeen lexical correspondences between Josh 2 and Gen 19.

14. For a study of these two texts together, see L. Daniel Hawk, "Strange Houseguest: Rahab, Lot and the Dynamics of Deliverance," *Reading between Texts: Intertextuality and the Hebrew Bible*, ed. Danna Nolan Fewell (Lousville, Ky.: Westminster/John Knox, 1992), 89–97. To his parallels, I would add the fact that they both happened in the same plain.

15. This is the conclusion reached by Hawk, ibid.

16. Exod 12. For the allusion, see Engar, "Old Testament Women."

17. Verses 19–21 are sometimes considered a later addition in order to explain the scarlet cord. Taking another tack, Hawk suggests that the scarlet cord *(tiqwat ḥût hašānî)* may be nothing more than the 'hope' *(tiqwâ)* associated with the 'two' *(šnê)*. However, the many references to the Exodus redemption throughout this story indicate that this episode is both original and a reminder of the saving of the first-born.

18. See Dennis McCarthy, "Some Holy War Vocabulary in Joshua 2," CBQ 33 (1971): 228–30.

19. Exod 15:15–16. The connection was noted by the ancient Rabbis in *Mekhilta Shirata* 9. Rahab reverses the order of these two sentences, as is the rule in biblical quotations (see Zakovitch, "Humor and Theology," 89).

20. See Gordon Mitchell, "Together in the Land: A Reading of the Book of Joshua," JSOT 134 (1993): 152–90.

21. Ottosson, "Rahab and the Spies."

22. K. M. Campbell, "Rahab's Covenant," VT 22 (1972): 243–45.

23. Deut 7:2, and see Deut 20:17.

24. For discussions of this issue, see Lyle Eslinger, *Into the Hands of the Living God* (Sheffield: Almond, 1989), 24–54. Polzin's theory that the story itself is a meditation on the issues of justice and mercy is unconvincing in that it requires him to make Rahab deserving of extermination and entirely undeserving of being saved (*Moses and the Deuteronomist: A Literary Study of the Deuteronomic History* [Bloomington: Indiana University Press, 1993]).

25. See Mitchell, "Together in the Land."

26. They, like Rahab, seem to have studied Deuteronomy.

27. They pretend to be from far away by aging their clothes and equipment, patching their sandals and bringing dry crumbly bread as they come to a people for whom God has performed the miracle of not allowing their clothes and shoes to wear out during the forty years in the desert.

28. Lawson Stone, "Ethical and Apologetic Tendencies in the Redaction of the Book of Joshua," CBQ 53 (1991): 25–36.

29. Eslinger (*Into the Hands*, 24–54) attributes this to a "failing" by God, who did not perform the divine duty.

30. To the Deuteronomistic historian, Solomon's one flaw was the fact that he loved foreign women, including the daughter of Pharaoh (1 Kgs 11:1–3).

31. Deut 7:1–5, 20:18.

32. The most negative valuation is given by Lyle Eslinger, who states unequivocally, "Rahab is characterized as a whore precisely because she is the door, left open by the divine whoremonger, through which the Israelites are led to stray, 'a-whoring after other Gods'" (*Into the Hands*, 46).

33. We can assume that the Israelites at Jericho included Phineas the priest but not the same narrative character full of murderous zeal.

34. Phyllis A. Bird, "The Harlot as a Heroine: Narrative Art and Social Presupposition in Three Old Testament Texts," *Semeia* 46 (*Narrative Research on the Hebrew Bible; 1989*), 119–39.

35. See particularly the Philistines in Zech 9:7.

36. See Martinus Beek, "Rahab in the Light of Jewish Exegesis (Josh 2:1–24; 6:17, 22–23, 25," *Von Kanaan bis Kerala: Festschrift für Prof. Mag. Dr. Dr. J.P.M. van der Ploeg*, ed. W. C. Delsman (Neukirchen-Vluyn: Neukirchener Verlag, 1982), 37–44.

37. See Heb 11:31.

38. Jas 2:25.

39. In *Midraš Tadše* 21, *Midraš Chronicles* iv 21, *Rabbah,* she is one of the righteous of the world and proof that God accepts sinners.

40. B. *Meg.* 14b.

41. Ruth Rab. 2:1; and cf. Numbers Rab. 8:9.

42. *Midraš Hagādôl Hayye Sarah* 94.

43. Even though some doubts have been expressed (Jerome Quinn, "Is Rachab in Matt 1:5 Rahab of Jericho," *Bib* 62 [1981]: 225–28), there is general consensus that Rahab of Jericho is the Rahab in Matthew (Raymond Brown, "Rachab in Matt 1:5 Probably Is Rahab of Jericho," *Bib* 63 [1982]: 79–80).

FEMINIST PERSPECTIVES II: GENDER AND THE LAW

15 / Patriarchal Family Relationships and Near Eastern Law

1981

The stories of Genesis are so much a part of our own culture, and so vivid in and of themselves, that we tend to treat them as timeless, almost universal, pieces of literature. Whether or not we regard them as sacred Scripture, we analyze them for their literary structure, their moral import, and their psychological truths. In this there is a danger that we will forget that even though the very durability of the Bible proves its ability to transcend cultural and temporal boundaries, nevertheless it comes out of a specific cultural milieu and manifests many of the features of the culture from which it sprang.

This has been made abundantly clear during the last one hundred years, during which time we have witnessed the discovery of the cuneiform culture, the dominant culture of the ancient Near East, and the mother-culture—if you will—of Israel. There were published in short order such documents as the *Gilgamesh* epic, which contains a flood story exceedingly similar to the biblical account, paralleling it in such detail as the sending forth of birds to determine the emergence of dry land. The discovery of the Laws of Hammurabi, with their close affinity to the Covenant Code of Exodus, must have seemed even more threatening to the traditional biblicists of the time. The emergence of these documents at the beginning of Assyriological research effected a radical transformation in our perception of the Bible. There was an initial period of shock during which the similarities to Babylonian material seemed so vast as to be explainable only in terms of gross plagiarism. Now, however, the intimate relationship of Israelite culture to earlier and contemporary traditions is taken as axiomatic. Attention is increasingly focused on the nature of that relationship and on the ways in which Israel adapted, utilized, and transformed the cultural materials at hand.

This is all in the realm of ideas, and such comparisons serve primarily to illuminate the formal legal tradition and the great cosmological cycle of Genesis 1–11. The rest of the Book of Genesis is of a very different order: we have an anthology of ancestral stories, centering first around Abraham (12:1–25:18), then Jacob (25:19–37:2a), and finally a coherent cycle of tales about Joseph and his brothers (37:2b–50:26). These stories are not uniform. In form they represent a wide variety of poetry and prose pieces; some of them are folkloristic. A whole school of Bible study, called form criticism, has developed to analyze these different forms and their import.

The stories are, furthermore, not all from the same stylus. It is now generally accepted that there are three main streams of tradition represented and partially united in the Book of Genesis. There is a tradition that developed in the southern state of Judah and which, it is commonly believed, began to be composed in a unified form in the tenth century B.C.E. This tradition is usually referred to as J, originally because of its distinctive use of the tetragrammaton YHWH as the name of God in the patriarchal period, but better termed J for Judean. There is a second, parallel tradition that probably developed in the north and was composed in unitary form just slightly later than J. This tradition used to be called E or *Elohist*, because of the way it refers to God. Now, with our increased sophistication, we usually refer to it as *Ephraimite*, conveniently E. Finally there is a Priestly recension of these origin-traditions, known as P, whose date of composition is still a matter of considerable dispute. To increase our sense of insecurity, we must remember that these traditions, sometimes called "sources" or "documents," themselves represented compilations and unifications of other, earlier material, some of it oral, and some more probably written at a time contemporary with, or soon after, the events they portrayed.

Genesis, then, is a very complex book, and the question of how to understand and interpret the patriarchal stories is a complicated one. As is usual in biblical studies, the first publication and general acceptance of the theory of separate sources (which has come to be known as the "documentary hypothesis") led to a period of such radical skepticism and doubt that some prominent groups of biblical scholars—most notably the school of Alt—refused to believe in the reliability and reality of any of the patriarchal narratives, maintaining that recoverable Israelite history first began with the entry into Canaan.

Paradoxically, it is the cuneiform evidence that elucidates and illuminates the patriarchal material, indicating its historical authenticity by demonstrating its fidelity to the cultural mores of the ancient Near East. There are many customs reflected in the patriarchal tales that did not exist in classical Israel and must have seemed peculiar to the compilers of J, E, or P, not to mention the final composer of Genesis. The wide variety of documents that we possess from Mesopotamia, and from diverse cultures strung out along its periphery, has revealed these customs to us, indicating some of the subtleties of their meaning, and, in so doing, causing us to give more credence to the historical value of Genesis. In particular, the discovery in the 1920s of such peripheral centers as Ugarit, Alalakh, and Mari provided us with enormous amounts of material with which to illuminate the patriarchal homeland of Haran. Among these, the city of Nuzi, an unimportant town (at that time) near the city of Arrapha (modern Kirkuk), had yielded thousands of documents from the private archives of one single prosperous family over a span of four generations, thus giving us our closest picture of family relationships in the Near East.

So many of the customs reflected in Genesis are paralleled by documents from Nuzi that it is tempting to think of all this as Hurrian law, unique to Haran, and learned there by the patriarchs. This was the view of Speiser (1964: 91–92 and passim) and was commonly accepted among scholars. However, new discoveries have tended to contradict this by indicating that the parallels first found in Nuzi are themselves paralleled elsewhere in the cuneiform cultures. Recently, reaction has set in and the "Hurrian hypothesis" has been attacked by van Seters (1975), who claims that the patriarchal narratives belong more properly in the first millennium, and by Thompson (1974), who denies the value of these comparisons in establishing the historicity of the patriarchal narratives. A careful study of the material indicates that the patriarchal stories are clearly a part of the general cuneiform tradition, and although the parallels may not enable us to pinpoint the date of the patriarchal era, they can illuminate the patriarchal stories themselves.

One of the key issues in the patriarchal narratives is the problem of succession and its accompanying inheritance of the covenant with God, an area in which we have particularly rich information from the cuneiform materials. Before studying this question, however, I would like to pause to give some picture of the various types of cuneiform evidence and the value of each to biblical studies. The first important body of cuneiform material bearing on the patriarchs is the cuneiform legal tradition, the so-called "codes." Early in the Sumerian south there developed a tradition of composing collections of legal cases. The impetus for this was apparently scholarly and jurispruden- tial rather than statutory, and the compilers combined and elaborated upon legal type-cases that illustrated the ideal legal principles. These collections are commonly known by the name of the ruler who com- missioned them, the first major identifiable one being the Laws of Ur-Nammu, king of the city of Ur in southern Iraq from 2111–2098 B.C.E. This collection is written in Sumerian, as are the Laws of Lipit- Ishtar and the as yet unidentified group known as YBT 28. Around 1800 B.C.E. we begin to get such texts written in Akkadian, the Semitic language of Babylon. The first such collection known to us are the Laws of Eshnunna, a city on the Dyala River prominent at this time. In this case the laws are called by the name of the city because the king's name was apparently in the broken beginning of the tablet. The next is the Laws of Hammurabi, by accident of discovery the first one known to modern scholars, the most extensive and detailed of all these collections, and the one most often copied and studied in the schools of Babylonia. All of these codes are from southern Mesopotamia in its classical period. The tradition of the study of law through such documents spread from there to the other cuneiform civilizations, and we have such documents from Assyria, from the Hittites, and again from Babylonia in the Middle Babylonian period. In fact, we probably should consider the Book of the Covenant in Exodus to be a document in this tradition.

In all these law books the laws themselves may change. Certain type- cases, like the Goring Ox (criminal negligence) or the problem of two men brawling and accidentally hitting a pregnant woman who promptly miscarries (grievous battery without assault), illustrate important juridi- cal situations. They therefore appear in the laws over and over again, not because of the frequency of such occurrences—pregnant women usually know enough to keep out of fights, and miscarriages are rarely caused by a blow—but because they illustrate well the principle involved. The penalties imposed may vary from society to society, and it is in the care- ful study of these changes and differences that we get some insight into the fundamental legal principles of these societies.

In addition to these groups of law-as-it-ought-to-be, we have a large assortment of humble documents of law as it was practiced daily: bills of sale, marriage contracts, lawsuits, court depositions, letters from creditors, adoption contracts, and so forth. These are harder to study because there are so many of them and they are not organized, but when sifted they yield close details about the nature of societal relationships in those days.

The family, as seen through these documents, is a large extended family which is patrilocal in residence, patripotestal in authority, and patrilineal in descent. This means that all the sons stay together in one household with the father, who remains the undisputed head of the family until his death. The father contracts marriages for his children. In the case of a daughter, he has unlimited authority to dispose of her in any way he sees fit, whether by contracting a marriage for her or even by giving her as a slave. He provides his daughter with a dowry, which she gets in lieu of an inheritance, and she leaves his house. The father is also expected to obtain wives for his sons, either by actively negotiating and contracting the marriage, or by acquiescing to it and providing the bridal payment. The daughter-in-law then enters the father's house and becomes a member of the family. The bond between the father-in-law and the daughter-in-law is a very strong one and is, I believe, the strongest new legal relationship created by this marriage, which must be seen as a transfer of membership from one household to another. When the father dies, the eldest son takes over as the head of the household: he is given the charge of the household emblems, insignia, and deities and presides over the management of the estate. The brothers may, for one reason or another, continue to hold the land in common for some period rather than divide the inheritance immediately, or they may divide the smaller property, such as houses and orchards, and maintain corporate ownership of the productive land. Whether or not they divide immediately, they must first provide dowries for their unmarried sisters and insure the bridal payment (in some cases) for their younger brother from their joint holdings, only dividing the remainder of the property. The eldest son thereupon receives a preferential share at the division of the estate.

This, then, is the pattern. It is not unique to the ancient Near East but is rather a common pattern for patriarchal families in many societies. The distinctive character of Near Eastern law appears in the ways that this pattern is perceived and understood, for in the ancient Near East such apparently self-evident kinship terms as "son," "brother," and "eldest son" are not limited to their biological referents, but rather define special juridical relationships, relationships that can be created artificially through various types of adoption and specification. Problems and unusual situations are therefore resolved in characteristic Near Eastern ways.

CHILDLESSNESS AND SUCCESSION

A problem that must have arisen quite frequently is that of a childless man, as was Abraham for a very long time in his marriage to Sarah. He may choose to adopt a son, and adoption is very common in the Near East even though it does not seem to have been used in classical Israel. Adoptions are not confined to cases of childlessness, and we have a number of texts (e.g., HG iii 23 and vi 1425) in which it is quite clear that the adopter already has children. Adoptions may occur for a wide variety of reasons, and the adopted son, moreover, need be neither an orphan nor a child. He is frequently a member of the adopter's family (e.g., a nephew). Occasionally he may be a member of the household who is made a son and heir in return for taking care of the man in his old age and providing for him in his death. Such an arrangement may underlie Abraham's complaint in Genesis 15:2–4 that, since he was childless, "Dammesek Eliezer" would inherit from him (Speiser 1964: 112; Prevost 1967: inter alia; for other interpretations of this difficult passage see Snijders 1958: 268–71; Thompson 1974: 203–30, and the literature cited there).

Adoption of an heir is not the only recourse a childless man has. In Genesis 16 Sarah gives Hagar, her own handmaiden, to Abraham, declaring her desire to produce a child through her. This is not the only time that a barren matriarch gives her handmaiden to her husband in the hope of bearing children: Rachel, also barren, gives Bilhah to Jacob. Here again the reason is so that she might have Bilhah give birth on her, (Rachel's), knees and thus reproduce through her (Gen 30:3). When Bilhah thereafter bears a son, Rachel calls him Dan (30:6), declaring that God has thus vindicated *(dn)* her cause. We find allusion to this rather peculiar custom in the Laws of Hammurabi in a section dealing with a man who marries a *naditu*—a priestess. This is a special class of women who may have been whores or nuns, but it is at least clear that whatever their sexual condition, they were not legally allowed to have children. Here we find:

144. If a man married a *naditu* and that *naditu* has given a female slave to her husband and she (the slave) has then produced children: if that man then decides to marry a *šugitu* (a secondary wife),[1] they may not allow that man (to do so); he may not marry the *šugitu.*

145. If a man married a *naditu* and she did not provide him with children and he decides to marry a *šugitu,* that man may marry a *sugitu,* bringing her into his house—with that *šugitu* to rank in no way with the *naditu.*

146. If a man married a *naditu* and she gave a female slave to her husband and she (the slave) has then borne children: if later that female slave has claimed equality with her mistress because she bore children, her mistress may not sell her, (but) she may mark her with the slave-mark and count her among the slaves.

147. If she did not bear children, her mistress may sell her.

Apart from the insights that this section gives us into the relationship between Sarah and Hagar, these provisions also indicate the reason behind this apparently peculiar custom. A woman was expected to bear children for her husband. If she could not do so, whether prohibited by law, as the *naditu* in Hammurabi, or otherwise incapable, he might marry another. Possibly to forestall this, the woman might give her own personal slave to her husband to bear the children for her. This handmaiden, although no longer a mere servant, must not become a rival to the original wife nor consider herself her equal.

One of our problems in interpreting the Laws of Hammurabi is that many of the domestic laws are cited only for the *naditu*, and for each provision we do not know whether that stipulation is unique to that class of women or typical of the status of all women. This is also the case with the grant of concubines, and we do not know if barren women in Babylon also gave their husbands concubines. Elsewhere in the Near East, however, we find documents relating to ordinary women that also mention this custom. In an interesting adoption tablet from Nuzi (HSS V 67 [Speiser 1930: 31–32]) a man gave his son Shennima in adoption to Shuriha-ilu so that he could become his heir. As part of this adoption agreement, Shennima is given a wife, Kelimninu. He must not take another wife, but if she does not bear children she will give him a woman from the Lullu-land (i.e., a slave girl) as his wife. The parallel is not exact, for Kelimninu goes abroad to get a servant girl rather than give Yalampa, the handmaiden mentioned in the same text as part of her dowry, to her husband. Nevertheless, the custom is the same, and it seems to have had a long history in the ancient Near East. We have a contract from Nimrud, one of the capitals of the Neo-Assyrian Empire, in which a certain Amat-Assartu gives her daughter Subietu in marriage to Milku with the proviso that should Subietu prove barren she should take a slave girl and give her to her husband, the sons thus born being her sons (Parker 1954: 37–39; van Seters 1968: 406–8; Grayson and van Seters 1975: 485–86). We also have an Old Assyrian text from Anatolia (ICK 3), twelve hundred years earlier than the Neo-Assyrian text, that records the marriage between Laqipum and Hatala. If within two years she does not provide him with offspring, she herself will purchase a slave woman. Later on, after she will have produced a child by him, he may dispose of her (the slave woman) by sale wheresoever he pleases (Hrozny 1939: 108–11; Lewy 1956: 8–10, and cf. text I 490 [Lewy 1956: 6–8] in which the man may himself buy a servant as a concubine).

These documents do not show uniform treatment of the proper relationship between the wife and the concubine, or the wife and the concubine's children. In Hammurabi the concubine who has borne children cannot be sold, although she can be demoted to the status of a slave. In the Old Assyrian text she can be sent away even after she has borne children, and this also seems to be indicated by the Neo-Assyrian text (according to the collation of line 46 by Postgate in Grayson and van Seters 1975: 485). In the Bible Sarah has Abraham send Hagar away, but only after much agonizing on his part and after the direct intervention of God. Similarly, the Neo-Assyrian text declares that the children born from the concubine are to be considered Subietu's children. This is the intention expressly stated by Rachel, who gives Bilhah to Jacob so that she can produce through her (Gen 30:3) and then declares that God has heeded her pleas by giving her a son (30:6). In Nuzi the situation is unclear because the broken line of HSS V 67 can be restored either *u šerri Gelimninu ala u-mar*, "and Kelimninu shall not send away the offspring" (Speiser 1930: 31, text 2:22) or, more probably, *u šerri Gelimninu-[m]a uwar*, "and Kelimninu shall have authority over the offspring" (Speiser 1964: 120). It is clearly Sarah's intention to "be built up" by giving Hagar to Abraham (16:2 [Speiser 1964: 121]), but Ishmael is never treated as Sarah's child, and he is ultimately sent away with Hagar (perhaps for this reason). The proper intrafamily relationships may have been subject to local customs or individual contract, but it is clear that the concept of the barren wife giving her husband a concubine is well established in the Near East.

SUCCESSION AND THE FIRST-BORN

As is often the case, no sooner does a couple adopt a child than the wife immediately becomes pregnant, and such adoptions have even been considered a treatment for infertility (Kardiman 1958: 123–26). When a hitherto childless man has acquired a child either through adoption or by being given the female slave of his wife, many very complex questions arise about the status of the children and their relationship to each other. The boys are certainly brothers, and any attempt to deny this was considered a serious matter. We have the record of an Old Babylonian lawsuit from Nippur (*Althabylonische Rechtsurkunden* 174) in which one brother claims that Shamash-Nasir is not his brother, that his father did not really adopt him. Witnesses are called who prove that Shamash-Nasir was truly adopted, and he is thereby reinstated to his inheritance. The brother who had attempted to deny him is himself disinherited. As an Old Babylonian text from Susa tells us (MDP 23 321:16): "According to the custom established by the gods Shushinak and Ishmekarab that brotherhood is brotherhood and sonship is sonship, the possessions of my father PN now belong to me." The child of the slave or second wife and the adopted son are thus real children and share in the inheritance. But who is the "eldest son," the one who receives the double portion? When all the sons are adopted, the heirship of the first may be stipulated in the contract, and one of the conditions to an adoption in fact may be that the adopter does not adopt any more children. But when a man acquires a natural son the situation is quite different. On one Nuzi adoption tablet, in which a man adopts his own brother as his son-and-heir, we read (HSS V 7): "If a son of my own is born to me, he shall be the oldest, receiving two inheritance shares. Indeed, should the wife of Akabshenni [the speaker] bear ten sons, they shall all be major (heirs), Shelluni following after." The term here used for "major heir" is the same as "eldest," chronological age is not always the determining factor and the natural son may precede, as here, all adoptive children in status as "eldest" even though he follows them in date of birth.

Although we have no justification for assuming that natural children *always* superseded adoptive ones, such a stipulation is not confined to the one document just discussed. We mentioned before an adoption tablet (HSS V 67) in which Shuriha-ilu adopted Shennima and gave him a wife. There are other contingencies in this contract. If Shuriha-ilu does have a natural son, that son will be the eldest and will inherit the double portion, with Shennima coming next. This text is very interesting for yet another reason. It is clear-cut, and one would think that Shennima would have no trouble in putting forth his claim to be the heir. Yet when Shuriha-ilu was about to die, another text (HSS V 48) tells us that a dispute about succession did in fact arise. A committee then went to visit Shuriha-ilu, who was apparently on his deathbed, and said to him, "Now you are alive, and claims are being raised against you. Since you may die, point out your son to us that we may know him." We must assume that Shuriha-ilu was not bound by the other document, which is not mentioned in this text, and could have appointed whomever he pleased.

He does appoint Shennima (who is, incidentally, his nephew) as his son and heir. From this case one might infer that even though Esau had sold Jacob his birthright, Isaac could nevertheless have appointed Esau his heir when he announced his intention to make a deathbed pronouncement with the formulaic phrase, "Now that I have grown old and know not the day of my death" (Gen 27:2), a phrase used elsewhere for just this purpose (Speiser 1955: 252–53). However, we really should await more evidence on this point.

To get back to the crucial problem of inheritance, it is clear that an adoptive son could be displaced as the eldest by a natural son. Similarly, when there was contest between the sons of a prime wife and the children of a slave, there was in fact no contest. In the Laws of Hammurabi we read:

> 170. If a man's wife bore him children: if the father during his lifetime has ever said "my children" to the children that the slave bore him, thus having counted them with the children of the first wife, then, after the father has gone to his fate the children of the slave shall share equally in the goods of the paternal estate, with the first-born, the son of the prime wife, receiving a preferential share.

The parallel is not perfect, i.e., this law refers to the children of any slave, rather than specifically of a slave given by a wife to her husband in fulfillment of her marital obligations. Nevertheless, it seems clear that Isaac, as the son of Sarah, the prime wife, could be legally considered the first-born even though he was chronologically younger than Ishmael. Sarah, however, is not really satisfied with this preferred status for her son—she does not want Ishmael to have any part in the inheritance, and wants him sent away. Such a situation is not unknown, for the Laws of Hammurabi continue:

> 171. If the father during his lifetime has never said "my children" to the children that the slave bore him: after the father has gone to his fate the children of the slave may not share in the goods of the paternal estate along with the children of the prime wife. Freedom for the slave and her children shall be effected, with the children of the prime wife having no claim against the children of the slave for service.

This is what Sarah wants to arrange while Abraham is still alive. He, however, is reluctant to do so, for we read in Genesis 21:11, "concerning his son." By calling him "his (my) son," he had legitimatized the boy. This was the reason for his having slept with Hagar, which he did at

Sarah's request and for the express purpose of bearing legitimate children. God intervenes, for it was his will that Isaac should be sole heir to the covenant. In the narrative as it stands God had already told Abraham (Gen 17) that Sarah would bear a son through whom the covenant would be renewed. God does not have to act arbitrarily against the laws and customs of his times in order to arrange his plan of having the son of Sarah inherit the covenant, for the times permit the choice of the son of the prime wife as the heir.

The situation is not much different when a man marries a second wife rather than take a slave girl as concubine. We have a Neo-Babylonian text (*VS* VI 3 1411 [Szlechter 1972: 106]) in which a man requests a girl named Kulla from her father, explaining that he has no children and that he is extremely desirous of having some. The contract stipulates that whenever Esagilbanata, the first wife of the man, has a son, he will get two-thirds of the patrimony. When Kulla gives birth, her son will get one-third of the patrimony. If the first wife has no children, then Kulla and her son are to inherit the entire property. Here we are not dealing with slave girl vs. mistress, but with two freeborn women both married by proper contract. Nevertheless, the chronological age of the son does not matter: the son of the first wife is automatically the "first-born" and major heir.

This brings us a little closer to the most ticklish situation of all—the plight of Jacob with his two unequal wives and two handmaidens, twelve sons, a daughter, and the necessity of choosing a chief heir. Reuben, as we know, was born first, and quite obviously expected to be the preferred heir. Joseph, the first-born of the beloved Rachel, seemed to think that he ought to be considered the first-born; he naïvely let his brothers know it by telling them his dreams of glory and power and by flaunting the preferential treatment that their father had given him. Was he simply being an obnoxious spoiled brat, or did he really have a legitimate claim? Was Jacob simply behaving like a silly old man doting on the son of his beloved Rachel, or was something legally significant involved? The law of Deuteronomy is quite clear that should a man have two wives, one beloved and the other despised, he may not give preferential status to the son of the beloved wife but must take the chronologically older son as the first-born who gets the double portion. Deuteronomy may have been composed (in the main) long before its promulgation in 621 B.C.E., but not before Sinai, and neither God nor Jacob could be expected to be bound by laws not yet in force. Furthermore, Jacob did marry two sisters at the same time, a marriage forbidden by Leviticus 18:18. It is clear that neither the pre-scription in Leviticus nor that in Deuteronomy had any bearing on the patriarchal period, and we cannot simply assume that Joseph had no claim to be heir. Leah, it is true, was married first, but only by a ruse, and Rachel's marriage agreement was made first. Rachel is clearly por-trayed as the desired wife, and Leah has to ask Rachel to send Jacob to sleep with her in return for the mandrakes (Gen 30:14–16). Jacob did manage to choose Joseph as chief heir. Although he had been rather clumsy in his early preferential treatment of Joseph, particularly in the incident of the "coat of many colors," in his old age he had learned to be cunning and devious. On his deathbed (where such pronounce-ments should be made) he adopted Joseph's two children, Ephraim and Manasseh, as his own sons, making them equal to Reuben and Simeon, and declaring that any other sons would inherit from them (Gen 48:5). He thus bypassed Joseph in order to give him the double portion due an heir through his children, and in that way accorded him the right of the first-born.

The Bible contains a consistent motif of the choosing of the younger son over the older. Isaac and not Ishmael, Jacob and not Esau, inherit the Covenant; Joseph (through his children) and not Reuben inherits the double portion. Moses outshines Aaron; David, and not his elder broth-ers, rules; and Solomon, and not his elders, inherits. More examples could be added to this list. God's plan unfolds through such choice, and primacy is not automatically achieved by birth rank. In order to achieve this aim, however, God does not have to act in an arbitrary or capricious manner, or to disorient society by disrupting the expected norms, for in the Near Eastern milieu the term "first-born," like the terms "son," "father," "brother," and "sister," is essentially a description of a particular juridical relationship which may be entered into by contract as well as by birth. People adopt others as brothers, brothers adopt each other as sons, brothers adopt women as sisters, and the designation of an indi-vidual as "first-born" can also be a matter of choice.

This article is based on a paper delivered 9 May 1975 to a symposium on "Biblical Themes in Western Literature: Brothers in Conflict" at Wayne State University.

NOTES

    1. In standard translations the *naditu* is usually translated "hierodule," and *šugitu* is translated "lay priestess." These, however, are misleading terms. There

is no evidence that *šugitu* were priestesses of any type, and the term seems to be limited to secondary wives, particularly when a *naditu* is prime wife. It is probably best to leave the terms untranslated.

BIBLIOGRAPHY

Grayson, K., and van Seters, J. "The Childless Wife in Assyria and the Stories of Genesis." *Orientalia* 44 (1975): 485–86.

Hrozny, B. "Über eine unveröffentlichte Urkunde vom Kultepe (ca. 2000 v. Chr)." *Symbolae ad iura Orientis Antiqui pertinentes Paulo Koschaker dedicatae Studia et Documenta* 2 (1930): 108–11.

Kardiman, S. "Adoption as a Remedy for Infertility in the Period of the Patriarchs." *Journal of Semitic Studies* 3 (1958): 123–26.

Lewy, J. "On Some Institutions of the Old Assyrian Empire." *Hebrew Union College Annual* 27 (1956): 1–79.

Parker, B. "The Nimrud Tablets 1952—Business Documents." *Iraq* 15 (1954): 29–30.

Prevost, M. "Remarques sur l'adoption dans la Bible." *Revue international des droits de l'antiquité* 14 (1967): 67–78.

Snijders, L. A. "Genesis XV: the Covenant with Abraham." *Oudtestamentische Studien* 12 (1957): 261–79.

Speiser, E. A. *New Kirkuk Documents Relating to Family Laws.* Annual of the American Schools of Oriental Research 10. New Haven: American Schools of Oriental Research, 1930.

———. "I Know Not the Day of My Death." *Journal of Biblical Literature* 74 (1955): 252–56.

———. *Genesis.* The Anchor Bible. Garden City, N.J.: Doubleday, 1964.

Szlechter, E. "Les Lois Neo-Babyloniennes (II)." *Revue international des droits de l'antiquité* 19 (1972): 43–128.

Thompson, T. L. *The Historicity of the Patriarchal Narratives: The Quest for the Historical Abraham.* Beiheft, Zeitschrift der alttestamenliches Wissenschaft 133. Berlin; New York: deGruyter, 1974.

Van Seters, J. "The Problem of Childlessness in Near Eastern Law and the Patriarchs of Israel." *Journal of Biblical Literature* 87 (1968): 401–8.

———. *Abraham in History and Tradition.* New Haven: Yale University, 1975.

16 / Law and Philosophy: The Case of Sex in the Bible*

1989

For the modern scholar, ancient law offers many challenges and types of inquiry. First and foremost, of course, it demands to be studied for itself, as a legal system of a society: how are problems adjudicated, what is to be done in the case of theft, what is the nature of property rights, and so forth? Second, it is a record of the socioeconomic system of that society: what are the social classes, who holds the property and how, what are the economic concerns addressed by the laws? Third, it presents questions of intellectual history: where did a given law come from, what is its relationship to other legal systems, what if any is the inner development within that society itself? And above all, it is an intellectual mirror of the philosophical principles of a given society. Through a culture's laws, we can see its values and some of its basic ideas about the world. Sometimes, our only access into the mind-set of a culture is through its laws. This is the case with sex in the Bible.

Sex is inherently problematic. At once cultural and physical, it defies categorization. In pagan religions there is a mystique, expressed through the sacred marriage ritual, in which sex has an important role in the bringing of fertility. The sacred marriage also gave rise to songs and poems that provided for the expression and celebration of sexual desire in a religious setting. Furthermore, the goddess of sexual attraction imparts a divine aspect to erotic impulse and a vocabulary to celebrate it and to mediate and diffuse the anxieties it may engender.

* For previous studies see Cosby, Dubarle, Larue, and Perry. This essay is based on my forthcoming book, *In the Wake of the Goddesses* (The Free Press: Macmillan, 1989).

SEX AND THE BIBLICAL GOD

But what about the Bible? Whatever may have been the case in empirical Israel, all the pagan sexual trappings disappear in the Hebrew Scriptures. The God of the Bible is male, which would make it difficult for him to represent the sex drive to a male. Even more, the God of Israel is only male by gender, not by sex. He is not at all phallic, and cannot represent male virility and sexual potency. Anthropomorphic biblical language uses body imagery of the arm, right hand, back, face, and mouth, but God is not imagined below the waist. In Moses' vision at Mount Sinai, God covered Moses with his hand until he had passed by, and Moses saw only his back (Exod 33:23). In Elijah's vision, he saw nothing, and experienced only a "small still voice" (1 Kgs 19:12). In Isaiah's vision (chap. 6), two seraphim hid God's (or the seraphim's) "feet" (normally taken as a euphemism), and in Ezekiel's vision (chaps. 1–2), there is only fire below the loins. God is asexual, or transsexual, or metasexual (depending on how we view this phenomenon), but he is never sexed.

Nor does God behave in sexual ways. God is the "husband" of Israel in the powerful marital metaphor. But there are no physical descriptions: God does not kiss, embrace, fondle, or otherwise express physical affection for Israel. By contrast, in the erotic metaphor that describes the attachment of Israel to Lady Wisdom, there is no hesitation to use a physical image, "hug her to you and she will exalt you, she will bring you honor if you embrace her" (Prov 4:8). Wisdom is clearly a woman-figure, and can be metaphorically embraced as a woman. But God is not a sexual male, and so there can be no physicality.

God could not model sexuality, hence it could not be a part of the sacred order. In order to underscore this, God also does not grant sexuality, erotic attraction, or potency. These are taken as matter-of-fact components of the universe and are not singled out as part of God's beneficence.

There is a concern to separate the sexual and the sacred. Before the initial revelation of God at Mount Sinai, Moses commanded Israel to abstain from sexual activity for three days (Exod 19:15).[1] This temporal separation between the sexual and the sacred also underlies the story of David's request for food during his days of fleeing from King Saul, in which he assures Ahimelech that his men can eat hallowed bread because they have been away from women for three days (1 Sam 21:4–5).

The priests, guardians of Israel's ongoing contact with the Holy, were to be conscientious in preserving a separation between Israel's priestly functions and attributes and any kind of sexuality. They were not celibate, a totally foreign idea, but their sexual activity had to be a model of controlled proper behavior. The unatonable wrong of Eli's sons was sleeping with the women who came to worship; for this they lost forever their own and their family's right to be priests (1 Sam 2:22–25). The priest's family also had to be chaste. His wife had to be a virgin, for he was not allowed to marry a divorcée. His daughters had a particular charge to be chaste while under their father's jurisdiction: he could not deliver his daughter into prostitution, and, should a priest's daughter be improperly sexually active, she was considered to have profaned *her father* and was to be burned.

Any sexuality was to be kept so far from temple service that even the wages of a prostitute were not to be given to a temple as a gift.[2] All hints of sexuality were kept far away from cultic life and religious experience.

The separation of sexuality and cult is also embedded in the impurity provisions of the sacral laws. Israel's impurity rules were intended to keep intact the essential divisions of human existence: holy and profane, life and death. They conveyed no moral valuation, and even doing a virtuous and societally necessary act, like burying the dead, would result in entering the impure state. There was also no danger involved in such "impurity"; the impure individual was not expected to die or to become ill. Such impurities were characterized by two major features: the major impurities (which last a week) were contagious, in that all who come in contact with someone impure in this way will themselves become impure for a day. And all those who are impure are isolated ritually: they cannot come to the temple or participate in sacred rites for the duration of their impurity.[3] Under these regulations, any man who has had a sexual emission, or anybody who has engaged in sexual intercourse must wash and will nevertheless be ritually impure until that evening (Lev 15:16–18). In this way, there was a marked temporal division between engaging in sexual activity and coming into the domain of the sacred.[4]

CONTROL OF SEXUAL ACTION BY LAW

Sexuality has been desacralized. It has not been demonized or condemned. On the contrary, it is not given sufficient status and importance to accord it a conscious valuation, even a negative one. It is talked about (or, most often, not talked about) as part of the social realm, as a question of societal regulation. The proper sphere for considering or mentioning sexuality was the law. The ideal state of existence envisioned by the Bible is marriage.[5] The monogamous nuclear family was established by God at the very beginning of human existence: "therefore a man leaves his father and mother and cleaves to his wife and they become one flesh" (Gen 2:24). Furthermore, "he who finds a wife, he finds a good thing and gets favor from the Lord" (Prov 18:22).[6] Within this marital structure, sexuality is not only permitted, it is encouraged. In God's description of life in the real world, he tells Eve, "your desire is for your husband, and he shall rule you" (Gen 3:16). Deuteronomy includes a provision for the exemption of a new bridegroom from campaigns for a year so that he may be free to cause his wife to rejoice (Deut 20:7, 24:5). The enjoyment of marriage is sexual as well as social:

> let your fountain be blessed:
> find joy in the wife of your youth—
> a loving doe, a graceful mountain goat,
> let her breasts satisfy you at all times,
> be infatuated with love of her always (Prov 5:17–18).

And the wise man is encouraged to enjoy his marital sexuality.

Sexuality has a place in the social order in that it bonds and creates the family. The sex laws seek to control sexual behavior by delineating the proper parameters of sexual activity—those relationships and time in which it is permissible. Sexual behavior was not free. Despite the indubitable double standard in which adultery means sex with a married woman, men were also limited by the sex laws. In the case of homosexuality, men were more bound than women, since homosexuality was considered a major threat requiring the death penalty (whether real or threatened) and lesbian sex was not a matter of concern. The unequal definition of adultery results from the fact that for a man to sleep with a woman who belonged to some other household threatened the definition of "household" and "family"; for a married man to sleep with an unattached woman is not mentioned as an item of concern, and the very existence of prostitutes indicates that there were women with whom a man (married or unmarried) could have sexual experiences. This was not an unusual definition of adultery, and it has been suggested that this unevenness is the essence of male control over female sexuality, and that possibly it demonstrates a desire to be certain of paternity. Within Israel this treatment of adultery is not examined: it is part of Israel's inheritance from the ancient Near East and, like slavery and other elements of social structure, it is never questioned in the Bible.

The Pentateuchal laws also rule on sexual intercourse with a girl still living in her father's house, at which time she is expected to be chaste. According to Exodus 22:15–16, if a man seduced an unbetrothed girl he had to marry her; he has engendered an obligation that he cannot refuse, and must, moreover, offer the customary bride-price. Her father had the option to refuse her to him, in which case the seducer must pay a full virgin's bride-price. The assumption in this rule is that the father has the full determination of his daughter's sexuality, a situation also assumed in the two horrible tales of the abuse of this right, Lot's offering of his daughters to the men of Sodom (Gen 18–19) and the man of Gibeah's offering of his daughter and the Levite's concubine to the men of Gibeah (Judg 19). These men were attempting to cope with an emergency situation in which they felt their lives were at risk, but the narrative considers them within their rights to offer their daughters, and Lot, in particular, is considered the one righteous man in Sodom.

The obligation a girl had to remain chaste while in her father's house is underscored in Deuteronomy 22:20ff., which prescribes that a bride whose new husband finds her not to be a virgin is to be stoned, because "she did a shameful thing in Israel, committing fornication while under her father's authority." There is good reason to suspect that this law was not expected to be followed. According to the procedure laid out in Deuteronomy 22:13–4, after the accusation, the case was brought before the elders at the gate, and the parents of the girl produced the sheet to prove that she was a virgin; once they did this, the man was flogged, fined, and lost his rights to divorce her in the future. Since the parents had plenty of time to find blood for the sheets, it is unlikely that a bridegroom would make such a charge; if he disliked the girl he could divorce her. If he nevertheless made such a charge, she and her family would have to be very ignorant not to fake the blood. But the law certainly lays down a theoretical principle very important to Israel, viz., that a girl is expected to be chaste while in her father's house. Stoning, moreover, is a very special penalty, reserved for those offenses which completely upset the hierarchical arrangements of the cosmos. In these cases, the entire community is threatened and endangered, and the entire community serves as the executioner.[7]

Stoning is also prescribed when a man comes upon a betrothed woman in town; in this case both are stoned; the girl because she did not cry for help (which would have been heard, since they were in town) and the man because he illicitly had sex with his neighbor's wife (Deut 22:23–24). The law assumes that the act was consensual: even though the word ענה is often translated "rape," it rarely corresponds to forcible rape but rather implies the abusive treatment of someone else. In sexual contexts, it means illicit sex, sex with someone with whom one has no right to have sex.[8] The sense of the law about sex with a betrothed woman is that a girl, although still a virgin, is legally considered married to the man to whom she has been betrothed; hence the two are guilty of adultery and are deserving of death. Moreover, death by stoning is prescribed, whereas in regular adultery the penalty is death, but not by stoning. Sex with a betrothed girl is compound adultery: the rights of the future husband have been violated, and the girl has offended against her obligations to her father.[9]

There is a question as to who properly exercises control over sexuality. In Exodus, the father can refuse to grant his daughter to her seducer; and this kind of paternal control is also implied in Lot's offering his daughters and the man at Gibeah offering his. But Deuteronomy indicates that the father's rights were not all that absolute (at least by the time of Deuteronomy). In Deuteronomy 22:28–29, if a man grabs an unbetrothed girl and they are found, the man is to give the father fifty shekels, and he must marry her without the right to divorce her in the future. Unlike the comparable law in Exodus, there is no mention of the father's right to refuse to give his daughter to this marriage. The laws have superseded his discretion and now require what had once been the father's discretionary act.

Husbands also do not have limitless control over their wives' sexuality. According to Assyrian laws, a husband has a right to determine the penalty for his adulterous wife, or even to pardon her outright; his freedom is limited only by the fact that whatever he chooses to do to his wife, the same will be done to her adulterous partner. Israel also may have known of such husbandly determination, for the Book of Proverbs, in warning the young man against adultery, warns him: "the fury of the husband will be passionate; he will show no pity on his day of vengeance. He will not have regard for any ransom; he will refuse your bribe, however great" (Prov 6:34–35). In the formal, scholastic formulation of the laws, however, the penalty for adultery is officially death, with no option of clemency.

Deuteronomy vests some of the control over these matters in the hands of the elders of Israel. It is their responsibility to uphold the social order and eliminate dangers to it. They try the recalcitrant son

(21:18–21); they investigate the question of the bride's virginity (22:13–19); they oversee the release of a *levir* (25:7); and they perform the decapitated heifer ceremony (21:1–9).

But above all, the laws place the locus of control outside the discretion of individuals, by prescribing mandatory sentencing for certain offenses and leaving others for divine sanction. In the prohibited relationships of Leviticus 20, adultery, homosexuality, bestiality, and sex with stepmother, mother-in-law, and daughter-in-law are all to be punished by death; sex with a sister, sister-in-law, aunt, uncle's wife, and menstruant are also prohibited, but they are outside social sanctions and are to be punished by God.

The Bible defines the parameters of permissible sexuality by forbidding intolerable relationships. One may not have a sexual relationship that infringes on another family (adultery or sex with a girl still in her father's household), but within one's own family there are strong incest prohibitions, detailed in Leviticus 18 and 20, and Deuteronomy 27. One cannot have sex with father and mother, stepmother, paternal uncle[10] and his wife, and both maternal and paternal aunts.[11] In one's own generation, both sister and brother's wife are prohibited.[12] In the next generation, one's daughter-in-law and, we presume, one's daughter[13] are prohibited, as are one's children's daughters. Furthermore, once one marries, one's wife's lineage is off limits: mother-in-law, wife's sister (while wife is still alive), wife's daughters and granddaughters.

These incest laws seem particularly complex, and it has been suggested that the laws sought to include all those women who might be found in the same household in an extended family. However, mothers-in-law would not have been expected in these households and prohibitions on father's daughters is explicitly said to include those daughters born outside the household. Moreover, these laws took their final form when Israel already had nuclear households. The laws are defining and clarifying family lines. There is a sense, expressed in Genesis, that the marital bond creates a family even though there are no blood ties, and so father's wife, father's brother's wife, and brother's wife are said to be prohibited because the "nakedness" (the conventional translation of Hebrew (הורע) of the woman is tantamount to the nakedness of her husband. So too, since one's wife is also bonded to him, her bloodlines (שאר) are parallel to his own and thereby prohibited. Sex within the family would blur family lines and relations and cause a collapse of family relations, and sex with daughter-in-law is explicitly called תכל–"mixing," in Leviticus 20:12.[14]

SEXUALITY AS DANGER TO BOUNDARIES

The power of sex to cross over the lines between households or blur distinctions between units of a family is an example of sex's power to dissolve categories. This is problematic on a national scale. This issue is clearly highlighted in Genesis 34, a chapter often called the "rape of Dinah," even though it is probably not about a forcible rape, and really is not a story about Dinah at all. Dinah had "gone out to see the daughters of the land."[15] Shechem saw her and lay with her, thus treating her improperly. In this way, he treated her as a whore (v. 31), a woman whose consent is sufficient because her sexuality is not part of a family structure. Even though Dinah may have consented to the act, the fact that he had not spoken to her parents in advance constituted an impropriety. The integrity of the family has been threatened, and Dinah's own wishes are incidental. Shechem, who loved her, asked his father, Hamor, to acquire her for him as his wife. But there are implications to this, made explicit by Hamor, who not only tendered the offer, but extended it, saying to Jacob, "Intermarry with us; give your daughters to us and take our daughters for yourselves; you will dwell among us, and the land will be open before you" (34:9–10); he further says to his own fellow townsmen, "the men agree with us to dwell among us and be as one kindred," even intermingling "their cattle, substance and all their beasts." This intermixing was the great threat to Jacob's family. Even though the generation of Jacob's sons was the first to intermarry with the local inhabitants, they had to do so under controlled conditions in which they could remain a distinct unit. The free exercise of erotic love by Shechem threatened that type of control. There is, of course, also a concern that intermarriage with non-Israelite women would make it possible for them to influence their husbands to worship other gods (Deut 7:1–5), as reportedly happened to King Solomon. Ultimately, after the return from Babylon, when the community of Israel was small and in danger of being overwhelmed by the other people in the land, these dual concerns resulted in a ban on foreign wives during the time of Ezra.

The desire to maintain categories is also a cosmic issue. The primeval history of Genesis, which underscores the basic features of human existence, is concerned to divide humanity from the divine realm, on the one hand, and the animal realm on the other. As humans become more cultured creatures, they become more god-like, not resembling the great monotheist conception of God, but certainly like the divine beings to whom God speaks in Genesis 1–11, the בני אלהים. To preserve the difference between humans and divine, God takes steps to insure the ultimate mortality of humans. This difference is threatened when the בני אלהים find human women fair (they were, after all, created in the physical likeness of the divine beings) and begin to mate with them. To further reinforce the difference, God limited the human lifespan (Gen 6:1–4).

As a practical matter, one did not have to be overly concerned with human-divine matings. No divine beings were observed in the post-flood era seducing human women; presumably women were not successfully attributing unexpected babies to angelic intervention; and there is no record in the Bible of divine females coming to seduce the men of Israel, even in their sleep.

But the animal-human boundary was more problematic. The primeval history acknowledges a kinship between humans and animals: Genesis 1 understands God to have created the land animals on the same day as humans, and Genesis 2 records that the animals were first created as companions to Adam. After the flood, action was taken to establish a clear and hierarchical boundary between the human and animal world: humans could kill animals for food (sparing the blood), whereas no animal could kill a human without forfeiting its own life. In reality, this uncrossable boundary of human existence could be easily crossed by mating with animals. Such mating could threaten the very existence of humanity, for the blurring of borders would be a return to chaos.[16] Every legal collection strongly forbids bestiality (Exod 22:28, Lev 18:23, 20:15–16, Deut 17:21); Leviticus 18:23 explains that bestiality is תבל, "(improper) mixing."

The maintaining of categories is particularly important in the Priestly writings, for one of the essential Priestly functions was the maintenance of the categories of existence (pure and impure, holy and profane, permissible and impermissible foods, family lines, sacred time, sacred space). But preoccupation with neatness is not limited to Leviticus; Deuteronomy also manifests this concern, prohibiting even the wearing of linsey-woolsey cloth, which combines wool from animals and linen from plants (Deut 22:9–11, cf. Lev 19:19).

Deviations from these neat categories are dangerous, and Leviticus proscribes male homosexuality under penalty of death (Lev 20:13, cf. 18:22). This extreme aversion to homosexuality is not inherited from other Near Eastern laws,[17] and must make sense in the light of biblical thought. It does not really disturb family lines, but it does blur the distinction between male and female, and this cannot be tolerated in the biblical system. Anything that smacks of homosexual blurring is similarly prohibited, such as cross-dressing (Deut 22:5).[18]

It has long been noted that lesbianism is not mentioned. This is not because these Levitical laws concern only male behavior; bestiality is explicitly specified to include both male and female interaction with beasts. But lesbianism was probably considered a trivial matter: it involved only women, with no risk of pregnancy; and, most important, it did not result in true physical "union" (by the male entering the female).

PUBLIC INTEREST IN CONTROL OF SEX

Issues such as adultery, incest, homosexuality, and bestiality are not simply the private concerns of families. Like murder, they are treated as a national issue for, like murder, sexual abominations are thought to pollute the land. The very survival of Israel was at stake. Leviticus 18 relates that the inhabitants of the land before Israel indulged in the incestuous relations listed there, in bestiality and homosexuality and Molech-worship, and that as a result the land became defiled and vomited out its inhabitants. Israel is warned against doing these same abominations: "Let not the land spew you out for defiling it, as it spewed out the nation that came before you" (Lev 18:28). Israel's right of occupation is contingent upon its care not to pollute the land with murder, illicit sex, and idolatry. The people must not only refrain from murder, they must also not pollute the land by letting murderers go free or allowing accidental murderers to leave the city of refuge (Num 35:31–34) or by leaving the corpses of the executed unburied (Deut 21:22–23). So too, they must not only refrain from such illicit sex as adultery and incest, but must also be careful to observe even such technical regulations as not allowing a man to remarry his wife who has divorced and since remarried (Deut 24:1–3; Jer 3:1–4).

The danger to the nation that ensues from murder and adultery explains the mandatory death sentence; it also clarifies two very odd biblical rituals. In the ceremony of the decapitated heifer, when a corpse is found but no one can identify the murderer, the elders of the city nearest the corpse go to a wadi and decapitate a heifer, declaring their lack of culpability and seeking to avert the blood-pollution of the land (Deut 21:1–9, see also Patai and Zevit). The second ritual is the trial of the suspected adulteress (Num 5:11–21; Frymer-Kensky 1983), which provides that whenever a husband suspects his wife he is to bring her to the temple, where she is to drink a potion made from holy water, dust from the floor of the sanctuary, and the dissolved curse words while answering "amen" to a Priestly adjuration that should she be guilty the water will enter into her and cause her "belly to swell and her thighs to drop" (probably a prolapsed uterus). After this oath she returns to her husband. This ritual allowed a husband to resume marital relations after he suspected adultery. Otherwise, intercourse with a wife who had slept with another man could be expected to pollute the land in the same way as remarriage to a divorced wife who had been married in the interim.

Improper sexual activity had even greater danger than the threat to Israel's right to the land (which was certainly a serious consideration). The blurring of the categories of human existence through sexual activity was a danger to creation, for in biblical cosmology the universe is seen rather like a house of cards; if the lines are not kept neat, the whole edifice will collapse, "the foundations of the earth will totter." Wrongful sexual activity can bring disaster to the world.

CONCLUSION

This is the great problematic of sex. The ideal of the bonded, monogamous nuclear family conveys a positive place for sexuality within the social order. But at the same time, the same sexual attraction which serves to reinforce society if it is controlled and confined within the marital system can destroy social order if allowed free rein. Sexuality itself is good, but the free exercise of sexuality is a prime example of wrongful activity. The exercise of free sexuality (particularly by the woman, who owes sexual exclusivity to the man) is the prime example of a lack of fidelity and a failure of allegiance. In time, all wrongful behavior was seen through the metaphor of sexual activity, with the result that in the prophets, particularly Hosea, Jeremiah, and Ezekiel, there is so much sexual imagery that it is hard to sort out what might be a literal depiction of too much sexual license from a metaphorical depiction of allegiance to foreign powers and other gods.

There is no coherent biblical treatment of sexuality. On the surface, sexuality is treated as a question of social control: who with whom, and when. There is only one explicit statement that sexuality is a cosmic force: "For love is fierce as death, passion is mighty as Sheol, its darts are darts of fire, a blazing flame; vast floods cannot quench love, nor rivers drown it" (Sg 8:6–7). The stories of Pharaoh and Sarah, David and Bathsheba, and Amnon and Tamar show a sense that erotic attraction can cause men to abuse their superior position and strength.[19]

But all of this is inchoate and essentially inarticulate. There is no vocabulary in the Bible in which to discuss such matters, no divine image or symbolic system by which to mediate it. God does not model sex, is not the patron of sexual behavior, and is not even recorded as the guarantor of potency; and there is no other divine figure who can serve to control or mediate sex. Our only indication that the Bible considers sex as a volatile, creative, and potentially chaotic force is from the laws themselves. These laws of control reveal a sense that sexuality is not really matter-of-fact, that it is a two-edged sword: a force for bonding and a threat to the maintenance of boundaries. They cut through the silence on this topic, which we consider so important, but about which there is little explicit mention in the Bible. Through the laws we can find an inkling of biblical Israel's appreciation and anxiety about the topic of such vital concern.

The laws also reveal a great danger: when a society has such legitimate concerns about an important aspect of life, it needs a way to discuss and channel anxieties productively. This the Bible does not provide. We can see the concerns about sex expressed in the laws, but we cannot see how they were mediated, detoxified, expressed, and understood. The result is a core emptiness in the Bible's discussion of sex. This vacuum was possibly filled by folk traditions not recorded in the Bible. Ultimately, in Hellenistic times, it was displaced by the complex of anti-woman, anti-carnal ideas that had such a large impact on the development of Western religion and civilization.

NOTES

1. The point of this command is to separate the sexual from the sacred experience. This purpose is often obscured by the unfortunate male-centered wording of the passage. God is reported as having commanded that the people wash and sanctify themselves and wash their clothes, making preparations for the third day (Exod 19:10–11). When Moses relayed this to the people, he added his own command, "do not approach your wives" (Exod 19:15). By this addition Moses explains how the people are to prepare for the third day, but he adds his own perspective, suddenly erasing half the people, addressing only the men. It is interesting that the Bible records this as Moses' invention rather than God's; it sheds new light on the Deuteronomic injunction to the people not to add to the laws.

2. On the basis of the interpretation of the term קדשה, "holy one," as a cult prostitute, scholars have long argued the existence of sacred prostitution in Israel, which the Bible was trying to stamp out. More recent work has indicated that there is absolutely no evidence that a קדש was a prostitute, nor that any sexual rites ever existed in ancient Israel. In any event, the wages not to be vowed to the temple are those of a זנה, which everyone agrees is an ordinary prostitute for hire, not attached to the temple.

3. For a detailed discussion of these issues, see Frymer-Kensky, 1983; Douglas. My analysis is somewhat different from that of Mary Douglas's classic study in that she does not distinguish between the "impurity" beliefs, which deal with a contagious state which is neither morally deserved nor dangerous to the individual, and Israel's separate set of dangerous pollutions, a noncontagious state caused by misdeeds which bring the perpetrator into the danger of divine sanction.

4. Menstrual taboos are also to some extent sexual taboos. In Israel, a woman was impure for seven days after the beginning of her menses. During this period, her impurity (as all impurity) was contagious, and could be contracted by anyone who touched her, or even sat in her seat. Intercourse with a menstruating woman was considered absolutely forbidden, and was sanctioned by the כרת penalty, which means the belief that one's lineage would be extirpated. The reminder in menstruation of a sexual dimension of existence would not by itself account for the seven-day duration of the impurity, however. Another element is at play, the blood and its association with death, for contact with death also results in a weeklong impurity. It is noteworthy that only intercourse with a menstruant results both in temporary impurity and in the divine sanction of כרת.

5. That marriage was evaluated positively throughout the ancient Near East, see Lambert.

6. For Proverbs, see Snell. Snell notes the structural parallel to 8:33, in which Dame Wisdom says "he who finds me finds life and gets favor from the Lord."

7. On stoning, see Finkelstein. In addition to the two cases discussed here, stoning is used for the ox that gores a man to death (Exod 21:12–14), one who lures others into idolatry (Deut 13:7–8), the practitioner of child sacrifice (Lev 20:3d), a sorcerer or necromancer (Lev 20:27), blasphemer (Lev 24:10–11), violator of the Sabbath (Num 15:32–35), and, by inference, the seditionist (1 Kgs 21).

8. In the sexual uses of this root, there are instances where it means rape: in Judges 19–20, where the concubine in Gibeah was raped to death; and in the story of Amnon and Tamar, in which he is said to have overpowered her (2 Sam 13:12–13); and in Lamentations, in which the women of Zion are said to have been raped (Lam 5:11). But forcible rape is not always the issue. Some cases are ambiguous. In Deuteronomy 22:28–29, a man has grabbed

an unbetrothed girl; he must marry her and not divorce her, because he has illicitly had sex with her. The same scenario is involved in the story of Dinah and Shechem (Gen 34). There is no indication in the story that Shechem overpowered her. The issue is that she was not free to consent, and he should have approached her father first. Similarly, the man who sleeps with a menstruant (Ezek 22:10) or with his paternal sister (Ezek 22:11) is said to have "raped" her only in the sense of "statutory rape," i.e., that he had no right to have sex with her even if she consented. In Deuteronomy 21:10–13, the verb paradoxically seems to imply a failure to offer a sexual relationship. This is the case of a man who takes a captive woman as a wife. She must first spend a month in his house mourning her past, after which the man can have sex with her. If, however, he does not want her, he must emancipate rather than sell her, for he has "violated" her. He has put her in a position in which she expected to become his wife, and then has not carried through. The verb does not always have sexual connotations; in nonsexual contexts it means to treat harshly, exploitatively, and/or abusively. Sarah treated Hagar oppressively (Gen 16:6, 9); Laban warns Jacob not to treat his daughters badly (Gen 31:50). The most common subject is God, who is said to treat Israel badly (Deut 8:2, 3, 16; 2 Kgs 17:20; Isa 64:11; Nah 1:12), David and his seed (1 Kgs 11), the suffering servant (Isa 53:4), and individual sufferers (Pss 88:8, 89:23, 119:71, 75; Job 30:11). The most common victim is Israel, which is treated badly by God, by Egypt (Gen 15:13; Exod 1:11–13), and by enemies (2 Sam 7:10, Isa 60:14; Zeph 3:10; Ps 94:4; Lam 3:33).

9. In the case of actual rape, as when a man grabs the betrothed girl, the offense is capital, but only the man is culpable. Forcible rape is explicitly likened to murder, a realization that rape is a crime of aggression and violence rather than sex, and that the girl is a victim (Deut 22:25–27).

10. Occasionally in these laws, a male is mentioned, which seems to indicate that the law also considers women and their permissible relations, but does not consistently list all of a female ego's choices.

11. It is hard to know whether the omission of mother's brother means that mother's brother and his wife were permitted as being of a different family, or whether they would have been prohibited. A similar question arises with father's brother's children (first cousins) and with brother's and sister's daughters. In this case it would seem that since father's brother is prohibited, brother's daughter must also be, even though it is not mentioned.

12. This was not always so in Israel. In Gen 20:16, Sarah and Abraham are described as having the same father by different mothers. A similar situation lies behind Tamar's entreaty to her would-be-rapist paternal brother Amnon: "Speak unto the king, for he will not withhold me from thee" (2 Sam 13:13). This is not the only instance in which the patriarchal and Davidic narratives differ from later biblical law. Jacob is married to two sisters, which is

not allowed in Leviticus. Jacob's and David's sons vie for inheritance position while, according to Deuteronomy, the first to be born is considered the first-born, whatever the wishes of the father.

13. The omission of daughter in the prohibited relations is another glaring omission. One might argue that since grandchildren are prohibited, children must also be, but one might equally argue that the idea of paterfamilias was still strong enough that the laws could not absolutely prohibit a father's access to his daughter. From the expectation of virginity in unmarried daughters, however, it is clear that father-daughter incest was neither expected nor encouraged.

14. It is also called זמה in Lev 20:14, a term reserved in these laws for incest outside blood kin, applied to mother-in-law, wife's sister, wife's daughter and granddaughter.

15. Probably a snide remark on the order of "she asked for it."

16. On the importance of categories in Israel, see Douglas; Frymer-Kensky, 1983; and Finkelstein.

17. Though the Sumerian laws consider an accusation of catamy as parallel to an accusation that one's wife is fornicating.

18. Having eunuchs is not considered the same kind of blurring. A eunuch, like people with visible physical defects, could not serve in the Temple. But eunuchs were found in Israel, particularly in the royal court (2 Kgs 20:17–18, Isa 56:3–4; Jer 29:2, 34:19, 38:7, 41:16).

19. John Van Seters believes this a particular motif in the Succession History and the Yahwist corpus. He also considers the concubine tales of Abner and Rizpah, and Adohijah and Abishag to be instances of this, but he does not sufficiently consider the political rather than sexual motivations of these acts. See further Blenkinsop. I cannot agree that the emphasis is on love leading to death, though I agree with Van Seters that in none of these stories is the woman blameworthy.

BIBLIOGRAPHY

Blenkinsopp, J. J. "Theme and Motif in the Succession History (2 Sam 11:2f.) and the Yahwist Corpus." *VTSup* 15 (1966):44–57.

Cosby, Michael R. *Sex in the Bible*. Englewood Cliffs, N.J.: Prentice Hall, 1985.

Douglas, Mary. *Purity and Danger: Analysis of Concepts of Pollution and Taboo*. New York: Praeger, 1966.

Dubarle, A. M. *Amour et fecondité dans le bible*. Toulouse: Privat, 1967.

Finkelstein, J. J. "The Ox That Gored." *Transactions of the American Philosophical Society* 71 (1981):26–29.

Frymer-Kensky, Tikva. "Purity, Pollution and Purgation in Biblical Israel." In *The Word of the Lord Shall Go Forth: Essays in Honor of David Noel Freedman*, edited by Carol Meyers and M. O'Connor, 399–414. Philadelphia: Free Press, 1982.

———. "The Strange Case of the Suspected Sotah (Numbers v 11–31)." *VT* 34 (1983):11–26.

Lambert, W. G. "Celibacy in the World's Old Proverbs." BASOR 169 (1963):63–64.

Larue, Gerald. *Sex and the Bible.* Buffalo, N.Y.: Prometheus, 1984.

Perry, Frank L. *Sex and the Bible.* Atlanta: Christian Education Research Institute, 1982.

Patai, Rafael. "The 'Egla 'Arufa or the Expiation of the Polluted Land." *JQR* 30 (1939):59–69.

Snell, Daniel C. "Notes on Love and Death in Proverbs." In *Love and Death in the Ancient Near East: Essays in Honor of Marvin H. Pope*, edited by John Marks and Robert Good. Guilford, Conn.: Four Quarters Publishing Co, 1986.

Van Seters, John. "Love and Death in the Court History of David." In *Love and Death in the Ancient Near East: Essays in Honor of Marvin H. Pope*, edited by John Marks and Robert Good, 121–24. Guilford, Conn.: Four Quarters Publishing Co, 1987.

Zevit, Ziony "The 'Egla Ritual of Deuteronomy 21:1–9." *JBL* 95 (1976):377–90.

17 / *Halakhah*, Law, and Feminism

1995

The last three decades have seen an enormous paradigm shift in our perception of reality and history. The old ideas of "objective science" on which many of us were raised, the old conceptions of History as "what actually happened," of Text as having "one correct reading and original meaning," and of Law as "what is legislated" have yielded to a view of complex interactions of the viewer and the viewed, the text and its readers, the law and its adherents. These decades have also witnessed sweeping sociological changes, and together they have created a renewed interest in *halakhah*, in the way that it works (or does not work, according to one's viewpoint), and in the relationship of *halakhah* to the theological and ethical teachings of Judaism. The collapse of legal positivism and the rise of contemporary philosophies of law have contributed to this new discourse, as has feminism, which has been both cause and result of our current intellectual and social revolution. This article looks at one important statement of the feminist critique of *halakhah*, that of Judith Plaskow in *Standing Again at Sinai*. In this very serious book, full of expert analysis and excellent insights into the workings of Judaism, Plaskow delineates the problems of traditional Judaism and suggests ways in which Judaism can be modified to be a truly feminist religion. This article is not a review of her book, for each section of her book deserves a careful reading. Rather, it takes her feminist analysis of the *halakhah* as a springboard to continued halakhic reasoning; doing so can lead to perhaps a new contribution to the current halakhic discourse.

To Plaskow, as to many other Jews, *halakhah* is the central defining element of Judaism; it is observance of the law rather than adherence to theological principles that marks one as a religious Jew; "law takes precedence over beliefs and feelings, which are expected to flow from action rather than to ground it" (p. 22). Nevertheless, she is very

255

suspicious of the claim that without *halakhah* there is no Judaism, and she rejects any predetermination of a Judaism rebuilt to include women's experience (p. 72). She presents a multitiered critique of *halakhah*. Her first layer of objection is the content of many laws, laws that exclude women from public worship and thus make them peripheral Jews, and laws that affect women's status in the family and sometimes result in the life-destroying problem of divorce. On these issues, as Plaskow admits, discussions easily polarize along denominational lines. Orthodox feminists are concerned with halakhic change, and non-Orthodox feminists see such change either as relatively straightforward or as irrelevant. The next layer of her critique addresses the problem of the androcentricity of the law. The law is male defined, and women are objects. As a result, in the religious sphere women are considered enablers and in family matters they are essentially passive, often not having control in important areas of their lives. Woman is the Other, and this fact shapes the questions that the legal system asks as well as the answers that it gives.

Plaskow poses a further question to explore: Is this androcentric law completely man-made, or have women had a role in shaping and transmitting it? On this, she remarks that legislators often formalize already prevailing customs, that the tradition itself records that certain laws were initiated by women, and that women took certain extralegal obligations upon themselves. But even if women actually had considerable input into the law, nevertheless the issue may be that law is not a form that women would normally use to express themselves.

Plaskow realizes that this last question is problematic, for it seems to presuppose an innate female nature. The very question is suggested by Carol Gilligan's now famous work on the games of girls and boys, in which girls were shown to be more interested in preserving their relationships and boys more interested in following the rules.[1] Gilligan's work has provoked a storm of controversy in feminist ethical theory and legal philosophy.[2] Plaskow understands the issue. She is not an essentialist and realizes that Gilligan's work revealed the result of socialization rather than innate male-female difference. Nevertheless, she suggests, *halakhah* might not have been the way that women chose to express their religious spirit had the choice of determining Jewish religion been theirs.

Much of Plaskow's critique of *halakhah* is a critique of traditional Orthodox Judaism. Not all forms of Judaism are halakhically oriented. Reconstructionist and Reform Jews consider themselves post-halakhic, and it is understandable that issues of halakhic change are not burning issues for feminists of these movements. But Plaskow does not really consider the issues of Conservative Judaism, a movement that considers itself bound by *halakhah* but that has been very receptive to changing *halakhah* to reflect a changed understanding of women. On the issues with which feminists are concerned there are *two halakhahs*, the old (Orthodox) *halakhah* and the new *halakhah*. The content of the new *halakhah* reflects somewhat the issues of the feminist movement. Women are no longer peripheral in religious matters: they can consider themselves enablers, but they can also make themselves obligated to the same public and private ritual obligations as the men.

In family law, things are much less sanguine in the new *halakhah*. The agonizing problem of the *agunah*, the married woman who cannot obtain a religious divorce, has been alleviated by the Conservative *halakhah* through their reactivation of an old procedure in which the religious court takes the initiative and dissolves the marriage when the husband is not willing to do so. This is not a complete solution, for it leaves the essential passivity of women in marriage intact. The man takes a woman in marriage, the man (or the court) releases her. The situation is often painful and humiliating for women, who must undergo intimate questioning by the court so it can determine whether it will indeed act. Furthermore, since most rabbinic courts are composed of men, the woman seeking divorce may (in the heat of divorce bitterness) see this tribunal of people as naturally allied with her husband. The woman who is ultimately released from the marriage does not have to suffer the fate of the *agunah*. Nevertheless, it is reasonable to hope for a better solution. In Reconstructionist Judaism, both husband and wife can issue the divorce decree *(get)*. Conservative Judaism could accomplish the same result through a rabbinic ordinance, passed by the Law Committee and the Rabbinical Assembly, that would establish women as active agents in the taking in marriage and the granting of divorce. That they have not done so is an indication of the incompleteness of feminist awareness in the Conservative movement. As more and more women become rabbis and vocal religious leaders, they have a chance to make the new *halakhah* ever more inclusive and egalitarian.

Women have always had a role in shaping *halakhah*. The Talmud records that women extended the monthly period of sexual abstinence by a week.[3] Whether they actually did so or whether the Rabbis were eager to convince them that they did is moot. There are other indications that women have had input into law. They could simply ignore the law. For example, we have evidence that they did so with the law against women's voices being heard in song; the "law" is clear, but men are not allowed to enforce its application. Similarly with the "laws" prescribing the missionary position for sex, other positions are "prohibited," but the courts must not inquire into what people actually do in their bedrooms.

There are also cases where women demanded to be included in the law or simply began to perform the obligations. Strictly speaking, in the old *halakhah* women were not required to eat in the sukkah or hear the shofar blown on Rosh Hashanah. They began to do so in such numbers, however, that even among the Orthodox many halakhic authorities now believe that women are obligated to do so by virtue of having taken this obligation upon themselves.[4] Another example of the process of women's influence on law is the question of who lights Hanukkah candles. The Talmud records that women are obligated to light the Hanukkah candles because women had a part in the miracle of Hanukkah. A thousand years later women had ceased to light them and the custom (at least in Europe) was that women would ask men to light them. In this century the pattern of observance has changed again as more and more women light their own candles.

The old *halakhah* reflected old family arrangements, which were caused as much by socioeconomic patterns as by laws, and which encouraged survival in the premodern age. The furthest-reaching example of women's ability to influence the development of *halakhah* is the great sea change of our current generation which has produced the new *halakhah*. In the early 1970s a group of women who had been educated in Jewish matters constituted themselves as *ezrat nashim* (the women's section) and demanded equal treatment under Jewish ritual law. They stressed the unfairness of a situation in which women who were learned could neither be counted in a prayer quorum nor be honored by being called to bless the Torah or lead in prayers, while any adult male would automatically receive these privileges. The press laughed at them—but the Conservative rabbis listened, studied these matters, and asked for input from the people. All of the demands of this group have now been met by the movement: women may be counted in a minyan, they may perform all ritual acts that men perform, they can be ordained rabbis and cantors.

The revolution in women's religious roles has not been easy and has had some schismatic consequences. Furthermore, not all Conservative synagogues have adopted the egalitarian innovations. Some synagogues are totally egalitarian, some are not at all, and most have an illogical and presumably temporary pattern of the inclusion and exclusion of women. The changes are nevertheless tantamount to a revolution.

As the position of women in family law indicates, the revolution is not complete. The current battleground is the question of including avowed homosexuals into the rabbinate, and at the moment the forces of change do not seem to be prevailing. But there is at least a history of change, and an indication that *halakhah* can be responsive to liberal demands. Just as it was unimaginable to the Rabbis that the values they lived by were not contained in Torah, and just as feminist midrash is fueled by the conviction that the Torah can be made to speak to today, so too it is unimaginable that the values taught through Torah cannot be lived through *halakhah*.

We call *halakhah* "Jewish Law," but it has no sanctions. There is no state enforcing compliance, and even rabbinic courts depend on persuasion and informal social sanctions. In non-Orthodox circles, concepts of reward and punishment after death or in the messianic world have only symbolic meaning for most Jews. In the Jewish Diaspora of the twentieth century, *halakhah* has strictures without consequences. The performance of a commandment (mitzvah) is its own reward, and there is no punishment for its nonperformance or violation. The etymology of the term "*halakhah*" also indicates that the system is not quite "law." In the language of the Babylonians and Assyrians the words *tertu*, Torah, and *alaktu, halakhah*, both refer to divine instruction from oracles.[5] "Torah" is what the god teaches, "*halakhah*" is the path of the god. The *halakhah* is the path of God in the world and the path of the world to God, the path that we travel through the infinite possibilities of lifestyle and life. More than just legal decisions, it is our *ho*.[6] It is also our *nomos*, the way we conceive alternative (ideal) reality and the bridge that links our reality to this vision. A community's shared vision entails rules and procedures for reaching and attaining it. These need not be coercive; rather, they provide the "map" to follow to approach the shared vision.

The vision of the Torah is *malkhut shamayim*, the kingdom of God on earth, which means a more perfect universe. This vision determines the map and provides a way to judge individual rules. But our vision of what the perfect universe would be changes over time, and we must both constantly refine this vision and continually adjust the rules so that they continue to lead to the kingdom of God and not to some travesty of it. For example, the talmudic Rabbis realized that slavery cannot be part of the perfect universe, and so Rabbinic *halakhah* did away with slavery. During our generation we have realized that patriarchy cannot be part of this universe, and the new *halakhah* has at least begun to dismantle religious patriarchy.

Feminist principles involve more than simple egalitarianism. As Plaskow points out, the feminist experience also emphasized relationships, an open structure, and a commitment to fluidity. The key question is whether these values cannot also be realized through *halakhah* or whether they are inherently nonnomian.

As Plaskow realizes, feminism and Judaism share an emphasis on the importance of community, their understanding of personhood as self-in-community. Jewish law serves to foster and sanctify the relationship of Israel to God; it also understands that the only way to promote a good relationship to God is to demand good relationships between people. The laws enacted and the legal decisions were intended more to create a harmonious community than to define and protect individual rights. There are, in fact, many ways in which Jewish law (the product of a marginalized and often oppressed people) resembles the "Different Voice" of feminine jurisprudence: Litigants are urged to have their case settled by compromise, judges are given great individual discretion, individuals are instructed to be more concerned with their obligations than with their "rights."[7] Sometimes, indeed, individuals have suffered because of this concern for relationships. For example, divorce courts have refused to coerce husbands to grant divorces, forcing the couples to try to work out the disputes by themselves. The principle under which the courts do this is not the rights of the husband, but rather the often cited principle of "family harmony" *(shalom bayit)*. Of course, a focus on community and on maintaining relationships is no guarantee that the law will serve the oppressed; indeed it often reinforces the status quo unless other principles of equity and communal vision are held higher than the web of community. The concern for relationships implicit in feminist jurisprudence must be balanced against other principles, but this is so for *halakhah* as well as for feminism.

The next serious concern is the question of an open structure. The current halakhic structure is highly centralized: The individual listens to his or her rabbi (the local authority, *mara d'atra*); the rabbi in turn addresses questions to recognized legal decisors or (in the Conservative movement) to the Law Committee. Is this hierarchy absolutely essential to the law, or can it be decentralized? In practice, the pyramidal structure already is often modified: the current generation of rabbis frequently decides matters of *halakhah in consultation* with the members of their community. Similarly, local rabbis (with or without prior consultation) sometimes ignore decisions of the Law Committee. A close analysis of the system indicates that these are not exceptions to the rule but are an inherent part of the *halakhah* process. The Talmud speaks of discovering *halakhah* by seeing what the people are doing. There are, moreover, examples in Jewish history (*Tashlikh* comes to mind) in which the people ignored rabbinic dictates until finally the rabbis went along with the people. Halakhic rebellion, like civil disobedience, is a very effective mechanism for halakhic change. A modern liberal philosophy of law must acknowledge and incorporate the role of the people in the ongoing interpretation of Torah. This is not a radical change in *halakhah*—it is a radical change from the narrow way in which *halakhah* has been conceived in the last several hundred years. An understanding of the role of the community, in fact, raises the question as to whether anyone should have the right to give up his or her responsibility for the formation of *halakhah*.

An acknowledgement of plural sources and multiple perspectives in the halakhic process also admits to a plurality of opinions. Norms and principles are a necessity for any group that wants to transform the world or at least its own existence. The difficulty arises when these rules are codified in such a way as to eliminate multiple options. The Mishnah usually records dissenting opinions, and the Gemara is as interested in the arguments as in the final decisions.[8] It is not until the Geonic period that the idea develops that one must have only one authoritative halakhic answer, and it is even later that the impulse to codify takes over. The codes take *halakhah* out of the context of process and thereby distance the statutes themselves from the goals of Torah. A more fluid approach to *halakhah* is not contrary to Judaism and can, in fact, create the kind of halakhic excitement that entails a real commitment to the ideals of Torah.

One cannot remove law from the rest of a culture's ideas. The *halakhah* is an integral part of the Jewish vision of a better universe. The halakhic statutes themselves must lead to this universe, and the principles of this vision should form the backdrop according to which individual judgments can be judged. Some of these metahalakhic principles are made very explicit in the Torah. "Be Holy!" and "Peace." Others certainly include the imperatives to care for each other in the community and to do no harm, as well as the concept of the full humanity of all people. With our contemporary understanding, we should include the idea of inclusivity—bringing the maximal number of people under the wings of *Shekhinah*. There are other principles that need to be discussed by the community as it formulates its vision of the perfect universe. When adherence to a status quo becomes more important than the obligation to continually create a moral order, then the particular *halakhah* is getting in the way of the job of *halakhah*, which is to show us the way to the kingdom of God. This is a standard by which to judge the life of norms and rules. Statutes and practices must be subordinated to this cultural vision.

This contemporary theory of *halakhah* is informed by the very principles that feminism holds most dear: the importance of community, the ethics of care, the full status of women, the value of diversity. It is also animated by a full recognition that the law comes out of and informs both a social order and the aspirations of that society. When we recognize that these principles are the source of the law (rather than divine or governmental dictation), then we must recognize our responsibility to keep adjusting the law to keep us pointed toward a better reality.

NOTES

1. Carol Gilligan, *In a Different Voice: Psychological Theory and Women's Development* (Cambridge, Mass.: Harvard University Press, 1982).

2. For feminist ethics, see Alison M. Jaggar, "Feminist Ethics: Projects, Problems, Prospects," *Journal of a Social Philosophy* 20 (1989), 1–2, and the bibliography cited there; for feminist jurisprudence see the bibliography in Steven Friedell, "The 'Different Voice' in Jewish Law: Some Parallels to a Feminist Jurisprudence," *Indiana Law Journal* (1992);915–49.

3. BT *Niddah* 66a; *Berakhot* 31a.

4. This position is articulated by the Magen Avraham (d. 1683). For discussion see Moshe Meiselman, *Jewish Woman in Jewish Law* (Krav, 1978), 47–52.

5. See Tsvi Abusch, "Alaktu and *Halakhah*: Oracular Decision, Divine Revelation," *Harvard Theological Review* 80 (1987);15–42.

6. See George Fletcher, "Ho and Halakha," *Sevara* 1:1 (1990);13–15.

7. For details see Steven Friedell, "The 'Different Voice.'"

8. For a review of these issues from an Orthodox perspective, see Michael Rosensweig, *"Elu va-Elu Divre Elokim Hayyim*: Halakhic Pluralism and Theories of Controversy," *Tradition*, vol. 26, 1992.

18 / The Feminist Challenge to *Halakhah*

1994

Halakhah[1] has faced many challenges during the several thousand years of its existence, some of them quite fundamental and far-reaching, that have resulting in major changes in the way we look at *halakhah*. An example is the dialogue with Aristotelianism which has so much to do with the codification of Jewish law and the change of *halakhah* into a statement of norms rather than a record of processes. Today's challenge, which comes mostly from feminism and other forms of postmodernism, is just as radical and far-going as any that have come before. Feminism challenges *halakhah* on a number of different levels.

The simplest feminist challenge is on the level of the many *halakhot*, the many individual norms and roles that are detrimental to women. Many of these have been discussed widely—and I understand that you have heard about some of them in this series and are aware of the problems of the *agunah* (the "anchored woman" who cannot get a religious divorce) and the question of inheritance. There is a whole checkerboard of practices which disadvantage women. These are being identified, and in many segments of the Jewish world (somewhat reluctantly in some circles and somewhat more eagerly in others) there is a serious attempt to try to rectify most of the gross inequalities perpetrated on women by the legal system. But this layer of individual laws and rulings is just the very first layer of the challenge of feminism to *halakhah*. It is the layer most often spoken about by Orthodox feminists who are concerned to work within the system to effect change, and by rejectionist feminists who are eager to find points of disagreement on which they can walk away from the system. But it nevertheless just scratches the surface.

At the same time, the deepest level of the feminist challenge to law and ethics, the feminist distrust of the deep structure of legal systems, is not applicable to *halakhah*. Feminism often worries about a system which pays greater attentions to norms and rules than to people and relationships. This is not a problem for *halakhah*. (I use the word *halakhah* rather than say Jewish law because to call *halakhah* "law" is to prejudice our understanding of the nature of *halakhah*.) *Halakhah* is noteworthy for the fact that it has historically been willing to sacrifice and to bend norms for the sake of relationships. This manifests itself in the huge enterprise of decision-making within *halakhah*. Legal rulings attempted to cope with the fact that individuals may suffer from the generalizations that are necessarily inherent in lawmaking. The decisions of halakhic courts frequently urged (and urge) compromise rather than victory. They also often subordinate individual rules to general relation-statements such as harmony within the home. In fact, it has been said that in many respects *halakhah* speaks with what used to be called "the feminine voice," a term that is mercifully quickly passing into oblivion.[1] We should probably not be surprised that Jewish modes of ruling and decision-making are similar to female processes: after all, Jews, who developed *halakhah*, have been people on the periphery of the power bases of society, as indeed women have been. As non-empowered people, Jews and women were often socialized the same way to consider the role of the individual and the community vis-à-vis the violence of judicial legislation and punishment. The tendency of women to decide issues by thinking more of the people than of the rules turns out to be something that women share with the rabbis of the *halakhah*. It may, of course, be the only thing that feminists hold together with *halakhah*.

The real issue of the challenge of feminism to *halakhah* concerns the basic set of principles of feminism. As you know, there are many feminisms, and feminists do not agree on many things, and whenever you have two feminists together, they are as likely to disagree as two Jews. Nevertheless, the basic principle of feminism, the bottom line, is that women are human beings—that they must be considered full human beings, and that to do anything else is unacceptable. Anything else is patriarchy. It may be patriarchy with an oppressive face, or patriarchy with a paternalistic face, or patriarchy at its most benevolent, but it is always patriarchy to say that women are other than fully human. The basic principles seem to us so self-evident as to not need being said. But it does need to be said, over and over, for our newspapers and our history books tell us of the many ways in which that principle is violated abroad and at home every day.

Not all the world agrees that women are full human beings. And the *halakhah*, in fact, does not view women as full adult human beings. It does not allow them to act as witnesses; it does not empower them to act as determinative of their own destiny. The structure of family law in the *halakhah* always treats the men as subjects of the law, as those who are agents of the action, and treats the women as the objects who are taken in marriage, who are released from marriage. This orientation is fundamental to the system. It results sometimes in the classifying of women together with minors, slaves, idiots, deaf-mutes, and other people who are being considered by the rule of the moment as the "other" in legal determination. The law keeps women in this position by making them dependent economically, in that according to strict *halakhah* women do not inherit and cannot fully alienate the property of marriage, and it treats them frequently as *a priori* enablers of others to perform public actions. In other words, according to *halakhah*'s mode of discourse, the community of obligated people who constitute the public's decision-making and public studying and public prayer worshipping agencies of Judaism are all male, and each woman is the satellite that revolves around her male. These women may then have their own set of social networks with other women, but they are rarely topics of halakhic discourse.

Of course, I am not talking about any particular contemporary practice; I am talking about the way that *halakhah* looks at the whole issue of male-female and communal relationships. Even current attempts to rectify and ameliorate the situation of women have maintained this lack of mutuality; women continue to be objects of increasingly less harsh rules. This constitutes a basic contradiction between feminism and *halakhah*, not only in the traditional understanding of *halakhah*, but also in its contemporary manifestations. One result of this contradiction has been a rejection by feminists of *halakhah*. Not all, but many feminists, having seen this issue and seen it clearly, may or may not declare themselves post-Jews but tend to declare themselves posthalakhic in that they want nothing to do with the system that cannot recognize them.

The other way of understanding this contradiction is the road of contemporary Orthodoxy, which has absolutely embraced the distinction between men and women. Orthodoxy not only denies the impact of modern discovery on *halakhah*, it also embraces the idea that women and men are fundamentally different. During the past couple of decades, the Orthodox world has separated males and females at an ever younger age in order to socialize them differently with different expectations of what their role in religion should be. Talmudic generalizations about where a women's honor lies (inside, of course), and what a woman's way of behavior might be, and what constitutes shameful conduct, and what might disgrace the honor of the congregation, all of these *ḥazakot* (assumptions) have been embraced as ontological verities by many contemporary Orthodox thinkers. These modes are timeless, says this manner of thinking: this is the essence of women. God did not create human beings to be mirror images of each other and therefore women should glorify being women and men should glorify being men.

This essentialist thinking, like the romantic feminism that we know from American writings during the period of the "cult of true motherhood" at the end of the nineteenth century, often devotes attention to the "greater spirituality" of women: women are truly more in tune to the divine than men and therefore need less prescriptions; women have rhythms of their bodies that correspond to the rhythms of the universe and therefore need fewer time-marking and time-bound rituals; women are caring and nurturing because of their occupation with children and need fewer mitzvot. Women can be placed on an enormously high pedestal, given great honor as in the Talmud, where the mother is the most revered person of all and nothing is ever said against the impact of the mother on the child. According to one famous talmudic dictum, the woman is said to be the most determinant of the household; if she is good, the whole household will be good. Woman is Queen of the House. In some Orthodox circles today, women are encouraged to get a good education, and not essentially a secular one. It is assumed that many of the women will have modern careers. In all matters having to do with the nature of human aspirations, women are glorified and put on pedestals and normally offered a very happy, self-satisfied life. If you speak to Orthodox women in these communities, they will praise to you the glories of such a life for womankind, a life that the court in America once called "separate but equal."

But, as with all "separate but equal" systems, the equality is ephemeral, and sometimes the whole system tends to come crashing down. For women in these communities, this crash happens when women want out, when a woman seeks to leave her marriage and finds that she cannot do so without becoming an *agunah*, a woman anchored to a husband who will not give her a divorce. Or when a woman violently disagrees with her husband and finds that she cannot get her way because he threatens to walk out on her without granting her a *get* (a religious divorce). Or when her husband dies unexpectedly as a young man, as happened to many in Israel in the Lebanon Wars, and she has no children and suddenly his family refuses to release her so she can marry again. These are stress points within the system where the veils drop (speak of feminist click movements) and you get some very disillusioned, angry, and bitter women. These stress points are being addressed by Orthodox feminists and there really is, finally, a serious attempt going on in the Orthodox community to come up with some solutions to these problems of the *agunah.*

Nevertheless, at the same time, these communities have countermanded the basic idea of feminism by saying, by maintaining that women are women, and men are men, that there are permanent ontological differences created by God, and that no matter what women do, they cannot turn themselves into ontologically different creatures. Therefore, says the Orthodox *halakhah*, no matter what a woman does in terms of obligating herself to the practices of Judaism, she cannot really be treated as obligated for what would have her become a judicial male.

There is a second stream of *halakhah*—I like to call it the new *halakhah*—the Conservative *halakhah*, which has attempted to declare many of these "verities" to be socially and culturally determined and no longer applicable. And there are thinkers who are trying not to justify the exclusion of women on the basis of what women truly want or truly are like. Nevertheless, the new *halakhah* has not yet addressed the basic problem of *halakhah*, which is the skewed view of male-female relations in which men are the agents and women the other.

In order to address this issue, we need to stand back and look at what *halakhah* is and what it should be, not only what it has become in the end of the twentieth century. The word *halakhah* ultimately has a Babylonian source. It is perhaps not insignificant that both the words Torah and *halakhah* have their analogue in Akkadian words, *tertu* and *alaktu*, both of which refer to oracles that receive from God, to instructions from the deity. Torah comes from the same word as *moreh*—to teach—and *halakhah* comes from the word "to go." In technical Babylonian religious text, *tertu* refers to liver omens and *alaktu* to astrological omens.[2]

However, it is not the technical definition that is important so much as the notion of how the term *alaktu* is used outside the technical divinatory realm. When we look at the word *alaktu* in religious literature, it means "the way" of the god, not only its way among the stars but also its way in ethics and justice. The god's way of dealing with human beings is its *alaktu*, and the questioning Babylonian will say "her *alaktu*—who can fathom it, who can discern the way of the gods?" The Akkadian *alaktu* is the equivalent of the word *derekh* in biblical Hebrew, for the *derekh* of God is God's way of behavior, God's way of dealing with human beings, God's way in the Temple. *Halakhah* is God's way and the way in which we follow God's ways. It is, in other words, a goal-oriented term. Sometimes it describes a form of *imitatio dei*, of behaving like God, and sometimes norms as to how humans should behave even when they are not like God (as when they engage their bodies), but it is always a term of goal direction, signifying the way that brings the community closer to God, the way that keeps the community under God.[4]

The way is mapped: it is not forced. Even in their inceptions, halakhic rules may not have been enforced by what has been called the "violence of the law.[5]" The sanctions that the Mishnah and Talmud spell often demand a political power that the writers of these texts did not possess. They could not coerce Jews to follow these prescriptions. There have been periods when Jewish communities could enforce norms, and there have been threats of excommunication and the supernatural sanction of reward and punishment in the world to come. Today, particularly in less traditional communities, *halakhah* has no coercive sanctions at all; nothing will happen if you do something against the *halakhah*. There is no "God Police Force;" there is no official violence of the Jewish community; no one will kick you out because there is no real *herem* in most of Jewry today, and there is very little belief in at least the non-Orthodox circles that there will be an exact reward and punishment after death. In other words, you can break *halakhah* without fear that somebody's going to get you for it. This current lack of sanctions is not different from the ideals declared by the earliest Rabbinic writings which admonish everyone to perform the commands, not like a servant who's looking to get a reward but rather like a servant who doesn't expect any reward at all. As this statement indicates, the halakhic system is a prescribed set of norms that are performed voluntarily by the community in response to the divine calling rather than as a result of human coercion.

Modern philosophies of law enable us to understand better how such a system can work. Some of you have read Dworkin and are aware of his idea that there are principles behind the law to which the law is reaching and which must never be contravened by the law themselves. In American law, says Dworkin, we have to abstract from the law the principles that govern the law; then these principles become as important in making legal decisions as any particular rules that may have been enacted. When we look at the law of Torah and *halakhah*, we do not have to abstract the principles. The "metahalakhic" principles are stated very clearly: *tsedek, tsedek, tirdof,* "pure justice," *kedoshim tiheyu,* "be holy," *ve-ahavta le-reakha kamokha,* "love your neighbor as yourself," and a few others that are perhaps somewhat less important. The purpose of the rules is to instruct you as to how you can institute justice, be holy, and demonstrate other-love. As the laws develop, these principles lead to the whole enterprise of equity-seeking in *halakhah* and should be our guide in determining what rules need to be modified and, if necessary, abrogated.

Possibly even more important for our understanding of *halakhah,* and certainly much more fun, is the legal theory of Robert Cover.[4] In a review of the activities of the Supreme Court, Cover articulated his idea that all law is really a concretization of the narrative in which it is imbedded. The Supreme Court, holds Cover, decides or should decide cases on the basis of the American narrative of where we are and where we come from. Cover held that it was aberrant and wrong, to cite a famous example, for the judges in the Dred Scott case to send the fugitive slave back to his owner. Even though statutory legislation ("the positive law") demanded the return of a fugitive slave, this did not accord with what America was about.[5]

This type of relationship between narrative of the people and the legal statues is inherent in the organization of the books of the Torah in which the laws are given in context of the release from slavery to form a holy, just society. Jewish learning exhibits this kind of thinking when we talk about the relationship between the *aggadah,* the nonlegal theological and ethical analysis section of our tradition, and the *halakhah.* And our very system of laws gets its authority from a narrative, from a foundation narrative of what Jewish people are about and where they got their Torah.

The foundation narrative is really well known but let me kind of formulate it for you anyway—I think you will recognize most of it:[6]

Once upon a time, fifty-seven hundred some odd years ago, God created the world. Later, God chose people to bond with, the people of Israel. God rescued them from slavery so they could become God's people and establish the covenant at Sinai in which God expressed desires in the form of laws. Israel accepted the covenant and agreed to obey these laws. These laws are eternal and unchanging and in order to insure their applicability, God also revealed at Sinai the elaborations of these laws in the oral Torah and the ways in which the laws can be elaborated. The sages who lived after the destruction of the Second Temple applied these divine instruction to the written Torah and thereby constructed the Rabbinic *halakhah* as the divinely ordained extension of the Sinai tradition. Rabbis have continued to study and codify these laws and to respond to questions about *halakhah* so that Jews would know the proper way to achieve the will of God and could rest assured that their obedience to the *halakhah* would fulfill God's will and bring blessings. In this way we know God's wishes and are obligated to them.

This is a coherent narrative which has served Jews for many generations. But it has been under concerted attack by all the discoveries of the modern world, the discoveries that have cast doubt not only on the age of the cosmos but also on the exact history of the Exodus narrative and the literal understanding of the Torah as revealed at Sinai. We also understand now, through our analysis of history, something about the motivation of the Rabbinic actions and recognize that there was a power vacuum in the Jewish people that the Rabbis filled with the idea of the oral Torah. One of the foundational premises of Orthodox Judaism is the principle that you do not apply the result of science to religious faith. For them therefore, the traditional myth remains intact, as does the obligation to observe every rule that can be traced back to Sinai.

Conservative Judaism, which declares itself more historically conscious, has modified the foundation story somewhat. It now goes something like this:

> Once, a long time ago, certainly much more then 5700 years ago, God created the world. Later, God maybe brought some people out of slavery who met up with other people who came to a mountain where something happened which the people interpreted as God speaking. The people wrote this revelation down as law because that is how they understood it. Throughout the period of the First Temple, and for much of the Second Temple, the Israelites contemplated, integrated, and reinterpreted these Commandments with the guidance of their priests and prophets. After the destruction of the Second Temple, the sages refused additional revelation. In so doing, they turned the written text of the Torah into the font of all order and knowledge and claimed the authority to read new meaning into the written Torah by the practice of *midrash* and to decide legal matters by majority rule. Generations of rabbis have constantly interpreted and amended their readings and their laws. Today we do not know the actual commands of God; we only know that neither the text that we have now, nor the laws that are based upon it, contain the actual statements of our divine commander. Nevertheless, we are obligated to obey them anyway.

This is an academically aware, historically responsible foundation story. It takes into account all we know of the processes of the law and the process of text making and the processes by which innovation has been made in Jewish tradition. The problem with this formulation is that the conclusion doesn't follow from the story, and it really isn't any wonder that Conservative Jewish leaders walk around saying that some of the people don't get it, that they're not observing the *halakhah*. In fact, and it is worth noting, Conservative Jews observe a tremendous amount of *halakhah*; I don't mean only the leadership of the movement, which is quite observant. I mean the normal people. Average Conservative Jews observe the ritual *halakhah*: the rules of observance of life-cycle events, religious rituals, performance of festivals. This is no accident. The traditional foundation story is recited liturgically and addresses contemporary Jews on a mythically powerful level. As such, it demands a ritual response, and gets this response in ritual observance. But neither the traditional nor the modified story can compel the observance of rules just because they are rules.

So we go to another variation of the foundation myth, that of Reconstructionist Judaism, which goes much like the Conservative myth except it has a different ending. It says:

> Generations of rabbis have constantly amended their readings and their laws, and the Jewish people have accepted the authority of the laws and of the rabbis who interpret them. Today, knowing that we do not know the actual commands of God, and that neither the text that we have now nor the text that we base upon it contain the actual statements of a divine commander, the Jewish people have refused to continue accepting this halakhic system. We now live in a post-halakhic age in which the language of obligation has no meaning.

In this posthalakhic age, says Reconstructionist Judaism, we observe tradition to honor our past, but no sense of obligation adheres to this observance.

One more fundamental myth, developed in most recent years, also highlights the response of *halakhah* to our changing understanding of history. This is the version of David Weiss Halivni, who is a leading talmudic scholar and spiritual leader of the Movement of Traditional Judaism. To paraphrase the sense of his myth-making foundational document *Peshat and Derash*:[7]

> The People of Israel were not ready to observe the Torah that God had given to them. The Bible records many instances of apostasy and backsliding throughout the period of the First Temple. During this time the people also did not care for the written Torah as well as they should have, and many errors of discrepancies entered the written text. As a result, the written text that we have now does not accurately reflect the word of God. Therefore, during the time of Ezra, God revealed to him the true word. God did not change the written text but revealed all the principles of exegesis by which the will of God could be discerned. These principles, the basis of *halakhah*, are not only divinely given, they bring us closer to the true meaning of written Torah than does the text that we have before us.

The rules and laws of the oral Torah transmit the divine commands and we are obligated to obey them.

This formation has many advantages; it includes the result of modern scholarship and acknowledges the problem of finding the literal unity in the written Torah, and it recognizes the fact of change of *halakhah* throughout the century. At the same time, its notion of the second revelation gives a compelling reason to observe the laws that doesn't depend on the laws themselves but takes it back to the authority of the divine commander. However, it enshrines the Rabbinic tradition to the point of idolatry, including all of the Rabbinic statements and provisions about women. This certainly cannot be a foundational document for feminists nor, in my opinion, can it be an approach to law which is conducive to the pursuit of justice and equity.

In fact, if you want to have a foundational myth that will incorporate both the current aspirations and the actual particulars of the law and provide *halakhah* guidance, you have to develop a new narrative. This narrative draws to some extent on the mystical tradition of Judaism but at the same time is a complete rephrasing of how we think the law got to be where it is and how we make halakhic decisions. Of course, such a foundation myth has to be developed by a community, not by an individual. But here is my sketch of such a myth:

> The universe has always been filled with God, and humanity developed an awareness of the transcendent immanent. They responded to the Presence and sought to establish connections with it as when Neanderthal people buried their dead with flowers. Humanity's vision of divinity raised living above mere subsistence and gave value and focus to human life and community. Written documents allow us to follow more closely our more recent ancestors' attempts to approach divinity. Sometimes their ways appear to be beautiful in our eyes, and other time ludicrous, but we acknowledge the fact of their faith.
>
> At Sinai, at the dawn of Israel, our people experienced God's presence as the determining factor of communal life. The people wrote this revelation down as laws because that is how they heard it. Throughout the period of the First Temple and for much of the Second Temple, Israelites contemplated, integrated, and reinterpreted these commands with the guidance of priests and prophets.
>
> After the destruction of the Second Temple, the sages refused additional revelation and made the written text of the Torah the source of order and knowledge, proclaiming the authority to read new meaning into the written text by the prophets of *midrash* and to decide legal maters by majority rule. Generations of rabbis have constantly interpreted and amended their readings and laws. We follow in the path of their vision, joining with them on the course that they have set, entering their symbolic universe to pursue the past and complete the journey, and in so doing we continue our creation in the image of God. Our goal is that we find in ourselves the

reflection and continuation of divinity in the life that we lead in the world and in community, that we as people live up to the injunction to be a holy people to the best of our understanding of what it takes to be holy.

The journey to holiness and Godliness is not an individual journey. The human self, encased in its own ego, lacks the expansiveness of divinity. An individual soul that opens its boundaries to connect to God in mystic union has achieved only half of its destiny. The self must find the key to connect and interlock with other selves for it is, above all, collective humanity that continues God's image. *Halakhah* is our way of acting in concert to reach God. It is our joint path on which we head for and help establish the divine order. Our task is easier because those who have come before us have indicated the way, and when we follow their way we establish connections not only to reach each other in the present but to all who stood at Sinai and walked along its path. *Halakhah* is our joint path with the generations of past and of future Jews allowing us to feel the presence of their religious yearnings in our present life and space and time. Establishing such connections across time and space is part of the enlarging of the self into the communal partner of God. Our religious duty is not only to follow that path but constantly to reexamine it to keep it heading us forward. We must continually monitor and adjust the path so that it leads to holiness and divine order, and this is the purpose of the halakhic process.

This narrative gives us a warrant to concentrate both on halakhic norms and on the *aggadic* principles that have animated *halakhah* as we attempt to live the command to be holy, pursue justice, and love each other.

The question that should rightly be asked and answered is: Does the tradition provide the same perspective in ways that don't come out of American reflections on the nature of law but come directly out of Jewish sources? What is the essence of the revelation: was the written Torah revealed, the written plus the oral Torah, or perhaps as the Jerusalem Talmud phrases it, "everything that an adept student will ever say before his master was already revealed on Mount Sinai" (JT *Pe'ah* 13a)?

Our written Torah is but a fragment of the revelation. And it is a flawed fragment. The Torah itself provides a sense of the imperfect process transmitting the divine word. A now classic example is the part of Exodus 19 where Moses tells the people to get prepared for the coming of God, to purify themselves and "do not go near a woman." In this one statement Moses looks out at the people of Israel and addresses himself to the men. And the women become the occasion for temptation. This statement of Moses is now well known to the point of infamy. Not as well known is the fact that earlier in the same chapter the narrator shows us God commanding Moses: God commands Moses to go and tell the people to prepare and purify themselves. God says nothing about "don't go near a woman." Something mediated Moses' transmission of God's word: patriarchy. Moses saw God in the way he was able to see God, and heard God in ways that he could understand God. This was the human contribution to the revelation.

Tradition also teaches us that God spoke in a very special multiplicative way. In the words of the Maharshal, God spoke through forty-nine *tsinorot*, forty-nine conduits between us and God, each seven times seven, purified fourteenfold, and every sound came through its conduit and everybody heard it according to his differential abilities. We hear what we can hear. Rabbi Levi Yitzhaq also explains that our differential understanding results from our diverse gifts from the holy Spirit. If you are a *mekil*, if you tend to be lenient in matters of the law, the reason is that your soul is in tune with *hesed*, and if you are a *mahmir*, meaning you tend to be more stringent in your legal decision, the reason is that your soul is in tune with the attribute of divinity that is known as *gevurah*. The word came in a multiplicative divine rather than human fashion, and was heard fragmentally according to the psychological abilities of what people could hear, what their makeup allowed them to hear.[8]

In effect, these mystical philosophers have deconstructed the authority of the written word. The written word relies for its significance and authority on the interpreters and their authority. The interpretation gives the normativity. These mystical maneuvers bring us back to the plain talmudic statement of *lo ba-shamayim hi* (the Torah is not in heaven). The decision of what to do, the interpretation of the rule to apply to the human circumstance, is in the hands of people and, said the rabbis, they should decide by majority vote of the rabbis.

In fact, during the history of Jewry, there have been very serious changes made in *halakhah* on the basis of the fact that we have the authority to change with the times, on the basis that the Torah itself doesn't change but perhaps the *halakhah* does in order to preserve the principles of Torah and the well-being of the Jewish people. Many changes have been made that affect women. The most famous is the Hafetz Hayyim's decision that times had changed and you could no longer keep women unknowledgeable in Torah. In his day, he said, you couldn't rely any more on the family to give them Jewish values because families didn't have values that strong, and you couldn't rely on women being willing to consider themselves ignorant in order to learn from their husbands, because the women were being taught to dance and play piano and speak French. For this reason, the Hafetz Hayyim made the dramatic change to formally educate women in Torah and the first schools for women were opened, and so it was in order to preserve the Torah that it could be changed.

There are even examples in the tradition of people changing their ontological status. One of the more radical examples is the question of deaf-mutes. Deaf-mutes are treated in halakhic sources as noncognitive beings who cannot be witnesses and do not have to fulfill any of the positive precepts of a human being. However, when the rabbis of Pressburg in the nineteenth century, the Sofer Simha Bunem and his father, dealt with this question, they went to the school for the deaf which was relatively new and decided that nowadays, in their time, the deaf were being taught to communicate; therefore, they should no longer be considered as possessing the status they once had had and should be included in the obligation to all precepts. This changes their ontological status to full adult Jewish people.[9]

Another great example of how you change ontological status is delicious. The *Gemara* (Talmud) sees a great difference between the sage, the *talmid ḥakham,* and the regular fold, the *Am ha-Aretz.* In effect, the *Am ha-Aretz* is defined by observing the mitzvot, and the *talmid ḥakham* by studying Torah. Social cleavages between these groups were so great that, at certain periods, the group would not intermarry. The *talmid ḥakham* was an elite so revered and privileged that the tradition ruled that anyone who insulted a *talmid ḥakham* had to pay a monetary fine. With changing times, this privilege was abused. Some *talmidei ḥakhamim,* sages with no visible means of support, who came to speak to audiences would badger and harangue them until someone in the audience would insult them back—at which point the sages would demand and would collect his fine. To stop such abuses, and because it no longer felt proper to have what amounted to a caste distinction within Jewry, the decision was made (ca. 1400) that nobody anymore was an *Am ha-Aretz*—since everyone had a little learning, they couldn't really be called an *Am ha-Aretz.* At the same time, nobody could truly be called a *talmid ḥakham* anymore because in order to deserve that title you have to be immersed in learning and nothing else. In this way, the ontological status of all Jew(ish male)s was changed.[10] Of course, this provision wasn't universally accepted—there were some communities that never adopted this change, that still called a sage a sage. But this provision is a good example of a major change in social status so that gross inequality could be removed while the framework of the law was preserved intact. The relevance for women is obvious.

Of course, when you discuss changes, the question that needs to be asked is, who can make the change: in certain circles it has been understood that only *gedolei ha-torah*, the greatest of all rabbis, only those recognized as the *posekim* (the legal decision-makers) of their generation, could make such changes. Not all rabbinical authorities, and certainly not all the people. There are also groups within Judaism today which will accept the authority only of a particular type of rabbi: not the master of the logic and precedent but the person who is acknowledged by the community as possessing a divine sanctity, a special *da'at* Torah (intimate knowledge of Torah). To them, only that person can pronounce a policy.

The question of religious authority is a very substantive one and the idea of hierarchy has to be examined. Who gets to decide questions of *halakhah*? Is it only the Rosh Yeshiva? Only the *tzadik* (the holy man)? Should only people with *semikhah* (rabbinic ordination) be listened to? Or how about Judaica-trained graduates from Harvard Law School? Or academically-trained Ph.D. specialists in Jewish law? Should they have a voice? Or perhaps—does the ongoing revelation of God operate through the *people* of Israel? After all, even the *Bavli* itself, the Babylonian Talmud, could not become important until it was accepted by the people. And any *takkanah* (special decree) had to be accepted by the people.

There are numerous statements in Talmud that the people themselves are the vehicle of the halakhic authority, and if you want to know the correct *halakhah*, you go out and you look, *puk hazei* in the Aramaic phrase. For example, can you keep a vicious animal? Go look. People keep guard dogs. If people keep guard dogs, it must be okay because the people are not trying to behave viciously toward each other.

The principle of *puk hazei* becomes less and less popular as time goes on, but in practice the people nevertheless sometimes asserts itself as the final arbiter of halakhic norms. A good example is the institution of *tashlich*—the ceremony of casting bread upon the waters to symbolize the carrying away of sins during the New Year holiday. This practice first appears in halakhic sources in the late Middle Ages. It was the object of concerted rabbinic effort to squelch it for two hundred years. The rabbis tried to convince the Jews not to do it, but the ceremony had a tremendous appeal and the people wouldn't give it up. And after two hundred years, the rabbis acquiesced, saying in effect the ritual must be in accord with the Torah, and proceeded to give some parameters and some definition to this people-driven ceremony.

In *tashlich*, the people as a whole acted as the determinants of their religious observance. There are a number of points in *halakhah* where the tradition declares that women were the agents of their destiny. Most of these are minor, but a few are highly instructive. According to the old *halakhah*, women are obligated to hear the *Megillah* (the scroll of Esther read ceremonially on Purim) even though not obligated to hear the shofar. Yet everybody will tell you that hearing the shofar is a far more momentous occasion in the Jewish year than hearing the *Megillah*. So why does the tradition privilege women (by obligating them) to hear the *Megillah*? Because, it is said, women (in the person of Esther) had a hand in the redemption that led to the reading of the *Megillah*. As a parallel case, women came before the rabbis declaring that they wanted to be obligated to light the Hanukkah lights, and the rabbis said yes, they should light Hanukkah lights because they had a role in that redemption. In this case, the reference is to the story of Judith, who in Jewish tradition was the daughter of Matityahu and killed the general as part of the Maccabean revolt. The extensive role of the midwives, mothers, and daughters in the redemption of Israel from Egypt is the reason that women are obligated by all of the ceremonial regulations of Pesach, such as drinking four cups of wine, even though they are not obligated to sit in the sukkah.

Women have also acted as the change agents for the *halakhah*. Even though the older *halakhah* did not require women to count the Omer, after hundreds of women had adopted the practice, a major halakhic authority, the Magen Avraham, announced that since women had been doing this for so long, they should be considered to have obligated themselves for all future generations.[11] In the same way (though in the opposite direction) women, who had been obligated to light the Hanukkah candles, simply stopped doing so, so that even today in many Orthodox circles women are not expected to light their own, but witness the lighting by men.

In the light of all these examples of the ability of women to change *halakhah*, I would draw the somewhat incendiary conclusion that it is time for women to begin to redeem themselves. If women want to be full moral agents, then they have to take the agency in their own hands. With few exceptions, women have not yet felt empowered to do so on matters of *halakhah*. It is ironic that despite the ever-growing number of women rabbis in Conservative Judaism, they have not yet reached the point of self-validation. They are still looking for approval from male halakhic authorities. The issue of *edut*, of allowing women to be witnesses, looms as a big problem for Conservative Judaism to solve in the coming years. It is becoming ridiculous to have a hundred women rabbis and still not be able to have them witness a document or to sit in on a *beit-din.*

What can you do? What are the options for changing the system: Can a group just come along and say "those times have passed"? Strict halakhic reasoning indicates that, since the prohibition of women as witnesses is formally derived from the Torah, it would take a *takkanah,* a special decree, to change it. Is there a group that will do so? And can it find good halakhic reasoning to justify doing so?

In fact, one can provide reasoning for an interpretive change. One can argue by analogy to the argument about the deaf-mute. It is undeniable that women were once kept in the private sphere and kept from direct experience of the working of the public legal system and polity. At such time there may have been justification for excluding them as witnesses except on private issues concerning their own families. Now, however, when women are an integral part of the body politic, their role has changed and so should the strictures on being a witness.

Another precedent might be Rashi's comment on the principle of *elu ve-elu divrei elohim hayyim* (lit., "these and these are the words of the living God" or, as the old joke states it, "you're right—and you're right too") and on the fact that contrary opinions are preserved in the *Gemara:* he says that these opinions might not be right now, but with a change in circumstances they could be right. In a similar vein is the Hatam Sofer's comment that in another *gilgul,* another eon, they could be right:[12] Why do you call a pig *hazir:* because it will come back *(hozer)* in the Messianic Era as kosher. The principles may be immutable, but not the details that explicate them. One could say that the modern world, with all its changes and the very different challenges and dangers it poses to modern Jews, constitutes a different *gilgul* and so the old social categories don't apply.

Of course, the old question remains: This may be a perfectly valid halakhic maneuver, but who is going to do it; who is going to bell the cat: who has the authority to get up and to it; and the answer is—no religious *posek* is likely to get up and do it. And no group that considers itself halakhic is going to do it for fear of being attacked as nonhalakhic by another group. It has to be done ultimately by the whole people, the only ones who can make a real statement on such a serious matter. And the agents of such change have to be the women themselves. They are the ones who must say "the old exclusion of women from *edut* (witnessing) simply doesn't pertain any more!" Women must be the self-defining group in Judaism that will get up and say "we declare."

A good example of women taking matters in their own hands comes, ironically, from orthodoxy. Because Orthodox Judaism refuses to allow women to play a role in public worship services, women began to come together in single-sex women's *tefillah* groups (prayer groups). Even though these groups avoided saying those prayers which Orthodox Judaism demands the presence of ten men to say, five eminent rabbis (the "Ritz Five") declared the practice of such prayer groups invalid. The reason they gave was "ontological," women are private individuals: Even if hundreds of women stand together, they cannot continue a public group for public prayer; they are simply hundreds of private individuals in the same place. The reaction to this ruling was the formation of an association of *tefillah* groups whose purpose was to support each other. This is an example of the process of women beginning their own redemption and becoming the agents of their own destiny. Of course, we shouldn't get too wildly optimistic on the basis of this example. The reason the women got away with what is essentially a halakhic rebellion is that the *tefillah* groups are actually an escape valve that defuses the impetus for change among Orthodox women. By satisfying the need of women to express their growing familiarity with Judaism and Jewish ritual though participation in public worship, they relieve the pressure that might build to make the official worship service more inclusive of women. In this way they serve to protect the "two state" system of Orthodoxy.

The strategy of halakhic self-determination is an important step for women. There is a great deal of anger about the *agunah*. If it is not solved, women may have to stop putting pressure on men to act and start acting on their own. Instead of only telling men that they shouldn't give honor to men who refuse to give their wives *gets*, there will come a time when they have to say, we will not raise the children or have sex with men who make their wives *agunot*. Similarly, if women want to be considered witnesses, they are going to have to declare that from now on they must be considered kosher witnesses. They are going to have to demand that their *ketubot* (marriage documents) be witnessed by other women or they won't get married.

This is, of course, a power play à la Lysistrata. It is also forcing the hand of the decision-makers by in effect becoming decision-makers. It is also a halakhic maneuver. We know that when the whole system is threatened, *et la'asot la'adonai*, "time to act for God," with a *hora'at sha'ah*, a legal ruling which doesn't have to be explained or interpreted but is sufficiently justified by the peril of the community and the necessity to act. Knowing this, the path is clear: If women want the rabbinate to change the ontological status of women, if women want to redress the basic inequity of the *halakhah*, the skewing of the law so that men are the agents and women the objects of actions, then we have to create a situation where the whole system is endangered without this change, and it becomes a *hora'at sha'ah* to declare women full proactive human beings. And that, maybe, only women can do.

NOTES

1. There is a very large bibliography on the *halakhah*. To suggest just a few sources on its nature: Eliezer Berkovits, *Not in Heaven: The Nature and Function of Halakhan* (New York: Ktav, 1983); Elliot Dorff and Arthur Rosett, *A Living Tree: The Roots and Growth of Jewish Law* (Albany: SUNY, 1988); Menachem Elon, *ha-Mishpat ha-Ivr* (English translation, Philadelphia: The Jewish Publication Society 1994); Robert Gordis, *The Dynamic of Judaism: A Study in Jewish Law* (Bloomington, IN, 1990); Louis Jacob, *The Tree of Life: Diversity, Creativity and Plurality in Jewish Law* (Oxford: Oxford University Press, Litman Library of Jewish Civilization, 1984); Ephraim Urbach, *The Halakhah: Its Sources and Development*, trans. Raphael Posner (Israel: Massada, Yad la-Talmud, 1986).

2. The term the "feminine voice" comes from Carol Gilligan, *In a Different Voice: Psychological Theory and Women's Development* (Cambridge, Mass., Harvard University Press, 1982). For the similarities of this voice to *halakhah* see Steven Friedell, *The 'Different Voice' in Jewish Law: Some Parallels to a Feminine Jurisprudence*, Indiana Law Journal 1992: 915–49.

3. Tsvi Abusch, "Akaktu and *Halakhah*: Oracular Decision, Divine Revelation." Harvard Theological Review 80 (1987): 15–42.

4. For the role of sanctions in law, see Robert Cover, *Violence and the Word*, 95 Yale Law Journal 1601–29 (1986).

5. For the applicability of Cover to *halakhah*, see Gordon Tucker, "The Saying of the Wise are like Goads: An Appreciation of the Works of Robert Cover," Conservative Judaism 45 (1993): 17–39, and Rachel Adler, "Feminist Folktales of Justice: Robert Cover as a Resource for the Renewal of *Halakhah*," Conservative Judaism 45 (1993): 40–55, and Tikva Frymer-Kensky, "Towards a Liberal Theory of *Halakhah*," Tikkun 1995.

6. See the very important work by Robert Cover, *The Supreme Court 1982 Term Foreward: Nomos and Narrative*, 97 Harvard Law Review 4–68 (1983); and also Bryan Schwartz, *Individuals and Community*, Journal of Law and Religion 131–71.

7. These narratives have been separately published by Tikva Frymer-Kensky, "Towards a Liberal Theory of Halakhah," *Tikkun* 1995.

8. David Weiss Halivni, *Peshat and Derash: Plain and Applied Meaning in Rabbinic Exegesis* (New York: Oxford University Press, 1991).

9. The forty-nine cunduits are from the Maharshal (R. Shelomo Laria), sixteenth century, in the introduction to *yam shel shelomo* on *hulin*; R. Levi Yitshaq's formulation, nineteenth century, is from *Kedushat Levi*. Both are cited by Moshe Sokol, *What does a Jewish Text Mean: Theories of elu ve'elu divrei elohim hayim in Rabbinic Literature,* da'at 32–22 (1994): xxiii-xxxv.

10. See Jacobs, *A Tree of Life*, 139.

11. The change was stated by R. Joseph Colon and R. Jacob Weil. See the discussion in Jacob's, *A Tree of Life*, 138–39.

12. See the discussion by Moshe Meiselman, *Jewish Women in Jewish Law*, 1978, 47–49.

13. Rashi's comment is to BT *Ketubbot* 57a, *ka mashma lan;* the Hatam Sofer to BT *Pesaḥim* 3b, *ke-gedi*. They are discussed in Moshe Sokol, *What does a Jewish Text Mean?: Theories of elu ve'elu divrei elohim hayim in Rabbinic Literature* da'at 32–33 (1994): xxiii-xxxv.

THEOLOGIES I:
BIBLICAL THEOLOGY

19 / Revelation Revealed: The Doubt of Torah

2002

The institution of *torah* and the appropriate attitude toward and use of *torah* is so well established in Jewish tradition that it is hard to imagine that its use in the Bible is not as well established or as simple as we might have believed. The priestly books of the Pentateuch speak only of "the *torah* of *x*" (where *x* is the issue), a usage shared by the later part of Ezekiel, as in 43:10 (*torot* of Temple). This usage accords well with the root meaning of the term "divine instruction," the Hebrew equivalent of the Akkadian *tertu*, "oracular instruction," in technical literature, the liver omen. The expression "*torah* of Y" (where Y is a person) never appears in these sources, but it is the standard use in Proverbs (for example, "the *torah* of your mother") and in Psalms. In the prophetic literature, the phrase "Torah of God" appears in the eighth-century prophets and continues as the dominant form in the prophetic corpus, although the "Torah of Moses" also appears (Mal. 3:22).

The written Torah, the book of the Torah, appears prominently in the Deuteronomistic history in such phrases as "the book of the Torah of Moses" (Josh. 8:31; 23:6; 2 Kgs. 14:6), "the Torah which Moses wrote" (Josh. 8:32) and "the book of Torah of God" (Josh. 24:25–7) with the clear understanding of fulfilling it (2 Kgs. 23:24; see also Dan. 9:13) and doing as written (Josh. 1:8; 23:6). This, of course, reflects Deuteronomy's emphasis on writing down the Torah (Deut. 31:19–28; 17–18). Deuteronomy provides for public reading to the people (Deut. 31:9–13), a provision reiterated by Joshua (Josh. 8:30–4; 24:25–8) and, much later, by Josiah (2 Kgs. 23:1–3), and much later still, by Nehemiah (Neh. 8). These public readings were occasion for a renewal of commitment, a renovation and reinstitution of the conventional relationship.

Deuteronomy also provides for monumental use of the written rules. They are to be inscribed on plastered stones for all to see (Deut. 27:1–8). This is quite different from the treatment of the tablets in Exodus, where they were put inside the Ark and behind the veil. Joshua did, however, create a monumental version, setting up inscribed stones on Mount Ebal after the conquest of Ai (Josh. 8:32). Like the reading, the setting up of the monument was a public ceremony with all the people attending.

The monumental use of the Torah of God is reminiscent of the code of Hammurabi that was inscribed on tablets but was also on a shoulder-high stele visible in the Temple. It is worth looking at the code to understand how such a monument functioned. The Laws of Hammurabi begin with a prologue, in which Hammurabi relates how the gods chose him to be king to make justice prevail in the land and *inūma Marduk ana šutēšur nišī matim usim šūhuzim uwa'eranni kittam u mīšarim ina pi aškun šīr nišī utib:* "When the god Marduk commanded me to provide just ways for the people of the land in order to attain appropriate behavior, I established truth and justice as the declaration of the land and I enhanced the well-being of the people." The text then says, "at that time" and continues with its approximately two hundred legal provisions. Then, in the epilogue, Hammurabi provides evidence of how the collection is intended to be used:

> Let any wronged man who has a lawsuit come before the statue of me, the king of justice, and let him have my inscribed stele read aloud to him. Thus may he hear my precious pronouncements and let my stele reveal the lawsuit for him: may he examine his case, may he calm his heart, and let him say "Hammurabi the lord who is like a father and begetter to his people, submitted himself to the command of the god Marduk his lord . . . and he secured the eternal well-being of the people and provided just ways for the land." May he say thus, and may he pray for me with his whole heart before the gods Marduk my lord and Zarpanitu, my lady. (Also may any future king observe the pronouncements . . . and may he too provide just ways for all humankind in his care).

The stele of Hammurabi is a testimony to Hammurabi's care. It is not here as the authoritative source of judgments, and the only two references we have to the stele instruct the receiver to disregard the stele. At first glance, this seems very different from the Deuteronomic idea that one should observe the laws and that one should not deviate to the right or left. However, another reason for the reading of the law in Deuteronomy is "so that they may listen and learn to fear the Lord," and so the children will also hear them and learn to fear the Lord (Deut. 31.9f). The book thus serves as witness to God's power and care (and so the tablets are called "the testimonies"). Yet another twist to this witnessing function of the book of the law is given in Deuteronomy when Moses has the Levites take the book and place it beside the Ark so that it will be a witness against Israel when they stray, as they inevitably will (Deut. 31:24). Later, in the covenant renewal ceremony at Shechem, Joshua also writes a book and then takes a rock (which the story does not say that he inscribed with the laws) and sets it up to be a witness against the people, a testimony that they have heard (and therefore should be accountable).

There are expected differences between Israel's book of the Torah and inscribed rock and Hammurabi's stele. The stele testifies to the king's concern; the Israelite book and rock testify to God's power and Israel's obligation. But, in both, the visual representation of the collection as a whole is an icon of the legal collection that testifies to its purposes.

This, however, applies only to the collection as a whole, and its authority. The legal provisions that are contained in Israel's book of the Torah have a different history. In reality, they do not come from God's mouth to a people who have had no experience of law. Their similarities—and their differences—from the ancient Near Eastern law provisions indicate that they almost always arise, like other collections, from reflection on the legal tradition of the Near East, an occupation and reflection that took place mostly among the sages in the academy. Whatever the role revelation may have played, it did not come *yesh me 'ayin* (ex nihilo) to a barbaric world. But this, of course, is a modern scholar's view. Did ancient Israel accept all the laws and decrees as the direct word of God, or did they also have reservations about the authentically divine nature of the individual provisions of the law?

A careful examination of several texts in the Pentateuch (Exod. 19 and Num. 25), in the First Prophets (1 Kgs. 22) and in the Latter Prophets (especially Ezek. 20) leads to the inescapable conclusion that in fact there were distinct voices in Israel that did not automatically accept the God-given nature of statements declared to be from God.

PENTATEUCH

The chaotic impression of this chapter is purposeful. Historical critics ascribe different parts to different traditions. But the disjunctures are not only obvious; they are highlighted. Resumptive phrases are used to provide, in a linear text, an impression that we are more used to seeing done in screen cuts. The text is the linear equivalent of overlapping fade-outs and blackouts and all the film techniques that we use. The chaos is intended to represent (as much as we can talk about authorial intention) the overwhelming nature of the event—linear words conveying a mass of sensations.

So Moses keeps going up and down, a kind of shuttle diplomacy. And God calls him from the mountain and says, "this is what you will say to the people of Israel . . . how I carry you on eagles' wings and brought you to this place." This is a process of learning for us. "On eagles' wings" sounds so easy, a political spin on the difficulties Israel experienced in Exodus 16–18. But then I learned how eagles carry their young: the children fly and the mother eagle flies beneath them. As they are buffeted by winds and get weak, they land on the mother's wings and rest till they are strong enough to fly again. "On eagles' wings" really is an appropriate picture for the way that God brought Israel into freedom. As the Israelites got hungry enough or thirsty enough, God was there to support them. But they had to endure the difficulties first.

The chapter relates a dialogue between God and Moses, which we overhear and the people of Israel do not. Then Moses comes to Israel and relates matters, and all the people say "everything that God says we will do," and Moses returns their words to God. Moses is very much the mediator here. God does not hear what the people are saying and the people do not hear God. God says to Moses, "I am coming to you in a cloud so that the people will hear when I speak to you and therefore believe in you forever." One of the purposes of God's appearance is to give authority to the words of Moses. Then God says to Moses, "Go to the people and sanctify them today and tomorrow and let them wash their clothes. Let them be ready for the third day, because on the third day God will come down before the people on to Mount Sinai. And you shall draw a boundary around. Be careful, that you do not go up the mountain or even touch it on its edge, for everyone who goes up the mountain will surely die. You should not touch it even with a hand, or you will be stoned or shot; whether animal or person no-one should touch until the trumpet sounds." So Moses comes down from the mountain to the people and they wash their clothes, and Moses says, "be prepared for the third day, don't touch a woman." We have been told that one of the purposes of God's appearance is to give authority and trust to Moses, but we are also given two speeches: God to Moses and Moses to the people, and they are not the same. They are not the same in two very significant ways. One is the meaning of "people" (*am*). God wants Moses to address the people, but

Moses looks at the people and addresses only the males. He doesn't say "don't approach each other, don't have sexual congress"; he only sees the males. The men are subjects; the women, objects. Where did this come from? It didn't come from God. We can speculate that it came from Moses' own psyche, because in the previous chapter, chap. 18, when Jethro, the father-in-law of Moses, comes to see him, bringing his wife and children, Moses immediately goes in to the tent to talk to Jethro. What happened to the wife? No greetings for the children? Moses is one of these idealistic men, notoriously not so good as family men, who have their eye on the goal and don't really see domestic relations.

Someone who is psychologically inclined could talk about the fact that Moses owes his life twice to women: once when he is rescued from Pharaoh's decree by his mother, sister, and Pharaoh's daughter and once when he is saved from God's inexplicable attack by Zipporah his wife. And maybe because of this, he can't really see women. Whatever the reason, Moses brings gender exclusion into the story. It is his myopia, his inability to see women, which makes him look at the people and address only the men.

The exclusion of the women has been noticed before. Judith Plaskow brought it into contemporary discourse by making it the title episode of her book, *Standing Again at Sinai.* But, long before, Jewish tradition restored women to the revelation at Sinai. Rashi and later commentators note that in the critical scene of Exodus 19, God commanded Moses to "speak to the house of Jacob and tell the children of Israel." They explain that the "house of Jacob" *(beit ya'akov)* means the women, and the "children of Israel" *(bnei yisra'el)* are the men. But we should note that their very attempt to undo Moses' exclusion of women reflects the results of exclusion. Understanding the term "the house" for women has a good philological basis: the word "house" means "wife" in Aramaic, including the Aramaic of the Talmud. But the "house of Jacob" is not an autonomous entity; it is a dependent part of Jacob's orbit, an appendage that, like the physical house, should not be coveted. Even though the tradition may explain that this "house" is mentioned first because it is often responsible for the behaviors of the household, the "house" is considered separate from the "children of Israel." Moses' exclusion of the women from the people of Israel continued to have its effect in Jewish tradition.

The other issue that Moses introduced into the discourse is never noticed. The entire command not to have sex because God is coming on the third day does not come from God. Moses himself introduced the whole antipodal relationship between sexuality and spirituality from which contemporary religions are trying so hard to unyoke themselves. The origin of this critical rupture is not in God's speech, but in Moses'. So the question is, where did he get it from? David makes a similar statement when he flees from Saul and comes to Nob and requests food. When told that there is only sacral food there, he answers that he and his men can partake of the sacred because none of them have had sex in three days. David is also operating with the concept that you have to have three days between sex and contact with the holy. But this must be local custom or folk tradition. Even the Levitical rules don't require this much separation. Leviticus is quite clear: if a man and a woman have sex, they are to wash and they will be ritually impure until that evening. The next day they can go to the Temple and do whatever is done. There are no three days of separation. Moses did not get his three days from God, and they are not found anywhere attributed to the word of God. He must have got them from the customs he knew, the same customs that don't have anything to do with God's command, or with texts that even purport to be God's command.

At this defining moment of revelation, Moses has introduced into Israel both gender exclusion and the separation between sexuality and spirituality. Two major concepts—and they are not divine. And not only are these precepts not divine, but somebody, this narrator (the *stam ha-torah*, "anonymous voice of the Torah"), goes out of the way to show that these sex and gender issues are not God's teaching.

Going a little farther into Exodus 19, Moses comes down to the people and on the third day there are sounds and flashes and lightning and clouds on the mountain and a loud voice of strong trumpet, and the people are very frightened. Moses goes down to talk to God, and all the people are standing at the base of the mountain, which is smoking like a furnace. And the voice of the trumpet gets stronger and stronger and Moses speaks and God answers him very loudly.

The people see Moses speaking to God and hear only loud sounds. They are given a clear message that Moses hears God in a way they cannot. God gives Moses divine authority, but the narrator who relates this also subtly undermines the authority of Moses' commands by showing us that, after all, when you look carefully at what Moses says, the words of God are still being mediated by a human figure and are not accurately transmitted. Gender exclusion and sexual separation are the commands of Moses, not God.

Another text, Numbers 25, shows even greater disparity between the word of God and that of Moses (though introducing gender exclusion and sexual distancing is pretty major to me). This is a very weird text. The story takes place at the end of the years in the desert. The people are invited to dinner and begin to be faithless in the direction of the daughters of Moab. "The people ate and bowed down to their gods, and in that way Israel attached itself to Ba'al Pe'or, and God was very angry" (Num 25:3). In the traditional retelling of this story, the narrators suffered from the exact same myopia that afflicted Moses at Mount Sinai. They see the word *am,* "people," and they see only men. And when they see women, they see sex. The scenario related has always been that men of Israel went off and were sexually enticed by the daughters of Moab and in that way became idolatrous. Even feminist readings simply repeat this dominant reading and react negatively to it, claiming that "the women are punished for what men did." But in the biblical text, the *am,* the whole people, went to dinner. The verb *znh,* which is always translated as *porneia,* "gone whoring, played the harlot," has a very specific meaning: it means to break the trust, to break the bonds of exclusivity that a woman owed her husband or Israel owes God. Whenever Israel breaks God's command, the word *znh* is used: *ʾaše r zônîm laʿasot.* The verb does not always carry sexual connotations. In any event, the issue at Ba'al Pe'or is idolatry. Whether it comes through dinner or through sexual enticement is not a concern of the story; whatever the cause, the people have been idolatrous. We can easily imagine the scene. The festive dinner is a *zevah,* a sacrificial offering that includes the eating of meat. At the feast, there is a sacrifice. Through courtesy, one might be moved to join in the thanksgiving to the hosts' god. But the moment Israel does that, Israel's God becomes angry—plague-producing angry. God is angry and people are dying. And then God says to Moses: "Take all the leaders of the people and impale them for YHWH in the daylight, and my anger will turn away." God is clear: the impaling of the heads of the people will be a backfire to assuage the anger of God. But Moses goes to the leaders and says, "Kill each one of you his own people who have attached themselves to Ba'al Pe'or." The narrator tells us that God said, "impale the leaders," but Moses relates that God wants them to punish the evildoers. Perhaps we might speculate that Moses, knowing that he is chief leader, doesn't want to be impaled. But whatever his reasons, he tells each leader to ferret out the guilty party. There are two very different concepts here of how to stop the plague and of the nature of God's retributive acts. Moses envisions individual moral retribution:

kill the guilty parties. But God is providing collective punishment, and God holds the leaders responsible for bearing the burden of the people in their persons. They bear the fate of the nation. Embedded here is the same notion of the vicarious punishment of a leader that is found in the suffering servant of Deutero-Isaiah (and nowhere else in the Bible), where the kings may pay for the sins committed by their people, but not visa versa. Moses totally changes God's message into one of individual reward and punishment. Translations such as the New Jewish Publication Society (not so new anymore) try to soften the impact of Moses' change, translating God's words as "impale the ringleaders," but the Hebrew, *r͏ošîm,* "heads," does not refer to the ringleaders.

The story gets weirder as we read on, and indeed the rest may be from a different source. All Israel is crying because of the plague, and Zimri comes with the princess of Midian and takes her into a *kubbah.* The dominant tradition relates that he fornicated with her in front of all of Israel. But, at the very least, the *kubbah* is some type of enclosure, and that one possible explanation is that taking her into it, Zimri took her as a wife, a kind of dynastic marriage; he is the chief of Shimon, she is the princess of Midian. Yet a third possibility is suggested by evidence that in pre-Islamic Arabian, a *kubbah* was a divinatory tent, perhaps also of white magic. If that is the use here, he brings her to try to stop the plague in the Midianite way. In this interpretation, we have a further instance of idolatry in this story. My own inclinations lead to this interpretation, precisely since the word *kabah* in the preceding chapters refers to the oracle-producing activity of Balaam for the Midianites.

Whatever Zimri and Kozbi were doing inside the *kubbah*, Phineas kills them. This stops the plague and is rewarded with an eternal *brit shalom,* "Covenant of Peace," of the priesthood. There are some very weird ancient traditions being reflected and sorted out in the story. But there is no question that the finished narrative presents a major discrepancy between the word of God and the word that Moses "relays." Source criticism cannot lessen the discrepancy, for the divide in the text comes between Moses' statement to the elders and the episode with Zimri, not between God's statement and that of Moses.

FIRST PROPHETS

These two narrative hints in the Pentateuch give us an indication of some biblical skepticism as to how any particular dictate of Moses should be received. When we turn to the Prophets, we find another story that undermines belief in the "word of God": the story of Micaiahu ben Imlah related in 1 Kings 22. Ahab invites Jehoshaphat to come recapture Ramotgilead with him. Jehoshaphat, somewhat reluctant, asks for another oracle. Ahab assembles his four hundred court prophets, who will answer that Ahab should go and be victorious. Jehoshaphat, still reluctant, asks for another oracle. Ahab explains that there is yet another, Micaiahu, but Ahab doesn't use him because he never has any good news to tell him (*oyf shailos is teshuvos*, after all, "even questions bring answers"). But Jehoshaphat insists, and Micaiah is brought. Having been told by the attendant what the other prophets said, Micaiah also prophesies victory. But Ahab, suspicious, tells him to speak only the truth. So Micaiah relates his vision, in which he saw God planning to convince Ahab to go to battle so he could die. One spirit came forth and offered to convene him, explaining his plan to God: "I will be a lying spirit in the mouth of all these prophets." Micaiah then explains that his own vision is true, that Israel will be like sheep wandering who have lost their leader. Zedekiah, head of the prophets, is horrified at this suggestion and slaps Micaiah on the cheek, declaring, "When did it happen that prophesy left me and went to you?" Here is the quandary: Zedekiah is certain that he is accurately relaying the word of God. He really is relaying what he has been told. But Micaiah claims further knowledge: the revelation of God is sometimes a lie. There is no way of knowing if the prophet before you, sincere as he might be, is telling the truth. And there is no way to know if the particular word of God you hear is what you should really believe.

LATTER PROPHETS

This indeterminacy of trust is highlighted also in the classic prophets. Jeremiah's famous diatribes against "false prophets" are a polemic against those prophets who claim that God will always provide "peace in Jerusalem." But these prophets are simply continuing the Isaianic tradition of trusting God to protect Jerusalem, simply reinforcing the Psalms' foundational belief that YHWH *mošîᶜa lekal hahôsîm bô*, "YHWH saves all who rely on Him." Events proved them wrong, but before the Destruction, there was no predicting which prophets were true and which false, which "word of God" came from revelation and which from wishful thinking. As in the case of Micaiah (who says to Ahab, "if you come back, then God has not spoken to me"), history will tell if the prophet was telling the truth. Not surprisingly, this is also the opinion of Deuteronomy, which tells you that if what the prophet prophesies comes to pass, you know he is a true prophet.

But this is not the only opinion. The Book of Jonah clearly states that a prophet whose words will cause people to change so that the prophetic words will not come true is the really true prophet. Events are not after all the true judge and even with hindsight it is hard to tell if a particular oracle was true or not.

And there is yet another problem. Isaiah relates that his mission is to obfuscate, to "thicken the hearts" of the Israelites so that they do not perceive the true future. His mission is thus similar to that of the "lying spirit" in Micaiahu's vision. The spirit will deceive the prophets, Isaiah will deceive the people. And yet, Isaiah is on a true mission from God, and his words are divine proclamations. This issue arises in the strong dispute between Jeremiah and those people in his day who were sacrificing their children in the valley of Hinnom. Jeremiah tells them (in the name of God), "which I didn't command, which never entered my mind." They, however, obviously believed that they were commanded to sacrifice their children, and their belief is shared by Ezekiel. In one of the most horrific verses in the Bible, Ezekiel declares (in the name of God) *gam anî nattatî lahem huqîm lô ṭôbîm, mišpaṭîm, bāl yihyu bām*, "I for my part gave them laws that are not good, rules they cannot live by," explaining that God had to keep his promise to bring them into Canaan, but God was so angry that God resolved to make sure that they would ultimately lose the land by putting some deadly laws as booby traps. As his example, God gave the law of the first-born, which God intended the people to understand as demanding child sacrifice, "so that I would pollute them in their very act of giving to me." Ezekiel doesn't list all the booby traps, and the result is the very opposite of positivism: each law is suspect of being a potential booby trap; each law has to be examined individually to see whether it is a law by which we shall live. Jeremiah and Micaiah cast doubt on the truth-claims of individual predictive prophesies; the Pentateuch narratives show the same suspicion towards the individual perspective decrees of Moses, and Ezekiel manifests the same doubt about individual received and well-established regulations and traditions. The authority of the institution of God-given commands to Israel may be self-evident, but at least a minority doubts the authority of any specific command within the institution. It remains for later generations to establish the principle of the absolute acceptance, at least formally, of whatever has been written.

20 / Moses and the Cults: The Question of Religious Leadership

1985

A significant phenomenon of the contemporary religious scene is the continuing attraction of large numbers of people, mostly young, to such groups as the Society for Krishna Consciousness (Hare Krishna), the Unification Church (Moonies), the Divine Light Mission and a whole set of small groups, all of which are commonly called "cults." Their popularity highlights one of the most important facets of religious history, the issue of leadership and the proper relationship between the members of an emerging religion and their leader-originator. One of the primary characteristics of modern cults is the intensity of the attachment of members to their group and, particularly, to the leader. Despite their expressed allegiance to an ultimate god, the main thrust of their belief is the devotion to the group's leader. His strength and the promise of salvation that allegiance to him represents are, together, the centripetal force holding these people together. They concentrate around him in a tight cluster which removes itself from other, more ordinary, societal ties. These groups are thus particularly characterized by their willingness to give up any prior identity, individual self-determination and ego-control to leaders who, like Reverend Moon or Reverend Jim Jones, become, in effect, semidivine characters.

There are many factors that make individuals susceptible to the pull of a leader-led salvation cult. People tend to join them at transition points in their lives: between high school and college, toward the end of college, etc., when old ties are being broken and new ones have not yet been established. The feelings of rootlessness, loneliness and (at least partial) alienation that are felt in such circumstances make people vulnerable to the attraction of cult communities and the security of following the leader.

In their recruitment procedures, the cults frequently enhance the feelings of anomie that potential recruits may already be feeling. They may invite prospective members to weekend retreats, and then induce them to stay for an additional period. During this retreat, the visitors are isolated from their normal ties and activities and are introduced to many new elements in their lifestyle. They undergo a change of locale, a shift in waking and sleeping hours, a (for some) radical change in diet. These changes have the effect of disembodying them from their old life and eroding their sense of their own identity. The effect is somewhat similar to that reported by draftees: when stripped of their clothes for their physical examination, shorn of their former hairstyles and issued identical clothing, they begin to feel divorced from their formal life. This disembodiment from the familiar makes the individual more malleable and capable of being "molded into a soldier" (to use the army analogy); it also makes him respond more readily to promises of a new identity, a new life and salvation. This technique of recruitment, which is sometimes called "brainwashing," is not the drastic brainwashing described by Korean War prisoners. It is, nevertheless, a highly effective technique of ego manipulation. It strips people who are already susceptible to feelings of rootlessness and alienation of their old sense of self. Then, when a new identity is offered, a "self" centered in a group and its leader, this new "self" is seen as highly attractive and the recruit gives up his individual identity, his self-determination and his "freedom" to join the group.

If we look at the situation of the people of Israel immediately after they left Egypt, it is apparent that they shared many of the characteristics recognized in potential converts to the modern cults. They were totally removed from their old life, for they were no longer slaves and no longer in Egypt. They underwent a complete change of diet, from the "leeks and cucumbers" of Egypt to the manna of the desert. Moreover, they were clustered around a strong leader, and they believed that they were the founders of a new order. Despite this, they did not form a modern "cult;" the new religion did not center around the figure of Moses, and the group that emerged after the wilderness experience was not noted for its willingness to follow the dictates of its elders. In the narrative portions of the books of Exodus and Numbers, we have a record of how early Israel almost developed into a classic cult of world salvation, and the changes that it made in order to avoid that pitfall.

Israel did not glorify the people who came out of Egypt. It did not believe that they had an inherent genetic superiority, an innate religious genius inherited from Abraham. Even though God's decision to rescue the people from Egypt was the result of His promises to Abraham, the people who came out were not all descendants of Abraham, but, rather, a "mixed multitude," composed of Abrahamides and others who had joined them. They chose to be Israelites by marking their doorposts with the blood of a slain lamb. This act of identification was necessary because it contained an element of risk, for the people must have realized that if the death of Egyptian first-born sons did not pass, the Egyptians would take retribution against the people who had put blood on their doorposts. It was a positive act of faith that God would, indeed, carry out His threat against the Egyptians, and, a positive act of choice: by marking their doorposts the people signaled their intention to join the Exodus, to leave their old lives and embark on a new life.

These people who came out of Egypt had been "chosen" by performing an act of faith at a considerable risk to themselves. Lest we think that they were in this way (although not genetically) superior, the Book of Exodus immediately presents a "history" of the group which shows that they did not have the ability to sustain a life of trust. All of the events subsequent to the actual Exodus reveal the people as insecure, unable to endure a life of risk, and, in effect, unprepared for a life of freedom. The narrative portions of Exodus and Numbers are almost a case study of the evolution of such a group. The "plotline" demonstrates their initial lack of the qualities necessary for independence and their resultant ever-increasing dependence on their leader, along the lines of an authoritarian "cult." It dramatized the crisis to which this led, but then details the subsequent steps that were taken to prevent the group from becoming and staying an authoritarian "cult."

There are seven stories related in Exodus from the time of the Exodus from Egypt until the arrival at Sinai: 1) the deliverance at the Red Sea (Ex. 14:5–15:21), 2) the waters of Marah (Ex. 15:22–26), 3) the manna in the Wilderness of Sin (Ex. 16), 4) the water of Massah and Meribah (Ex. 17:1–7), 5) the battle with Amalek (Ex. 17:8–16), 6) the arrival of Jethro (Ex. 18:1–12) and 7) the appointment of the judges (Ex. 18:13–27). In these, two major themes can be discerned: the nature of the people and the relationship to their leader. The portrayal of the essentially weak nature of the people begins with the account of the victory at the Red Sea. As the Israelites caught sight of the pursing Egyptians, they were, understandably, frightened. This fright led to their complaint to Moses, "Was it for want of graves in Egypt that you brought us to die in the wilderness" (Ex. 14:11–12). Faced with danger or hardship, the new

Israelites preferred slavery. When they were hungry they repeated this refrain—"if only we had died by the hand of the Lord in the land of Egypt . . ." (Ex. 16:3)—and when they were thirsty—"why did you bring us up from Egypt, to kill us and our children and livestock with thirst" (Ex. 17:3). In all of these statements, they revealed a lack of appreciation for the "freedom" that they had just been granted.

Freedom, in fact, means very little to those who have not been trained to cope with the difficulties that it entails. The readiness of the Israelites to prefer the life of bondage in Egypt to the "free" life of danger, hunger, and thirst was paralleled by the choice of many newly freed slaves in the South of the United States to stay on the plantations after emancipation, and the return to their slave homes by many who did initially leave. Freedom entails choices and difficulties, and, as Erich Fromm described in *Escape from Freedom,* even those born in freedom often show a willingness to give it up in return for security. A people which has not been trained to expect choice and its difficulties cannot be expected to value its "freedom" and to be willing to sacrifice safety and security for it.

The Book of Exodus continues its depiction of the Israelites in a set of three stories that follow immediately after the Red Sea deliverance. These all exhibit the same pattern: the Israelites face hardship in the form of thirst or hunger, they bring their justifiable complaint to Moses, Moses approaches God, and God solves the problem. The first of these, the episode of the alkaline waters of Marah (Ex. 15:22–26), is included in the same chapter as the victory celebration after the Red Sea, an arrangement that highlights the fact that the great victory neither ended the people's difficulties nor gave them the assurance that they would be protected. They journeyed three days without water and when they came upon alkaline wells they "grumbled" against Moses. He, in turn, cried out to the Lord, who showed him how to throw a piece of wood into the water and make the water sweet. The next two stories, the manna (Ex. 16) and the waters of Meribah (Ex. 17:1–7), exhibit the same pattern: when the Israelites were faced with thirst or hunger they "grumbled" again against Moses, escalating their "grumbling" with an expressed preference for the Egyptian slavery. Once more, Moses interceded and the Lord solved the problem. These stories portray the Israelites as ordinary people, disoriented and embarked on a new life with which they were not prepared to cope. They could not rely on themselves and turned to their leader, both rebelling against him and waiting for him to solve their problems.

These stories reveal the crucial importance of Moses. In the eyes of the people, he was their deliverer, and he continued to be the person who solved their problems. Although the people were told that their savior was an invisible God, the figure whom they actually saw performing the miracles was Moses. The Red Sea divided when he held his arm over it (Ex. 14:21) and the waters came back and drowned the Egyptians when he again stretched his arm over it (Ex. 14:26). At Marah after he sweetened the waters he immediately told the people that the Lord was their healer (Ex. 15:26); the people had seen only the human leader giving them drink. When the people grew hungry, they turned to complain against Moses and Aaron, expecting them to fill their needs. This is the meaning of Moses' announcement to the people that when they received the manna they would see that it was Lord who had brought them out of Egypt, and that their grumbling was "not against us, but against the Lord" (Exod. 16:8). When they grew thirsty again, it was Moses to whom the people came, against whom their anger was directed, and whom they were almost ready to stone (Exod. 17:4), and it was Moses who struck the rock so that water could come out for the people to drink.

The other stories that are recorded from the period before Sinai further illustrate the stature and importance of Moses. When Jethro arrived to acknowledge God before Moses, he saw long lines of people waiting. Moses was not only supreme magistrate of the people; he was the sole arbiter of their disputes. At Jethro's urging, Moses appointed judges to settle the minor disputes; he remained, however, the final authority, and all important cases ultimately came to him. To the people, Moses was the savior, the political leader, the one with direct access to God, and also the judicial authority. The final story before Sinai, the battle with Amalek, indicates that Moses was also held to have mystic powers. When Amalek attacked, Joshua led the people into battle and Moses climbed a hill where he could be seen by everyone and held up his arms. When they were raised, the battle went well; when they dropped, the Israelites began to lose. Ultimately, Aaron and Hur had to hold up Moses' arms so that Israel could defeat the enemy. Moses clearly understood that this victory-power came from God: he held the rod of God in his hand and built an alter named "The Lord is my standard;" the people, however, saw only the arms of Moses bringing them victory, not the invisible God behind him.

In light of all of these events, it would have required an impossible degree of theological sophistication for the people not to have come to see Moses as somewhat larger than human. The Israelites, as they approached Sinai, were not sophisticated. They were a fearful group of people, not at all self-reliant, clustered around a leader upon whom they depended for all their needs, revering this leader as a conduit to a distant God, and marching behind him to the establishment of a new order. In other words, the classic picture of a world-salvation cult.

The initial events at Sinai could not have been at all reassuring to such a group. As they approached the mountain they were bound to a covenant whose content they did not know (Exod. 19:8). Then, after their three days of purification and abstention the mountain began to quake with thunder and lightning and to make great noises and smoke (Exod. 19:16–18). The people did not need God's warning not to approach the mountain (Exod. 19:12, 21), for they were so frightened by the eruption that they declared to Moses, "you speak to us . . . and we will obey; but let not God speak to us, lest we die" (Exod. 20:16). To complete the awesomeness and terror of the occasion, Moses bound the people to a covenant and sprinkled them with blood; leaders of the people ascended with Moses and feasted with God—and then Moses disappeared.

This disappearance was a major crisis for the people of Israel, for they, who had complained to Moses at every hardship and appealed for his intervention, did not have the ability to continue without him. In desperation they approached Aaron, saying, "Come, make us a god who shall go before us, for that man Moses, who brought us from the land of Egypt, we cannot tell what has happened to him" (Exod. 32:1). In the people's perception, Moses was the *man* who brought them from Egypt. Although they knew that Moses did not act without God, this abstract knowledge did not fill the vacuum created by his disappearance. They therefore demanded some other conduit to God: the golden calf. The episode of the golden calf was not a case of apostasy, for when Aaron made it he declared, "This is your god, O Israel, who brought you from the land of Egypt." Nor was there any confusion about the identity of the god that brought the Israelites out of Egypt, for Aaron declared, "Tomorrow shall be a feast to 'the Lord,'" using the tetragrammaton, the personal name of God. The golden calf was intended to be a visible "symbol" of God's presence, a more approachable object of veneration and power than a distant invisible god. The mechanism by which the calf was expected to accomplish this is not certain. There is no hint that the calf was a representation of God himself, i.e.., an "idol" and perhaps the best way of understanding its role is to consider it, like the cherubim, a "seat" for God—an earthly object that God could ride upon, or in which he could be immanent, as he led the people into the wilderness.

The motivation of the people in building the golden calf is clear: the "sin" was not the abandonment of God, but the collapse of trust. There is a form of idolatry involved, but the "idol" was not the calf; it was Moses. The people had rested all their faith and confidence in Moses and, when he disappeared, they could not find the courage and confidence to believe that they would not be left bereft. The idolization of Moses was a direct result of the pre-Sinai phase, in which he was the sole conveyor of the new religion. But this idolization presented a significant problem for the emerging religion: if it was to survive it could not be dependent on a human figure. New avenues of approach to God had to provide new assurances that God was in their midst. This incident of the golden calf was a critical event marking a turning point in Israel's history, for after Sinai the importance of Moses diminished and he was superseded by the institutions of a developing religion. They did not change the character of the people, but they did somewhat lessen their infantile dependence on him and, ultimately, provided the groundwork for a new order.

After Sinai, Moses himself became veiled (Exod. 34:33–35). Although this was a sign that he had been marked by a special closeness to God, it made him more remote from the people. He was now closer to, and more a part of, the distant God, but he was less accessible to the people and, therefore, less able to serve as the intermediary between them and God. At the same time, institutions were introduced which were to serve as the "intermediaries" between God and the people, to demonstrate God's will and to provide a way for the people to approach God. The first such "intermediary" was the law, in which God's will was recorded in an objective statement—represented here by the Book of the Covenant in Exodus 21–23—which could be learned and consulted. Moses would no longer be the sole conveyor of God's message, for others would be able to learn and to teach the law. Furthermore, this law could serve to test the authenticity of a leader's dictates, even those of Moses. It could not be changed at the command of individual leaders, and would serve as a permanent reminder to the people of God's will and as a permanent support to them that they knew the ways proper to God.

The next "intermediary" was the Tabernacle, and with it the cloud of God's presence and the cultic personnel. The Tabernacle had a dual function: as a focus of the people's attention and, at the same time, as a way that the distant invisible God could be more apparent to, and less remote from, the people. It was designed to be a physical symbol of God's presence, and the "cloud" rested upon it, visibly assuring the people that God was present among all of them. The Tabernacle was further designed to be a meeting place of God and Israel *(Ohel Mo'ed),* a place to which the people could to go to seek God without being deterred by a thundering mountain. It was, thus, a place where they might ultimately meet God without the mediation of Moses. Associated with this Tabernacle was the priesthood of Aaron, which constituted a chain of authority not connected with the political leadership and also served as an active intermediary between God and the people, and, especially, between the people and God. The priesthood was charged with knowing and applying the ritual law, instructing the people in ritual purity and ritual states, conveying God's wishes in the sphere of ritual action. Most important, the priesthood was the main intermediary by which the people approached God in normal, prescribed ritual patterns without the danger of encountering God's enormous power. The importance of the Tabernacle and the cult personnel in Israelite thought is indicated by the length of the description given to its building and installation (Exod. 25–31, 35–40).

There are six stories that deal with the events following Sinai: Taberah (Num. 11:1–30), the meat at Kibroth-Hattaavah (Num. 11:41), the rebellion of Miriam and Aaron (Num. 12), the story of the spies (Num. 13–14), the rebellion of Korah and Dathan and Abiram (Num. 17), and the waters at Meribah (Num. 20). Like the stories before Sinai, these revolve around the nature of the people and their relationship to Moses.

By the time they left Sinai, the structure of the religion had been changed. Moses was the political leader and was, moreover, revered as a prophet. In civil matters, conflict resolution was presided over by a system of judges. In cultic matters, in addition to Moses, the people were led by Aaron and could address religious questions to him and his subordinates. Religious life centered around the Tabernacle, and the people were assured of God's presence among them by the cloud that rested thereon. As a result of the dramatic changes in their institutions, we would expect to see a change in the behavior of the people, but when the narrative resumes after the departure from Sinai (Num. 11), we see the people reacting as before. The difference, however, is that now more is expected of them, and when they complain at Taberah, God becomes angry and punishes them with a fire (Num. 11:1–39). Nevertheless, we immediately hear of a new complaint, that the people are tired of manna.

It is clear that the new institutions, these objective assurances of God's interest and presence, did not change the people, nor had they been miraculously transformed by standing at Sinai. The experience of slavery had irrevocably molded them or, more exactly, the lack of freedom in their upbringing had made them incapable of coping with that hard independence of their new existence. The people who came out of Egypt remained the same: ultimately, they could not change. After the episode of the spies in the land (Num. 13–14), when, again, the people demonstrated both their lack of confidence in themselves and in God's ability to give them the land, God gave up his hope of transforming them. Although he did not totally abandon them (thanks to the intervention of Moses), he decreed that those who had come out of Egypt would not enter the land but would wander in the wilderness until they died (Num. 14:26). This was not simply a "punishment"; it was a realization that they had been so marked by slavery that they were incapable of an independent existence and could never learn to conquer the land of Israel and establish a just society. Only a new generation, growing up in the desert and trained into freedom and self-reliance, could undertake this task.

Although the people did not change, the new institutional elements introduced at Sinai did alter the dynamics of the group and expand their relationship to Moses. This change was not immediate, for when the people left Sinai (after the granting of the law, the Tabernacle, the priesthood, and the cloud) they still related to Moses in the old, almost idolatrous way, depending on him to meet their needs. And when there were complaints at Kibroth-Hattaavah, it was Moses himself who reacted, for he realized that all of the changes that had been made in Israel's structure were not sufficient and that he was still the parent-figure carrying the people alone "as a nurse carries an infant" (Num. 11:11).

At this point, therefore, yet another institution was added, the ecstatic communion of the seventy "prophesying" elders (Num. 11:10–30). They could bear witness to an experience of God that was more immediate than the vision of the thundering mountain, the cloud over the Tabernacle, or the priesthood. Moses would no longer be the only witness to God's direct presence, and the people would have yet another assurance that God was with them. Added to the objective law, the organized priesthood, the judicial system, the holy meeting place, and the divine presence (the cloud), the elders were the final step in the institutionalization of the function of Moses' leadership.

This dispersion of Moses' functions clearly posed a danger to his authority, a danger recognized by Joshua, who advised restraining Eldad and Medad from acting out prophetic communion in the camp. Moses, however, declined to restrain them, declaring that he would be pleased if all the people were prophets (Num. 11–29). He realized that he could no longer continue to be a parent-figure or god-figure to the people, supernormal and unique. Nevertheless, the danger to Moses was real, for the dispersion of his functions and power did lead to an erosion of his authority. The story of the prophesying elders is followed immediately by the rebellion of Miriam and Aaron (Num. 12), who declared themselves equal to their brother (Num. 12:2). The later rebellion of Korah and Dathan and Abiram centered on the lack of unique power in both Moses and Aaron, for their complaint is precisely "you have gone too far." For all the community are holy, all of them, and the Lord is in their midst. Why then do you raise yourselves above the Lord's congregation?" (Num. 16:3). These challenges to Moses' authority could not have happened in the pre-Sinai phase of Israelite religion; they are a clear indication of the success of the steps taken by God and by Moses to weaken the centrality and importance of the leader in the eyes of the people. But the revolts indicated that they had been too successful, and that the absence of recognized leadership authority could present as great a danger to Israel as did the earlier overreliance of Moses. God, therefore, intervened in these rebellions to reinforce the statue of Moses by miraculous acts, demonstrating divine support for his authority.

The question of the extent of Moses' uniqueness was not fully resolved during his life. Although God wrought miracles to buttress Moses' authority, he rebuked him for acting to demonstrate his power at Meribah striking the rock and declaring, "are we to bring you forth water out of this rock?" (Num. 20:10)

Two precautions were taken to ensure that Moses would not become a messiah figure after his death. One was that he did not complete the task of redemption derived from God. In addition, a dead-hero cult was prevented by keeping the site of Moses' grave unknown. He was remembered, therefore, as a great man, but he did not pass into folklore as a messiah who would return to save the people once again.

After Moses, care was taken to change the structure of community leadership. Joshua was the political successor; for religious matters he had to consult Eleazar, the priest (Num. 27:15–22). The priesthood, in turn, had its limits, for Eleazar had to divine the Lord's decision by the use of the Urim and Thumim. The priests could not claim direct divine authority for decisions that they might reach without divination, and the main decisions of Joshua's time—the determination of the guilt of Achan and the division of the land—were made through divination by lots. After Moses there were three separate chains of authority: political, religious and the divine word. This became the pattern in the Classical Israel of biblical times: the political authority rested in the king, the normal religious authority in the priesthood, and the authority of the divine word with the "powerless" prophets. It was this "separation of powers" within the community that enabled Israel to create a political system which was fundamentally religious, but which at the same time did not turn into a religious dictatorship or a cultlike theocracy.

21 / The Theology of Catastrophe: A Question of Historical Justice*

1982

Two passages in ancient Near Eastern literature are striking for their extraordinary view of historical justice. The better known of the two is the discourse between Abraham and God about the destruction of Sodom and Gomorrah (Gen 18) in which Abraham asks God, "Will the judge of the world not do justice? Will you destroy the righteous with the wicked?" Had God answered, "I will spare the righteous and punish the wicked," we could easily understand the moral universe of the discussion, for the passage's concept of reward and punishment would be like ours. Instead, however, God expresses the divine readiness to spare the whole city if fifty righteous people are found in it, and after a give-and-take, reduces the critical number to ten. And we are left wondering how such a small number of righteous people could commute the punishment of the wicked. Moreover, we wonder, how could such a bargain and compromise be considered an ethical discussion of divine right and wrong?

The second passage is found in the epic of *Gilgamesh*, and the version of the flood story contained in it. After the flood, when the gods have gathered to eat Utnapishtim's sacrifice, Ea says to Enlil:

> Let the sinner bear his sin,
> The wrongdoer—his wrongdoing,
> Be merciful, lest he be cut off
> Have pity, lest. . . . (*Gilgamesh* XI 180–182)

* The earliest version of this study was presented as a paper at the Midwest meeting of the Society of Biblical Literature in 1982. It was published in Israel as a tribute to my colleague and friend, the late Raphael Kutscher.

These words sound like the classic formulation of historical retribution. However, he goes on to say:

> Instead of your bringing the flood—would that a lion had risen and wreaked destruction among humankind,
> Instead of your bringing the flood—would that a wolf had risen and wreaked destruction among humankind,
> Instead of your bringing the flood—would that famine had wreaked destruction among humankind,
> Instead of your bringing the flood—would that Erra had struck humankind.
> (*Gilgamesh* XI 183–186)

What, if any, is the connection between the beginning of Ea's exhortation and its end? How can the apparently arbitrary reduction of the human race operate on the same standard as the saying, "upon the sinner lay the punishment for his transgression?" Ea's speech has a long tradition behind it, for the Old Babylonian *Atrahasis* epic has a plot that resembles Ea's "would that . . ." wishes. In this epic, after the increase in human beings created a situation in which the land was "bellowing like a bull" and the god Enlil (in charge of events on the earth) could not sleep, the gods brought successive reductions of the human race by means of plague, drought, and famine until they finally decided to put an end to humankind by bringing the flood. The *Atrahasis* epic does not present these tragedies as punishments, but rather as Malthusian solutions to the problem presented by the overpopulation of the world. The god Ea, however, is not as sanguine about these disasters as the narrator. In Ea's speech in the *Gilgamesh* epic, the "lion rising to minimize humanity" is the answer to "let the sinner bear his punishment," and seems to demonstrate how "let the sinner bear his punishment" is to be carried out. But if this is the connection between the beginning of Ea's speech and its continuation, what is the reasoning that underlies this exhortation?

The answer to these questions can be found in a particular Near Eastern understanding of historical justice, the theology of catastrophe. Both Mesopotamia and Israel shared a historical perspective that held gods responsible for the events that caused the fall of nations. Moreover, they believed, when a city encountered catastrophe, the catastrophe had been brought by the gods of that very same city. The common perspective on catastrophe in Mesopotamia and Israel gave birth to a similar literature of lament in each culture. There are striking parallels between the Book of Lamentations and the Sumerian *Lament over the*

Destruction of Sumer and the *Lament over the Destruction of Sumer and Akkad.* But these parallels do not indicate a direct dependence of the Book of Lamentations on these much older laments from the first half of the second millennium B.C.E., over a thousand years older than the biblical text. More precisely, they result from a common way of looking at such catastrophes and possibly from a common literary tradition of the description of such catastrophes and then lamentation over them. For similar reasons, there are also clear parallels between the descriptions of the Day of YHWH in Israelite prophecy and the descriptions of the Day of Erra in the Babylonian Poem of Erra. This similarity is particularly striking in that the parallels between biblical texts and the Poem of Erra are the only ones between biblical literature and texts from Mesopotamia from the first millennium B.C.E.. It appears that the biblical passages, the Sumerian Laments, and the Day of Erra in the Poem of Erra all have their source in an early tradition that understood historical catastrophe as destruction brought by the national god.

The Bible's conception of catastrophe is closely connected to its concept of pollution, which it considers an important element in historical causation. Sin or wrongdoing results in physical pollution, which pollutes the wrongdoer, the public at large, and the land. This contamination is not simply metaphorical, but is a stain or raggedness that can be seen (by the eyes of God) and, like contemporary pollution, can render the land infertile. There are ways to purify the individual from his pollution and limited ways to purify the people as a whole, but there are absolutely no ways to purify the land, no rituals to eradicate the land's pollution. As a result, the pollution of the land, and to a lesser degree of the people, is cumulative, a spreading stain that cannot be erased. When the number of "stains" enlarges, when the level of pollution passes some sort of critical stage, the process becomes irreversible and unstoppable. No regret or repentance can erase the damage that has been done; no prayers or rituals can halt the pollution and its consequences. According to this biblical conception of sin, after pollution reaches a certain critical point, there is no longer any room for repentance or expiation.

This idea of the critical point of no return beyond which there is no repentance has much in common with the "hardening of the heart" of Pharaoh and of Israel. As Maimonides (and others) have recognized, Pharaoh hardened his own heart at the beginning, for he was stubborn enough and firm enough in his convictions not to listen to God's request. For this, he warranted his fate, and God thereafter intervened in order to prevent Pharaoh from changing his mind, and thereby to ensure that Pharaoh would continue to deserve the punishment that he had brought upon his own head. God's strange command to Isaiah comes from the same motivation. In Isaiah's vision (in chap. 6), Israel had already deserved its punishment, and so God sent Isaiah on a mission to "fatten the hearts of this people and harden its ears and weaken its eyes lest it see with its eyes and hear with its ears and its heart will understand and it will repent and be healed" (Isa. 6:10). Israel was to be given no opportunity to repent "until the cities will languish without inhabitants and houses without occupants and the land will be waste and desolate" (Isa. 6:11).

In both these passages, God intervenes at a point at which it would not yet be too late to repent, for true repentance would still be able to prevent the imminent destruction. However, God has made up his mind; God has decided to bring the destruction and therefore acts to prevent the repentance that might do the job. Later on in Israel's history, during the reign of Manasseh (according to the historian of 2 Kgs.), matters reached that critical point at which destruction was unstoppable, and no amount of repentance could prevent the destruction. After that, there was no need for God to prevent repentance; as the prophet Huldah informed the repenting King Josiah, repentance was no longer able to reverse the doom. Josiah's repentance could only defer the destruction until after his death (2 Kgs. 22:14–20). The destruction was not to be final, for the purpose of the catastrophe was not to destroy, but rather to punish and to instruct Israel by means of the absolute destruction of certain parts of it.

The closest parallel to this conception of catastrophe is the phenomenon known in the field of nuclear engineering as "critical mass." Once a critical mass of a radioactive substance is reached, an explosion begins; nothing is needed to start the explosion other than reaching that critical mass. In the biblical concept of catastrophe, the critical mass is composed of sins, and the explosion is the destruction and exile of the nation. Possibly, the degree of punishment was considered variable according to the measure of sins and transgressions. However, we have no information on this question. The only partial punishment that is described in quantitative terms is the destruction of Israel; most of the nation will be destroyed, and only a tenth will remain (Isa. 6:13).

Even though the society as a whole deserved such punishment (a concept normally called "collective responsibility"), nevertheless, from the moment that the destruction begins it does not operate on principles of ethical judgment. Once the critical mass is achieved and the explosion begins, anyone in the path of the destruction is liable to be destroyed. The destruction proceeds without discrimination. The portion of the nation comprising the one-tenth that is to survive decimation will not be chosen according to its characteristics or attributes. There is no hint that the surviving one-tenth has a higher proportion of righteous people than the nine-tenths of the nation that is destroyed. On the contrary, the idea of "a tenth of a tenth" is an indication that at its core, the rescued tenth is still endangered and most of it remains to be destroyed until only a tenth of that tenth is left.

Holding that catastrophe is void of ethical discrimination is actually in itself an important moral consideration. One must not see the death of an individual in an epidemic, a natural catastrophe, or war as having anything to do with retribution for his or her deeds. And one should not attribute greater righteousness to those who survive. From the moment the catastrophe begins, all rules of individual retribution are suspended.

Two passages describe an almost total destruction from which there remained only one survivor: the flood story and the tale of the overturning of Sodom and Gomorrah. The two survivors, Noah and Lot, are not presented as perfect persons. Even Noah, righteous in his generation, behaved less than perfectly after the flood, becoming drunk, placing himself in a compromising position, humiliated by his son and cursing his grandson. Nevertheless, as single survivors, they are chosen in advance to be spared from the destruction. In less total disasters, those who survive are not chosen to be spared.

These two almost total destructions—the flood and Sodom and Gomorrah—are the background to the two puzzling pronouncements that began our study. The conversation between Abraham and God concentrates on the question of why it was necessary to send the decree of catastrophe. To Abraham's question, "will you slay the righteous with the guilty?" God answers in narrative historical terms rather than ethical deliberation: if fifty righteous people can be found in the city, there will be no need to destroy it. In that event, the critical mass that makes destruction necessary will not be reached, and therefore God can spare the city. But if fifty righteous people cannot be found in the city—a number reduced by bargain to ten—then the critical mass will be achieved and destruction will arrive. It seems strange that such a small number of people can prevent the destruction of a whole city, but here too a comparison with nuclear physics helps us understand the phenomenon. In a nuclear reactor, a small amount of nonradioactive materials prevents the aggregation of the critical mass and thereby stops an explosion before it can begin. In Jewish tradition, the idea that a minimal amount of positive elements can prevent disaster reaches its Rabbinic expression in the concept of the "*Lamed-vavniks*," the thirty-six righteous men upon whom the world rests. The merit of these righteous prevents the destruction of the world.

Rabbinic Hebrew has a special term for this concept of catastrophe or, to be exact, Rabbinic language has a Greek term for this concept: *androlomousia* or, more correctly, *androloumsia*. This term derives from the Greek verb *androlepsia (androlempsia)* meaning "to snatch people." *Androlepsia* is a technical term for an Athenian legal custom, mentioned in several passages,[1] by which Athens gave herself the right to avenge a murder on an Athenian. If an Athenian was murdered outside Athens, the Athenians had the right to demand that the people of the area in which the murder had taken place deliver the murderers to justice. If they could not, or would not, then the family of the murdered party, or other Athenians acting for them, had the right (they declared) to go to the city in which the murder took place and take three people—any three people—in retribution for the murder. These people would be held hostage until their city delivered the murderer to Athens for trial, and would be punished in his stead if the city did not deliver the murderer. Rabbinic texts use the term somewhat differently, and it appears that their usage reflects the politico-judicial practice of Rome. According to Rabbi Simlai, "wherever you find *znut* [faithlessness], *androloumsia* comes into the world and kills the good and the evil."[2] *Androloumsia* is a horrendous disaster—an epidemic, a battle, a hurricane—that kills everyone in its path. Rabbi Simlai is saying that *znut* brings on the horrendous disaster, but when it arrives, it kills anyone in the area without looking for those who practiced *znut*. Moral discrimination is suspended until after the disaster.

To the Rabbis, the flood was the first example of *androloumsia*, for "the generations of the flood were not eradicated from the world until after they wallowed in *znut*."[3] Then *znut* brought *androloumsia*, in this case, the flood. The Rabbis interpret the verse, "And YHWH closed [the ark] upon him" (Gen 7:16) in the light of this understanding of the flood as *androloumsia;* Rabbi Levy compares it "to a prince who decreed *[an]drolomousia* on his country and took his beloved and locked him in a dungeon and placed his seal upon it.[4] In this way he distanced him from the path of political and military disaster. The word *androloumsia*, borrowed from Greek by the Rabbis, expresses the theology of disaster that provided the basis for an important aspect of biblical thinking about the destruction and the Babylonian Exile.

Ea's objection to the flood in the *Gilgamesh* epic is connected to his opposition to the absolute destruction of humankind. Even though Ea acknowledges the principle of ethical retribution ("let the sinner bear his sin"), he argues that there was no need to destroy humanity completely, but only to minimize it. Lions, wolves, famine, and disease are, in his mind more "moral" than the flood. Yet this "morality" does not signify a distinction between good and evil people, for there is no hint that the lion will destroy only sinners. It does signify that disasters brought upon humanity in times of crisis will be limited in their scope. They will not cause total destruction, and the good will have at least a chance to escape. But in *androloumsia* it is all random: the destruction is massive, the good can be caught, and the evil escape peril.

The famous words of the Irish poet W. B. Yeats convey some sense of this horrendous disaster:

> Things fall apart; the center cannot hold
> Mere anarchy is loosed upon the world
> The blood-dimmed tide is loosed, and everywhere
> The ceremony of innocence is drowned.[5]

For Yeats, such all-consuming destruction is a sign of future events, some kind of "labor pangs of the Messiah," as a "new beast slouches towards Bethlehem to be born." In the Bible and the tradition of the ancient Near East that lay behind it, such dreadful tragedy was the ultimate result of past actions, a historical retribution to a society that has lost its way.

NOTES

1. Demosthenes, Oration 23 "Against Aristocrates," par. 82 and Or. 51, "On the Trierachic Crown," par. 13.

2. Rabbi Simlai's words are brought in several places: *Vayiqra Rabbah* 23, 19; *Be-midbar Rabbah* 9, 33 and cf. *Bereshit Rabbah* 26.

3. *Vayiqra Rabbah* 23, 9.

4. *Bereshit Rabbah* 33.

5. W. B. Yeats, "The Second Coming."

22 / The End of the World and the Limits of Biblical Ecology

2001

It was only a year ago, though it seems much longer, that the end of the world was in the air. Places were going to drop out of the skies, not because their pilots went up in the rapture, but because their computers crashed on encountering double zeroes. Panic over Y2K brought back memories of doomsday fever at the end of the first millennium, and reminded us that apocalyptic ideas are part of the way that we see the world. Nonrational, nonscientific ways of imagining reality have found a new receptivity in the last fifty years, perhaps accompanying the collapse of absolute faith in science and rationalism in the postmodern shift of the latter half of the twentieth century. There has been a resurgence of both scholarly and popular interest in magic, in mysticism, in the occult and in apocalypticism. People are searching for old ways to express their spiritual understanding; scholars are seeking to recover and present long-forgotten ancient literature on these themes, to understand how this literature developed and to achieve a nuanced reading of these newly reintroduced writings. Our colleague Hans Dieter Betz has been in the forefront of this movement, and his work on Greco-Roman magic and on apocalyptic literature has been crucial in developing these areas of study. As early as 1966, Betz laid down several essential principles: that apocalypticism did not develop solely from inner-Jewish discourse, but was part of the "Hellenistic-oriental syncretism"; that understanding the theological intentions of an author demands clarity about the religio-historical context and traditions at work; and that one needs to detect the underlying questions which cause older material to be transmuted and recast.[1]

To turn first to the question of the "Hellenistic-oriental syncretism," the Hebrew Bible itself has more in common with Hellenism than is usually noted. Israel sat on several cultural axes, and participated in the culture of each complex. One was the "fertile crescent," the cultural complex centered on Mesopotamia; another involved interaction with Egypt; and yet another was a set of traditions from the eastern Mediterranean. Certain biblical ideas have more in common with Hittite and Greek concepts than with Babylonian or Assyrian. These are ideas about purity, pollution, and blood, some of the very ideas that Betz discusses in later apocalyptic literature. His concrete example illustrates the intricacy of following the thread of these traditions. Betz demonstrated that the statement of the "Angel of the waters" in Revelation 16 involves ideas widespread in the literature of the day—ideas of the personification of the elements, and especially of their pollution through bloodshed. Ideas about the pollution of the earth, prominent in the Greco-Roman period, did not originate then. Pollution is a central concern of the Hebrew Bible. The pollution of the earth necessitated the primeval flood, and the pollution of the land of Israel brings exile. The chief cause of such pollution is murder, which forms a "gruesome threesome" with the other causes—serious sexual impropriety and (in Ezekiel) idolatry—and Israelite law warns the people to be careful not to pollute the land.[2] Pollution of the land through bloodshed is also a concern of ancient Athenian law. Is the presence of this concern in Jewish and Christian apocalyptic texts a feature brought in from other Greco-Roman literature of their times, or was it an outgrowth of the biblical idea? Perhaps the answer is "yes" and "yes." The pollution of water, on the other hand, is not an outgrowth from the Hebrew Bible.

Both the Hebrew Bible and later apocalyptic literature conceive of a future redemption in which God will purify. When God redeems, God purifies. But there is an underlying question that has to be addressed: can we be sure that God will always redeem? Will future destructions always usher in new beginnings? Will there ever be a destruction of humanity, and will it involve the end of the world? Will the end of history involve an eschatological new reality? Or will it all end someday?

The Hebrew Bible wrestles with this question, and with the underlying issue that it involves: does the world have a purpose? An old children's song expresses the difficulty of understanding this question:

> I know an old lady who swallowed a fly,
>   I don't know why she swallowed the fly.
>   Perhaps she'll die.
> I know an old lady who swallowed a spider,
>   which wiggled and tickled and giggled inside her.

She swallowed the spider to catch the fly,
　but I don't know why she swallowed the fly.
　　Perhaps she'll die.

Why did God create the world? God created humankind (Gen. 1 tells us) to administer the world, to have mastery over the world. But why did God create the world? God created humanity (Gen. 2 tells us) to work and guard the world. But why did God create the world? The Bible never answers this question, and in this silence lies the essence of biblical thinking about the earth, the environment, and ecology.[3]

In the polytheistic religions of the ancient Near East, this question simply didn't arise. Gods, after all, had to eat, and if they had to eat, they had to farm. The Babylonian *Atrahasis* epic tells us why the gods created humanity. After digging the Tigris and Euphrates rivers, those massive irrigation canals, the exhausted gods realized the advisability of passing on the work to others—a larger, subordinate workforce. And so they created human beings. The purpose of humanity and of the soil that they work is the care and feeding of the gods.[4]

Such an answer, of course, will not work in a monotheistic religion in which God neither works nor eats. As scholars who are trained to look at matters historically, aided by the tools of *Religionsgesschichte*, we can speculate that the idea that human beings were created to work the soil ultimately comes from a time when Israel believed that God ate. Nevertheless, Israel told this story and understood humanity's role through this story long after Israel ceased to believe that God had any physical need for soil and food. If there is no cosmic need for crops (beyond feeding humanity), then there must be a meaning for humanity's existence beyond the growing of crops.

The priestly view of earthly fertility makes the need to find a non-agricultural role for humanity even more acute. In Genesis 2, the earth was a barren place until God brought moisture and humans to work the soil. In Genesis 1, on the other hand, the creation of dry land on the third day is immediately followed—on the same day—by the creation of vegetation. The formal structure of Genesis 1 underscores the message. Only one "thing" was created on the first day (light) and only one "thing" on the second (the firmament dividing the waters). On the third day, one "thing" was created and pronounced complete—dry land—but on that same day God created vegetation. The meaning is clear: fertility is the normal created state of the earth, and there was not even a single cosmic moment in which the earth was barren. The refrain further intensifies the message: the earth brought forth vegetation "each bearing

fruit according to its own kind." The fertility of the earth is self-perpetuating. It does not require the intervention of deity or the ritual actions of
fertility cult, or the ongoing labors of humanity. Left to itself, the earth
will continue to be fertile. Left to itself, vegetation is self-propagating.
In this view, humanity cannot be created simply to farm, and humans
become administrators, tamers, and subduers of the wilder tendencies
of the earth, the stewards of the world with dominion over it.

The role for humanity is spelled out by the use of the phrase *tselem
elohim,* the image of God. The term *ṣalmu* is known from Mesopotamian
inscriptions, where the *ṣalmu,* the statue, can represent the king and
where the king can be the *ṣalmu,* "image," of the gods. The human being
is the avatar of God on earth, the one who keeps everything going properly. This role for humanity is the subject of Psalm 8:

> When I see the heavens, the work of your fingers,
> the moon and the stars which you established:
> What is humanity, that you should consider it?
> Children of Adam that you should take note of us?
> For you have made us only slightly less than the gods,
>   crowning us with glory and honor.
> You have given us dominion over the works of your hands,
>   placed everything under our feet.

This very famous passage has long been understood as the biblical
counterweight to the opposite valuation of humanity, Job's statement
"I am but dust and ashes." But the passage has even more profound
implications. The occasion for the poet's meditation on the status of
humanity is a contemplation of the stars. The night sky can be an awesome sight, and can certainly inspire feelings of smallness and crea-
turehood, feelings that might induce philosophical reflection. But here
the night sky may resonate with an allusion to the great Babylonian
myth *Enuma Elish,* "The Exaltation of Marduk." In this myth, Marduk
defeats Tiamat and becomes king of the gods. He sets out to organize
the world politically, on the model of a state. He turns first to the
heavens, where he assigns each god a "standing" place, a fixed place
in the heaven from which it can operate. The god is associated with
this place, its constellation in the sky. The word for "standing place,"
mazzaltu in Akkadian, is the Hebrew word for constellation (*mazzal*)
and, by extension, for fortune. Once Marduk has organized the heavens, he creates the rivers and mountains from Tiamat's body, and then
creates humanity so that the gods will not have to work. The latter's
role, instead, will be to supervise, to have the role and the power to

administrate the universe. In Babylonian thought, the stars in their courses (or rather the gods whose places are in these stars) rule the world. In Israel, the poet looks at the stars and makes this connection. The Israelite poet knows that the stars do not rule, that the administration of the world is humanity's job. Even though the humans are themselves works that God's hands have created, they have a role that other theologies attribute to some gods themselves.

But how does one administer a cosmos? The high role assigned to humanity is a prescription for disaster. Since humans are responsible for the running of the cosmos, they are responsible for anything that goes wrong. The Bible is a veritable catalogue of disasters that carry a clear and unequivocal message: we humans, and in particular, we Israel, are responsible. The primeval history of Genesis 1–11 sets the pattern, as human misdeed progressively impacts upon the fertility of the earth. The cause and effect relationship is clear in the stories and spelled out in the legal sections of the Pentateuch. The Priestly writers of Leviticus and Deuteronomy speak of the pollution of the earth that results from human misdeeds; the Deuteronomic passages concentrate on the cessation of rains that follows if Israel sins. Both consequences lead to the same ultimate result: the land (in particular the land of Israel) becomes infertile and the people must leave.

In the old Mesopotamian theology in which human beings were the workforce for the gods, the position of gods' laborers, lowly though it might seem, had a built-in security. The reassurance this position offers humans is made explicit in the *Atrahasis* epic, the same story that detailed the creation of humans to be the workers. After the creation, relates the epic, the human population grows to become such a problem for the gods that they "cannot sleep." The gods first bring drought, then plague, then infertile soul to prevent human growth, but humans keep bouncing back. The gods finally decide to bring a flood to destroy humanity. But as the flood covers the earth, the gods soon realize what they have done in destroying humanity. To quote the text, "their hearts were broken and they thirsted for beer." Nobody is feeding them, and their hunger brings them to a realization of the enormous consequences of their actions. The goddess Ishtar articulates the issue, lamenting that they have destroyed their own creation, and the gods become angry at the god Enlil who moved them to take such an action. The same gods who were eager and willing to destroy humankind when its numbers disturbed their peace now regret having made that decision. Once they are truly upset that humanity has been destroyed, the god Enki has

Atrahasis come out of the ark and offer a sacrifice from the animals on the boat, and the gods are so hungry that they swarm over the sacrifice "like flies." Once humanity has been saved, wise Enki presents a permanent solution to the problem of overpopulation by creating barrenness, miscarriage, perinatal death, socially nonbearing women, a limited lifespan, and other currently unreadable population safeguards. Thereupon the gods are so overjoyed that humanity has been saved that they reward *Atrahasis* with eternal life.

In this story, the gods' hunger for beer during the flood made them realize how much they depend on humanity for their physical comforts. Like all leisure classes, the gods have become dependent on their workforce to ensure the continuation of their lifestyle. Human beings may be a servant class, but their place in this universe is secure. The useful role of humanity means that the gods will never destroy them, not because of divine benevolence, but because the gods need them. Moreover, the Sumerian story of Lahar and Ashnan reveals that the gods will be benefactors of human beings—again, not because of abstract benevolence, but out of their own desires. Lahar and Ashnan tell us that the earliest human beings were primitive, naked, and eating grasses and drinking water. They gave the gods what they had, but the gods became tired of such primitive fare. To better the offerings that they themselves received, the gods gave humankind grain and wool and taught them how to work the wool into clothing. The enlightened self-interest of the gods makes them sustain the life of human beings.

Biblical theology cannot offer the same assurances. God does not need humanity, and humanity can only rely on divine benevolence to save them, and on the same divine agenda that brought God to create humanity to supervise the earth. But which is primary to God's agenda, the earth or humanity? There is an essential conundrum here. The farmer story of Genesis 2 seems to make the earth primary, and we are created to work and tend it. But even in this view of humanity, the question arises: if humans do not tend the earth well, will God destroy the earth? The flood does not answer this question; it only demonstrates how acute the problem is. When God saw that the earth had become polluted, God destroyed the old order, washing the earth clean of all animals and humans. But God saved Noah to begin again. God then promised not to bring a flood again. Does this mean that God won't destroy the world again? Or does it mean "the fire next time?" The Bible never spells out the answer to this question. It does depict God's determination not to continue to punish the earth because of human misdeeds. And it shows God providing laws that are supposed to prevent the contamination of the earth.

These laws, presented in Genesis 9, are revealing. They reinforce the executive nature of humanity, setting it apart from the rest of the animal kingdom. At the same time, they cannot eliminate violence. The solutions the law prescribes are violent as they introduce controlled violent measure to limit violence. Shedding the blood of those who shed blood is supposed to prevent bloodshed from contaminating the earth. But what will God do if the laws do not succeed, if they are not able to prevent humanity from polluting the world?

Israel's speculation on this issue must have been greatly enhanced by the series of ecological disasters that struck Israel in the eighth century, the same century that witnessed the destruction of the northern kingdom by the Assyrian Empire. The first prophecy of Amos bears a notation that it was given two years before the earthquake (which thereby bore out Amos' prophecy and established his credibility). This earthquake was so massive that Amos considers the population of Israel a remnant from destruction. "I overturned you as God overturned Sodom and Gomorrah. And you were like a brand saved from the fire" (Amos 4:11). The earthquake also brought Isaiah to think of Sodom and Gomorrah, for his famous statement "If YHWH of hosts has not left us a small remnant, we would be like Sodom and Gomorrah" (Isa. 1:9) is about the earthquake rather than a future destruction. The earthquake was not an isolated phenomenon, and the eighth century also witnessed widespread rainlessness, famine, and pestilence, with weird droughts that fell on one city and not on another: "I for my part have given you cleanness of teeth in all your towns, lack of food in all your settlements . . . I withheld the rain from you three months before harvesttime: I would make it rain on one town and not on another, one field would be rained upon while another on which it did not rain would wither" (Amos 4:6–7).

Amos recites hymns that emphasize God's role as creator: "For behold! He forms mountains and creates the wind . . . He makes blackness into daybreak and treads on the high places of the earth" (Amos 4:13). "The one who built his chambers in heaven and founded his vault on earth, who summons the waters of the sea and pours them over the land, his name is YHWH" (Amos 9:6). In the Hebrew Bible, God's creation is often mentioned in connection with God's redemption. But in Amos' "creation theology," God's creation is a reminder of God's power to destroy. This power to destroy becomes the major theme of the forthcoming "Day of the Lord" predicted by Amos and the prophets who came after him. The phrase *and the coming of God's day* may have been an established part of Israel's cult, based in an early nationalist idea that the Lord would arise and come some day to rescue Israel and take vengeance on her enemies. But Amos and the later preexilic prophets turned this idea on its head, proclaiming the Day of the Lord as a day of judgment and terror: "Ah, you who wish for the day of YHWH! Why should you want the day of YHWH? It will be darkness, not light" (Amos 5:18). In the new sense of the Day of the Lord, God's appearance has an impact on the earth itself, and beyond the earth to the heavens whose lights cease to shine. In the words of Isaiah, "therefore I will upset the heavens and the earth will quake its place, in the coming of YHWH of hosts in his day of wrath" (Isa. 13:11).

God's very movements shake nature, making mountains quake at his footsteps. Beyond this almost incidental effect, nature is both the weapon of God's judgment and its object, for the earth will suffer when God comes in wrath. As a result, God's relationship with Israel (and with all humanity) determines the destiny of the natural world. There is an old history to this idea, for in the Babylonian *Atrahasis* story, the gods were not focused on the well-being of the soil and the environment. They sacrificed it, sending droughts and soil pollution, and they concentrated on their problems with humanity and tried to destroy humankind. Droughts, famine, and pestilence were weapons and tools of the gods. The message of the prophets is not terribly different: the earth suffers because of human actions. In the Bible the earth suffers twice. As in Babylon, the biblical God uses the earth in God's retributive actions. In the Bible, moreover, the actions of humans have a direct polluting effect on the earth, which thereupon is "cursed" and becomes infertile. The process is expressed clearly in the "Isaian Apocolypse," Isaiah 24:4–20:

> The earth is mourning, dejected, the earth has become wretched,
> The inhabited world has become wretched . . .
> For the earth is polluted under her inhabitants because they have trespassed instructions, they have left and destroyed the eternal covenant.
> For this a curse has eaten the land, and her inhabitants are suffering.
> for this . . .
> The earth is breaking, breaking,
> the earth is crumbling, crumbling
> the earth is tottering, tottering,
> the earth is reeling, like a drunk,
> she is rocking to and fro like a hut.
> Her iniquity lies heavy upon her,
> she has fallen and does not rise.

At such a time when God appears in retribution, the whole earth is wiped out, including the humans and the animals, the fish and the fowl.

Can this devastation be the end of history? On this question the prophets are divided. Hosea and Joel speak of a future in which peace and fertility will be restored. Jeremiah, who depicts the devastation to come in terms that reverse the act of creation, nevertheless declares that the awesome destruction of creation will not be the end of the story.

> I look at the earth, it is unformed and void;
> at the skies, and their light is gone.
> I look at the mountains, they are quaking and the hills are rocking.
> I look: no human is left, and all the birds of the sky have gone.
> I look, the far land is desert, and all its towns are in ruin.
> Because of YHWH, because of his blazing anger.
> For thus said YHWH: the whole land will be desolate,
> but I will not make a final end to it (Jer. 4:23–27).

The Hebrew word that Jeremiah uses for "final end" is *kallah*. This is the Hebrew equivalent of the Akkadian word *gamertam,* the word that the *Atrahasis* epic uses to describe the decision of the gods for a "final solution" of humanity. In that story, the gods changed their minds once they became hungry and realized that they needed humanity to feed them. In the Bible, there is no such assurance. At least by the time of the later prophets, Israel knows that God does not need people to feed God: "Lebanon is not fuel enough, not its beasts enough for sacrifice" (Isa. 40:16). Humanity has no absolute guarantee of continued existence, and people must rely on God's benevolence and on God's mysterious agenda for creating humankind. Even God's promise never again to bring a flood upon the earth leaves open the possibility that God could interpret the promise narrowly and bring another kind of catastrophe to end the earth. Jeremiah, like the other prophets, has his eye on the restoration to follow God's wrath. But Zaphaniah considers a very clearly final end, using the same word *kallah* to envision the end of the earth:

> In the fire of his rage, the whole earth will be consumed,
> for God will make an awesome final end of all the inhabitants of the earth (Zeph. 1:18).

Suppose Zephaniah has it right, and God is willing to end the history of humanity? Can it be that the world could continue without us? Even if (horrors to contemplate) we thoroughly pollute the soil or deplete the ozone, even if we bring a nuclear disaster (God and humanity forbid) and a nuclear winter, might it nevertheless happen that the earth itself would survive and the cockroaches would still continue as they have endured since the age of the dinosaurs and so in a sense the world would still continue? A Gaia philosophy tells us that we will not have destroyed earth utterly: we will only have eradicated it as a habitable place for humanity. The earth, Gaia, the ecosystem, existed before us and will continue after us. . . .

Deutero-Isaiah addresses this issue. Isaiah concentrates on the creator aspect of God, on God's vastness and incomparability. The prophet who makes it clear that God could never be fed by the world knows that God's agenda for the earth must go beyond agriculture. To Deutero-Isaiah, God's purpose and activity in the world are intimately connected to the fate of "the worm Jacob" (Isa. 41:14). The redemption of Israel is the reason that the master of nature and history moves events, nations, rivers and mountains. At the same time, God's redemption of God's people has cosmic consequences: the whole world will prosper now that God has had compassion over God's people.

> Rejoice, O heaven and be happy, O earth!
> Let the mountains open in song,
> for God has compassion on his people
> > and redeems its wretched ones (Isa. 49:13).

God's return to his people means the resuscitation of Israel's land:

> He will change her desert to Eden,
> her desolate land to the garden of YHWH (Isa. 51:3).

God does not desire the ruined, uninhabited, (and to Isaiah) uninhabitable condition of the land of Israel. The land's ruination was a consequence of God's anger at Israel, and now that God has gotten over God's anger, God will restore Israel's environment to Edenic perfection.

Isaiah focuses on Israel, the people in exile and their return to Zion. But (s)he make it clear that this pattern has universal implications. God would not be satisfied with a wasted world:

כי כה אמר יי בורא השמים-
הוא האלהים
יצר הארץ ועשה
הוא כוננה
לא-תהו בראה
לשבת יצרה

For thus says YHWH, Creator of Heaven—
He is the God
Creator of the earth and her maker,
He established her.
Not for waste did He create her,
for inhabiting He formed her (Isa. 45:18).

A waste ecology, populated by cockroaches and bats, is not part of God's plan for the universe. The earth must include human inhabitation. Whatever God's final purpose for the earth, this is the bottom line. Human existence is the absolute limit of biblical earth-talk. Humanity and the earth are totally interdependent. Humans depend on the earth's creative powers, and the fate of the earth depends on human behavior. The well-being of the environment depends on the deeds of human beings, both because humans themselves can damage the earth's environment, and because God may damage the earth as God sacrifices the ecological well-being of the land in response to human actions. But even though God may bring various ecological cataclysms, God will not have the earth stay wasted, nor is the earth supposed to exist without people. The destiny of the earth is closely dependent on human beings, and the destiny of humanity is closely related with the earth. Humans, created from the earth and named as "earthlings" *(adam* from *adamah),* are intertwined with earth's destiny, at least for the next five billion years till the sun explodes.

Isaiah's prophetic statement that the earth was created in order to have inhabitants has a narrative parallel in the much misunderstood story of the Tower of Babel. When humans begin building their tower, God realizes their abilities, and declares that "now, nothing that they propose is impervious to them" (Gen. 11:6)—a statement made otherwise only about God (Job 42:2). This human ability presents both danger and opportunity: danger because, if they continue to cluster together in an increasingly tall city, they will lose their connection to the earth and become totally like gods, effectively canceling the purpose of creation; opportunity, because they now have the technological and other capacity to fulfill their destiny, which is to spread out and fill the earth. At creation God declared that humans should "increase and multiply and fill the earth." Now that humans no longer have the need to cluster together, the time to fully realize this mission has come. To this end, God mixes their speech and so fragments them to spread out and create an inhabited world.

Humanity and the ecosystem have to be held in equilibrium. For whatever reason God created the cosmos, God has great allegiance to it and will not allow humanity to continue to damage the earth for its own benefit. But, from the biblical viewpoints, humanity also had independent and equal importance. Forms of deep ecology, which place the earth above humanity, are not biblical theologies, for the biblical ideal of *shalom* must include the presence of human beings. There is no further destiny for the earth. If humans continue on a disharmonious path, the whole world will be destroyed. Even if the cockroaches and insects could then take over, the divine plan would end with the end of human history.

Isaiah did not have the final word. As new troubles made it clear that the return from Babylon would not bring eschatological perfection, the last prophets of the Hebrew Bible turned again to thoughts of the Day of the Lord, the punishment of the wicked, the vindication of Israel. Isaiah is determined to believe that after the coming of God's fire and whirlwind, "like the new sky and new earth that I am making stand before me, so will your seed and your name" (Isa. 66:22). Not only humankind, but Israel, will remain as long as the new perfected universe.

Zechariah has a similar message. He, too, foresees a terrible cataclysm with nuclear-like devastation, but when it finishes, "they will live in it and there will be no more total destruction, and Jerusalem will dwell securely" (Zech. 14:11). Zechariah extends to all nations the same insecure ecology that Israel has held: if they do not come to worship God they will not have rain (Zech. 14:18). The cycle of the earth is therefore not finished: now every nation's failures can have an impact upon the earth.

Zechariah's word for total destruction, *herem*, resonates in the last prophet, Malachi. He, too, prophesies a *dies irae* of awesome destruction, one in which those who "fear my name" will be saved and prosper (MT Mal. 3:19–21= English Mal. 4:1–3). But Malachi ends on the old disturbing note. God will send Elijah before the great and awesome day to reconcile father and sons "lest I come and smite the land with total destruction *(herem)*" (MT Mal. 3:24= English Mal. 4:6). When fathers and sons fall out again, and when people forget the Torah of Moshe, will there be a *herem*?

The legacy of the Hebrew Bible on this matter, as on so many others, is one of questions with no ultimate answers. The polysemy and indeterminacy of the Hebrew Bible are famous, but now newly appreciated. Perhaps they stem from the ultimate uncertainties of biblical monotheism. Not only is God not fully knowable, but God's agenda for the world is never spelled out. Since humanity's destiny is inextricably bound up with the world's, that leaves our own position in the universe fundamentally insecure. This angst goes beyond the uncertainties brought by the ordinary vicissitudes of history. It exacerbates Israel's tensions about being a small nation surrounded by empires, and its anxieties about being covenanted with such an awesome and mighty deity. The fate of the universe depends on the actions of humans, and from that fact stems the creative tension that fuels the many different opinions about the end of history.

The lack of clear answers to Israel's questions also meant that Israel would not cease its questioning. Israel's views were continually evolving. It continued to search its own scriptures to find new clues and new meanings through inner-Jewish exegesis even as it remained open to the wisdom and scriptures of the peoples with which it came in contact. The explosion of cultural horizons in the Persian and Greco-Roman periods created a ferment of intermingling motifs and ideas out of which Jewish and Christian apocalyptic literature developed. The basic questions and insecurity about human existence, never resolved in monotheism, became the engine that fueled the great literary creativity of apocalypticism.

NOTES

1. Hans Dieter Betz, "Zum Problem der religiongesschichtlichen Verstandnisses der Apokalyptik," *ZTK* 63 (1966): 391–409; published in English as "On the Problem of the Religio-Historical Understanding of Apocalypticism," ed. Robert Funk (New York: Herder and Herder, 1969), 134–56 and reprinted in Hans Dieter Betz, *Hellenismus and Ur-christentum: Gesammelte Aufsatze I* (Tübingen: Mohr/Siebeck, 1990), no. 4.

2. On pollution in Israel, see Tikva Frymer-Kensky, "The *Atrahasis* Epic and Its Significance for Our Understanding of Genesis 1–9," *BA* 40 (1977): 147–155 and idem, "Pollution, Purification and Purgation in Biblical Israel," in *The Word of the Lord Shall Go Forth: Essays in Honor of David Noel Freedman in Celebration of His Sixtieth Birthday*, eds. Carol Meyers and Michael O'Connor (Winona Lake, Ind.: Eisenbrauns, 1983), 399–414.

3. For writings on biblical ecology, see the seminal article by Lynn White, Jr., "The Historical Roots of Our Ecological Crisis," *Science* 155 (1967); Jeanne Kay, "Concepts of Nature in the Hebrew Bible," *Environmental Ethics* 10.4 (1988): 309–27; and recently J. Baird Callicott, "Genesis Revisited: Murian Musings on the Lynn White, Jr. Debate," *Environmental History Review* 14.1–2 (1990): 65–90.

4. The copy of the *Atrahasis* epic was published by W. G. Lambert and A. R. Millard, *Cuneiform Texts from Babylonian Tablets in the British Museum*,

XLVII (London: Trustees of the British Museum, 1967), no. 2965. Lambert and Millard published the edition and English translation in *Atra-Hasis: The Babylonian Story of the Flood* (Oxford: Clarendon, 1969). For a consideration of the importance of this text for Mesopotamian ecology, see A. D. Kilmer, "The Mesopotamian Concept of Overpopulation and Its Solution as Reflected in the Mythologies," *Orientalia* 41 (1972): 160–77; for biblical ecology, see Frymer-Kensky, "The *Atrahasis* epic," and idem, "Ecology in a Biblical Perspective," in *The Torah of the Earth*, ed. Arthur Waskow (Woodstock, Vt.: Jewish Lights, 2000), 55–69.

23 / Pollution, Purification, and Purgation in Biblical Israel

1983

MAJOR AND MINOR POLLUTIONS

The ideas of pollution, purity, and purification were fundamental concepts of biblical Israel. The desire for purity was so intense that a major social class, the priesthood, was entrusted with the task of determining and giving instruction about purity and impurity. Pollution, the lack of purity, could affect individuals, the Temple, the collectivity of Israel, and the land of Israel itself. Some forms of pollution could be eradicated by rituals; the performance of these purifications and expiations was a major function of the priesthood. The pollution caused by the performance of certain deeds, however, could not be eradicated by rituals; Israel believed that the person intentionally committing these acts would suffer catastrophic retribution. Wrongful acts could cause the pollution of the nation and of the land of Israel, which could also not be "cured" by ritual. There was therefore an ultimate expectation of catastrophic results for the whole people, the "purging" of the land by destruction and exile. Pollution was thus thought to be one of the determinants of Israel's history, and the concepts of pollution and purgation provided a paradigm by which Israel could understand and survive the destruction of the Temple. The idea of pollution was such an important part of Israel's worldview that its primeval history, its story of origins, was also seen as a story of cosmic pollution and purgation.

The simplest type of impurity is the impure state of the Levitical laws.[1] If an individual comes in to contact with a polluting substance, that person becomes impure for seven days or more, in the case of major pollutions, or until evening, for minor pollutions. During the period of his impurity, the polluted individual is highly contagious. He must avoid contact with others and must take care to avoid coming into contact with the sacred.

External causes (things) normally cause only minor contamination. The chief exception to this is death. Corpse-contamination is a most virulent pollution. Contamination for seven days results not only from contact with a corpse but also from being in a tent when someone dies, and even from contact with the human bones or graves of a corpse-defiled person (Num 19:11, 14, 16); everyone involved in purification rituals suffers minor contamination. In the ideal camp of the desert, therefore, corpse-defiled people were to stay outside the camp for seven days (Num 31:19). The other major external pollutant is the disease of leprosy (Lev 13–14). The leper's contamination is considered so intense that he must dwell outside the camp, alone, and he must indicate his condition by tearing his clothes, growing a mustache, leaving his hair disheveled, and calling out, "Unclean, unclean" (Lev 13:45–46). He remains impure for seven days after the leprosy is pronounced healed. We are not informed what happens to an individual who comes into contact with a "leper" (assuming of course that he does not contract the disease from casual contact); we might speculate that he would become impure, perhaps for the major period of seven days. Other external causes of pollution (see chart below) cause only minor pollution.

The extremely defiling nature of corpses has been explained as an attempt to avoid a cult of the dead (Wold 1979, 18). However, there may be a more fundamental reason: in Israelite cosmology it was considered vitally important to maintain the structure of the universe by keeping all distinctions (boundaries) firm (Douglas 1966, 53). The boundaries between life and death are crucial and no individual who has had contact with the world of death can be part of life. He must therefore sit in limbo—outside the camp—for seven days and undergo a special ritual (sprinkling with the "waters of impurity," Num 19) to enable him to rejoin the life-group. Before he has spent his time in limbo and been readmitted to the group he belongs at least partially to the world of death. The severe isolation of the leper may also be related to this distinction between life and death (in addition to its value as a medical quarantine). If the disease was at all similar to modern leprosy, its affect in an advanced state was similar to the decomposition of a corpse; the biblical association of leprosy and corpses is expressed in Numbers 12:12, where the leprous Miriam is compared to one born dead and half decomposed. The afflicted individual, like one who has been in contact with a corpse, might have been considered to be in a no-man's-land between two realms which must be kept rigidly apart. It may be relevant that disheveled hair and rent clothes are a sign of mourning (Lev 10:6); the leper may be mourning his own "death." The ritual that the healed leper undergoes before he can reenter the camp (Lev 14:4–7) may also indicate that this blurring of the demarcation between life and death lies behind the virulence of the contamination of leprosy. Two clean birds are taken, one of which is killed over a bowl with running water. The living bird is dipped in the blood of the dead bird, the leper is sprinkled with the blood of the slain bird, and the living bird is let loose in the field. The formal similarity between this ritual and the ritual of the Day of Atonement is apparent: both involve two creatures, one of which is killed and the other set free. In the case of the leper, the symbolism focuses on the living bird who has been in contact with death (dipped in the blood of the killed bird) and is then set free; so too the leper has been set free from his brush with death. The leper may then return to the camp, although he is still impure and must remain outside his tent seven days before undergoing a ritual of readmission and resuming normal life (Lev 14:10–32).

The other major pollutions are caused by emissions from the human body. The most enduring is that of childbirth (Lev 12). Birth of a male child renders a woman impure for seven days, birth of a female for fourteen days. After this period, although no longer impure, the mother is not totally pure and must avoid the realm of the holy for an additional thirty-three days for a male and sixty-six days for a female. This additional semi-impure period is known as the period of blood-purification (*dmy ṭhrh*, Lev 12:4, also *ymy ṭhrh*, 12:4). No reason is given why a male pollutes his mother only half as long as a female pollutes hers: one might speculate that the necessity of having the circumcisions on the eighth day made it impossible for the period of full impurity to last more than seven days after the birth of a male child, but why should the birth of a female contaminate for fourteen? The lengthy transitional periods ("purification") after childbirth is unique. Although childbirth involves emissions of blood and other fluids, and therefore could be expected to contaminate, like menstruation, for at least seven days, this does not explain why the contamination of childbirth lingers on, at least partially, after the seven- or fourteen-day period has elapsed. It may be that, like the person who has touched death, the person who has experienced birth has been at the boundaries of life/nonlife and therefore cannot directly reenter the community. She therefore must undergo a long period of transition before she can reapproach the sacred.

The other two causes of major pollution are menstruation, and genital discharge for males and females (Lev 15). Menstruation pollutes a woman and any man who has intercourse with her for seven days after (apparently from the onset of menstruation); genital discharge pollutes for seven days after the discharge has disappeared. The reason for the severity of this pollution, or for its cause, is not quite clear. In her pioneering study of impurity, Douglas suggested that the human body served as the symbol for the body politic. Since Israel, as a hard-pressed minority, was careful to maintain its boundaries, that which entered the body was carefully regulated, and that which left was a polluting agent (1966, 124; see 1975, 269). Douglas explicitly assumes (1966, 51, 124), that all bodily emissions were considered polluting. This, however, is not indicated in the Bible. On the contrary, only emissions from the genitalia were considered polluting agents. Despite the fact that food (entry into the body) was carefully regulated, the excreta involved in the digestive process—saliva, urine, feces—are not mentioned as polluting. Defecation is supposed to take place outside the ideal camp (Deut 23:13–15) but individuals excreting or even touching feces are not considered defiled until evening, nor is it prescribed that they must bathe. Even those emissions that might be considered somewhat diseased—nasal discharge, sputum, pus—are not mentioned as polluting agents. The most conspicuous human emission absent from the list of polluting agents is human blood (or, for that matter, any blood). Blood, of course, may not be eaten. However, despite the fact that menstrual blood is a major contaminant, and that (innocent) bloodshed is the most important pollutant of the land (see below), ordinary blood is not mentioned as a contaminant. Bleeding or touching blood is not considered polluting, and people who are wounded and bleeding are not defiled and are not forbidden to come to the Temple or to partake of sacrifices. The only bodily emissions that pollute are those involved with sex: menstrual blood and discharges as major pollutants, ejaculation (with or without intercourse) until the evening. The reason that these are considered polluting must lie in the social relations between men and women and in the culture's attitude toward sex.

Minor pollutions are generally contracted from external causes: contact with impure things, such as the carcasses of unclean animals, or contact with something that has become unclean through contact with someone under a major pollution; or contact with someone who is polluted with a major pollution. The only internally caused minor pollution mentioned is caused by seminal discharge through ejaculation or fornication. For convenience, I include a chart of the minor pollutions mentioned in the Levitical laws (see page 336).

The prime characteristic of the major pollutions is their contagion. People who have a major pollution can defile others, making them impure for the duration of the day. People with a major pollution can also defile things which, in turn, can defile other people for the day. The Levitical laws do not indicate whether a person under a minor pollution can himself defile during the day that he is impure. Our assumption would be that a person with a minor pollution cannot defile, because otherwise there would be no end,[2] and because we would expect some warning if minor defilement was contagious. This is indeed the way later Jewish law understood the issue of contagion.

These pollutions are contagious, but they are not dangerous. No harm is expected to come to the individual who has become impure in any of these ways, nor is there a hint that a man who, e.g., touches his menstruating wife would suffer harm or fail in his crops, only that he himself will become impure for the day. The only characteristic of *ṭm'h*, "pollution," is contagion; the only misfortune associated with the condition is isolation from the people and alienation from all things holy. The condition of impurity becomes actively dangerous to the individual only when it comes into contact with the sacred. Since the impure can defile the sacred, the sacred must be protected. This goal may be accomplished by direct means such as posting guards to prevent visibly impure people from approaching the Temple (2 Chr 23:19). It is also achieved by a belief that catastrophe will strike whoever approaches the sacred while impure: an impure priest who eats the sacred portions (Lev 22:3–9), an impure person who eats a sacrifice of well-being (Lev 7:20–21),[3] and anyone who comes to the Temple while impure. As long as the polluted individual avoids the realm of the sacred he is not expected to suffer any harm: he waits out his period of pollution, performs appropriate purification and readmission rituals, and returns to ordinary membership in the community. There is only one threat inherent in these pollutions. Since they are contagious, there is a danger that the contagion will spread throughout the community, thus effectively isolating the entire community from contact with God. Since the community believes its well-being to be dependent on its relationship to God, alienation from God could present impossible danger.

There is no onus attached to these pollutions, no idea that they result from forbidden or improper actions, no "guilt" attributed to the impure. Acts which are prohibited are not said to result in an impure state. On

verse	source of uncleanness	action of person	wait till evening	wash clothes	bathe
Lev 11:24,27	carcass of unclean animal	touching	x		
11:25,28	carcass of unclean animal	carrying	x	x	
11:31	carcass of unclean animal	touching	x		
11:39	carcass of unclean animal	touching	x		
11:40	carcass of unclean animal	carrying	x	x	
11:40	carcass of unclean animal	eating	x	x	
14:46	leprous house	entering while sealed before examination	x		
14:47	leprous house	eating, sleeping in	(x)[4]	x	
15:05	man with discharge	touching bedding of	x	x	x
15:06	man with discharge	sitting on seat of	x	x	x
15:07	man with discharge	touching person of	x	x	x
15:10	man with discharge	touching something that has been under (e.g., saddle)	x		
15:10	man with discharge	carrying something that has been under	x	x	x
15:11	man with discharge	being touched by with unwashed hands	x	x	x
15:16	ejaculation		x		x
15:18	fornication (for m and f)		x		
15:19	menstruant	touching	x		x

15:21	menstruant	touching bedding of	x	x	x
15:22	menstruant	touching seat of	x	x	x
15:26–27	woman with discharge	touching bedding or seat of	x	x	x
17:15	carrion	eating	x	x	x
action of priest					
22:4–7	impure person	touching	x	x	x
22:4–7	ejaculation	having; possible touching	x	x	x
22:05	unclean animal	touching	x	x	x
22:05	unclean person who can make unclean	touching	x		x
Num 19:6–7	red cow	putting hyssop, cedar, and crimson into fire of	x	x	x
action of person					
19:8	red cow	burning	x	x	x
19:10	red cow	gathering ashes of	x	x	x
19:21	waters of impurity	touching	x		
19:21	waters of impurity	sprinkling	$(x)^4$	x	
19:22	corpse-defiled person	touching	x		

the contrary, many of the acts which result in the polluted state are natural functions which cannot be avoided. Without childbirth (a major pollutant) and sexual intercourse (a minor pollutant) society would cease to exist. Avoidance of intercourse and childbirth is, moreover, an avoidance of the explicit command to procreate. Similarly, a corpse must be disposed of properly even though contact with the corpse results in major pollution. The world must come into contact with the dead— only the Holy has to be kept separate from it. Even priests may attend the deceased of their immediate family, and then remain in limbo until their corpse-contamination is over (Lev 21:1–6). Only the High Priest (Lev 21:10–11) and the Nazirite (Num 6:6–7) must avoid all corpses. If someone falls down dead right next to the Nazirite, the contamination of the death disrupts the vow and terminates his period as a Nazirite (Num 6:9–12). There is, however, no question of moral culpability for such inadvertent contact with death.

The only instance in which there was any moral opprobrium attached to a polluted state is the case of the leper. In narrative portions of the Bible, leprosy (like premature death or *karet*) is a divine sanction imposed for the commission of certain wrongs: on Miriam for her effrontery against Moses (Num 12:10–15), Gehazi for wrongfully taking money from Naaman (2 Kgs 5:27), and Uzziah for presuming to offer incense by himself (2 Chr 26:19–21). Since the tradition records instances in which leprosy was a divine punishment, there may have been a tendency to suspect lepers of wrongdoing. This, however, is simply folk suspicion, much as in nineteenth-century social philosophy the poor may have been suspected of being "shiftless." The formal tradition of Israel attached no blame to lepers, only impurity. Ritual pollution, even in the case of lepers, was not a moral issue.

The lack of wrongdoing involved in these pollutions distinguishes them from other forms of pollution which do convey a moral message. Biblical Israel had two separate sets of what anthropologists would consider "pollution beliefs": a set discussed extensively as pollutions in the Priestly laws, since the priests were responsible for preventing the contamination of the pure and the Holy; and a set of beliefs that we might term "danger beliefs." The deeds that involve these danger beliefs differ fundamentally from the deeds that result in ritual impurity. There is a clear implication of wrongdoing, for the individual has placed himself in danger by doing something that he and the people have been expressly forbidden to do; the danger is seen as a divine sanction for the deed. Unlike the ritual pollutions, which last a set period, the danger caused by these deeds is permanent (until the catastrophe strikes). The ritual pollutions cannot be ameliorated in this way, although there is a sense that repentance and sacrifice can avert some if not all of the calamity. The state induced by committing one of these infractions is also not contagious. No one can become impure by contact with someone who has committed one of these wrongful acts. One does not share the danger of an adulterer or of someone who has eaten blood by touching him. There is no immediate danger to others in allowing these people to walk around, and therefore there are no prescribed patterns of avoidance. There is, however, an ultimate danger to the people, for if too many individuals commit these deeds, then the whole society might be considered polluted and might thus be in danger of a collective catastrophe.

When an individual commits one of these wrongful catastrophe-deeds, the catastrophe may not be specified, but rather indicated by the phrase *nśꜣ ꜣt ꜥwnw*, "he shall bear his penalty," a phrase which always indicates divine punishment (Zimmerli 1954, 8–11; Frymer-Kensky forthcoming). More often, the individual may be said to be *nśꜣ ꜣt ꜥwnw* "cut off," a phrase which may appear alone (e.g., Lev 20:18) or with the *nśꜣ ꜣt ꜥwnw* warning (e.g., Lev 20:17). This *karet* provision is an integral part of the Priestly understanding of purity and was probably understood to mean the extirpation of one's lineage.[5]

The deeds that entail the *karet* sanction are acts against the fundamental principles of Israelite cosmology; in particular, acts that blur the most vital distinction in the Israelite classificatory system, the separation of sacred and profane. The protection of the realm of the sacred is of prime importance in Israelite thought in view of the belief that God dwells among the children of Israel. Since he is holy, they must be holy (Lev 11:44, 45; 19:2; 20:7, 26) and must not contaminate the camp, Temple, or land in which he lives. The protection of the realm of the sacred is a categorical imperative in Israel: it must be differentiated, not only from the impure, but also from the pure, which serves almost as a buffer zone between the sacred and the defiling. Violating the distinctions between sacred and profane disrupts the entire system. The violator is therefore expected to incur the *karet* penalty; in other words, his deed is expected to result in calamity to his entire lineage through the direct intervention of God ("automatically") and without necessitating societal action. This belief in automatic retribution protects the realm of the sacred by deterring acts which would encroach upon it.

The protection of the sacred was the prime purpose of the *karet* penalty. Israel considered itself a holy nation which was to keep itself distinct from other nations: failure to keep this distinction by not performing circumcision would result in *karet* (Lev 7:20–21; 22:3–9). The spread of impurity threatens the sacred by eliminating the "buffer-zone"; thus failure to be cleansed from corpse contamination results in *karet* (Num 19:13, 20), while failure to be cleansed from lesser contamination caused by eating carrion results in the doer "bearing his punishment" (*nś' 't 'wnw*, Lev 17:15–16). Unauthorized contact with the sacred is believed to result in death (Num 4:18–20, cf. 1 Sam 6:19; 2 Sam 6:6–7). Holy objects must not be subverted: lay persons, though pure, may not eat the holy offerings. The blood (Lev 7:27; 17:10, 14), the sacrificial suet (Lev 7:25), the oil of installation (Exod 30:33), and the sanctuary incense (Exod 30:38) are all protected from profane consumption by the *karet* belief; the holy altar is thus maintained as the only proper place for slaughter (Lev 17:4) and sacrifice (Lev 17:9). Even the prohibition against eating sacrificial offerings on the third day (Lev 7:18; 19:8), which seems to us to be an excellent hygiene measure, is explicitly understood to be a matter of profaning God's holy offering (Lev 19:8) and is therefore believed to incur the *karet* sanction. Similarly, the distinctions between sacred and profane time are a crucial part of the structure of Israelite thought, and failure to maintain the characteristic distinctions of holy time results in *karet:* eating *ḥāmeṣ* on the Feast of Unleavened Bread (Exod 12:15–19); working on the Sabbath (Exod 31:14); working and eating on the Day of Atonement (Lev 23:29–30); not performing the Passover sacrifice at its appointed time (Num 9:13).

In all of these instances the function of the *karet* belief is clear: it serves as a divine reinforcement of the boundaries between sacred and profane by providing a sanction for acts which violate these boundaries but which are not normally provided with legal sanctions. This is also its function in the two instances of *karet*-belief which do not ostensibly involve sacred/profane distinctions, the prohibition against sleeping with one's sister (Lev 20:17) and the prohibition against sleeping with a menstruating woman (Lev 20:18, the only instance in which a deed is believed to result both in a temporary pollution and *karet*). The two provisions are part of a group of sexual laws establishing the limits of permitted sexual contact. One subset (Lev 20:10–16) consists of relationships which society acts to punish with the death penalty. The other subset (Lev 20:17–21) consists of relations which society apparently will not punish, but which it seeks to prevent by threats of supernatural sanction, i.e., danger beliefs: sexual intercourse with a sister or menstruant by *karet*, with one's aunt by unspecified danger *(nśᵓ ᵓt ᶜwnw)*, with one's uncle's wife or brother's wife by childlessness. In Lev 18:29, in what seems to be a general statement, all forbidden sexual relations are sanctioned by *karet.*

POLLUTION OF THE TEMPLE

Fundamental to the function of the *karet*-belief is the idea that the sacred can be defiled and that there is a need to protect it from such contamination. The Temple in particular, as the site of God's presence, needs such protection. It could be defiled by enemies (Ps 79:1), corpses (Ezek 9:7), and idols or idolatrous practices (Jer 7:30; 32; 34; Ezek 5:11). It could also be defiled by impure people: by those who came to the temple while ritually impure (Lev 15:31), and those who indulged in molech worship and then came to the Temple (Ezek 23:38–39). Moreover, those who have not purified themselves of corpse-contamination (Num 19:13, 20) or who have indulged in the abominations of the Gentiles (2 Chr 36:14) are said to have defiled the Temple, either because they came in an impure state or simply because they spread impurity.

The Temple may also be defiled indirectly, from a distance. As Jacob Milgrom has explained (Milgrom 1976a), the Priestly image of the temple is that of a "Picture of Dorian Gray." The sanctuary can become polluted without direct contact with the impurity. All misdeeds pollute the outer altar, misdeeds of the whole people or of the High Priest pollute the shrine, and wanton sin pollutes the adytum. This pollution of the Temple would result in alienation from God, for God will not tolerate the pollution of his home: this alienation would have serious historical consequences.

There is, however, a cure for such pollution. The Temple cult is meant to expiate and atone for misdeeds. On an individual level, there is a danger-belief that inadvertently committing an infraction results in the doer "bearing his punishment"; if, however, he brings an offering, the danger will be lifted ("it shall be forgiven him," Lev 5:17–18). Individual and national sacrifices, particularly the *ḥatta't* sacrifice, purify the Temple from the pollution caused by misdeeds (Milgrom 1971a, 1971b, 1976a, 1976b). And the Day of Atonement rituals were intended both to purify the people (the Azazel Goat) and to cleanse the Temple from the pollution caused by the people (Milgrom 1971c). Within limits, therefore, the pollution of the Temple could be rectified by ritual means.

POLLUTION OF THE PEOPLE AND THE LAND

Karet is usually mentioned alone or together with *ns'ʿt wnw:* specific legal sanctions are not mentioned. The exception to this is the "gruesome threesome" of apostasy: idolatry, child-molech service, and necromancy. All three of these acts constitute serious apostasy from God and are thus sanctioned by *karet*, in each instance by the unusual formula *hkrty (w)*, "I (God) will cut (him) off," in which the divine nature of the sanction is manifest (molech-service, Lev 20:5; necromancy, Lev 20:6; idolatry, Ezek 14:8). These offenses, moreover, are particularly grave in that they strike at the very basis of Israel, its relationship with God. The society cannot wait passively for divine action, but is commanded to punish the offender actively. The punishment meted out in all three cases is stoning (molech-service, Lev 20:2–6; necromancy, Lev 20:27; idolatry, Deut 13:7–12; 17:2–7). This is a form of execution without an executioner, i.e., one in which the whole people act as the executioner since the people as a whole and the world order on which they depend have been endangered (Finkelstein 1981, 26–27). Stoning is limited in the laws to these three instances of apostasy, to the disobedient son (Deut 21:18–21), the nonvirgin bride (Deut 22:20–21), and both partners in the seduction of an engaged girl (Deut 22:23–24). The corporate execution of the offender indicates the collective responsibility of the people for the act. It is extended to the protection of the sacred by three cautionary tales that are included in the narrative portions of the Hexateuch; the tales of the blasphemer (Lev 24:10–16), of the man who violated the Sabbath (Num 15:32–36), and of the man who took from the *herem* (Josh 7). In all three stories the violator was stoned; whether these stories had the force of law, and whether there was any intent to prescribe stoning for violating the Sabbath or blasphemy, is unknown.

The provision of stoning in Deuteronomy is accompanied by the phrase "you shall exterminate the evil from your midst" *(wbʿrt hrʿ mqrbk)*, which implies that should society not act to punish the offender, the evil would in some way be imputed to it. This phrase is not limited to cases which demand stoning: ignoring a divine judgment (Deut 17:12), murder (Deut 19:11–13), false witness (Deut 19:16–21), adultery (Deut 22:22), and kidnap-and-sale (Deut 24:7) must all be punished by society in order to exterminate the evil from its midst. These provisions (and the concept of exterminating evil from the midst of the people) may predate the Book of Deuteronomy and may be part of an ancient criminal corpus (L'Hour 1963).

The concern about collective responsibility indicated by the stoning laws and the *bi'artā* provisions can also be expressed in the language of pollution. Necromancy is considered polluting (Lev 19:31), as are molech-worship (Ezek 20:26, 30–31) and idolatry (Ezek 14:11; 20:31; cf. 22:3–4; 23:7–38). All forms of apostasy pollute the people, and this pollution does not disappear with time (Josh 22:17). Sexual immorality is also a polluting agent: rape (Gen 34:5, 13, 27), incest with one's daughter-in-law (Ezek 22:11), and adultery (Num 5:11–31; Ezek 18:6, 11, 15). Adultery, moreover, results in the pollution of both parties (Lev 18:20), as does bestiality (Lev 18:23). All the improper sexual acts of Leviticus 18 are considered as defiling both people and the land (Lev 18:24). Murder, which is explicitly described as polluting the land, is not said to "pollute" the people in this terminology. It is clearly contaminating (McKeating 1975), but its contamination is expressed by the phrases *dam naqi*, "innocent blood" (Deut 19:13; 21:8), and *dammim.* General misdeeds and sins are also categorized as polluting the people (Ps 106:39; Ezek 14:11; 20:43), though this may be a late extension of the pollution concept as it refers to the people. Ultimately, the people are considered as having become polluted; at the restoration, according to Ezekiel, they will be purified by God (Ezek 36:25; 37:23).

There is no "cure" for the pollution engendered by these immoral acts, no ritual purification that can be performed until the sprinkling of pure water by God at the restoration. The progressive pollution of these people by these deeds is thus like the most catastrophic pollution, that is, the pollution of the land.[6] The crimes of the people are considered to pollute the very earth of Israel (Jer 2:7; Ezek 36:17), and certain acts are explicitly termed contaminants. Bloodshed (Ps 106:38) is a major pollutant, as is everything connected with it, such as leaving the body of an executed murderer exposed (Deut 21:22–23), accepting compensation for murder (Num 35:31–35), or letting accidental murderers go free from the city of refuge (Num 35:32). Idolatry pollutes (Ezek 36:18), and so do such wrongful sex acts as the illicit sexual relations prescribed by Leviticus 18, whoredom (of the individual, Lev 19:29; of the nation-as-female, Jer 3:9; Ezek 23:17), and adultery and remarriage to a previous wife who has been married in the interim (Deut 24:1–4). These three classes of pollutants—murder, sexual abominations, and idolatry—pollute both the people and the land. In later theology, they are the cardinal sins that a Jew must die rather than commit and from which (according to James in Acts 15) it is incumbent on all nations to refrain. The results of performance of these sins are catastrophic, for, as Rabbinic sources recognized, they (together with unfulfilled public promises) bring drought (y. *Ta'an.* 3:3 = 66C), and they (together with the nonobservance of the Sabbath and the Sabbath and Jubilee years) bring exile to the world (*b. Šabb.* 33a).

These acts have catastrophic results because they pollute the land that God protects as his own. Israel based its right of possession of its land on the idea that God dispossessed the original inhabitants because of their misdeeds. This concept is found in both Deuteronomic and Priestly traditions. According to Deuteronomy, it was not the goodness of Israel that caused God to give it the land, but the evil of the nations living there (Deut 9:4–5). Its right of occupation is therefore contingent on its actions. Israel is warned against performing the abominations of the nations that God dispossessed: passing children through fire, and engaging in magic, divination, and necromancy (Deut 18:9–12). The Priestly tradition is also quite explicit that the abominations of the nations made them lose the land. Leviticus 18 lists the sexual abominations practiced by the dispossessed nations, warns the people not to become polluted by them as the nations did, and explains that the land had become polluted by its inhabitants, that God had exacted the land's punishment,[7] and that the land had thereupon vomited its inhabitants. Israel is warned not to do these actions lest the land become polluted and vomit it out; people who engage in these abominations are "cut off" from the people *(karet)*. In Leviticus 20, some of these sexual abominations are reiterated, molech-service and necromancy are added to the list, and the people are again reminded that they are inheriting the land, that the previous inhabitants who did these abominations are being expelled, and that the land might vomit Israel out, too (Lev 20:22–25).

Israel thus considered the nonpollution of the land a matter of national survival. The people are warned not to pollute the land by letting murderers go free or allowing accidental murderers to leave the city of refuge (Num 35:31–34), by leaving the corpses of the executed unburied (Deut 21:22–23), or even by permitting a man to remarry his divorced and since married wife (Deut 24:1–4, cf. Jer 3:1–4).

The pollution of the land cannot be rectified by ritual purification. In the case of murder, the law explicitly states that the blood of the slain cannot be expiated except by the blood of the shedder. The only ritual at all connected with the pollution of the land is the ritual of the decapitated heifer, the *ʿeglâ ʿarûpâ* (Deut 21:1–9; see Patai 1939–40, Roifer 1961, Zevit 1976). This is clearly designed to avert the contamination of the land and the people by a murder whose perpetrator cannot be found. Although the people cannot properly expiate the blood of the slain, by performing this action they may eradicate *(br)* the blood-contamination.

The pollution of the land may build up and ultimately reach a point beyond the level of tolerance, when a cataclysm becomes inevitable. There can be no "repentance" in the face of such pollution; it should be noted that repentance is seen as a privilege that is not automatically available. The concept of pollution was thus understood as one of the motive principles of Israelite history: the pollution of the land cleared the way for Israel to enter it; its pollution during their occupation presents a major danger. The idea of pollution was a major theoretical paradigm which enabled Israel to absorb and survive the eventual destruction of the state. It existed alongside but is not identical to the better-known theoretical explanation of the destruction, the legal paradigm of misdeed and punishment.

By the time of the prophets, Israel is seen as a land which has become polluted. In the Deuteronomic historian, there is a stress on the abominations performed by the disinherited peoples set into the record that the people or their kings performed these abominations (1 Kgs 14:24; 2 Kgs 16:3; 21:2); the destruction of Samaria is attributed to its having acted like the dispossessed nations (2 Kgs 17:7–8). At the time of the Assyrian threat, Hosea viewed Israel as a contaminated people and land (Hos 5:3; 6:10); the term used, *ntmʾ*, is later applied to Judah (Ezek 36:18; Ps 106:38). The land is seen as defiled, *ḥnp* (Isa 24:5; Ps 106:38). The people have polluted the land (Jer 2:7; Ezek 36:4), they have defiled it (Jer 3:9). The land of Israel is described as full of blood (Hos 6:8). Judah is described as full of *ḥāmās*, "unlawfulness" (Ezek 8:17; 12:19, see discussion below) and bloodshed (Ezek 7:23; 9:9), murderers (Hos 6:8), gods (Isa 2:8), and adulterers (Jer 23:10); the city is full of *ḥāmās* (Ezek 7:23) and blood (Ezek 22; Nah 3:1). Judah and Jerusalem are described as whores (Hos 1:2; Isa 1:21; Jer 2:20; 3:3; Ezek 16:30–35; chap. 23; Mic 1:7; Nah 3:4). By the time of the destruction the nation is portrayed in the image of the ultimate defiled woman, the menstruant (Ezek 36:17; probably Lam 1:8, *nydh*, and Ezra 9:11) and, even more, the menstruant whose skirts have become soiled with blood (Jer 13:22, reading *nĕgoʾălû šûlayik;* cf. Lam 4:14). Even the ultimate image of defilement, the image of the leper, is applied to the nation, who sits alone (Lam 1:1; cf. Lev 13:45). In the face of such pollution, the Temple and its cult could not be enough to save Israel, and this necessitated the land being destroyed and the people being sent into exile. The exile is thus seen as a necessary result of the pollution of Israel.

THE EXILE AND THE FLOOD

The exile was necessitated by the polluted state of the land. It was not, according to this paradigm, an act of vengeance or even a result of anger. It was also not intended to be a final destruction of the people. The prophesies of doom are frequently accompanied by mention of the remnant which is to be saved and restored to the land. In this respect the Exile resembles the flood, which also allowed a remnant—Noah—to be rescued and restored. The connection between the Exile and the Flood, moreover, is not simply a matter of destruction and restoration. As narrated in Genesis, the Flood is the grand cosmic paradigm of the Exile. Genesis has taken the ancient flood story and the old structure of a "primeval history" (now Genesis 1–9) and retold it in the light of Israel's ideas about pollution. According to the Genesis story, the prerequisites of human existence are laws. Man has inherently evil impulses and man without law polluted the world to such an extent that the Lord had to bring the Flood to erase the pollution that man had brought (Frymer-Kensky 1977).

With this reinterpretation of the flood story, the flood was seen as a cosmic paradigm of the exile, and the retelling of the story of the flood became a way for Israel to assimilate its own fate. We must, of course, ask when Israel looked at the flood in this light. There is no reason to look for a late postexilic date for this. Source analysis cannot provide a solution. Genesis 9 is conventionally assigned to P, but I would not like to venture to date the material in P, nor do I believe it likely that the J version of the flood did not conclude with a remedy for the cause of the flood, although J's remedy, which may also have been laws, is lost to us. Pollution ideas are certainly not new to Israel, and there is no reason to suggest that the purity laws are late, even though they are preserved primarily in P. The characteristic Israelite notion that the pollution of the land leads to its desolation is already attested to Hosea. Hosea describes Gilead as defiled with blood (6:8), defiled by the doing of perversion and by "whoredom" (6:9–10). Furthermore Hosea states that because Israel has become defiled it will be desolated (5:3, 9, note key words *hznyt*, *ntm²*, and *šmh*). The concept of pollution as a historical force is thus attested long before the exile: it may be an innovation of Hosea, or it may already have been part of Israelite cosmology.

The idea that misdeeds pollute the land is also attested in Isaiah 24:5–6, part of the "Isaian apocalypse": "And the land was defiled under its inhabitants for they transgressed the teachings, violated the laws, and broke the ancient covenant. Therefore the curse[8] consumes the land and the inhabitants pay the penalty." There is some question about the dating of his passage; despite the conventional wisdom it should probably not be taken as postexilic since Jeremiah 23:10 appears to be dependent on it. Certainly the idea of the pollution of the land is well established by the time of Jer 3:1–9. We therefore do not have to look for a postexilic date for the understanding of pollution as a motive force in Israel's history or for the retelling of the flood story as a case of cosmic pollution. It is possible that the anticipation and/or experience of the Assyrian threat and the experience of the destruction of the northern kingdom led to a profound awareness of the pollution problem and occasioned a retelling of the flood story in light of it. The belief in the corruptibility of the land of Israel and the catastrophic consequences of such corruption may even be earlier than the Assyrian period, for all we know.

There is also no reason to think that the midrashic perception of the flood and the exile as parallel events is an exilic innovation. I am tempted to take Hos 6:7 as evidence that Hosea, who clearly believes that the pollution of Israel will lead to its desolation, also saw a connection between this destruction and the primeval cataclysm. The translation of 6:7a, *whmh kʾdm ʿbrw bryt*, as "They like men have transgressed the covenant" seems needlessly weak and obscure. In the context of the pollution described in 6:8–10 it may be more proper to translate, "They like Adam have transgressed the covenant" and see an indirect allusion to antediluvian events. Jeremiah, who is so conscious of the pollution of the land (Jer 3:1–9), also uses cosmic parallels. A cosmic paradigm, i.e., the flood, seems to underlie the so-called "Jeremiah apocalypse" in Jeremiah 4:23–27. Jeremiah here describes the coming military destruction of Israel (cf. 4:20–21) in terms that are clearly reminiscent of Genesis 1; he depicts the event as a reversal of creation: the world is returned to chaos *(tobu wabohu)*, there is no more light in the skies, the mountains are quaking, and there are no more people. In this vision, however—as at the original, cosmic undoing of creation (the flood)—the destruction will not be final: "All the land will be made desolate, but I will not finish it off completely" (Jer 4:27). This passage has been understood—or misunderstood—as an apocalyptic vision, but to understand it this way it was necessary to posit later accretions to the passage (Eppstein 1968). The context, however, makes it clear that we are dealing with the imminent destruction of Israel rather than a future cosmic upheaval. It may be that the use of the cosmic symbolism is the primeval parallel in such passages as this and the "Isaian apocalypse" of

Isaiah 24 laid the groundwork and provided the symbolic imagery for the later development of universal apocalyptic.

The parallelism between the flood and the destruction is well developed by Ezekiel, and the early chapters of Ezekiel are replete with flood imagery, particularly with the repetitive statement that the land is full of ḥāmās (Ezek 7:23; 8:17; and cf. 12:19; 45:9; for the flood story, Gen 6:11) and with the emphatic use of the term qes (Ezek 7:2–7, esp. vv. 2–3): "Thus says the Lord to the land [or (?) ground?] of Israel, the qēṣ is come, and the qēṣ on the four corners of the earth; now the qēṣ is upon you and I send my anger against you and judge you as your ways"; and cf. v. 6; for Genesis, see 6:13). Another allusion to the primeval story may be the marking on the forehead of those not to be killed (Ezek 9:4–5), possibly an allusion to the mark of Cain.

The parallelism between the flood and the exile does not involve only pollution and destruction, but also additional themes which are an inherent part of the parallel. The flood and the exile were necessary purgations; they were not ultimate, permanent destructions. Just as humankind was saved from permanent destruction by Noah's survival, so too God will not exterminate the people, but will rescue a remnant to begin again. The flood and the exile are also not viewed as repeatable acts. The flood is immediately followed by God's promise not to bring a flood again (Gen 9:11). It is significant that one explicit reference to the Flood outside of Genesis 1–9 occurs in a passage dealing with the restoration of Israel. In this passage (chosen by Jewish tradition as the prophetic reading to accompany the liturgical recitation of the Genesis flood story), the flood paradigm is taken as assurance that, just as the flood was to be a unique occurrence, so too God will not again punish the people of Israel: "As the waters of Noah this is to me, about which I swore that the waters of Noah would not (again) pass over the earth; so too I swear that I will not get angry at you and rebuke you" (Isa 54:9).

The flood was not to be repeated because it was followed, not only by the restoration of mankind but also by the establishment of a new order, the "reign of law." Jeremiah and Ezekiel (possibly anticipated by Hosea) develop the concept of the exile in line with this cosmic parallel. They consider the destruction the result of the pollution of the land, and see it as followed not only by the restoration of the remnant but also by the inauguration of a new order. The flood inaugurated the Rule of Law: humankind's evil impulses were recognized, and therefore laws were given to educate and restrain it. This would prevent the pollution of the earth and eliminate the need for a future flood. This reliance on law culminated in the covenant of Sinai, in which one people (Israel) was given a more elaborate and demanding set of laws, with the expectation that this would enable it to be a holy people entitled to live in God's country. However, the covenant of Sinai was "broken." The misdeeds of the people polluted Israel, and God had to exile the people. The land had to rest; after the purgation (evacuation of the land) it needed time to recuperate. As the impure individual becomes pure after a set period of time even without purification rituals, so too time can eliminate the impurity of the land.[9] After the land has "fulfilled its Sabbath" (2 Chr 36:21; cf. Lev 26:32–45; see Ackroyd 1968, 153, 242) God will restore the people. He will purify them (Jer 33:8; Ezek 36:25, 33) and reestablish relations with them; he will be their god and they will be his people (Jer 31:32–33; Ezek 36:28).

There will be fundamental changes at the restoration, for the world after the exile is to be different from the world before it, just as the world after the flood was different from the antediluvian world. There is a radical change in the mechanism of sin, for the new stress on individual retribution (Jer 31:29–30; Ezek 11:16–21; 14:12–23; chap. 18; 33:12–20) represents a reversal of the concept of the national responsibility of Israel for the sins of its members (see Weinfeld 1976), and a removal of the idea of the build-up of pollution across generational lines. In this context it may be significant that Ezekiel's formulation of this change refers to the proverb which is spoken about the "land/ground of Israel."

The renewed relationship with restored Israel is to be established by a covenant which is called a "new covenant" (Jer 31:31), an eternal covenant (Jer 32:40), and a "covenant of peace" (Ezek 34:35). This covenant is fundamentally different from the Noahide covenant and from its typological extension, the Sinai covenant (see Jer 31:32 for its differences from Sinai). The covenant of Noah and even more the covenant of Sinai were covenants of law to be studied and obeyed. At the time of the "new covenant," however, no one will have to study the laws anymore; everyone will know the law (Jer 31:33–34). The law of God will be engraved on the heart (Jer 31:33); everyone will have a "new heart and a new spirit" (Ezek 36:26). Internal law is not "law." This radical change is projected for the restoration after the exile. After the flood, God instituted the rule of law to cope with man's evil instincts. These instincts, part of the nature of man, would continue to exist, but they would be held in check by an increasingly detailed set of laws. To Jeremiah and Ezekiel, this approach to the problem of evil and the pollution of the world has failed.[10] Man's evil instincts were not effectively restrained by law, even by the Law of Sinai and God's ongoing instruction by history and the prophets. Israel continued to do evil and ultimately, as in the time before law, the microcosm of Israel became so polluted that another cataclysm, the exile, became necessary to destroy that polluted world. In the restored Israel, therefore, the attempt to control man's instincts will be abandoned. Instead, God will effect a fundamental change in the nature of man: his evil impulses are to be eradicated, the "law" internalized, and he is to receive a "new heart and a new spirit."

It should be noted as a postscript that this search for an alteration of man's spirit, with the concomitant abandonment of the Law as the agent of God's instruction, was later developed in the early Christian Church. Israel, however, ultimately rejected this vision of Jeremiah and Ezekiel in that it never abandoned its belief in the ability of the Law to control man's evil instincts. The Law in all its ramifications became the defining characteristic of the Judaism that emerged after the biblical period.

NOTES

1. This is not a complete picture, for the laws do not mention all cases. An example is the status of the person who eats impure food. In the case of carrion we know that the ordinary people (unlike the priests) were not forbidden to eat it; however, they would become impure until evening and must bathe and wash their clothes (Lev 17:15–16). In the case of impure animals we know that lay people were not to eat them (Lev 20:25), and we therefore do not hear of the pollution of such people (as discussed below, pollution terminology is not applied to those who do forbidden acts). The question is the status of the person who eats food that has been tainted by contact with an impure person, given especially that meat rendered impure should be burned (Lev 7:19). From Hosea we know that whoever eats impure food will himself become impure (Hos 9:3–4). The laws, however, do not discuss what happens to the person who eats impure food. We can only assume that the resultant pollution would be minor, like that from eating carrion.

2. There is clearly a desire to prevent infinite contagion in the provision in Lev 14:36 that all things in a house suspected of "leprosy" be removed before the house is examined, so that they will not be "made unclean": the contagion does not start until the declaration, rather than with exposure prior to the determination of impurity.

3. From Num 9:10 it is clear that impure people (here, specifically from corpse-contamination) may not perform the Passover sacrifice; calamity is not explicitly mentioned.

4. Assumed but not explicitly mentioned.

5. The major study of *karet* is that of Wold (1979, 1–46), who realizes that *karet* should be seen in the context of the purity laws, and who argues convincingly that it means extirpation of one's lineage. The analysis of *karet* presented here does not always agree with Wold's.

6. Although the emphasis in Deuteronomy is on the pollution of the people and that of the Priestly sections on the pollution of the land, this may simply be a question of style; one should note that Lev 18:24 mentions the pollution of the people and Deut 21:1–9 is clearly concerned with the pollution of the land as well as the people. Deut 21:22–23 is clearly concerned with the pollution of the land. See also the discussion by Weinfeld (1973) and Milgrom (1973).

7. This punishment is probably drought, infertility, and famine. According to Israel, rain, so necessary to Israel's agriculture (Deut 11:11) is to be withdrawn in case of apostasy (Deut 11:13–17). Drought is a clear indication of chastisement (1 Kgs 17–19; Amos 4:7; Isa 5:6; Jer 14; Ezek 22:24). Even after the restoration, the infertility and drought prevalent are attributes of Israel's failure to rebuild the temple (Hag 1:6–11). See also Ackroyd 1968, 157; Roifer 1961, 136; and Patai 1939.

8. The "curse" probably also refers to drought and famine. See note 7 above.

9. It may be particularly relevant that women do not have fixed purification rituals. Although both men and women are to bathe after intercourse, women become pure after their set period of impurity for menstruation and childbirth: there is no mention of bathing. In light of the feminine conception of the land, one would expect that the land too would have to wait out its impure period, and that time alone would make it pure.

10. It is difficult to say whether the idea of the new covenant originated with Hosea. Hosea clearly anticipated a restoration, with a covenant and God betrothing Israel forever (Hos 2:20–21); nothing, however, is said about fundamental changes in the covenant or in the people.

BIBLIOGRAPHY

Ackroyd, Peter. *Exile and Restoration: A Study of Hebrew Thought in the Sixth Century B.C.* Old Testament Library. London: SCM Press, 1968.

Douglas, Mary. *Purity and Danger: An Analysis of Concepts of Pollution and Taboo.* New York: Praeger, 1966.

———. *Implicit Meanings.* London: Routledge and Kegan Paul, 1975.

Eppstein, Victor. "The Day of Judgment in Jeremiah 4:23–28." *Journal of Biblical Literature* 87 (1968): 93–97.

Finkelstein, J. J. *The Ox that Gored.* Transactions of the American Philosophical Society 71/2. Philadelphia: The American Philosophical Society, 1981.

Frymer-Kensky, Tikva. "The *Atrahasis* Epic and Its Significance for Our Understanding of Genesis 1–9." *Biblical Archeologists* 40 (1977): 147–54.

———. "The Strange Case of the Suspected Sotah: Numbers 5:11–31." *Vetus Testamentum* (forthcoming).

Milgrom, Jacob. "Sin Offering or Purification Offering?" *Vetus Testamentum* 21 (1971a): 237–239.

———. "Kipper." *Encyclopedia Judaica* 10 (1971b): 1039–43.

———. "Day of Atonement." *Encyclopedia Judaica* 5 (1971c): 1383–87.

———. "The Alleged 'Demythologization' and Secularization in Deuteronomy." *Israel Explorational Journal* 23 (1973): 156–61.

———. "Israel's Sanctuary: The Priestly 'Picture of Dorian Gray.'" *Revue biblique* 33 (1976a): 390–99.

———. "Two Kinds of Hatta't." *Vetus Testamentum* 26 (1976b): 333–37.

Patai, Raphael. "The 'Control of Rain' in Ancient Palestine." *Hebrew Union College Annual* 14 (1939): 251–86.

———. "The Egla Arufa or the Expiation of the Polluted Land." *Jewish Quarterly Review* (1939–40).

Roifer, A. "The Breaking of the Heifer's Neck." *Tarbiz* 31 (1961): 129–43 (Hebrew).

Weinfeld, Moshe. "On 'Demythologization' and Secularization in Deuteronomy." *Israel Exploration Journal* 23 (1973): 230–33.

———. Jeremiah and the Spiritual Metamorphosis of Israel. *Zeitschrift fur die Alttestamentliche Wissenschaft* 88 (1976):17–56.

Wold, Donald. "The *kareth* Penalty in P: Rationale and Cases." In *Society of Biblical Literature 1979 Seminar Papers*. Vol. 1. Edited by P. J. Achtemeier. Missoula: Scholar Press, 1979.

Zevit, Ziony. "The Egla Ritual of Deuteronomy 21:1–9." *Journal of Biblical Literature* 95 (1976): 377–90.

Zimmerli, W. "Die Eigenart der prophetischen Rede des Ezechiel." *Zeitschrift fur die Alttestamentliche Wissenschaft* 66 (1954): 1–27.

24 / Ecology in a Biblical Perspective

2000

We have become accustomed, in both Judaism and Christianity, to attribute to the Bible the origin of everything good and evil. Needless to say, such an attitude has no basis in fact: the world was not a barren wasteland before the writings of the Bible. Nevertheless, it has become the conceit of the Western religious tradition to imagine that the Bible came to bring light to those in utter darkness and to write God's word on the tabula rasa of humankind.

It should therefore not be surprising that ever since the publication of Lynn White Jr.'s seminal article,[1] the Bible, in particular the Hebrew Bible, has stood accused of teaching us to kill the earth. White's article has been refuted hundreds of times on many different grounds, not the least of which are the many articles showing that the Bible simply doesn't support the "conquest of nature" theology that was imposed upon it a few hundred years ago.[2] Despite all the refutation, it remains constantly cited whenever people once again discover that there is an earth and that the Bible has given us some problems with it.

THE BABYLONIAN CREATION STORY

I would like to take a different path, and tell a story from prebiblical ancient Babylonia that gives us a good indication of what a prebiblical Near Eastern view of the relationship of God and the earth was like. The story has a long history. Our copy was written around 1550 B.C.E. This copy is probably not the original composition, for the copyist tells us that he is a junior scribe.[3] The story had at least a thousand-year history and we find tablets from a thousand years later that contain parts or all of this text, which we call the human *Atrahasis* epic, and they called, "When the gods act as humans."

The story begins when there was an earth, but before the creation of humankind. It is a primordial history of humankind, and tells us of the defining characteristics of that prehuman world: the gods had to work. They had to work because they had to eat, and since this text was written in Iraq, the work that they engaged in was digging irrigation ditches. Seven gods seized power and became the administrators, and everybody else worked at backbreaking labor for a very long time. They were, of course, gods: the irrigation ditches that they produced were the Tigris and Euphrates Rivers, and the dirt from the excavation piled up as the mountains of Iran. But even for gods, this was a lot of work, and they got very tired of it.

One day, one of the gods (whose name is not given)[4] instigates the others and calls them to strike, and the gods decide they do not want to work anymore; they are going to create a disturbance. In the middle of the night, they set fire to their pickaxes and their spades, and they march to surround the palace of the chief administrator, the god Enlil. The watchman sees them and rouses the vizier; the vizier rouses Enlil, and he immediately wants to set the defense and defeat these rabble-rousers. The vizier halts him, reminding him that "these are your sons." They call a council of the seven power wielders. Anu, the god of heaven, comes down and the god of the subterranean world, the wise god Enki, comes up, and they decide that they need to find out what is happening and why the gods are doing this.

One can imagine this story as an early D. W. Griffith movie, or better, a Pete Seeger song, because when the council tells Enlil to find out what is happening, he directs his servant to find out who started it. But when the servant goes and asks who proclaimed this rebellion, who started this revolt, then (to the strains of "Solidarity Forever") all the gods answer, "We all did, every one of us declared rebellion." When this word is brought back, Enlil, the very personification of power, says, in effect, "Well, we gotta break the strike, let's just go in and mash a few heads and set an example of our power." The heaven god, Anu, admonishes that the council has been hearing the worker gods groaning and muttering in the pits for a long time and that they should find a solution to the workers' hard labor.

At this point the wisest of all the gods, the friend of humanity, the god Enki (or Ea, depending on whether you name him in Sumerian or Akkadian) has a brilliant idea: that the gods need a substitute workforce, a permanent underclass. Enki proposes a procedure: the gods should purify themselves in a ritual immersion, should moisten the clay that

Enki provides with their spittle, and the mother goddess should create a worker person.

The mother goddess, Mami, mixes the clay with the blood of a god slain for this purpose,[5] a god whose name has never been heard of before, in this text or any other myth. His name is We-ilum, which is a play on the word for humankind, *awilum*. Moreover, Weilum is said to be a god *ša-išu ṭemu*, a god who has sense. Once again, this is a wordplay on the word *eṭimmu*, the ghost that we have when our body is dead.[6] By infusing the clay of the earth with this god's blood, they give this new creature rationality and create a being who can remember that it has been created. Mami creates seven pairs of this *lullu*, the primitive worker-human, and they create seven pairs of men and women.

The gods then load upon this creature the tasks of the gods. A break on the tablet obscures a long speech about the duties of humankind and when the text picks up again, we hear about an unexpected problem: "twelve hundred years had not yet passed when the lands extended and earth multiplied, the land was roaring like a bull." The god Enlil cannot sleep from the noise, calls his council, and they send a plague on humankind.

This devastating plague continues until the god Enki, our friend the wisest of all the gods, tells his human devotee, *Atrahasis* (literally "supersage" or "megabrain"), that all human beings should stop worshiping any gods or goddesses except Namtar, the god of the plague. They should devote themselves to him, build him a temple, and bribe him into lifting the plague. Once they do so and the plague stops, then the text continues: "twelve hundred years had not yet passed when the earth extended and the land multiplied, the earth was roaring like a bull."

Once again, the god Enlil cannot sleep. The problem has recurred, and this time Enlil gets the gods to agree to send a drought. When the drought comes and decimates humankind, once again Enki tells *Atrahasis* that people should worship only Adad the god of rain, once again humans respond and the drought lifts. But the problem recurs yet again: the text is broken, but it is clear that the gods now pollute the earth and make the soil saline. Once again, Enki saves humankind. The gods then gather to try to find a final solution to the problem, an ending, a *gamirtam*. They decide to bring a flood, and they bind Enki by an oath that he will not inform humankind of this flood. They are determined to end the problem that humans pose.

Needless to say, Enki is not so dumb, and neither is Megabrain—*Atrahasis*. The next time *Atrahasis* comes to the temple on a vision quest, he overhears Enki talking to the walls, saying, "Wall, listen to me: reed, but attend my words. Break down your house, build a boat, leave your possessions and save your life." *Atrahasis*, realizing that this message might have something to do with him, builds a boat, and loads animals and humans on it. The flood comes and destroys all of the earth except for this one boat in which *Atrahasis* and his family and animals survive.

The gods soon realize what they have done in destroying humanity. To quote the text, "Their hearts were broken and they thirsted for beer." Nobody is feeding them—and their hunger brings them to a realization of the enormous consequences of their actions. Ishtar gets up and articulates the issue, lamenting that they have destroyed their own creation, and the gods turn angry at Enlil, who moved them to take such an action.

Once they are truly upset that humanity has been destroyed Enki has *Atrahasis* come out of the ark and offer a sacrifice from his animals. The gods are so hungry that they swarm over the sacrifice "like flies." While they are eating, Enlil, the god who instigated the flood, comes and is dismayed that humanity has been saved. But the gods will no longer listen, and wise Enki presents a permanent solution to the problem:

> Let there be a third class among people,
> the women who bear and women who do not bear;
> Let there be a pashittu-demon to snatch babies away
> from the women who bear them;
> Let there be Entu, Ugbabtu and Igiṣtu women
> who are taboo, and thus stop childbirth. . . .

Here, still in the middle of Enki's solution to the human problem, the texts gets very broken, but clearly another innovation is death, or timely death. No longer, after the flood, do people live for thousands of years.[7] After this broken speech comes the poet's summation, "I sing of the flood to all people; listen!"

The *Atrahasis* story is a primeval history that seeks to tell us that the great danger in creation is overpopulation, that the gods try "nature's" methods of controlling population (drought, pestilence, famine), and that when none of these prove anything more than temporary solutions, they are ready to destroy the whole world. In nonmythological language: if overpopulation is not controlled, then the world will be destroyed.

The story depicts a new order in which the universe is changed so as to contain built-in population safeguards that should prevent a recurrence of overpopulation. These safeguards are perinatal death, barrenness (natural and social), and a shortened life span of at most 120 years.[8] The myth thus provides a framework for viewing personal tragedies as cosmic necessities. It also contains a reassuring note about humanity's place in the cosmos, for it turns out that the gods, who are able to destroy humankind, ultimately discover how much they need humanity. To be the workers of the god may imply subservience and dependence on the gods' goodwill, but it also makes humans indispensable and assures our continued existence. The world of gods and humans is thus interdependent.

The myth does not have such a happy message for the earth itself. The gods are willing to sacrifice the soil and the environment. They send droughts and pollution on the earth in order to decimate humankind. Of course, from our nonmythological perspective, droughts, famine and pestilence are a direct consequence of overpopulation, but the myth does not see it that way. Instead mutilation of the earth is the weapon that the gods use against humanity.

The myth does not present an integrated view of nature and humanity, and the gods; on the contrary, the purpose of the soil is to nourish humans, and the purpose of humans is to nourish the gods. This tale presents a clearly defined hierarchical order, gods-humans-earth, in a mythological setting of a definitely nonmonotheist religion.

THE GENESIS CREATION STORY

When we look at biblical mythology, the situation is much more complicated. I will concentrate on the much-discussed creation story in Genesis 1, in order to point out one facet that has been overlooked.

In this chapter, the Priestly celebration of creation, God creates by introducing distinctions, divisions, and hierarchies: the very essence of creation is the bringing of order to the formless mass of chaos depicted as the featureless deep. On the first day, God creates light and declares it good. On the second day God creates firmament and declares it good. On both days there has been a one-step process and one thing has been created, making one distinction: light/dark, waters above/below, and pronouncing this new creation good. On the third day, God creates the division between the sea and the dry land and pronounces it good, but the third day doesn't end with the creation of earth. On that very same day, God has the earth bring forth vegetation, which is self-perpetuating and seed-bearing and will maintain its own distinct varieties. Only then does the third day end.

This compositional strategy has a significant implication: there is not one moment in cosmic time that the earth exists barren. The earth is created as a fertile, self-sustaining unit. In Genesis 1, there is no need for fertility rituals and no need for humanity to produce a fertile earth: this is the way that earth was created and this is the way it remains if it is not interfered with.[9] By doubling the creations of the third day, Genesis 1 conveys an important theological point. The cult neither has to produce fertility nor even to offer thanksgiving for the fertility because a good universe is fertile, and God created a well-ordered universe.

Genesis 1 uses a similar technique on the sixth day. Both humans and animals are created on the sixth day. The earth did not have animals without humans; the two are interconnected, and humans administrate. The essential position of humankind in the cosmos is not the farmer, but the executive. This is spelled out: humans are to be the *ṣelem elohim*, image of God. *Ṣalmu* (cognate of *ṣelem*) is a term we know from Mesopotamian inscriptions, where the king is the "image" of the god. It means the avatar of God on earth, the one who keeps everything going properly. This is humanity's proper human role in the cosmos.

The following chapters, the primeval history of Genesis 2–11, show (among other things) a progressive diminution in the fertility of the world; the world is created fertile, say the priests, but chapters 2–11 show us that every time humans do something wrong, the world becomes that much less fertile. From the garden that at most has to be tended, humans go out to the world, which has to be tilled by difficult agriculture. After the murder of Abel, that land is no longer fertile and can no longer be successfully planted: the blood of a murdered victim has ended the life of that soil and Cain is told that if he tills it, it will not answer. By the time of the birth of Noah, Noah is named Noah because, the text says, "this one will give us consolation"[10] "from the ground which God had cursed" (Gen 5:29). The world has become a very infertile place.

In chapter 6, God looks at the world and sees that is has become contaminated, *nišḥatah. Nišḥatah* is also used to describe the rotten cloth that Jeremiah first buries and then digs up (Jer 13:7–9). God sees that this earth, which was created fertile and beautiful (chap. 1) and which humans were supposed to guard and cultivate (chap. 2), has instead become rotten and full of stains. In this context, the flood comes as a response to this problem. Unlike in Mesopotamia, the problem is not too many people and the post-flood solution is not to build in population safeguards. In Israel the problem is the undirected and lawless activity of humankind and the pollution that results, and the post-flood solution is the giving of law.[11]

After the flood collapses the old creation by undoing the separation of the waters, then God reasons that God no longer wants to curse the earth because of the deeds of humans. God creates a regular order of nature: summer and winter, cold and heat, so that nature will not constantly fluctuate according to human acts. God also seeks to bring order to human activity, in chapter 9, by declaring that humans must guard and avenge human life. A clear hierarchy is made very explicit—humans are in control of nature, and their authority reaches over all the animals. Moreover, both animals and humans will forfeit their lives if they kill a human. Humans can kill animals for their own use (without eating the blood), but no one can kill a human being, the avatar of God.

There are three specific regulations in chapter 9. In the first, humans are told to be fruitful and multiply and fill the earth, probably the only command of God that we've ever fully obeyed. Next, they are told to refrain from eating blood because that is the life: hierarchy does not imply total domination. The third regulation emphasizes that no one (human or animal) can kill human beings, those responsible for the earth, and demands the death penalty for that terrible crime. These laws do not eliminate violence, indeed they include violence, the violence of the law. Violence is ordered and sanctioned as the antidote to violence: "whoever shed the blood of a human, by a human his blood will be shed" (Gen 9:6). The blood of the murder is not expurgated except with the blood of the murderer.

These laws do not prevent violence. However, they do protect the earth from being polluted by lawless behavior. The laws are meant to protect the earth. God makes it very clear that God no longer wants to have the earth cursed because of human deeds. Why God wants an earth, we have no idea; for God has no need to eat food. Chapter 2 links the creation of humans with the earth: they are to tend it; but it never tells us why God wants an earth. Chapter 9, a Priestly text, explains that God gives the whole legal structure of the world to protect the earth from suffering, but once again, it doesn't tell us why God wants the earth. The entire creation is an act of absolute divine desire ("grace"); we don't know what motivates it.

BIBLICAL PROPHECY: THE LAND AND PEOPLE OF ISRAEL

After Genesis 1–11, the biblical discourse of the Pentateuch and the Prophets is not about humanity and the cosmos, but specifically about the people and the land of Israel. These books talk about the responsibility of Israel and the protection of the sacred land of Israel. As modern readers, we extrapolate and restore a universalist sense to the text. The universalism may have always been there, but the text expresses itself in the immediate terms of its audience, the people of Israel.

In the Pentateuch, the sense that human behavior is responsible for the condition of the earth is very strong. Moral misdeeds pollute the earth: Israel is told to refrain from murder because it will contaminate the land; to refrain from allowing killers to go free because it will contaminate the land (Num 35); to refrain from acts of sexual abomination in order to keep the land pure (Lev 18,20)

The Book of Deuteronomy, produced by the teachers, makes this explicit. Deuteronomy 11 states the responsibility of humanity starkly: if you do good, God brings rain and abundance and you live a long time on the land; if you do wrong, then skies dry up, the earth will not produce, and you lose the land.

In such a text, we get a strong sense that humans are the intermediary between God and nature, and that God's behavior towards the earth is very reactive to human deeds. In this tradition, unlike the Priestly tradition of Numbers 35 and Leviticus 18, God does not show any more allegiance to the earth than did the gods of Mesopotamia who were prepared to send a drought to decimate humanity. Not only do human misdeeds immediately pollute earth but God also adds to the earth's suffering by stopping up the skies.

In Israel's prophetic books, particularly Hosea, Jeremiah, and Ezekiel, the contamination of the land of Israel will lead to disaster. The most extreme formulation of this idea is found in Jeremiah's vision in chapter 4: here, because of the deeds of Israel, Jeremiah sees the entire collapse of creation. The skies go dark, and no Adam can be found. So, too, Isaiah sees the very earth broken and falling apart (Isa 24:19–23).

In all these passages, the Bible presents a very strong statement of human responsibility. The centrality of humanity means that human beings are the intermediaries who influence the condition of the earth both directly, by the immediate polluting impact of their misdeeds, and indirectly, by causing a divine reaction that ends the rain and further pollutes the earth.[12] Humanity has long run away from facing this responsibility, but it has become hard to ignore now that technology increasingly gives us the power to impact on the environment and really create destruction by our social misdeeds. At this point, a statement that what humans do determines whether the earth continues or not is a simple statement of fact.

Of course, a statement that human actions determine whether the world continues is only a statement of fact if our definition of the world includes humanity. However, even if (horrors to contemplate) we thoroughly pollute the soil or deplete the ozone; even if we bring a nuclear disaster (God and humanity forbid), it may be that the earth will stand and the cockroaches will still survive as they have survived since the age of the dinosaurs, and so in a sense the world will still continue. We will not have destroyed it utterly: we will only have eradicated it as a habitable place for humanity. The earth, Gaia, the ecosystem, existed before us and will continue after us. Somehow, such thinking, characteristic of the Gaia-thinkers, is supposed to make us feel better.

We should note that this approach is almost totally unbiblical. The late prophetic tradition does consider the question. The prophet Zephaniah's terrible prediction of doom might envision earth remaining even though life has gone: "I will utterly sweep away everything from the face of the earth, I will sweep away humans and beasts, I will sweep away the birds of the air and the fish of the sea . . . I will cut off humankind from the face of the earth (Zeph 1:2–3). But this is not a prophecy that Zephaniah utters with any consolation. Deutero-Isaiah constantly emphasizes the importance of human life in the creation scheme: "[God] who creates heavens and stretches them out, who hammers out the sky and its teeming life, who gives breath to humankind and life-spirit to those who walk upon it" (Isa 42:5). Isaiah further tells us that when God created the world, God didn't create it to be unformed *(tohu)* but to be inhabited and inhabitable *(la-ševet)* (Isa 45:18). God's ultimate purpose for the earth, whatever it may be, includes a functioning human and animal community.

THE PRIESTLY VOICE: AN AWESOME EARTH

I would like to praise another voice of the Bible, one which is very often maligned in all contexts, including the ecological discussion: P, the Priestly tradition of ancient Israel. It is in the Priestly writings and in Temple writings that we find a profound sense of the awesomeness of nature, of the revelation of God through the beauty of nature, and of the place of humanity as a creature within nature. This love of nature is explicit in such psalms as 104 and 98. It also underlies Priestly legislation, where it is concerned with the land of Israel.

To these priests, the land of Israel is sacred and primary. Leviticus 18 and 20 explain that when the peoples before Israel polluted the earth, the land vomited out these people. This land belongs to God, and God will protect it. Israel's tenure includes a mandate to protect the land of Israel from becoming polluted by the performance of abominable acts. In this Priestly sense of the sacredness of the very soil of Israel, no less than in the prophetic tradition of Hosea, Jeremiah, and Ezekiel, Israel loses its right to the land if it doesn't protect it; the forced exile of the people separates the land from this contaminating force. This exile does not mean that God abandons Israel: the priests hold that God has great allegiance to Israel that goes beyond the land, and present the covenant of circumcision as the sign that land or no land, the relationship with Israel continues forever.

But the land itself is holy, and Israel may be separated from the land and sent far off to a land unknown. In Priestly theology, two elements, the land of Israel and the people of Israel, are both extremely vital to God, and neither will be sacrificed for the other.

Interestingly enough, with all the Priestly purification rituals, there is no ritual to purify the land.[13] Pollution must be prevented; once it settles in, it cannot be remedied by religious action or petition. The cult helps purify the people and the Temple, not the land itself. But the Priestly cult did not ignore the land; in fact, the *tamid* sacrifices, offered according to the calendar, were directed toward the whole cosmos to help keep the entire system going.

As we apply the Priestly concept of the two independent foci to our current understanding, we must hold both elements, humanity and the ecosystem, in equilibrium. For whatever reason God created the cosmos, God has great allegiance to it. Humanity cannot continue to damage the earth for its own benefit. But, in the biblical viewpoints, humanity also has independent and equal importance.

In biblical theology, the earth must be a place where human ideals of harmony can be fulfilled, a place where humans behave well toward each other, so that the earth is both fertile and inhabited. Forms of deep ecology that place the earth above humanity are not biblical theologies, for the biblical ideal of *shalom* includes the presence of humanity

This ancient language does not tell us whether, if humans continue on their current disharmonious path, the whole world will be destroyed, or just the people removed and the land preserved for the cockroaches. But it does bring home the recognition that we cannot escape the consequences of the human impact on the world. It further insists that today, now that we have technology that greatly magnifies our powers of destruction, if we do not make and obey rules of harmony and equity, then our connection with the earth will somehow be broken, and whether the cockroaches survive or not, the end of human history will have come, and with it the end of the divine plan.

NOTES

1. Lynn White Jr., "The Historical Roots of Our Ecologic Crisis," *Science* 155 (1967).

2. See, e.g., Jeanne Kay, "Concepts of Nature in the Hebrew Bible," *Environmental Ethics* 10:4 (1988): 309–27; and recently J. Baird Callicott, "Genesis Revisited: Murian Musings on Lynn White, Jr. Debate," *Environmental History Review* 14:1–2 (1990): 65–90.

3. This copy of the *Atrahasis* epic was published by Lambert and Millard, *Cuneiform Texts from Babylonian Tablets in the British Museum*, XLVII, 2965; Lambert and Millard published the edition and English translation in *Atrahasis: The Babylonian Story of the Flood* (Oxford: Clarendon Press,1969).

4. Moran constructed the text differently, understanding the "one god" in the tablet who instigates the rebellion not as "a god," but as a specific god, whose name may have been in a break, and who is identical to the god We-ilum, who was killed in the creation of humankind. See William Moran, "The Creation of Man in *Atrahasis* I, 192–248," BASOR 200 (1970): 48–56.

5. For Moran, it is not "a god" but "the god"; instead of "one who has sense" he translates "the one who had the plan."

6. For a study of these wordplays, see Steven Geller, "Some Sound and Word Plays in the First Tablet of the Old Babylonian *Atrahasis epic*," in *The Frank Talmadge Memorial Volume I,* ed. Barry Wahlfish (Haifa University Press, 1993): 137–44.

7. In the Sumerian King List (ed. Thorkild Jacobsen, *Assyriological Studies II*), the kings before the flood had reigns into the thousands of years; after the flood, their reigns were more normal.

8. Jacob Klein, "The 'Bane' of Humanity: A Lifespan of One Hundred Twenty Years," *Acta Sumerologica* 12 (1990): 57–70.

9. This is not the view of Gen 2, where the earth is barren until humanity is created. Gen 2 is a farmers' myth; Gen 1 is not.

10. Or "this one will give us rest," reading the Hebrew word as *yenihemenu*, which would conform to the Greek, as the standard *yenahahemenu*, "will comfort us," also matches the Greek, for the technical use of the word *nhm* means

to have release from work-bondage. However, since Noah's name is not Naḥum, "give us rest" fits his name better.

11. See Tikva Frymer-Kensky, "The *Atrahasis* epic and Its Significance for Our Understanding of Genesis 1–9," *Biblical Archaeologist* 40 (1977): 147–55.

12. For further discussion of the nature of human responsibility, see Tikva Frymer-Kensky, *In the Wake of the Goddesses* (Macmillan, 1993): 83–107 and 243–49.

13. The closest rite is the ritual of the decapitated heifer, performed when a corpse is discovered and the murderer cannot be found. This ritual seeks to prevent the pollution from settling in; once it does, nothing can remove it and it builds up until it reaches a critical mass. For further understanding of this concept of pollution, see Tikva Frymer-Kensky, "Pollution, Purification and Purgation in Biblical Israel," in *The Word of the Lord Shall Go Forth: Essays in Honor of David Noel Freedman*, ed. Carol Meyers and Michael O'Connor (Eisenbrauns, 1983): 399–414.

THEOLOGIES II: CONSTRUCTIVE THEOLOGY

25 / The Emergence of Jewish Biblical Theologies

2000

At one time, not too long ago, writing on "Jewish biblical theology" would have been considered unthinkable. It was a truism that Jews don't do theology, and the long roster of distinguished Jewish theologians of the twentieth century, Hermann Cohen, Martin Buber, Franz Rosenzweig, Abraham Joshua Heschel, Mordecai Kaplan, and Emanuel Levinas (to name only the most prominent), did nothing to dispel this axiomatic understanding. Somehow, each of these theologians was considered an aberration and, at any event, more a "philosopher" than a "theologian." Jews, after all, didn't do theology.

As strange as the concept of Jewish theology may have seemed, at least there were some writers who wrote "Jewish philosophy." The enterprise made some sort of sense, and the negative Jewish reaction to the concept of Jewish theology was mostly an issue about the definition of "theology." Theology was narrowly understood as the study of God, and writing about God was not considered a Jewish activity. But Jews did write about religious dimensions of life and had a long history of serious contemplation of the universe, life, and humanity. Most Jews preferred to call such contemplation "Jewish philosophy" or even מחשבת ישראל, "Israel's thinking," but there was a tradition of reflection on such issues. On the other hand, Jewish biblical theology was simply incomprehensible. The Bible was simply not the axis around which "Israel's thinking" revolved.

The Bible plays an enormous role in Jewish ritual life. Many psalms from the Book of Psalms have been incorporated into the synagogue liturgy, forming an essential component of the regular daily, Sabbath, and festival services. A group of psalms forms the core of the special service for Sabbath eve (קבלת שבת), and another group of psalms is the core of the additional celebration on festivals and new moons (the הלל). On Jewish festivals, entire books of the Bible are read aloud as part of the service: the Song of Songs on Passover, Ruth on Pentecost, Lamentations on the Ninth of Ab, Jonah on the Day of Atonement, Ecclesiastes on Tabernacles, and Esther on Purim.

But the main ceremonial use of the Bible in Jewish worship involves the Torah (the Pentateuch), for the Torah is at the ritual center of the Sabbath morning prayer service. The architecture of a synagogue entails an "ark," an ornamental, ceremonial cupboard at the front of each synagogue, on the eastern wall, usually upon a raised platform. This ark houses at least one Torah scroll, a scroll that contains the first five books of the Bible, carefully inscribed on parchment with a quill pen. Every Saturday morning, the Torah is taken out of the ark and promenaded around the synagogue, touched and kissed and loved by the congregation. The Torah is then "undressed," for the scroll normally wears a velvet cloak, with a silver breastplate over the cloak. Even the wooden poles around which the scroll is wrapped are ornamented, for they wear either a crown around the two, or individual caplets, רמונים "pomegranates," on each pole. After the procession and the unveiling, the Torah is ready to be read. Individual members of the congregation receive the honor of being "given an *aliyah*," being called up to the Torah to bless God for granting the Torah to Israel. A portion of the Torah is then chanted aloud. In traditional services, seven such honors will be awarded. The portions to be read are consecutive, so that each year the entire Torah will be read aloud from Genesis 1:1 to Deuteronomy 34:12. An alternate tradition allows three years for the reading of the entire Torah, but in this tradition also, the entire Torah is chanted from start to finish. When each Torah reading is complete, the individual being granted the honor will once again offer blessings of thanksgiving. After the seven readings, a companion piece is chanted. This piece, called the haftarah, is a selection from the prophetic books that tradition decrees complements the Torah portion. When the readings are finished, the Torah is dressed and adorned once more and is conveyed back to the ark in ritual procession. A minor version of this service takes place on Monday and Tuesday mornings. At that time, three people are called up, only the first section of the week's portion is read, and there is no haftarah. A macro version of the Torah service takes place once a year, on the festival of Simḥat Torah, "Rejoicing in the Torah." All the Torahs in the ark are taken out for procession; there are seven processions; each procession is an occasion for dancing and song; and most of the people present take turns dancing with the Torah scrolls. On this holiday, every-one in the congregation is given the honor of being called up for the blessings of thanksgiving. Some congregations call the people up to the Torah in seven groups; other congregations call each person up, one by one, for as long as it takes. In this latter case, in order to speed up the action, several people may chant from the different Torah scrolls simultaneously. The final section of the Torah is read, and then the Torah is begun again with a special ceremonial chanting of Genesis 1.

In all these liturgical ceremonies, the Torah is the central icon of the long relationship between God and Israel and a visual symbol of the regal nature of God the king. Through participation in these rituals, Jewish worshipers receive a deep sense of the awe and the joy of the Torah. At the same time, this centrality of the Torah is more symbolic than real, more celebrated than maintained. The liturgical and symbolic central-ity of the Torah functions strongly on an emotional level. But in many respects, the Torah, and indeed the whole Bible, has been marginalized in Judaism. Symbolically central to the faith, the Bible has been placed on a pedestal in Judaism. But being placed on a pedestal has its negative aspect, for it entails a certain degree of isolation: the Bible is not directly involved in matters of halakhah, Jewish practice and law. Authority in halakhah lies in a chain of tradition that begins with the Rabbis of the Talmud. The Bible is the source of halakhic authority, but it does not function on its own and is not an independent source of authority in traditional Judaism. A new reading of the Bible never has the power to upset Rabbinic laws or attitudes. The Rabbis turn to biblical passages to legitimate and give great weight to Rabbinic concepts or provisions. The Bible is of paramount importance as a source of legitimation. But it does not have the power to delegitimate or to invalidate Rabbinic provi-sions. One cannot argue that the Rabbinic reading of a biblical passage is misguided and expect that this argument will uproot the practices that were based on that Rabbinic reading. New readings of the Bible do not change old customs. In traditional Judaism, the Torah, regal as it is, is not sovereign; it is yoked to the Rabbinic system that it serves. In effect, the Torah was (and is, in most traditional circles) a king or queen in captivity. It is well known that the Christian church was explicitly "supersessionist." It showed honor to and interest in the Hebrew Bible and claimed it as its heritage, but it considered the New Testament as its foundational Scripture and drew its behavioral conclusions from there. Judaism was almost equally supersessionist, but it did not make its supersessionism apparent. It behaved ritually as if the Torah was the central facet of Judaism, but it dictated the way that the Torah should be read. In effect Jewish tradition subordinated and domesticated the Bible. Rabbinic readings declare the sense of Scripture. These Rabbinic readings of biblical passages are rarely judged wrong or misguided. They have so much weight in tradition that new readings are not only extraneous and irrelevant—they are practically unthinkable or inconceivable. The traditional readings overlie the biblical text so extensively that they obscure the readers' view of it. The Queen on her pedestal is hidden by veils.

This domestication of the Bible had ramifications in the way the Bible was taught and was in turn reinforced by Jewish religious pedagogy. The Bible was taught as an entry-level book. Little children learned their Bible, mostly concentrating on the Torah. But children would "graduate" from the Bible to "higher" forms of Jewish learning. By the time they were eight or ten, they would be studying the Mishnah, a Jewish law book that was produced around 200 C.E. When a little older, they would enter the world of Talmud study, which they would continue to study in adulthood, later perhaps also studying mystical or philosophical literature. Grown-up children did not come back to the Bible with more sophisticated eyes. They had learned their Bible and were expected to know it. But the Bible they had learned remained the text of their childhood and of ritual.

There is a form of Bible study that continues into adulthood in traditional Judaism, a semiritual form of study in which the portion of the Torah read aloud that week is studied as a devotional activity. In this study, the Torah portion is augmented by the comments that medieval teachers wrote about it. Of these commentators, the most important was Rashi, who lived in the eleventh century. He was a master educator with an important goal: he wanted to enable people to continue to study the Bible. To this end, he distilled the bewildering array of postbiblical study of the Bible and legends attached to it into a simple line-by-line commentary. Rashi's eyes became the lens by which Jews read the Bible. His commentary became so authoritative that Jews often did not distinguish between what the Bible says and Rashi's interpretation. Later readers and commentators built new ideas and commentaries on top of the foundation that Rashi laid, but they very rarely went beneath his commentary into the biblical text to find alternate readings.

As time went on, the "Rashi lens" through which Jews looked at the Bible was joined by a translation lens. Most Jews read the Bible in English, or French or German, alongside their Hebrew. But all translation is interpretation, and modern translations are in the tradition of the great translations of the Renaissance/Reformation, in which one of the goals of translation was to remove ambiguity from the text in the interest of opening the Bible to the masses. Like Rashi, the translators streamline and simplify the Bible to make it easier to read. With two such lenses "helping" the reader to see the Bible, the actual text could easily be simplified and amplified into almost total invisibility. The Queen on the pedestal had even more veils.

Things have changed. The many discoveries of modernism have had an enormous impact on our knowledge of Judaism. They have revealed the existence of many different streams of Judaism in antiquity and later, thus removing the impression that Rabbinic choices were the only possible Jewish choices. There have also been enormous changes in the way we read the Bible. The modern disciplines of biblical studies have increased our knowledge of biblical Hebrew and have led to approaches to biblical ideas that are at least partially independent of the classic traditional way of reading the Bible. Ancient Near Eastern studies and Assyriology have given us perspectives on the Bible that come from times prior to the Bible and contemporary with it. These and other avenues of approach to the Bible have been added to the traditional "vertical" approach that descended chronologically to the Bible through the layers of later tradition. At the same time, the modern development of Jewish studies has led to an explosion of our knowledge of ancient texts from Qumran and from the Cairo Genizah. Ancient Jewish magical texts have been discovered, and there has been a reawakening of interest in Kabbalah. All of these discoveries and methodologies have multiplied our resources for the study of Bible. The growth of contemporary philosophy and literary theory has also given Jews a new appreciation for the plurifold approach of midrash, which declared that there were seventy facets to the Torah and that everything could be found in it. Perhaps the most significant impact of biblical and Judaic studies has been the creation of a core of highly educated Jewish scholars who have not "moved on" from Bible to Talmud but have remained focused on the Bible, applying their reading of the Bible to everything else they learn and all their learning to read the Bible.

These modern developments were not always caused by modernism itself. Modernism challenged the validity of certain biblical claims, often juxtaposing biblical claims with scientific knowledge. But it very rarely looked to see whether the "biblical claims" it challenged were actually the Bible's claims. In fact, modernism often increased the simplified approach to the Bible that tradition generated. The trajectory of reading in the modern period has been to achieve a single authoritative reading of the biblical text. Modernism, with its belief in univocal objective truth, intensified the expectation that there could be ever more exactness in the one true reading. Early biblical scholarship, imbued with the attitudes of modernism, sought to use philology, historical criticism, and scientific data in order to achieve ever more precision in reading. With scientific precision, modern scholars "corrected" old readings and challenged the authority of traditional commentators by undermining faith in the accuracy of their traditional readings. But the modernist scholars shared with the medieval commentators the effort to determine a clear and unequivocal reading of Scripture that could command the allegiance and submission of its readers. Authority demands submission, but one must know to what one is expected to submit. So authority must present a clear, unambiguous statement to which allegiance is required. The text cannot be allowed to have a rich texture of multiple meanings, or how would people know to what meaning one is required to submit? Modern biblical scholarship displaced the source of authority from the traditional clergy and medieval traditions to the scholar and the new modern traditions. But the approach of scholarship, like the approach of the religious traditions, was to claim authoritative readings and understanding. A new approach to reading the Bible, and a new understanding of its theological significance, had to wait for the collapse of the authority of the same modernism that had itself challenged the authority of the old approaches.

The last twenty years have witnessed a collapse of all the old certainties, the demise of modernist ideas about objectivity and even about rationality. Much more attention is now paid to the impact of the researcher in science, interpreter in history, the reader in literature. Contemporary students of texts or events know that the texts and events acquire much of their meaning through the interaction of events, objects, or written documents with the person studying them. The interests and agenda of those doing the reading always affect the results of their reading process, sometimes unconsciously and sometimes with full intention. This new attention to the mutable and subjective nature of knowledge pervades much contemporary thinking. But it is especially strong in biblical scholarship, which has not only learned these contemporary principles from contemporary theory but has also come to realize them empirically through the inclusion in dialogue about the Bible of groups who had been on the margins. This dialogue revealed that different groups had different readings of the text, different readings influenced by the presuppositions and agendas of those who were doing the reading. Jews had their traditional authoritative readings that were sometimes quite different from traditional Christian readings. The poor read with their own experiences in mind, the third world readers with their own experience of marginalization and colonization, and groups of women in turn read the Bible with eyes conditioned by their own experiences. Dialogue among these groups began to highlight the great amount of interpretive content that lay underneath interpretations that masqueraded as simple reading.

The ongoing reinterpretation of biblical texts and the dialogue about interpretation and about these texts have made it clear that there was nothing essentially "true" about the traditional religious or scholarly readings. They were "hegemonic readings," readings that depended for their authority on the hegemonic power of those doing the reading, the authority of the church or the academy. The church or academy spread their interpretations by the power of their position. At the same time, the demands of power and the interests and agenda of the readers in power helped shape the particular content of these traditional readings. The traditional readings reflected the experiences of men of power. These hegemonic readings, it became clear, made choices in interpretation, and other people could make other choices. Today, the hegemonic readings continue to hold their authority within authority-driven circles, but within the world of scriptural studies and more open environments, the inclusion of new voices in the wider interpretative community has created a climate in which the old hegemonic readings have collapsed.

The collapse of hegemonic authoritative readings has resulted in a liberation of the text itself. Instead of being forced into the straight-jacket of the "one true truth," a biblical passage can now demonstrate its complexity and ambiguity. The contemporary babble of views has begun to reveal the multivocality of the Bible, its complexity and ambiguity. Knowing that many different interpretations of the text have in fact existed and held authority has caused us to carefully examine the nature of biblical writing that makes multiple readings possible. We have begun to gain understanding of the literary techniques of the biblical story, in particular the technique of "gapping," the most important tool of ambiguity in the Bible, leading us to see how the biblical authors created a story that changes with different reading communities. The gapped writing of the biblical story makes the interpreter or interpretative community fill in the gaps according to their presuppositions. As presuppositions change, the way that communities fill in the gaps also

changes, so that the text begins to have many different variations, allo-
morphs of the biblical story.

We have begun to recognize other biblical modes of complexity, other
techniques that allow the biblical story to change with its readers even
more than literature usually does. One such technique involves intertextual allusion. Biblical stories are often written intertextually, so that situations and key words in one story draw allusion to another story. Paying
attention to intertextual allusions shows us how stories and laws relate to
each other and cluster in discourses. The story or law has meaning when
read by itself but adds another layer of meaning as part of a discourse that
may present a whole spectrum of ideas about any given topic.

Another source of ambiguity is contained in the oracular nature of
biblical rhetoric. Famous statements, long "understood," like ורב צעיר
יעבד (Gen. 25:23) and שלח־נא ביד תשלח (Exod. 4:13) turn out to be much
more problematic than once believed. Does Rebekah's oracle declare
that "the elder will serve the younger" or "the elder, the younger will
serve"? Rebekah chose the first reading and acted to make it so. But
is that understanding required by the oracle? And Moses' statement is
translated "send someone else." But the words mean, "Send by whomever you send." Moses has learned to speak as cryptically as God, and
God gives him his own prophet, Aaron, to interpret him.

The Bible begins with an enigmatic construction: בראשית ברא. The
traditional translation, "in the beginning," ignores the ungrammatical
nature of this phrase. The word בראשית is a noun in construct, "the
beginning of," and a construct should be followed by a noun: "the beginning of something." Rashi emends the vowels, reading בראשית ברא, "at
the beginning of God's creating." But the text says, "At the beginning
of—he created." Assyriologists point to the Akkadian *awāt iqbû*, a gram-
matical construction in which a construct is followed by a verb. *Awāt
iqbû*, which literally means "the word of—he spoke," is a way of forming a relative clause with the meaning "the word that he spoke." Thus
perhaps בראשית ברא should be translated as "when God began to create
(the heaven and the earth)." In support of such an understanding, the
two major Babylonian creation myths both begin with a "when" clause.
The *Enuma Elish* begins "When on high the heavens had not yet been
formed," and the *Atrahasis* epic begins "When the Gods, like men, (had
to work)." There are enormous theological implications to such a change
in translation. "In the beginning" speaks of the beginning of all things,
the start of God's activity. Earth and humanity are the first entities that
God created. In this translation, the Bible is profoundly geoentric and

anthropocentric. Nothing existed before our own cosmos, God did nothing before God created us. A translation, "when God began to create," on the other hand, says nothing about the beginnings of God's activities, nothing about events before the six days of creation, nothing about the primacy of our world. There is time before the creation of our space, space before our own. In this translation, the Bible is picking up the story at the beginning of our universe, but *in medias res* in the story of God, and says nothing about the beginning of time or the primacy of this or other worlds. For these reasons, I prefer this translation. But it is not certain. בראשית ברא is not exactly an *awāt iqbû* formation. This formation occurs once in the Bible, תחלת דבר־יהוה בהושע, ("When God began to speak to Hosea," Hos. 1:2). The true *awāt iqbû* formation in Genesis 1:1 would be ראשית ברא. Why does it have an extra ב *(bet)*? And as for the Mesopotamian parallels, the few Sumerian tales about creation start with the words *u-rí-a,* or *u-úl-la,* meaning in *illo tempore,* "at that time," in other words, "in the beginning."

The composers of the first chapter of Genesis knew Hebrew at least as well as I do. They could say something clearly when they wanted to. Moreover, the beautiful litany is carefully, poetically constructed. They were not being sloppy or racing for deadline when they wrote בראשית ברא. The ambiguity of the phrase must be purposeful. The two possible translations reflect our own uncertainty and lack of clarity about our role in the wider cosmos. An intentionally ambiguous phrase mirrors the mystery of creation. People who do not know whether eternity preexists creation and creation preexists terra can refrain from writing in such a way that would reflect a certainty that is not there. The ambiguity is also a foreshadowing and a tip-off about things to come in the Bible. The world the Bible considers is complex, and the text reflects the world: different voices compete and clash, claim and disclaim.

It is difficult to talk about the intentionality of authors, divine or human, but the more we look at the Torah, the more oracular it seems, and the more Delphic in its oracularity. The very word *torah,* after all, means "divine instruction." It is related to the Akkadian term *tertu,* divine instruction by means of oracles, a word that ultimately became specialized as a technical term for instruction through liver omens, the chief way in which the Babylonians received their divine instruction. In Israel, the term *torah* originally referred to a specific teaching. By the time of Ezra, the people sought divine instruction within the written tradition of Israel, and Torah became the term for the entire collected Pentateuch. People could "seek out" revelation within the book precisely because the book is complex, ambiguous, and difficult. Like the world itself, like historical events, the book in which divine instruction was sought was full of riddles wrapped in enigmas.

The God of the Bible is not easily known. First Genesis, then the Pentateuchal narrative in Exodus through Numbers and the narratives that follow in the historical books trace a trajectory in which the God who once walked in the Garden in Genesis 3 and actively spoke to Abraham removes the divine presence from human affairs. God remains to be sought, not confronted simply and unambiguously. Even the High Priest in the holiest section of the holiest place, on the holiest day of the year, could not confront God directly. He experienced a God who was doubly veiled, obscured first by the cloud in which God hovers, then by the cloud of incense the priest created, a cloud of incense that prevented him from even glimpsing the divine cloud. God is seen through veils, experienced through visions and glimpsed through events. And God's presence can be felt through the writings that record these experiences and consider these events. But these writings cannot be simpler or more obvious than the God they represent.

The complexity and multivocality of Scripture need not deter those who read it. Nobody has to understand the full meanings of the text: indeed, the text, like life, can be so multivocal and complex that only the mind of God can fully comprehend it. There is no obligation to understand, no demand to spend one's life looking for fuller, deeper, more comprehensive meaning. One can live, Deuteronomy tells us, with only the simple truths: that God made us God's people and that we owe God the behavior appropriate to God's people. A life lived in accord with a simple truth is a simple life, and there is great ease, beauty, and peace in a simple life. When our lives become more complex, we may react by longing for simple truths and simple lives, or we may be led to look for more complex truths, to seek fuller meanings and more understanding. It is then that we begin to "seek" the text, and when we do, we find that the simple truths no longer look as true or as simple.

There are yet other reasons that the Bible was written with such complexity and ambiguity. First, the Bible is a text, a written document, and written documents from the ancient world were not "records" in our present sense of the word. A text was a witness to an event, not a complete or accurate recording of events or ideas. The very sight of the *stela,* or tablet, or scroll, as much as their content, served as witness to the reasons they were written. Even as a witness, the text was limited: it could not be entered as evidence in a law dispute unless there were witnesses to attest to what was on it. The text could not stand by itself. To use it in law, you had to have witnesses; to use it in study, you had to have interpreters. The texts are written laconically and often need explication. In the Near Eastern and biblical law collections, two cases will differ from each other by at least two variables. Oral discussion is needed to discuss which variable is determinative and what the result will be if only one change takes place. The written text will never replace the interpreter. And the rights of interpreters depend on their authority, their ability to convince others to listen and be convinced by their interpretation.

The authority of interpreters depends on their power, but the vagaries of history, not the logic of inevitability, determine who will have such power over the text. The biblical text does not itself determine who will be the authorized leaders. In fact, the Bible finds its final shaping under the impact of the collapse of all biblical systems of authority. Judah had a monarchy that claimed divine election and privilege. There had been antimonarchic forces in Israel, which claimed that with God as king, there was no need for the apparatus of state. But the Book of Judges invalidates the antimonarchic point of view even as it presents it, arranging the stories to show the utter collapse of premonarchic society. The Book of Kings ultimately loses faith in the Davidic dynasty of Judah as well and blames its kings for the destruction of the kingdom. Even the other basic tenet of Judah, the Jerusalem ideology that considered Jerusalem God's inviolate city, lost its power as God allowed Jerusalem to be destroyed. The Davidic promise and its ideology were destroyed along with the Judahite state. Much later, the Davidic king and Jerusalem became the centers of messianic and eschatological hopes, and that language is still used today. But that development came later. The disillusionment at the destruction of Judah was so great that, Haggai's wishes to the contrary, the monarchy was not restored when Israel was returned to its land.

The other sources of authority in Israel, the priests and the prophets, also lost their authoritative aura and their hegemonic power by the time of the destruction. The longstanding prophetic critique of the priesthood and its sacrificial system was compounded by the Priestly failure to ensure that God continued to dwell in the Temple. Nor was prophecy the answer. The ability of the prophets to determine policy was always somewhat problematic. The prophet Elisha was active in instigating the revolt of Jehu against the Omride dynasty—but the prophet Hosea clearly disliked Jehu's actions. The biggest problem with prophecy is the veracity of the prophets and their reliability. Whom can you believe? Deuteronomy demands that the people listen to prophets and insists that signs and wonders are not a good indicator—Deuteronomy claims that God might send prophets with signs in order to test the steadfastness of the people. The true indicator, says Deuteronomy, is the content of the message: the prophet must be telling hearers/readers to stay faithful to God (13:2–6). But this standard is only helpful when the false prophet advises abandoning God: when the issues are subtle and complex, how can the people know what action constitutes staying faithful? Deuteronomy considers this problem, "And if you question in your heart, 'How will I recognize the matter which YHWH has not spoken to him?,' the prophet who speaks in the name of YHWH and the matter does not come to pass—that is the matter which YHWH did not speak to him" (Deut. 18:21–22). But history cannot be the test of a true prophet. It cannot determine what to believe now, only what should have been believed then. Moreover, the Book of Jonah argues that the best result a true prophet can hope for is to have his prediction made false by inspiring repentance. During Jeremiah's blasphemy hearing, elders recalled that in the days of Hezekiah, Micah prophesied that Zion and the Temple would not destroy the city (Jer. 26:17–19). At that time, those who prophesied the Isaianic message, peace on Jerusalem, were proved right. But Jeremiah denounced as false prophets those who delivered that message in his day—and the destruction proved him right.

The Bible relates stories that illustrate the danger of following a false prophet and the great difficulty in understanding when a prophet is false. Even a prophet cannot always tell. At the time of Jeroboam's revolt, a Judahite prophet went to Bethel on a mission to denounce Jeroboam's religious innovations. As he returned home, an elderly prophet invited him to eat and drink. The traveling prophet declared that God had demanded that he fast till he get home, but the other prophet replied, "I too am a prophet, like you," relating that an angel instructed him to have the first prophet eat. But when the first prophet sat to eat, the word of YHWH informed him that he had disobeyed and as a result would not receive proper burial. A lion then dismembered him on his way home (1 Kgs. 13:11–25). The old prophet was not evil; when he heard what had happened he buried the remains of the traveling prophet and asked to be buried with him. The old prophet may not even have known that he was inducing a prophet to rebel against God's word; he may have believed his own prophecy about his duty to show him hospitality. This is the core problem with prophetic authority: even prophets do not know when they are not speaking a true prophecy. The story of Micaiah's vision (1 Kgs. 22:2–26) dramatically illustrates this problem. King Ahab wants Jehoshaphat king of Judah to join him in battle for Ramotgilead. Jehoshaphat wants a prophecy, and Ahab brings out four hundred court prophets who predict victory. Jehoshaphat wants still another prophet, and Ahab sends for Micaiah even though "he never prophesies good about me." Micaiah comes and tells Ahab to go, but Ahab is suspicious and demands that he tell him only truth. Micaiah then prophesies doom and relates his vision: he has seen the heavenly court, with God on his throne asking for someone to entice Ahab to battle so that he can die in battle. A spirit volunteered. When God asked how the spirit would do this, the spirit declared, "I will be a lying spirit in the mouth of his prophets," and God sent him to do so. Zedekiah, the head of the court prophets, is horrified at this story; he strikes Micaiah on the cheek, declaring, "How is it that the spirit of God passed from me to speak to you?" Zedekiah is convinced that he is a true prophet; Micaiah is convinced that God has deceived Zedekiah. In the face of such deception, nobody can tell what to believe. By the time of Ezekiel, the people have lost faith in prophets, and Ezekiel records a proverb, "the days are prolonged and every vision fails" (Ezek. 12:22).

The destruction discredits all the old systems of authority. As Zephaniah says (3:3–4), "Her princes in her midst are raging lions, her judges are wolves . . . her prophets are reckless men of treachery and her priests have polluted the holy and turned the Torah into lawlessness." It is no wonder that people seek the will of God in a book rather than turn to their leaders. But even the law is somewhat problematic. Allegiance to laws of debt and debt slavery, declared Amos, is וחמס שד, "criminal lawlessness and brigandry," and because Israel collects debts and holds debt-slaves, they are worthy of destruction. Jeremiah shows us that the child sacrificers in the valley of Hinnom really believed that God had commanded them to sacrifice their children. To Jeremiah, God says, "I didn't command it; it didn't enter my mind" (Jer. 7:31; 19:5)—but they believed they were commanded by God. Even more horrifying, Ezekiel tells us that God really did command them, that some of the laws are booby traps intended to doom the people (Ezek. 20:25).

The written law depends for its authority on Moses, for it is the "Torah that Moses commanded," but Moses himself is subtly undermined by the narrator on at least two occasions. In one, the people are at Sinai, and the narrator shows us two dialogues: God's command to Moses to tell the people to prepare for revelation, and Moses' charge to the people.

There is a significant different between them, for when Moses commands the people, he adds, "Do not approach a woman," a command never given by God (Exod. 19:15). Moses, on his own, without God's command, has introduced the separation of sex from sanctity into Israel's law, and gender inequality into Israel's congregation. And the narrator, the anonymous voice of Torah, shows the reader that God never commanded this. Another story is equally serious. The people have angered God by attaching themselves to Ba'al Pe'or, God has brought a devastating plague, and God now commands Moses to "take all the leaders of the people and impale them for YHWH before the sun" in order to stop the plague (Num. 25:4). But Moses never relays this message; instead he tells the leaders to search out and punish the guilty parties. Moses has rejected the idea of the vicarious punishment of leaders and substituted individual responsibility and retribution. And the narrator has shown that that important principle of law is from Moses, not God.

If some laws are from God, but shouldn't be followed, and other laws are from Moses rather than from God, there is no room for legal positivism. Every law has to be examined on its own merits; no law can simply rest on its own authority as "God's word." The written word has no more unquestionability than the priests who teach it, the prophets who proclaim it, or the state authorities who enforce it. This lack of trust in any given authority contributes to the complex multivocality of the Bible.

The Torah was completed during a time of complexity and new horizons. The rest of the Bible was finished in yet another period of complexity, the Roman era. To deal with a complex, shifting world, we need a complex text, and the Writings and the Prophets abound in diverse opinions and contradictory thoughts. Much of the complex variety has been simplified or ignored during the eons since the composition of the Bible by authorities who have claimed hegemonic power to determine the interpretation of Scripture. Now, however, the world is once again exploding with new horizons, and the old hegemonic authorities have come under suspicion. Indeed, the very idea of hegemonic power clashes with some of our contemporary approaches to reality. The genie and genius of indeterminacy have come out of the bottle, and the multiple facets of the Bible are once again compelling attention. Indeed, in our contemporary world, this very negotiating between voices gives the Bible a new centrality in Jewish religious thinking. The new interpretations of the Bible show that the Rabbinic interpreters made choices and that other choices can be made. By presenting alternative voices in the central iconic text in Judaism, the study of the Bible helps undermine the authority of any single biblical voice, any one particular biblical reading. Biblical theology presents an alternative source of authority to Rabbinic thinking and creates a very fertile opportunity for dialogue between biblical and Rabbinic ideas. The Bible offers us an ability to triangulate our contemporary sensibility with two major systems of our past. Above all, the Bible offers us a model of how to react to the collapse of old hegemonies. It shows us that we need not fly into a new absolutism or to nihilistic despair, but should proceed with a determination to keep faith and an understanding that revelation and sacrality do not lie in any particular word, but in the very process of sifting and negotiating and wresting. This is the process of the Torah.

26 / Constructing a Theology of Healing

1997

In ancient Mesopotamia, a person who felt sick would go to a diagnostician, a *baru*, or diviner, who would investigate the cause of the illness. If he deemed that the cause was "natural," a chemical imbalance or something like that, then the sufferer would call for a master of herbal medicine. If the *baru* declared that the illness was caused by witchcraft, then the sufferer together with the ritual experts would perform a long ritual, *maqlu*, burning effigies of the witch and sending the witchcraft back on the witch's head. If the *baru* declared that the patient could offer penitential prayers, if the sick person's personal god was angry, he or she could write a letter-prayer asking the god to come back. If the culprits were demons, the patient could exorcise them, and if the patient had done something wrong but didn't know quite what, or had angered some god that couldn't be identified, he or she could perform a phenomenal ritual called *shurpu*, which contained invocations and prayers for all the gods to stand by and help, a long prayer-litany with the refrain "O Marduk, giving life and healing is in your hands," and physical rituals to rid the client of the wrongful aura. These rituals were symbolic acts in which you would rub yourself with flour and then scrape it off while reciting the message with words like "As this flour is scraped off, so may the harm (and the disease that it caused) be scraped off me." Or you would be tied up in knots and then would cut the knots: "As the knots that are tied are loosed, so too the knots that bind my illness." Or you could peel an onion: "As the onion is opened, so am I opened and rid of all the evil within me." With every possible diagnosis, there was a prescribed remedy to alleviate the suffering.

In Judaism, or course, there is no diagnostician. Our theology tells us that there is only one cause, God; and what to do is not always so clearly mapped out. God may cause our illness by abandoning us. Deuteronomy 31:14ff contains an interesting statement in which God warns Moses that in the future Israel will be unfaithful, and then "I will be angry at them and leave them, and hide My face from them, and [Israel] will be devoured, and many evils and troubles will find him, and he will say 'These evils have found me because there is no God in my midst.'" In this paradigm, God is our "protective shield"; when God leaves us, external forces are free to destroy us.

In the more common biblical understanding, God's anger does not lead God to abandon us, but to punish us. The paramount paradigm of reward and punishment is repeated so often, with so many formulations, that it left a profound impression on Israel. The Deuteronomic paragraph included in the *Shema*, of course, is the best-known expression of reward and punishment, but the most pointed formulation is in Exodus 23:25, at the end of the Book of the Covenant: "You will serve the Lord your God, and God will bless your bread and your water, and I will take away every sickness from your midst." When you obey, you will have no sickness. When you do not obey, you will suffer all the illnesses of Egypt.

Even though the promises and the warnings are expressed in the national ("you, Israel"), the proverbial wisdom of Israel has always understood the same scheme to apply to the personal: the good prosper, the evil get theirs. This thinking is carried to the extreme by Job's friends, who reverse the truism: if you are not doing well, you must have done wrong.

Job's friends are doing what Deuteronomy is trying to do, and what people tried to do even before Israel, in the Babylonian and even Sumerian tales of the righteous sufferer: they are attempting to maintain their belief that there is an order and a justice to the world. If they can do this, they can also keep their hope for the future, a hope that God is just and will someday relent and restore us all. The best way to do this, or at least the easiest way is to do this, is the Deuteronomic way, by blaming the sufferer: *hata'nu, ašamnu.*

This self-blame is ingrained in all of us, reinforced by teaching, by penitential prayers like *Tahanun*, and by rituals of *Vidui.* Since we are bad, we suffer; and by inversion, if we are good, we should be healthy, wealthy, and wise. But our lived experience of reality is very different. As the famous comparative religion T-shirt says, "Shit happens," and the Jew says, "Why does shit always happen to me?" Our texts are full of the anguish of this central question and the answers in the history of Jewish theodicy, the justification of God. Sometimes we take all the blame upon ourselves: "I deserve to suffer." Sometimes we say that the fire of our pain means that God is purifying us through the crucible of our suffering: "it will make me a better person, and then I will be more deserving to be with God." Sometimes we want to believe that our suffering is redemptive: "if I suffer, I am adding to the merit of the world." And then sometimes we imagine that God is absent, that God is seated or asleep, and we cry out to God to get up, "*kumah Adonai*, answer me, (ʿanēni), do something! Act like you used to in the days of your redeeming miracles."

And often we simply feel that we do not know enough to know why we are suffering. If we could only see the world from God's eyes, we say, then we would know. At times, we have been passionately angry at God, we have been hopefully beseechful, we have been determined to hold God accountable for every bit of unmerited suffering by each and every one of us and by Israel. We have argued with God, presenting *din torahs* and writs of accusation; we have wept with the God we are sure weeps with our suffering. And we have kept the faith with God by constantly wrestling with the just God and the real world.

This wrestling with theodicy keeps our relationship with God fresh and engaged. But as far as healing is concerned, it is almost certainly a blind alley. The whole enterprise is founded on the idea that reward or punishment follows from the nature of human deeds, and that we can predict the consequences of our actions. This has always run counter to our experience of reality, in which we ask, as does Jeremiah, "Why does the way of the evil prosper?" (Jer. 19:1), and in which we struggle to understand the sufferings of the righteous and the deaths of the innocent. It may run counter to contemporary thinking about the nature of God, which has difficulty in believing that God intervenes directly in human lives to reward and punish. The idea of predictable results now also runs against our contemporary scientific understanding of causality, which posits that even if we assume intervention, it would be impossible to predict what the practical effects on the system of any one individual would be.

Let us state the proposition in its simplest form. Our actions cause God's reactions. But God's reaction is also influenced by the complex interaction of God's judgment and God's compassion, *middat ha-din* and *middat ha-rahamim*. In algebraic terms if x represents *din*, and y, *rahamim*, and God's action is 1 (one act of reward or punishment), then $x + y = 1$. But this means that $y = (1-x)$ and God's reactions are $R = x + 1-x)$. This is a simple equation, and an extreme oversimplification of the concept of reward and punishment. But even this simplistic formation, this very simple-looking equation, is known as a logical-difference equation, and such equations are notoriously unsolvable. In cases of low input, where one action is dealt with in isolation, you can predict the result. But when there are more people (each exerting a pull on the others) and more deeds, the reactions become, it seems, chaotically unpredictable. For as our science has finally realized, the butterfly batting its wings in China may cause a storm wind on the other side of the world (or may not); the world is enormously sensitive to the tiniest variation in initial circumstances—we cannot predict the exact results, but now (with computers, fine microscopes, and superpowerful telescopes) we can see the exploding consequences of a single factor. Contemporary chaos theory, plotting such equations through time, has mapped this kind of chaos, drawing this map of apparent chaos that charts as a "strange attractor," an eerie pattern that looks like a masquerade mask or a butterfly's wings. But this mask is the image of the reactions through time; it does not indicate what any particular reaction will be; on the contrary, the whole chart indicates the wide variability of any particular reaction.

We have to remember that the innocent equation was itself a gross oversimplification of the theology of reward and punishment. It doesn't even consider the many other factors that influence God's actions: the concept of merit, *zekhut*, which takes account of a person's whole record of past deeds and the merit of one's ancestors and of the ancestors of Israel; the idea of grace, *hesed*, that runs freely though the world by God's will; the notion of *berit*, covenant, in which God has made promises that must be kept; and the principle of God's freedom to have a divine agenda rather than being totally a reaction machine. It also doesn't consider how people's deeds impact on each other, and how many nondivine causes an intervening God would have to support or thwart. The dimensions of the problem are infinite, and when such complications are considered, it becomes clear that even if we posit a divine reward and punishment operating in the world, when it is applied to complex dynamic systems like society or the individual human body we have such an intricate structure of interlocking factors that it defies the ability to predict the fate of any one element in the system. The world need not be haphazard, and the system is not truly random, but we cannot understand the individual tit-for-tat.

Theodicy, searching for God's justice, is not a productive or effective way of responding to illness. It cannot answer the question, "why me?"

and it also doesn't consider that the question can have a direct impact on the questioner. Such questions can have enormous ramifications on the intricate mind-body network that we call a *nefesh,* a living being. Let us focus for a moment on what happens to a person in health and in sickness.

The *nefesh* of a healthy person has a fuzzy boundary. Our body is the medium though which we interact with the world, and so its boundaries are permeable and constantly responsive to the "outside." Our eyes, ears, nose, mouth bring the world into us and us into the world. We take in oxygen, we give off CO_2 and water. Our hands, legs, and feet touch and move through the space of our universe. And at the same time, our consciousness pays attention to the world beyond the body, and the boundaries of our egos expand to feel the joys and sorrows of others, to empathize with them, and to love them. Those of us who have a mystical bent are very conscious of this and cultivate this expansion of boundaries of the ego (or even their temporary disappearance), seeking out occasions when our own mind will stretch even farther, when love will make us reach out yet more to another person until we feel almost at one with this other person, with our family, with the Jewish people, with the universe.

All this changes dramatically when we fall ill. We should distinguish between mourning and sickness. A mourner sometimes has gaping wounds right on the surface that may admit and seek contact with God. When we are sick, really sick, we have to cope not only with loss but also with the violation of our bodily integrity. Victims of burglary feel violated and trespassed upon beyond the extent of material loss: their private space has been invaded. How much more so when our own bodies have been attacked. As a result, we withdraw into ourselves, a kind of psychic drawing the wagons around ourselves. This is a defensive gesture and an instinctive one. A sentient being withdraws from pain. We contract our egos, we focus on ourselves. This gives us the space to be safe, safe to mourn the self we used to be, the body we used to have. Safe to lick our wounds and to grieve at the process that is transforming us. It is also a safe space to make a *heshbon ha-nefesh,* a self-examination: Did I do something to cause this? Why did this happen to me? Have I contributed by sins of commission or sins of omission? Sometimes in this reckoning we find our answers: Yes, I took risks or ate poison, and now I must live with the result and wrestle with guilt. And sometimes we find our answer: No, I cannot imagine what I could have done differently. I have eaten healthily, I have taken all my vitamins, I jog three miles a day—why did I get a heart attack? I have taken care of myself and others—why have I been struck down? And then we wrestle with rage.

At such times, when we have turned inward, we are profoundly alienated from both God and other people. We have nothing left in the world but the tiny space, the four *amot*, of our own troubles. It is in this sense that we can best understand why the word for trouble is *tzarah*, "narrowness": we find ourselves in the narrow confines of our contracted ego. We are isolated and alone with our sorrow, our guilt, and our rage. And we also suffer from the depression that the loss of bodily vigor can bring in a culture that values fitness and activity. We are not worthy, we cannot make our own way in the world, we can no longer compete.

The safe space in which we lick our wounds is also the closed arena of anguished emotions. At such a time, more guilt will only make us feel even more apart from everything and compound the loss of self-esteem that inevitably accompanies our loss of control over our own bodily functions. We do not need inappropriate guilt, theological guilt that tells us that God is punishing us. Trying to believe that God is just, that the illness is a deserved punishment for misdeeds, makes us turn on our own uprightness. We already have feelings of guilt that we have not taken care of ourselves; to think that we are also being punished by God can make us feel worthless as well as negligent. Our *nefesh* suffers insult in addition to the ongoing injury.

There is another response well known in our tradition: rage. Anger that we are being punished when we don't deserve it. Rage, anger, and bitterness against an unjust God. We call God an abuser, we call God a wounder, we call God otiose, one who fails to protect. We summon God to a *din torah*, an indictment of God's justice. This raging at God is an art form long practiced in Judaism, and has turned into the lynchpin of theologies of the post-Holocaust era. In illness, such anger can perhaps help in the short run by deflecting negativity from ourselves: blaming God may be less destructive to the ill person than blaming oneself. But if rage becomes the dominant mode of our relationship with God, it alienates us even more and isolates us not only from the God at whom we are so angry but also from our community, which still holds fast in its notions of goodness and order. The anger, *ka'as*, becomes part of the ongoing affliction itself: "My eye is consumed by anger," says the psalmist (Ps. 8:8); "for all his days are pains, and anger is his preoccupation," writes Ecclesiastes (2:23). In that narrow space where anger consumes us, we are alone in a prison of our own making and we cannot heal.

In the narrow confines of illness, we are alienated from our bodies. We who have only recently learned again to appreciate, to love and depend on, the working human bodies—when these bodies fail us, we feel that our bodies are somehow separate from our minds. The body is out there, covering the real me. It's right there, but it is not really me. I'm divorced from it. It is discontinuous from my psyche. Suddenly, we fall into a dualist way of thinking; we see our bodies withering and react by trying to become talking heads. Of course, this is impossible in health and doubly impossible in illness: our bodies will not let us forget them.

In the narrow confines of illness, we are often also alienated from our friends. Some of them cannot cope with us as ill people. We are so different from the friend we used to be—and they withdraw from us. At other times, the sick person withdraws: they are not sick, they cannot fully understand. And even more, we envy them that they are not sick and feel ashamed at that envy. And we are angry that they have failed us by being healthy, by being different from us at the moment of our greatest need: "I envied the foolish, for they have no pangs; their strength is sound and healthy" (Ps. 73:4).

We may be alienated from our bodies, which no longer feel like part of us. We may be alienated from our friends, who do not suffer. And we are often alienated from God. If we hold on to our naïve faith that everything is predictable and God is always right, and we do not believe that God is punishing us for some unknown misdeed, then God seems to be absent. If we believe that God is wholly light and goodness, only "the power that makes for salvation," then if trials come and we do not deserve them, God cannot be there. We call out to God to answer, to arrive, to reveal God's face, giving voice to our enormous sense of loss. And so we are left totally alone, in our hard-core contracted ego, with a sense of God's disappearance. The theology of the absent God allows us to maintain the absolute goodness of God, but it increases our desolation and our pain: we have been abandoned.

But there is a strong biblical lesson that God is also there when disaster happens. God may be too much there: God has *paraṣ*, "broken through" uncontrollably, beyond our ability to tolerate it. God warned the people at Sinai not to approach the mountain *pen ʾefroṣ*, "lest I break through." And God broke through and killed Uzzah at Perez-uzzah, and may have broken through in the deaths of Nadab and Abihu, sons of Aaron. God is a force for order and for disorder. God brings disorder as well as order; in Hosea's metaphor, God is a lion that comes out of the dark, out of his cave, and snatches away suddenly, and you cannot know when, and you cannot know what to do about it. Isaiah tells us very clearly that God is not absent in the evil: "I make well-being and create evil" (*oseh shalom u-vorei ra*, Isa. 45:7); on this verse, Exodus Rabbah (28) comments, "God does everything simultaneously—causes to die and brings life, wounds and heals." God is present in the darkness as well as in the light. This is a hard fact to accept, and we often try to soften our realization of it, as in our siddur's euphemistic substitution *u-vorei et ha-kol*, "who creates everything." But our traditional attempts to suppress the association of God and evil cannot erase the fact that God brings death as well as life, God wounds and God heals, and God does all of these things simultaneously. God is present in the dark as well as in the light. The darker side of God can be a vivid presence in suffering, and the experience of illness or trouble can bring us vividly face-to-face with the power of this God. When we pray to God to heal us, we need to remember that the healer is also the wounder; and the wounder wounds by fact as well as by action.

Sometimes we prefer to visualize God suffering along with us. This lessens our alienation. But we pay a price: we give up the certainty of the eschatological hope that someday it will all come out right. The suffering God cannot offer the hope that the perfect punishing God offers, the hope that God is perfect and just, and that when God relents, God can make everything good (if not in this world, then in the next). If God is absent, God can come back. But the image of the suffering God, of the God who is present with the suffering person, is an image of a God who is wounded as well as wounding, a deity who suffers because it cannot not wound. This is a God who cries, "Be careful or I may break out," knowing that a divine breakout can destroy. Illness and suffering can result from too much presence of God, not from divine absence. This image of a God whose overwhelming presence causes our suffering may help us to heal in the face of our own suffering.

For the essence of healing is "breaking out": breaking out of the narrow confines of aloneness to which we have retreated in our pain; healing is the learning of truths about reality that we have learned and even taught and yet paid no attention to: healing is finding trust in the assurance of the order that lies beyond the disorder of our lives. It is the rediscovering of the integrity of life, the realization that our connection to others and to the Other is deeper than, and stretches beyond, the integrity of body,

In this healing, our friends can be our greatest helpers. Even when they say nothing, and do not know what to say, even when they say the wrong things and make light of our suffering in order to "cheer us up," even then, their very presence is supportive. Even Job's friends, intent as they were on convincing him that God was just in causing his suffering, nevertheless sat with him and listened so that he kept engaged with them, with human company, and with God. The presence of friends may start to call forth response from us, begin to poke a hole in the narrow confines of our contracted ego. This is the true sense of *bikkur holim*, visiting the sick. We come and intrude on the sick person's sense of global disorder with the steady power of a presence that does not go away. For presence exerts a magnetic force that pulls at our prison of *ṣarah*, gradually focusing our attention back on the world and on our own place in it.

Personal friends cannot do this alone. They also need the formal presence of a community, of a public minyan. Once again, we need to distinguish between the needs of a mourner and the needs of a sick person. They are not quite the same. A mourner needs a public minyan to say *Kaddish*, both because *halakhah* restricts the *Kaddish* to public recitation and because mourners have gaping wounds of which they are well aware and are looking for and receptive to the energy of others to make them whole. But the sick person may need a different kind of public space, a "*gevalt minyan*," a time and place to come together with other suffering people. We need to support each other—and we also need a safe space to express rage and "vent" bitterness and share disillusionment. When we are suffering, we need to experience the fact that we are not the only afflicted ones (why me?) and to understand that there is room in our love of God to express our negativity and God's darkness. We need to know that our own dark thoughts do not have to remain hidden in the confines of a contracted ego.

To be healed, we must open the tightly gated walls of our withdrawn selves. We must be receptive to the presence of people and of God. Healing services, now becoming so popular, bring together the power of healthy beings, healthy *neshamot*, to come knocking at the gated walls of the ego, to hurl power and goodwill and love to chip away at the wall of pain and isolation. When they do so, they provide a window for God's presence to enter. To be healed we must find our way to let God back to us. The healing service, the presence of friends, the *gevalt minyan*, all help stretch the once-elastic walls of our ego, helping gradually to restore the open-spaced fuzzy boundary of the ego of the well person, interactive and participating.

What else can help us open ourselves to God, to community, and to cosmos? If we are very, very lucky, we can study Torah. The Talmud states, "If he has a backache, let him study Torah; if he has a toothache, let him study Torah" (BT *Eruvin* 54a). Those of us who are blessed with the gift of Torah can lose ourselves in study no matter how contracted our ego, lose ourselves in the words of a page and the pages of the Word. This study connects us beyond ourselves, into the past, into the minds of others, and to God. For us, Torah is the way to the world. But not all of us can do that. Many of us need other words, words and rituals to help us expand once again.

The old fixed rituals of Judaism were not created for healing, and may not be of much help. Regular rituals and services are designed to create a bridge between "normalcy" and God; they often cannot cut through the wall of need and pain that separates the unwhole from the well, and they cannot connect God to the soul that has withdrawn from the overwhelming and wounding presence of God's power. Much standard ritual can seem alien to us in our suffering—we have to be healed in order to engage in it once again. The eternal cyclicality of the daily and weekly services may not resonate with us at a time when we are superconscious of our one-way linear march toward entropy and collapse. Our rituals point to the world beyond nature. Shabbat creates a sacred time by cutting through nature with an abstract counting that is divorced from nature's rhythms and natural processes. But these rituals and the Shabbat may not be as meaningful to us when we are sick, when we are obsessed with nature, with the diseases of nature. We cannot rest from our pain and our struggles. We cannot taste the taste of Eden, and even the Sabbath may lose her delight and her power to point the way to God.

We need other rituals to bridge our way to God and help bring us to the point where we can again feel the presence of normal human life and engage in communal response to God's presence. Other rituals, foreign and strange to our normal communal existence, may bring us back to community. Mimetic, meditative, and prayerful rituals may tap our sense of the immanence of the dark side of God and channel into the experience of the wholeness of God. Rituals like peeling an onion and praying that the disease peel away may smack of "magic," for they use transparent symbolism as we peel an onion. Casting out bread on waters and praying that evil be borne away has found its way into the communal Rosh Hashanah liturgy; a personal use to rid oneself of sickness taps into the same power of symbolic thought. Some therapeutic rituals may appear shamanistic, for they involve visualizing the illness as a demon and then visualizing our own powers and blood cells marching to battle with it. But, they go well with the Bible's own image of God as a triumphant warrior. "The Lord is a man of war," says the great song of the sea. "As God threw horse and rider into the sea, so may God help me destroy the power that afflicts me."

One of the simplest healing practices is using an amulet. Amulets have a long, respected history in Judaism, but were cast aside by "enlightened" thinkers as primitive and magical. But one can use an amulet without attributing magical powers to it. For an amulet is a perpetually visible prayer which involves many of our senses. When our voices are too choked by tears to speak the prayer, we can look at the amulet. And when our eyes are blinded by tears, we can touch it. *Shiviti Adonai le-negdi tamid:* by means of an amulet I can see the presence of God in front of me always; it heals me by bringing me into the presence of God.

This kind of healing may make us well. We keep discovering that the mind and the body are one mind-body, and that healing the soul, *refu'at he-nefesh,* may bring healing of the body, *refu'at ha-guf.* It also may not make us well. We can be healed and still be dying. When we understand that we can be whole without the return of bodily integrity, then we are healed. We are healed when we realize that the structure of the world that we live in does not reside in our immediate arena but in the order that lies on the other side of the experience of chaos and underlies it. Our realization of the order of the universe may not lengthen our days, but at least it asserts that we have our role. We can realize the enormous complexity of life in and out of the body, the beauty of this dynamic complexity, and our own role in it. Every life changes the world enormously, keeping the universe ever changing, ever renewing. We may have one destiny, one *mikveh* (to use Koheleth's term), but on the path (our *ma'aseh*) we have changed the world and kept it from stagnating.

Our tradition teaches us that this complex, dynamic, and infinitely interconnected world of creation is *tov me'od,* "very good," and that the God who underlies it really does wonders, *mafli' la'sot.* But there may be a heresy here in this healing theology. When we were children, we asked, "Can God make a rock so heavy that God cannot lift it?" Our experience of evil, suffering, and illness may make us realize that yes,

God has performed a great miracle, God has created a world so complex that even God cannot control it. Our postmodern science realizes that the world is infinitely sensitive to the smallest events. Tiny variations may result, not in tiny results, but in enormous changes of world proportions. Every minute change in even a single factor of a complex dynamic system can have exploding effects. So, too, every miracle, every intervention by God, will have infinite effects. We may pray to God for cures, but at the same time we realize that every time God intervenes to save somebody, the intervention has infinite consequences. The effort to control them could damage the very order, causality, and structure that constitutes the universe. This God has promised not to do, in God's promises to Noah and to all creation.

The process of healing is an opening to this infinitely complex world. When we can quiet our mind enough, we can hear the *kol demamah dakkah,* not the "still small voice" but the thin sound of humming, the humming of the universe, of the atoms and the quarks and the immune system and the blood and the stars humming away, moving away. That is where we feel the presence of God—not in the raging whirlwind of sudden intervention, but in the quiet hum of the ongoing dynamic system.

Sickness and suffering make us lose our sense of bodily integrity, and with it, the integrity of God and the world. We can no longer maintain faith in a God who is perfect and just and sweetness and light and in control, we can no longer believe in the fairness of life. We withdraw in pain and disillusionment, unable to believe the simple truths we wanted so much to be real, and alienated from the world whose moral underpinnings we have cause to doubt and more. And we contract to protect ourselves from the falling sky and the flying shards of our brittle pre-suffering truisms. Our friends and communities pull at our boundaries, and we venture to start opening up again, our way facilitated by their old abiding love that may use new techniques and new rituals and services. When we can feel again the wholeness of the universe and know that we are an integral part of it; when, knowing all that we have learned, we can once again say, *Zeh'eli ve'anvehu,* "this is my God whom I will praise," then we can truly know that we are healed.

27 / On Feminine God-Talk

1994

Passover is here as I write this, and we have been singing songs around the Passover table. Joyfully we raise our voices: *Adir Hu, Barukh Hu, Gadol Hu, Dagul Hu. Hu. Hu. Hu. Hu.* "He. He. He. He." He is noble, He is blessed, He is great, He is outstanding. It is hard to miss the message, applied as it is with a sledgehammer: God is a He. As we say seven times at the end of Yom Kippur: YHVH, He is God, YHVH, *He* is God.

Every time we say a blessing in Hebrew, the message is underlined: *barukh ata* YHVH, "Be blessed, you-he YHVH." Masculine verbal forms, masculine adjectives, masculine nouns unremittingly deliver the subliminal message: God is male. Even the nouns in the liturgy are masculine, in content as well as form: our father, our king, our mighty hero.

Alongside this liturgical message goes a theological one: God is not really male. God has no form, so *He* cannot be a male. Language is gendered, and that limits us, but God was never really male, and the *He* should be understood as generic or neutral. Religious leaders sometimes seem almost surprised that they should have to state this: since God is not human, how could anyone believe *Him* to be male. Like a secret message to the initiates recorded at 33 ⅓ r.p.m. on a 45 r.p.m. record, the theological message gets overwhelmed by the drumbeat of He's, Him's, King's and Father's. Every child hears that God is male; only the religiously sophisticated learn more.

There is some truth in the theological message that God, not being human, is also not male. The God of the Bible is not sexually a male, not a phallic figure. There is no worship of male sexuality, potency, or virility in the Bible. In stark contrast to the veneration of the phallus of male pagan deities, the penis of God is never mentioned. Nevertheless, there can be no doubt that the God of biblical Israel is *grammatically* male: all the verbal forms, adjectives, and pronouns are masculine. God in the Bible is also sociologically male: the husband, the father, the king.

393

FROM LANGUAGE TO STATUS

This cumulative impact of male-centered language and imagery is profoundly alienating to women. At the simplest level, it seems to carry intimations of masculinist theology: if God is male, then perhaps every male is a little bit of God. Even when this equation is avoided, we are left with a kind of "male club" to which God and men belong. God and men share *something* (indefinable) that women lack. This *something* is, more often than not, power, privilege, and status. A vicious circle develops. Male images are used for God because they are images of status and power. The fact that these images are used for God then reinvests these male images with even more status and power. Women are completely left out of both the imagery and the power loop.

There is warrant in the Bible for using nonmale, nongendered and inclusive imagery for God. The Book of Hosea (in which the gendered image of God-the-husband features so prominently) also draws many other metaphors for God. These include animal metaphors, notably the lion, and nonanimal metaphors such as the tree. We can build on these and other nonpersonal biblical metaphors, such as God as Rock.

God-the-mother may be more problematic. The Bible abounds in passages describing God's role in procreation, God's formation, supervision, and birthing of children. These are often taken as descriptions of God as mother. However, the imagery is still accompanied by masculine verbs, so that it conveys a message of a male God birthing. The cumulative effect can therefore be that as birthing is considered divine it is also considered less female. If the God with womb and breasts remains male in our consciousness, then "He" will diminish women. The language with which we think about God has to become more gender-flexible before individual metaphors can begin to offset the masculine impact of our God-talk.

There is an undeniable need to introduce female God language. But the decision to do so immediately presents a whole set of questions.

WHAT NAME CAN WE USE?

1. *Shekhinah* is the most obvious name that comes to mind. This is a name with a long venerable history. In Rabbinic writings, the term refers to the immanent presence of God, and it is not clear whether this immanence was conceived in specifically *female* guise. In later writings, particularly mystical texts, the *Shekhinah* is that emanation

of God closest to our world, and is decidedly female. Moreover, in kabbalistic writings, the ultimate unity of God toward which we aim is conceived as *yihud qudša berikh hu ušekhinteyh* "the (conjugal) union of the Holy One blessed be He and his *Shekhinah*." Moreover, the name has come into use among contemporary feminists and is now a well-established name for God, particularly in the blessing formula *berukha at Shekhinah*.

However, the very popularity of this name presents a difficulty, for *Shekhinah* has become almost the female deity, rather than a female facet of God. This presents the real danger that a message of God's duality will be delivered subliminally in much the same way that the maleness of God is currently conveyed. Moreover, the associations of the name *Shekhinah* with immanence, with the indwelling presence of God, severely limit the use of the name. It is difficult to use the name *Shekhinah* in contexts of awe and transcendence, in those moments in which we acknowledge divinity beyond the limits of human sensation or conceptualization.

2. The Queen of the World, *Malkat Ha'olam*. This is certainly an epithet that expresses transcendence. It would seem logical to express the *malkhut* in our blessing formula with the female. Should we say *Shekhinah malkat ha'olam* or YHWH *malkat ha'olam*? The former gives us a nice balance between immanence and transcendence, but reinforces the idea that *Shekhinah* is somehow separate from YHWH. The latter is clearly a mix-and-match, but do people react to the concept of Queen the same as the concept of King? In English the problem can be finessed by using the de-gendered terms "ruler" or "sovereign," but Hebrew has no such neutral word. Even in English these gender-neutral terms do not have the rich associations or emotional affect of "king" or "queen."

3. The Queen of Heaven, *Malkat Hašamayim*. At first sight, this has a nice ring, and seems a good poetic variant of *malkat ha'olam*. It conjures up images of the celestial heavens and the infinite reaches of space, and has a resonance that seems biblical. Though its resonance is indeed biblical, it is quite negative. *Malkat hašamayim* is the Queen of Heaven that Jeremiah angrily tells us people were worshiping in the last days of the Kingdom of Judah. In Sumerian, the same words refer to Inanna, whose very name means "queen of heaven." The words are innocuous, but their associations may carry undesired connotations. In the same way, the word *elah*, "goddess," seems at the same time

appropriate and dangerous, as does the word *ba'al*, "master." The historical use of these terms to refer to pagan gods gives them connotations far beyond the normal meanings of the words.

4. *Raḥamema*, "the merciful one." This term has recently begun to gain currency and status. It has the advantage of referring to one of the more appealing attributes of God: the compassion that extends beyond judgment. It seems particularly appropriate for the female for two reasons. "Mercy" and "compassion" are two attributes that have long been associated with women, even in the most Pythagorean male-female dichotomization of the universe. The term itself is ultimately related to *reḥem*, "womb" and reinforces the female-appropriate sense of "mercy." However, the fit carries its own dangers.

The derivation of "mercy" from "womb" has a long history in the ancient Near East and is found in the Sumerian *arḫuš*, "womb," and *arḫuš-sùd*, "merciful," and in the Akkadian *remu*. It is certainly less misogynist than the Greek-derived connection of "hysteria" with womb (Greek *hyster*). But it is not kept as an attribute of goddesses: *arus-sùd* is an epithet often applied to male gods. Does using *rah amema* as a name of God reinforce the idea that mercy is a female quality? If so, does that give human males the right or the obligation to act without compassion?

GENDER-NEUTRAL NAMES

Because of the difficulty inherent in using specifically feminine names, it may be best to stick to gender-neutral names. The term *elohut*, "divinity," while gender-neutral in meaning, has the advantage of being feminine in form. This demands grammatically the use of feminine verbs and pronouns, thus countering the use of grammatically necessary masculines with *elohim*.

It is equally important to degender YHWH and Yah. These have always been considered the personal name of God, and need not be gender-specific. The name may derive from an imperfect verb ("the one who causes to be")—indeed the imperfect was used for females in many Semitic dialects. In addition, this derivation may be false or folk etymology, for the name may derive from the sound of the wind in the desert rather than from a verbal form. Whatever its origin, the name is a *name* and can be degendered by being used with feminine verbs and adjectives.

The English term "God" also needs to be degendered. It too is not etymologically male. The female "Goddess" not only contains intimations of paganism, but, like "poetess," "authoress," "Jewess," and "Negress" is an outdated and basically sexist female form that actually has a diminutive connotation.

Beyond the choice of names lies the gender of the adjective, the verb, the phrase, the sentence, the paragraph. The feminine needs clearly need to be used in order to repair the universal masculinity of religious texts, but the moment that we try to do so, we are faced with the necessity of making choices. Here the dangers are considerable, because there is a risk of undoing one of monotheism's chief advantages. In a polytheistic system, where the divine is divided into masculine and feminine, earthly gender relations and expectations get projected into the divine sphere. This, in turn, gives sacred warrant to the status quo and acts to impede changes. To call upon God as father when we seek protection and God as mother when we seek compassion is to endorse and perpetuate a system in which men do not have to be compassionate and women do not have to be strong.

The epithets that we apply to God are the archetypes of our thinking. We need to avoid perpetuating stereotypes by our choices. We also need to understand the reason that we choose certain images. What does it mean to choose a young virile (man) soldier—*'ish milhamah*—as our defender rather than an Ishtar-figure, an Amazonian woman-warrior? Does it mean that we believe that the man-warrior is more trustworthy? Or more malleable and controllable? And what would it mean to reintroduce this woman-warrior image?

ARCHETYPES AND ETHICS

Old, familiar images sometimes slide past our consciousness, their way facilitated by the fragrant oils of history, community, nostalgia and devotion. But problems arise whenever we try to modify them so that we can pay attention. If the "True Judge" is *dayan 'emet,* a male judge, then do we reinforce the idea that men are the most trustworthy at forming legal decisions? How does that reflect on the women judges that we find in our courtrooms? At the same time, our discourse about justice and law has itself acquired gender connotations. If we call God our *dayenet,* our female judge, does that imply that we are rejecting a "masculine" idea of judgeship for some putative notion of "the ethics of caring" or "relational justice," which may or may not accord better with the "female voice"?

Can we use *dayenet* without bringing the whole current discussion of ethics into our prayer? Or does *dayyenet*, like *raḥamema,* carry subliminal statements about this issue?

The other great metaphor for God, God-the-parent, can be kept in gender-neutral terms in English. But is gender-neutral also devoid of emotional resonance? And can we choose in Hebrew between "father" and "mother" without modifying the emotional timbre of each sentence? On what principle should we do this? Who is the economic support who gives *kalkalah* and *parnasah*? Who provides succor in sorrow or support in disaster? Who has unending grace?

In determining new gender language, we are trying to steer clear of the old and now-recognized danger of divinizing maleness. But as we avoid this Scylla, we must also steer clear of the Charybdis of gender-stereotyping and sexualizing. God-the-female is not simply the mother who gives birth or the mother who nurtures. Women are more than wombs and breasts, and God-as-woman must reflect a transcendence of these sexual characteristics. To honor our mothers by understanding God as mother may include honoring gestation and lactation; it cannot be limited to this aspect of femaleness, however, without doing violence to the many different ways that women can be women.

TOWARD A MULTIPLE IMAGE

Many of these difficulties can be met at least temporarily by a conscious decision to randomize the choice between male and female images and to mismatch the gendered names with the (in)appropriate adjectival and verbal forms. This might be our best way to approximate our newfound ability to convey multiple images visually, without words. In biblical times, words were chosen over graven images because of their relative impermanence and plasticity. A statue engraves a metaphor permanently, creating the distinct possibility that the metaphor will become confused with reality and will blot out the possibilities of using other metaphors. But with today's technology, images have become more plastic than words. The technology of "morphing" presents exciting possibilities for visually representing the multiple facets of divinity. Morphing images dissolves them into each other in what looks like a seamless way, compiling a visual image of transformation. A morphed image of God could incorporate all metaphors and genders into a constantly changing image of God-the rock-the tree-the father-the mother-the lover-the judge-the male warrior-the woman-warrior-etc., etc. We need to invest effort, time, and money in creating morphed films of God and in using them extensively in our religious education, so that the concept of multifaceted oneness sinks into our collective consciousness and remains there as we pray in randomly gendered language.

The advantage of morphing is that it avoids the great danger of creating permanently gendered images of the attributes of divinity. Once the morphed image is primary, language can attempt to refer to it by multiplicity of images in multiple gender. But this is a very difficult task, because it requires great sensitivity to the dangers of gender stereotyping and to "biology as destiny." We cannot impose the burden of innovation and sophistication on each individual prayer-leader. Instead, we must consciously compose gender-random prayer language to accompany this morphed image.

GOD'S CONSORTS

Uniting the genders into a single nondifferentiated image of deity may have an unavoidable side effect: We may lose the many female "consorts" that Judaism has provided for God. In polytheism, consorts do not do much. Basically, they consort, and they give birth to the god's children. But the consort-image has provided one of Judaism's most powerful images for God: the lover/husband.

Once upon a time, in ancient Israel, God may have had a consort, Asherah, who may herself have been a reflection of God's immanence and nurturing qualities. She was not an active deity, for even the ancient inscriptions, such as the one from Kuntillet Ajrud, indicate that it is God (not Asherah) who is the active source of blessing. Then, when biblical religion moved beyond the Asherah image it still acknowledged the power of erotic bonding by imaging "Israel" as the wife of God. The marital metaphor of Israel and God as husband and wife summons all the emotional power of male-female bonding and applies it to God's relationship to Israel. It captures both the intimacy and the terror of our closeness to God. Since Israel does not have equal power to God, the model of the marriage is patriarchal, and indeed the relationship contains great pain. Yet the metaphor also contains the promise of a future bonding without difficulties, a hope expressed by the prophets in the image of Zion as the future wife of God: "As a bridegroom rejoices over a bride, so will God rejoice over you," says the exilic prophet Isaiah to Zion (Isa 62:5).

We sing these words every Friday night to another one of God's consort-images, the Sabbath. As the Sabbath is the foretaste of the perfect world to come, so too the Sabbath is the weekly "bride" who foreshadows this eschatological marriage. "Come, my beloved, to meet the bride," we sing to each other (and to God) in our beloved hymn *Lekhah Dodi*. This poem contains many biblical verses originally addressed to the restored Zion. As Zion is the manifestation of divine "consort-ness" in space, so too Sabbath is its manifestation in time. And what about Israel? Elsewhere, Israel is also God's consort. But in this poem, (male) God and (male) Israel merge with each other as each unites with the Sabbath bride/queen.

The metaphor of God-and-consort also shines through our love of the Torah, whom we often image as a beautiful woman, desirable forever to God and to those who learn her. The impassioned love of Israel for wisdom, and for the Torah that is wisdom, is a feature of both our literature and our liturgy. The alluring woman Torah is another avenue through which (male) Israel and (male) God come together.

In this understanding, the *men* of Israel are the husbands of Zion, of Sabbath, and of Torah. God-in-heaven and man-on-earth share this love for the divine female and meet each other *in her person: on* the Sabbath, *in* the pages of Torah, *at* Jerusalem. The actual, physical women of Israel are invisible. The (men) kabbalists of Safed called out to each other and to God, "come, my beloved friend," as they went to the fields to meet the bride on Sabbath Eve. The women were at home, not included in this salutation.

The women are no longer invisible, no longer waiting at home. What then can we do with this imagery? We could, of course, toss it out, but in doing so we would not only lose a large part of our traditional imagery but we would also deprive ourselves of its emotional effect.

RECONSTRUCTING THE EROTIC

We can retain the power of the image of this beloved female in several ways. The simplest is to confine the image to woman-Israel and male-God, so that all of Israel is subsumed under the "beloved" image—but this brings us right back to the problem of the essentially male-God. Another step would be to encourage women to merge with the Torah and the Shabbat and explore what it means to become one with Torah or Shabbat. The possibilities for mystical merging are exciting, but there is a serious drawback. Such a metaphor of men merging with God and women with *Shekinah*/Torah/Shabbat may not only reinforce masculine divinity but may also provide sacral justification for considering females secondary in all relations: after all, we do not pray to the Torah! Moreover—and equally dangerous—it perpetuates a notion of male activity and female receptivity, since the "lover" is God/Israel and the "beloved" is the Torah/Shabbat.

The third way to retain this erotic imagery is to specifically include women in the invitation to become lovers of Torah, of Sabbath, of Zion, not by "translating" themselves into men, but by keeping their identity as women and being encouraged to feel passionate devotion to the woman-imaged Shabbat/Torah/Zion. This means abandoning or transcending the heterosexual aspect of the erotic metaphor. It acknowledges the power of female-female bonding and, at its best, creates an image of love that goes beyond heterosexuality/homosexuality and reaches for an eros that goes beyond gender. The dangers in attempting to use homo-erotic imagery in our current, homophobic intellectual climate are obvious and do not need repetition. The value, however, is equally enormous, as it would be liberating for both men and women. Women could be included fully in this traditional mode of Jewish spirituality; men and women could be released to express passion and devotion to *elohut* in all divinity's forms.

There is danger in degendering the image of God, danger in incorporating feminine forms for God, danger in reimaging erotic sexuality. But these dangers cannot be deterrents. We have eaten of the fruit of knowledge, and innocence can be maintained only by a conspiracy of silence. Once someone has pointed out that the traditional language is not inclusive, that women are not really included in a "He" and that motherhood is not honored by a "Father in Heaven," then it is clear that the emperor has no clothes. We cannot go back. Despite all the difficulties involved in determining the best way to make God-talk less dehumanizing, we cannot abandon the attempt. May the Force be with us!

28 / Woman Jews

1991

Judaism is a religion, a thought-system, a tradition, a history, a community, and a way of life, all intertwined. The very richness of the tapestry makes it difficult to define or pin down the Jewish belief and practice system. There are many voices, many periods of history, many disputes and agreements to disagree. The story of women in Judaism is similarly complicated, constantly in flux, and even more so today.

We should probably begin to consider the experience of women in Judaism with the reflection that Judaism is a religion and lifestyle with a built-in "mommy-track." Ever since the beginning of Judaism, and doubtless long before that, it had been assumed that a woman's life would be occupied with bearing and rearing children, providing for their economic and spiritual well-being. The Biblical poem "A Capable Woman" (sometimes called "A Woman of Valor," Prov. 31:11–21) shows an appreciation of women in this role and an assumption that women will fulfill it. In this poem, the woman of the house, wise and intelligent, is mistress of all the many economic tasks of women and an expert in buying and selling land. Because of her many capabilities, her husband praises her as he sits in the town gate. At this gate, the site of communal deliberations and legal judgment, the community made its decisions and adjudicated its disputes. The capable wife was not there—she was taking care of her household. It was her husband, together with the other men of the community, who engaged in these public affairs, and it was the strength and capability of the women that enabled their men to attend such matters. The division of labor was the ideal of the scribes and scholars who wrote the biblical Book of Proverbs at the beginning of the Second Temple. Later, the founders of Rabbinic Judaism further refined a system that had different expectations for women and men.

In many religions, one might ask: what do social arrangements have to do with *religion*? But in Judaism, society is at the core of religious thinking. The fundamental idea of Judaism is that there is one power, one will, supreme in the universe, and that this will, God, is in partnership with humanity to form a more perfect universe. The divine ruler demands our allegiance, fidelity, love, and commitment to the establishment of a righteous order. The way to do this is found in the Torah, the divine instruction, a term that refers both to the Pentateuch and the whole content of divinely inspired tradition. The Rabbis elaborated this central commitment into a series of *mitzvot,* "commandments," which spell out the parameters of proper behavior. There are two kinds of *mitzvot:* negative *mitzvot,* meaning proscriptions of impermissible behavior, and positive *mitzvot,* prescriptions of actions that one is required to do. These are part of the system of *halakhah,* religious law, which prescribes and regulates all the details of life and society.

In this system, all girls become obligated to the performance of *mitzvot* at the age of twelve (when a girl becomes a *bat mitzvah,* "daughter of the commandments"), and all boys at the age of thirteen *(bar mitzvah).* But the *mitzvot* to which they become obligated have not been identical for boys and girls. Everyone is equally obligated to observe the negative *mitzvot,* that is, to refrain from improper behavior. But there is a difference in the positive prescriptions. Females are particularly admonished to obey three commandments, sometimes known as *ḥanah mitzvot* by the acronym of their names. The first is *hadlakah,* the lighting of the Sabbath candles. The second is *niddah,* the observance of the system of menstrual taboos (avoidance of male contact during the first half of the cycle), and the third is *ḥallah,* a formal destruction of a small portion of dough in memory of the portion reserved for priests during the existence of the Temple. There are, of course, no penalties in Jewish religious law for failure to observe commandments. But these three have a special sanction: according to the Mishnah, failure to observe them can result in death in childbirth. Postmenopausal women are not exempted from these commandments. In fact, in the absence of women, a man is also expected to light Sabbath candles and, if baking bread, to destroy the *ḥallah* portion. But the three *mitzvot* are particularly singled out as the woman's *mitzvot:* taken together they define and sanctify the traditional woman's domain. Active in the household, she is to guard its purity by being scrupulous about menstrual laws, preserve its communal acceptability by not making the priest offering into food for the family, and make it into sacred space by ushering in the Sabbath through the lighting of the Sabbath candles. In doing these three, she perpetuates Judaism in the home and makes it possible to transmit it to the next generation.

At the same time, women have been exempt from commandments to which men are obligated. Of the 248 positive commandments, women have traditionally been exempted from 14 (by other counts 18):

- Recitation of the *Shema* (the central prayer of Judaism)
- The study and teaching of Torah (sacred law and lore)
- Wearing of tefillin on head and arm (2)
- Wearing tzitzit (tallit)
- Writing a Torah
- Recitation of the Priestly blessing by male priests
- Counting of the Omer (the days between Passover and Shavuot)
- Hearing the shofar
- Dwelling in the sukkah (the festive booth of the fall holiday)
- Taking and blessing the *lulav* (a stalk made of four types of plants)
- Procreation
- Circumcision
- Making one's wife happy during the first year of marriage.

These are very few mitzvot, but collectively they can make a big difference. In this system, the central public acts of Judaism (study and communal prayer), the visible symbols of the worship community (tallit and tefillin), and the central call to accept divine sovereignty (the blowing of the shofar) all may legitimately take place without the required participation of women. For at least two millennia, the public life of the community was a life of men. Even the commandment to procreate is addressed only to men, despite the physical impossibility of male single-sex generation. There are many reasons for this, not the least of which was the fact that a woman could not be obligated to pursue a course of action that might very well end in her death. But essentially, the reason for exempting women from the law is not important. The message that the exemption of women from this commandment gives is the same as that conveyed by the other exemptions for women: the men who comprise the community have, or rather had, the obligation to perpetuate it.

The Rabbis of the Talmud, already faced with a group of commandments from which women were exempted, suggested as explanation that women were exempt from those commandments that are "time-bound" (i.e., that have to be done at a set time). Thus, the blessing after meals (which can be done any time after eating) is required of women, while the recitation of the *Shema*, which has to be done at set points of the day, is not. Of course, this rule about time-bound commandments does not really fit the pattern of exemptions: fringes on one's garment are not time-bound, yet women are exempt from wearing them; and nothing is more time-bound than lighting the Sabbath candles, which cannot be done after the Sabbath has begun. But this idea of "time-bound" commandments shows the understanding and assumptions of the Rabbis. Household work, particularly with children, was considered to be a woman's proper highest priority, and she was exempted, say the Rabbis, from anything that might interfere with this.

There were consequences to this exemption of women. Not being required to attend public prayer, they were not able to be counted as part of the quorum of ten men who constitute the minimal public community necessary to have the special elements of public communal prayer. Not being obligated, their action in performing these ritual acts was considered an act of self-gratification rather than obedience to divine command, and there was dispute about whether women should recite the blessing that accompanied the ritual acts.

The Rabbinic system assumed that a woman would be occupied in the private domain, and this domain began to occupy her. She was increasingly defined as essentially and inherently "private." It is on this basis, still popular in many Orthodox circles, that women were defined as essentially private persons, so that no number of them can constitute an official public assembly, which requires ten men. The pattern of the optional *mitzvot* changed subtly. In home-centered rituals, such as counting the Omer, taking the *lulav*, and eating in the sukkah, women gradually became participants in such numbers that halakhic authorities began to consider that women—as a group—had obligated themselves. Thus the Magen Avraham, a halakhic authority of the seventeenth century, argued that women had become obligated to count the Omer, and others extended the argument to the Sukkot rituals (eating in the sukkah, taking etrog and lulav). On the other hand, in public rituals the direction of change went in the opposite direction. In the case of study, which in Judaism is a central *devotional* exercise and not only an intellectual pursuit, the exemption of women developed into a presumption that women would not study, and then into a cultural pattern in which women were not taught. Public worship followed a similar pattern, with women increasingly shunted out of visible participation in the community. Even the obligation to light Hanukkah candles underwent change. Women had been obligated to do this, but the public/private distinction became so important that this *mitzvah*, which was a *public* demonstration of the Hanukkah deliverance (and was moreover done outdoors until recently), became performed by men for the women.

The absence of women from the public life of the community was intensified by rules of segregation and "modesty" that developed in the first few hundred years of the Common Era. Among these was the *mehitzah*, the physical barrier between men and women as they pray. By the fourth century, it seems, women were physically separated from men by being in balconies or behind curtains. The family did not pray together. The men congregated near where they could participate in the action (which was all being performed by men); the women were out of sight. All the men could see were other men. This system of separation, probably borrowed from the Greco-Roman world, was explained and justified on the principle that women were a sexual distraction that would take men's minds off prayer. As women became more private, as men had less opportunity to interact with women other than their wives, they thought of these other women primarily as sex objects, and the fear of sexual temptation loomed ever larger. The men of Israel told stories about how the sight of a beautiful woman could cause men to perform almost superhuman feats in their drive toward immorality. They developed laws to guard against opportunities for sexual misconduct, chief among them the mishnaic law of *yihud*, which prohibits a man and a woman from being alone together. They protected themselves from lustful thoughts by decreeing that women should be dressed "modestly" (covered from elbow to toe), that their hair should be covered, and that their voices should not be heard. The women of Israel, out in public on their tasks and labors, should not attract attention: the goal of "modesty" regulations is the invisibility of women.

The community of Israel did not ignore women, nor consider them less than Jews, but it also did not see them as independent members of the community. All the active members of the public life of the Jewish community in synagogue and school were men. Each man, in turn, represented his household, his wife and children. In this way, the male of the household mediated the message of the community, the learning and heritage, to his family. His family, in turn (particularly his wife), encouraged his active participation in this public devotional life and did everything possible to enable the man to participate. The women had become "other," a separate group that intersected with the public Jewish community. They were the "wives and daughters of Israel" rather than woman Jews. The woman enabled the men to live their lives in the divine presence and were praised and honored for this role. Judaism evolved through the millennia of our era into a sort of "benevolent patriarchy," a community of God-centered men prescribing respect and affection for the women who provided them with their opportunities of divine service.

Women have long found security and fulfillment in this type of a system, but it is archaic and maladaptive to contemporary ideas of the proper relationship between the sexes and the real identity of women. It also lends itself to abuse. If the husband is the head of the household, responsible to the community for maintaining it, the well-being of its members depends on the goodwill of the man and, failing that, the strength of communal persuasion. But if this should fail, what can a woman do? In traditional Judaism, the right to create and dissolve a marriage was the husband's. If the woman was dissatisfied in her relationship, she had to depend on the community's ability to persuade her husband to grant her a formal divorce. When community control was weak (as it is today), this could lead to husbands permanently shackling their wives, creating *agunot*, "anchored" women who were no longer living with their husbands but were not free to marry anyone else. Any system in which the women are individual satellites to the men who comprise the community contains within it vast potential for abuse.

WHY, THEN, AM I A JEW?

In truth, I have no real choice. There is no "me" that is not a Jewish "me," no "I" to stand outside the people and choose to belong or not to belong to the faith. When I was about thirteen, one of my teachers told me a story. He had just been to a celebration of Martin Buber's eightieth birthday at the Ethical Culture Society. As he told the story (the scholar in me knows that I have no independent verification), a guest speaker praised Buber, claiming that he was neither Jew nor Christian, but the "universal man." This was high praise indeed at the Ethical Culture Society, and everybody was full of good cheer and fellow feeling. Except Buber. When he arose in response, he slammed his hand down on the lectern and said, "I am not a universal man. I am a Jew.

I feel it in my blood and in my bones: I stood at Sinai." That story has stayed in my memory, for Buber expressed something deep in the soul of many Jews—a sense of eternity and community, a deep experience of linkage and history.

I am not naïve. A twentieth-century scholar, I know how I came to feel this way. Every year at Passover I remember the primal event of Judaism, the Exodus from Egypt. Every year I read in the *haggadah*, the liturgy recited at the Passover feast, that "in every generation a person must look at him/herself as if she came out of Egypt." Throughout the year, the signposts of the seasons carry me once more into my Jewish identity. In June, at Shavuot (Pentecost), the start of the summer brings the revelation and the coming of the Law; in September-October, at Sukkot, the fragile hut in which I eat the season's harvest of fruits and vegetables recalls the desert journey of the Hebrews to the Promised Land. I sit and taste the food, and invite Jews from past generations to come and share this memory with me. In the spring, at Passover, I celebrate freedom, beginnings, and rebirth. To these three harvests of history, the Jewish calendar adds remembrances of good times (Purim) and bad (Tisha b'Av), momentous happenings (Hanukkah) and small (Fast of Gedaliah). Even in my lifetime, more days have been added—days to commemorate the horror (Holocaust day, Memorial Day) and the glory (Israel Independence Day) of Jews in our times. In the passing of the present, Jews see their past; in the marking of days we meet our history.

To these annual events, shared by (I hope) most Jews, I add the events of my own life. When I was a very little girl, my father took me to a rally. There I listened to the vote at the United Nations that established the State of Israel, and then I rose with a huge crowd to sing the "Hatikvah," the song of national Jewish identity. I am not sure where that really was, perhaps at Madison Square Garden, perhaps at Yankee Stadium. I was four years old at the time, and my memory of this event, my first real memory, is more mythic than historical.

Israel, Jews, the Holocaust—all were an important part of my life. Zionist youth groups and summer camps, years in Israel, Hebrew songs, Hebrew dances, all enhanced my identification with Israel and with the Jewish people. They did not make me an Israeli. I am an American, and like other Jews in America I mark my years in two calendars, journeying also through the American civic remembrances by which our nation of immigrants transforms itself into a people. Every Thanksgiving, we rehearse the arrival of the pilgrims and retell the stories of Jamestown; every Fourth of July we are reminded of the Revolutionary War, of independence, freedom, and the ideals of our founders. We reinforce these journeys through time with visits to Philadelphia, Boston, Williamsburg, Valley Forge, Gettysburg, and our many other national monuments and historical sites. Holidays, pilgrimages, and our studies in school all help us internalize our history until it becomes a part of us, inseparable from our hope and values. In the communal memory of past events we realize our identities as Jews and as Americans.

The heritage of Jewish history and modern Jewish events provides a deep sense of community and a rich feeling of connectedness to past and present. But this is only a small fraction of Judaism. I have always felt somewhat ill at ease with the same Buber story that had such an impact on me. When I first heard the tale in my teens, I wanted to change Buber's answer. "Why," I responded (in the innocent effrontery of adolescence), "didn't he say 'I *stand* at Sinai'"? I still feel the need for this philosophical-grammatical change. The synagogue in which I grew up had a verse inscribed in Hebrew above the holy ark: *da' lifnei mi atah omed*, "know before whom you stand!" This ark, the cabinet in which the Holy Torah scrolls are kept, is the focal point of synagogue architecture. Throughout the service, as I looked at it, I was reminded of the presence of One I could not see. The ark, the Torah, and this verse all directed me beyond myself, even beyond the community in which I stood, to an eternity of time, space, and will.

This transcendent message is reinforced every year with great impact on the solemn High Holy Days of September. In the majesty of Rosh Hashanah, the year begins anew with a joyous proclamation of creation and the sovereign authority of the Creator. God sits on the universal throne. Then, in the days that follow, we focus on us humans, on our deeds and misdeeds and the sense of responsibility that they engender. These "days of penitence" culminate in the solemn day of Yom Kippur, a day of fasting, penitence, and hope. These solemn High Holy Days, the "Days of Awe," reinforce our sense of transhuman nexus in our lives. They speak to our connectedness and obligations to each other, to the universe, and to God. This, the central message of Judaism, has become part of my own essence.

For all these reasons, I am a Jew and always will be. Ecumenical modern American that I am, I know that there are many religions, that they strive to give their believers a sense of belonging, responsibility, and fervor. I believe with fervor and conviction that there are many paths for the human quest. But as for me, I am a Jew. I can do no other, nor would I want to.

This being a Jew is a matter of destiny, education, and identification. Nevertheless, above all, it is also a matter of choice. The forces that make us a Jew do not *compel* us to be so. If Judaism were a misogynist religion, I could not continue to choose to participate. A Jew I might remain, by tradition and upbringing, but a Jew in rebellion or, even worse, a Jew in silence and solitude, alienated from the tradition and the community that give energy to the Jewish spirit. Instead, I study and learn (which are devotional exercises), I train students to be rabbis, I send my children to Jewish day schools so that they too can learn to learn, and I not only belong to a synagogue, I go regularly to pray in community. To me there is no doubt that Judaism provides a home for my spirit, a faith that allows me to grow and contribute.

As a woman, I know that the wellspring of Judaism is not in conflict with either my love of Judaism or my woman-ness. The classical Rabbinic tradition of women's separateness is foreign to my life and beliefs, and the systematic exclusion of women from the men's club of prayer and learning is a history to be mourned. Whenever I approach the ancient texts that heralded the domestication of women, I feel again the same anger that I felt when I first realized that I could never have lived my life of involvement with Jewish learning had I been born before my time. But the rage recedes before the realization that the past can be laid to rest. Rage seems to be only valuable as an incentive to change, so that one develops the determination to lead the type of vigorously Jewish and feminist life that will keep at least some groups of Judaism open and receptive to all their members. We need to grieve about the past, and, having grieved, set aside our grief in order to create a new order. This is easier to do in Judaism than in some other religions, for even though Judaism has been totally androcentric in its focus, it has not been anti-woman. There have been misogynist statements from time to time, but they are neither consistent nor dominant in the tradition. In many respects, Jewish tradition exploited women, but it did not malign them. The result has been that Jewish women are famously strong-willed and proud. The women of Israel never were Victorian maidens. The Rabbis knew that they were strong, assertive mistresses of their households, and they encouraged this, proclaiming that the woman was queen in her household, the religious home observances, and the well-being of family members. Their responsibilities often brought them into what we normally consider the "public" domain, not only physically into public space but actively as wage earners and businesswomen. Judaism has always had an often-expressed appreciation for women in their place.

This approval, of course, was conditional of their staying in their place, and was an important incentive to women to accept their lot and the approval that went with it. Nevertheless, Judaism did not tell women that they were inferior, or evil. With the explicit approval of the men, the women were openly capable.

There is another reason for the strength of Jewish women. Beyond all the patriarchal concerns and attitudes, there has always been another, deeper message of Judaism, sometimes not acknowledged, but always there. Beyond the Talmud lies the Bible, always proclaimed the most sacred of all texts, held to be divinely originated and divinely inspired, celebrated and studied liturgically as part of sacred service. And the Bible simply does not depict women as sex objects, or weak, or reticent. Of course, the Bible, written for its time, never imagines egalitarianism. The Bible inherited a social structure that we could call "hierarchical" or "patriarchal," complete with inequities between rich and poor, slave and free, ruler and ruled, men and women, and never questioned the fundamental premises underlying such social divisions. Some of these divisions, indeed, have never been eradicated. Slavery was abolished in Jewish law in Rabbinic times, and in Western culture only in our recent past. Male-female distinctions are disappearing only today, painfully, in fits and starts. And the poor are still very much with us, with the inequalities between rich and poor in America growing enormously in our own lifetime. Probably, none of these divisions could have been eradicated in biblical Israel. Certainly there could have been no gender egalitarianism. At a time when half of all women could expect to die in childbirth, when it took multiple pregnancies and births to produce one child who would survive past the age of five, and when women rarely lived past thirty, and men not much longer—how could egalitarianism or unisex lifestyles be conducive to survival?

Biblical Israel never questioned the legal subordination of women to men. But the way that Israel *justified* its skewed social order has had important ramifications for the way Judaism looks upon women. The social order is legitimated by divine fiat (Gen. 3): husbands are to be dominant over their wives. This divine prescription is really a description of historical reality. Attributing this social order to God doesn't open the door for much argument or dissent, but it also removes the onus from women for their social position. Nowhere in the Bible are women considered inferior, less wise, less moral, or in need of keepers. They have the life they lead because God announced that it would be so—a theistic way of saying "it is so because it is so." Social subordination is not a reflection of a lesser character. In fact, the biblical portrayal of women shows them to be much the same as men. Neither sexy nor weak, they have the same goals as the rest of Israel, and pursue them with the same strategies and powers as the out-of-power men who formed the bulk of the population.[1] There are no characteristics that we can call "feminine" in the Bible that men to do not also share, no attributes of "masculinity" not manifested by women.

The metaphysics of gender unity finds expression in the creation stories. In Genesis 2, after God creates the earthling (Adam), Adam is lonely. God sets out to create other creatures to accompany Adam. But even in his earliest, most primitive naïveté, Adam cannot find suitable companionship in cows or chickens. So God creates "woman" and "man."[2] The significance of this story becomes apparent when we compare it to two tales from the Babylonians. In the beginning of the *Gilgamesh* epic, Gilgamesh is oppressing his city and the gods realize that his arrogance results from having no peer. They rectify the situation by having the mother goddess create a new creature who can be a counterpart to Gilgamesh, and she creates Enkidu—another male. When the two meet, they recognize their suitability to each other and become close companions. The second tale, the Agushaya hymn, has a similar plotline. Ishtar, most ferocious and "virile" of the goddesses, is terrifying to the gods. The god Enki realizes that she needs a companion to occupy her attention and creates Saltu—another ferocious female goddess. In these Babylonian stories, the closest bonding possible is between male-male and female-female. By contrast, in the Bible, the suitable companion for a male is female and the male-female bond is proclaimed as the closest possible connection between humans: "therefore a man shall leave his father and mother and cleave to his wife and they shall become as one flesh."

The other story of the creation of human beings also delivers the same message of mutuality and equality between men and women. In Genesis 1, on the sixth day, God created humanity in the image of the divine, "male and female created he them." Once again, the implication is that male and female, both in the image of the divine, are essentially similar to each other and that all differences are secondary to this congruence. The separate creation of Pandora in Greek mythology, and the Greek concept of the "race of women" that it illustrates, are a sharp contrast to this biblical message of homogeneity. Just as there is no plurality of divine powers in Judaism, so, in reflection, there is no multiplication of different types of humanity. In Genesis 2, one human being was created, and when the solitude proved too lonely, the one was divided, with the second coming directly out of the first. In Genesis 1, both humans were created at once, but they were each created in the image of the one God.

The Bible sends a double message, for alongside these creation stories is the divine fiat that men will rule their wives. Further reading of the Bible shows that the court and the Temple (though not prophecy) were in the hands of men. But in the household, there is no echo of the divine fiat. Where is the woman who does what her husband or father says simply because he tells her to do so? In Genesis, in the stories of the matriarchs, the husbands have the right to control the succession. But women are not automatically assumed to be willing to follow their husbands and fathers in all their decisions. They are not obligated to move away from their home. Before she is sent off to marry Isaac, Rebekkah is asked if she will move to the land of Canaan (Gen. 34:57–58). Even Rachel and Leah, already married, must be asked if they are willing to move with their husband, Jacob (Gen. 31:4–13). Nor are the matriarchs assumed to acquiesce in their husband's choices of heirs: Sarah persuades her husband to eliminate Isaac's rival (Gen. 21:8–14); Rebekkah tricks her husband into awarding his inheritance blessing to Jacob (Gen. 27).

The law codes and the narratives of Samuel and Kings sometimes show different pictures of the position of women. The law codes tell us that a husband can immediately annul a wife's vow if he overhears it, presumably because he controls the goods that she is vowing to present to God. But women such as the great (wealthy) woman of Shunnem do not consult their husbands before deciding to bestow gifts or offer hospitality (2 Kgs. 4–8). In fact, biblical narratives abound in strong decisive women who act for the benefit of Israel: from Deborah and Jael through Abigail, the great woman of Shunnem, and the Wise Women of Abel and of Tekoa, the women of Israel act with strength and decisiveness. Throughout the millennia of Jewish history, the power of these narratives has gripped the Jewish imagination and helped form its expectations of human behavior.

The impact of these stories was particularly strong on Jewish women precisely because of the Rabbinic exclusion of women from serious study. While the men were studying the Talmud, with its worry about sexual temptation and its determination to create a pure and purely male system, the women were learning the Bible stories, with their subliminally revolutionary message that women are not sex objects, victims, or submissive and meek. Jewish women have had other strong role models:

from the talmudic period came Beruriah the scholar, wife of Rabbi Meir, whose learning was famed and respected, and Rachel, the self-sacrificing wife of Rabbi Akiba, who worked to send him to school; from later in history came figures of wealth and charity such as Donna Gracia Mendes and the Americans Rebecca Gratz and Henrietta Szold. Different stories have had their greatest impact at different periods. The story of Rachel, Akiba's wife, was particularly important when scholarship could exist only when some women were willing to shoulder both household and economic burdens; the story of Beruriah had a renaissance when women themselves were encouraged to study. But in all the stories, women were glorified for strength and determination, perseverance and achievement. With these models in mind, women were able to live under the *halakhah* (the legal system that defined everything, including the proper patriarchal relations between the sexes) without being effaced by it.

Religions are never static: they always entail process and growth. Every generation learns from its past and adapts to its present. Consciously or unconsciously, each community chooses anew the foundation message of the faith and, in so doing, modifies it so that it can continue to live. With very few exceptions, religions cannot live only in the past: they must respond to the human ideas and needs of each present generation. There are differences between biblical and Rabbinic Judaism. The world changed, and the religion, always faithful to its core, changed in response to new needs and new ideas. From the standpoint of today—in other words, according to the needs and ideas of the late twentieth century—some of these changes were "advances"; the abolition of animal sacrifice, the increased emphasis on interior values, the abandonment of war as a means of expression or persuasion. Other changes aren't as appealing to us, particularly the establishment of separate spheres for men and women and the reinforcement of this separation by rules of "modesty" (invisibility). This separation is not biblical: it is deeply influenced by Greek ideas about categorical differences and about the dangers of sexual attraction. It is also part of the great emphasis on the household by a society that had lost its institutions of Temple and Palace.

But the changes introduced by the Rabbis were not irrevocable. They were adaptive to their own situation, and helped ensure the people's survival then and throughout the medieval period, but they have no place in a postindustrial society. Judaism has changed and will continue to change on all sociological issues. The modern revolution concerning women has been underway a long time, long before we were actually aware of its magnitude. Women began to be educated seriously in Jewish studies a hundred years ago, in response to the new reality created by the industrial revolution in which there were women of leisure, ready to be educated and being educated only in non-Jewish matters. Some voted with their feet, opting to abandon the Jewish lifestyle and community. Others found that they had nothing in common with their Jewish-educated husbands, leading to disrupted home relationships. To ensure the continuation of the Jewish family, a leading and brave halakhic authority, the Hatam Sofer, decreed that in the modern world women needed to be educated in Torah, thus paving the way for the establishment of the first religious schools for girls. The education of women in Judaism had great consequences, for it meant that they would no longer be quite as dependent on traditional male interpretations of the traditional sources. Another major change happened without any particular legal decision or authority. Jews in America in the Conservative movement began to pray with "mixed seating": men and women sat together, there was no women's section and no *mehitzah* barrier. And somehow services didn't become orgiastic, men didn't abandon fervor for frivolity. Slowly, mixed seating had a profound psychological effect: as the worshipers looked around at the congregation with whom they were praying, they saw both men and women. The message delivered subliminally by an unsegregated congregation is that the community of Israel is both men and women.

These new directions have turned into a fundamental seachange in Jewish thinking and practice. I feel that I, and many other women still fairly young, have witnessed a revolution. I had my own small part to play in this revolution. I was the first woman undergraduate at the Jewish Theological Seminary permitted to be a Talmud major and take part in the Talmud major seminar. It seems incredible to believe that there was a time when a woman's registering for a class in Talmud was a major achievement. As with most other barriers, once breached, it was almost as if it had never existed. There were soon several women studying Talmud seriously, a woman graduate student was admitted to the seminar of the grand master of Talmud, and there were women Talmud Ph.D.s. Of course, we say now: the study of Talmud, like any study, is not the property of any one gender! How could anyone ever have thought that women could be excluded from *study*? And yet, they were—until our generation.

Change had come very rapidly. In the early 1970s, as the first Reform and Reconstructionist women rabbis were being ordained, a group of women called "Ezrat Nashim" (Women's Section) presented a list of demands to the Rabbinical Assembly of the Conservative movement. They expressed their extreme discomfiture that they, highly educated and knowledgeable in Jewish texts, liturgy, and practice, should not be able to lead services and even to attend as full members of the prayer community. There could be no prayer community without ten men—no matter how many knowledgeable and devout women were sitting there. They could not be honored with a blessing over the Torah, while a man who set foot in a synagogue once in a decade and had to mumble the blessings from an English transliteration could be so honored. They could not read liturgically from the Torah that they loved, they could not represent in song the prayer community they felt such a part of. Some Conservative Jews laughed at them, not even comprehending the pain out of which they spoke. But the Conservative Rabbis listened, and less than twenty years later, the agenda of Ezrat Nashim has been completely fulfilled. Women are full members of congregations, they receive equal honors with men, and they can be rabbis and cantors.

From derision to fulfillment in twenty short years! There was no way to predict how quickly change could take place. Those of us who were raised before the change sometimes have to play "catch-up" with our own children. I had my religious bat mitzvah celebration when I was thirty (rather than twelve or thirteen), when I learned for the first time how to chant the haftarah, the reading from the Prophets sung liturgically. I am still learning liturgical skills that my daughter, not yet bat mitzvah, has already mastered. She knows chants that I am now learning, and assumes that she will master them all. She has been raised to expect to pray and lead prayers, and sometimes finds virtue in doing as little, rather than as much, as she can get away with. Her very nonchalance teaches me how peacefully she can follow the path carved by revolution.

The task is not yet finished, the sexes are not completely equal: this very rapid revolution has its turmoils. The past is not yet past. Orthodoxy still teaches an extremely gender-segregated lifestyle and religious practice, and declares all change in the other branches of Judaism to be fundamentally non-Jewish. The other branches are evolving, but even in non-Orthodox circles there are many who do not accept and agree to change. Jewish life today is a checkerboard of egalitarian and non-egalitarian practices. In Reform and Reconstructionist Judaism, there is unanimity; in Conservative Judaism, there is division. Officially, the movement, committed to *halakhah*, has not yet found a halakhic argument to allow women to serve as witnesses (it has now). But the clear majority of the Conservative movement appears headed for complete egalitarianism between the sexes. A small group bands together to encourage each other to resist this change, talks of schism, and establishes its own women-exclusionary seminary. Obstructionist as they are, the dissenting reactionary voices are fighting a rearguard action. Their objections are vestigial elements of the old separatist system. For the majority of Jews in America, the last two decades have witnessed a major transformation in the thinking and practice of liberal Judaism.

Even the Orthodox may change, but in Orthodox circles change is in its infancy. Officially, many elements of Orthodoxy deny that change is possible. Still others require that change always be dictated from above. Yet there have been major changes. Women are educated in the Orthodox community, though separately from the men and not to the same level of talmudic knowledge. Women do not lead prayers, but they are not silenced from joining in the singing of Sabbath songs. And there are women actively working and agitating for change. Voices such as Arlene Agus,[3] Blu Greenberg,[4] Rivka Haut,[5] and Norma Josephs[6] express the sentiments of many modern Orthodox women, committed to Orthodoxy but anxious for fuller female participation. The many women's prayer groups and the National Women's Tefillah (prayer) Network attest to the active desire of women to participate in a community of worshipers. The developing Orthodox women's religious expression is different from women's experiences in the other branches of Judaism, for among the Orthodox the newly developing public ritual for women is a parallel community, separate from the male but giving public expression to women's devotion and spirituality.

The Orthodox movement has not yet made peace with the idea that women want to be part of public devotional community. There are rabbis vigorously opposed to the women's prayer groups in the United States, rabbinic leaders who argue vociferously that women need to remain private and individual in their devotions. This year, the newspapers have been full of reports of the struggles of progressive women (Reform, Reconstructionist, Conservative, and Modern Orthodox women together) to achieve the simple right of being allowed to gather at the Western Wall in Jerusalem and be a congregation of women, praying together at the site of the ancient Jewish Temple. Their dignity has been stripped, they have been insulted and physically mauled. Their very presence as an independent congregation of Jews, proudly praying together without the mediation of men, has sent shock waves through groups that are used to thinking of the community of Israel as an assemblage of *men*, each with his mother, wife, and daughters.

The drama of the Western Wall is the result of a major change. Not because women came together, but because they continue to do so. Once, I too was attacked at the Wall. I had gone there to pray as soon as I arrived in the country. I had worn my most modest outfit: pants with a full dress over them, somewhat in the Yemenite fashion. The dress was high-necked and long-sleeved, but it was eyelet, fully lined except for the sleeves. If you stood very close and looked very hard, you could see pinpoints of arm flesh through the eyes of the fabric. As I stood praying silently, I suddenly felt blows around my head and shoulders. Behind me there was a woman, beating me with a pocketbook and yelling at me that I was shamefully immodest, and insulting to the holy place and its worshipers. I told her to go away and I think she did—I never wore that dress to the Wall again. I conformed to her norms, concerned that I insult her traditions. Ultimately, I gave up on the Wall, going rarely and reluctantly, having internalized the sense that my ways were foreign to the Wall, a modern intrusion. No more. The women at the Wall today have announced by their persistence that the old structures against women's public being are simply *wrong*. They are simply wrong, and the women creating new patterns stand more genuinely in the ongoing tradition of Judaism.

Other legal barriers to women's equality and self-determination have no place in Judaism. The Orthodox community is agonizing over how to prevent the abuse of women under a legal system that holds that a woman is not free until her husband grants her a divorce. *Agunot* (anchored women) are multiplying as modern mobility enables husbands to move away, as husbands blackmail wives out of large sums of money before they agree to grant the bill of divorce.[7] Tens of thousands of Orthodox women live shackled by this regulation, unable to marry again. This is an ethical disaster, never intended by the Rabbis. It is a fossil of an age in which rabbinic authority and community pressure made sure that men properly freed their wives. But the modern abuse of the ancient law shows the inherent danger and ethical error of leaving a woman's future in the hands of her husband. In Reform Jewry, there is no religious bill of divorce; in Reconstructionism, either the husband or the wife can apply to have the divorce issued. Conservative Judaism has solved the problem by reinstituting the ancient court that can free the woman by annulling the marriage. This action frees women whose husbands simply leave or obtain a civil divorce, and the existence of this possibility eliminates threats and blackmail. Halakhic experts, Conservative and Orthodox, have shown the antiquity and authority of annulment. But the Orthodox community has not adopted it, probably because of the threat it poses to male autonomy.

Orthodoxy attempts to assert the dominance and centrality of males. But it has nothing to do with me. The Orthodox voice is not the voice of ancient tradition; it is one voice among the many interpreters of Judaism today. There are many paths in Jerusalem. My own is egalitarian and traditional in liturgy and observance. Other people, including Orthodox women, may opt for the Orthodox system, may accept it and support it. Patriarchy offers security, rigid rules offer a conviction of righteousness. Patriarchal Orthodox Judaism, male-centered but not misogynist, offers the women who accept the system a sense of appreciation and purpose. This is not my way, and it has no authority over me. Patriarchy is not my ideology and, moreover, any view of Judaism that freezes tradition at a particular point in the past seems to me misguided and in some cases idolatrous. As a pluralist, I cannot object to Orthodoxy. However, I do not have to justify myself before it. It lays no claims on my attentions or emotions, for Orthodox Judaism is one form of modern Judaism. It does not embody the ancient Jewish tradition any more than any other branch of Judaism does. Orthodoxy, too, has developed in response both to external circumstance and its own internal dynamics. At every point of change, there were choices that were made. I see no reason to demand absolute allegiance to early nineteenth-century versions of Judaism when Judaism continues to evolve, and I feel no need to consider these early nineteenth-century formats as normative in any way.

The barriers to women's participation are coming down in the rest of Jewry. But anti-woman feelings find other expression. Threatened by advances and achievement of women in the world, and denied the bastion of the synagogue as a "men's club," anti-woman sentiment finds its expression in cruel humor, in the proliferation of "JAP" (Jewish American Princess) jokes, crudely misogynist and anti-Semitic. This development is sad, and needs to be combated. It erodes women's self-esteem and heightens divisions between women. It reinforces sexual and ethnic stereotypes and can cause estrangement between Jewish men and women. But in the long run, it is a rearguard reaction and cannot stop the tides of change.

In the long history of Judaism, on practically any point at issue, there were many voices eager to speak and be heard, many opinions, equally learned, based on antiquity, faith, and love of God. That is what makes

Judaism so exciting. There are many voices today, an array of opinions both bewildering and inspiring. That too is exciting. And now, many of these voices are female. A whole new dimension of experience is being brought to the ancient tradition. Women's lives, women's needs, are heard. Women have always had their own *aggadah* (philosophy, interpretation, folklore, customs), but it was separate, women's own, superceded by the high tradition of Jewish learning with which it never interacted. Now the dialogue has been opened. Now that women speak the language of learning and have access to ritual and ministry, they are offering their insights to everyone: feminist interpretation of the Bible, new liturgy without hierarchical dualism, changing images of God, new liturgy for life cycles, inclusive theology and liturgy, theology of birth and nurture. Some new developments:

- *Rosh Hodesh*—there was an ancient tradition that on Rosh Hodesh (the beginning of each month), women refrained from certain work (particularly washing and sewing) and gathered together for a celebration. This custom has been revived as a women's occasion, when women come together for fellowship, devising their own creative rituals to mark the year.

- Ministry—as more women enter the clergy, trends already present have been intensified. The rabbinate is becoming ever less authoritarian and more pastoral, ministering to the needs and addressing the spiritual desires of the people.

- Blessings—in traditional Judaism, the events of the day—eating, drinking, washing, seeing nature, studying—have all been sanctified by the saying of a blessing, recalling the presence of God, and focusing attention on the transhuman in the midst of the mundane. New forms of these blessings are being written by Marcia Falk and others, forms that stress the activity of humanity and immanence of God.

- Theology—the central ideas and institutions are being reexamined in the light of what they mean to an inclusive community. A feminist Jewish theology is emerging, particularly in the works of Judith Plaskow.[8]

- Scholarship—the presence of women in Judaic studies is opening up new areas of research and providing new perspectives on ancient traditions. There are now so many women in Jewish Studies that it would be unfair to try to enumerate them all. Ancient Near Eastern scholars, biblical scholars, ancient and modern historians, anthropologists, and sociologists are both studying Jewish women and providing women's perspectives on all scholarly issues.

- Life Cycle—Jewish women have expressed the need to sanctify the biological events of life, and there has been a profusion of prayers, rituals, and poems for the naming of a daughter, for puberty, menstruation, marriage, birth, and menopause. My own work on "Motherprayer"[9] seeks to expand traditional insight and vocabulary to encompass a theology of pregnancy and birth.
- Song—spirituality is joined to creativity. Women's voices, long silent from the religious arena by law and custom, are now being heard. The songbook of Gecla Reezel Raphael,[10] the liturgical music of Shefa Pelicrow (both students at the Reconstructionist Rabbinical College), and the liturgical music of Debbie Freedman are creating a new form of spiritual music, centered in liturgy and expressing modern spirituality.

There are many more contributions of women to midrash, to scholarship, liturgy, and thought. The list has grown too great to enumerate, and only random names come to mind. There have always been women thinkers; now their offerings enter the mainstream of Judaism and enrich the ancient traditions. Indeed, with all the difficulties and turmoil, it is an exciting time to be a Jew.

NOTES

1. For a detailed presentation of the image of women in the Bible, see my *In the Wake of the Goddesses: Women, Culture, and the Biblical Transformation of Pagan Myth* (New York: Free Press, 1992).

2. It has been noted, and deserves to be noted again, that Adam is not called 'ish, "man," until after the woman is created.

3. Arlene Agus, "This Month Is For You," in Elizabeth Koltun, ed., *The Jewish Woman: A New Perspective* (New York: Schocken, 1976), 84–93.

4. See Blu Greenberg, *On Women and Judaism: A View from Tradition* (Philadelphia: Jewish Publication Society, 1981).

5. Rivka Haut is head of the Jewish Women's National Tefillah Network.

6. Norma Josephs, who is Professor of Judaism at Concordia University, Montreal is well known as a lecturer in Orthodox women's circles and is currently working on a study of the women-related response of Reb. Moshe Feinstein.

7. There is a difference in the status of men and women who are civilly, but not religiously, divorced. A man can apply for permission to take a second wife;

and even if he does not do it, any children born of his subsequent unions will be fully legitimate. A woman may not, and future children of a woman who has not received a proper religious divorce are considered *mamzerim*, bastards, and are not permitted to marry Jews. Because of this difference, men have leverage over women and can subject them to blackmail.

8. See most recently Judith Plaskow, *Standing at Sinai* (New York: Harper & Row, 1989).

9. Tikva Frymer-Kensky, *Motherprayer: Reading Toward a Theology of Birth*. Forthcoming, 1992.

10. Sponsored by the Melton Foundation.

29 / Like a Birthing Woman

1995

On coming to Jerusalem, kings stand in wonder
trembling seizes them—hil kayoleda   (Ps. 48:7)

It is not the stone that is astonishing
Babylon is bigger
Nineveh is stronger
Rome is more powerful.

It is the nearness of the Presence
the greatness of the Presence
the awesome might of God—hil kayoleda.   (Ps. 48:7)

Today—a sudden tightening,
my body shakes,
my fingers tremble.
The time has come.

On the high mountain of my pain I climb,
I who brings glad tidings.
I lift my voice with strength,
I cry aloud,
Behold our God!   (Isa. 40:9)

Sound the trumpet, for I hear the rushing of a
mighty force.
I howl: the divine day is at hand.   (Isa. 13:4–9)
The coming of the Lord shakes the earth—
shakes the people,
shakes the soul.
We howl, we quake, our faces flame.
We feel the power of the divine host.
My hands grow limp,
my heart is trembling,
pangs and throes—hil kayoleda.

It is in battle that men have felt this power,
felt the trembling,
the coming of God,
the danger and the glory of the cosmic forces.

Sound the trumpet, they have called.
Sound the alarm!
The day of the Lord comes and is near.   (Joel 2:6)
The nations tremble,
the hills tremble,
the earth shakes.
A mighty force is coming.
The men of Israel heard,
the king of Babylon heard the mighty hordes.
His hands also trembled—hil kayoleda.

Scream! for I, too, hear the sound of mighty combat.
The battle is on!
The forces near!
Like a rocking war chariot,
like a bucking plow,
I feel the movement,
the heat,
the sweat,
the dust of battles swirls around me.
I feel the coming of God's mighty force.
I tremble and I quake—hil kayoleda.

A mighty force is coming,
in awe, in terror,
I pray that I will not bear wind,   (Isa. 26:18)
that the child can bear the battle,   (Hos. 13:13)
that in the wake of this great coming,
God will leave our blessing.
And in the terror and the struggle of this great battle,
I work for life.

30 / Shaddai

1995

It is the twelfth week of gestation,
fourteen weeks in the counting.
A body grows and becomes.
There, on its form, is stamped its destiny:
To be a person,
image of God,
partner in creation,
lover of the world.

The body in which it will know life
is taking shape.
On its face, there is a nose.
The human nose, beacon of the face.
The nose that breathes the air of the world,
smells the creation,
tastes the pleasures of life.
The nose of a human being stretches forward from the face.
Not a beak,
not a snout,
center bone and two nostrils.
The letter shin ‍ש sha.

From the body stretch forth the arms and the hands,
the humanoid arms and hands.
Mark of us creatures who stand upright.
With these arms we reach,
we lift,
we carry,
we hold.
We stretch forth our arm, we bend it.
We hold others to us,
body to body,
face to face.

As we reach with our arm our hand stretches forward,
the humanoid hand,
able to write, to grasp, to feel, to caress.
Four fingers and a thumb,
playing the music of the world:
Hands writing the wisdom of the world,
Hands molding the creation.
Hands touching others in love and sharing.

Wondrous arms with bends and angles,
wondrous hands with bends and angles.
The bent arm—the letter daled
the fingers and thumb—a daled
the bend of the fingers—a daled
Shin and daled ד shadd.

And finally, at the core,
a letter yod.
A boy's yod is open, in front.
A girl's yod is hidden, in her midst.
The yod י.
Site of a joy not bounded by time,
site of a love that knows no seasons.
The yod of a human being:
future-creator,
pleasure-bringer,
binder of love.
A gift from God of God's own name,
for us to use in love of God.

Shin, Daled, (ד), Yod,
Shaddai.
The great Almighty of our ancestors
has sealed this divine name on our bodies.
Shaddai.
Every child comes with the name of God.
Blessed be the one who comes in the name of God.   (Ps. 118:26)
Blessed by the child,
Blessed be God.
Shaddai.

Bibliography of the Published Writings of Tikva Frymer-Kensky

BOOKS

2005   *Studies in Bible and Feminist Criticism.* Philadelphia: The Jewish Publication Society.

2002   *Reading the Women of the Bible: A New Interpretation of Their Stories.* New York: Schocken Books. Reprint, 2004.

1995   *Feminist Approaches to the Bible: Symposium at the Smithsonian Institution September 24, 1994.* With Phyllis Trible, Pamela J. Milne, and Jane Schaberg. Edited by Hershel Shanks. Washington, D.C.: Biblical Archaeology Society.

        Motherprayer: The Pregnant Woman's Spiritual Companion. New York: G. P. Putnam's Sons. Reprint, New York: Riverhead Books, 1996.

1992   *In the Wake of the Goddesses: Women, Culture, and the Biblical Transformation of Pagan Myth.* New York: Macmillan, Free Press. Reprint, New York: Ballantine, 1993.

1977   *The Judicial Ordeal in the Ancient Near East.* Reprint, Ann Arbor, Mich.: University Microforms International, 2000. Photocopy.

EDITED BOOKS

2000   *Christianity in Jewish Terms.* Edited by Tikva Frymer-Kensky, Peter Ochs, David Novak, Michael A. Signer, and David Sandmel. Radical Traditions. Boulder, Colo.: Westview Press. Reprint, 2002.

1998   *Gender and Law in the Hebrew Bible and the Ancient Near East.* Edited by Victor H. Matthews, Bernard M. Levinson, and Tikva Frymer-Kensky. Journal for the Study of the Old Testament, Supplement Series 262. Sheffield, Eng.: Sheffield Academic Press. Reprint, Edinburgh: T. & T. Clark Publishers, 2004.

BOOK CHAPTERS

2006 "The Image, the Glory, and the Holy: Aspects of Being Human in Biblical Thought." In *Humanity Before God: Contemporary Faces of Jewish, Christian, and Islamic Ethics*, edited by William Schweiker. Minneapolis, Minn.: Fortress. In press.

2003 "Israel: Anatolia and the Levant." In *A History of Ancient Near Eastern Law*, vol. 2, edited by Raymond Westbrook, 975–1046. Boston: Brill.

2002 "Revelation Revealed: The Doubt of Torah." In *Textual Reasonings: Jewish Philosophy and Text Study at the End of the Twentieth Century*, edited by Peter Ochs and Nancy Levene, 68–75. Grand Rapids, Mich.: Eerdmans.

2001 "Biblical Voices on Chosenness." In *Covenant and Chosenness in Judaism and Mormonism*, edited by Raphael Jospe, Truman Madsen, and Seth Ward, 23–32. Madison, Wis.: Farleigh Dickenson University Press.

   "The End of the World and the Limits of Biblical Ecology." In *Antiquity and Humanity: Essays on Ancient Religion and Philosophy: Presented to Hans Dieter Betz on His 70th Birthday*, edited by Margaret M. Mitchell and Adela Yarbro Collins, 15–26. Tübingen: Mohr Siebeck.

   "Israel." In *Security for Debt in Ancient Near Eastern Law*, edited by Raymond Westbrook and Richard Jasnow, 251–63. Leiden: Brill.

2000 "Ecology in a Biblical Perspective." In *Torah of the Earth: Exploring 4,000 Years of Ecology in Jewish Thought*, vol. 1, edited by Arthur Waskow, 55–69. Woodstock, Vt.: Jewish Lights Publishing.

   "The Emergence of Jewish Biblical Theologies." In *Jews, Christians, and the Theology of the Hebrew Scriptures*, edited by Alice Ogden Bellis and Joel S. Kaminsky, 109–21. Society of Biblical Literature Symposium Series, vol. 8. Atlanta: Society of Biblical Literature.

   "The Image: Religious Anthropology in Judaism and Christianity." In *Christianity in Jewish Terms*, edited by Tikva Frymer-Kensky, Peter Ochs, David Novak, Michael A. Signer, and David Sandmel, 321–37. Radical Traditions. Boulder, Colo.: Westview Press. Reprint, 2002.

   "Memories of a 'First Woman.'" In *Wise Women: Reflections of Teachers at Midlife*, edited by Phyllis Freeman and Jan Zlotnik Schmidt, 135–46. New York: Routledge.

   "What of the Future? A Jewish Response." With Peter Ochs, David Novak, Michael A. Signer, and David Sandmel. In *Christianity in*

Jewish Terms, edited by Tikva Frymer-Kensky, Peter Ochs, David Novak, Michael A. Signer, and David Sandmel, 366–73. Radical Traditions. Boulder, Colo.: Westview Press. Reprint, 2002.

1999　"Law and Philosophy: The Case of Sex in the Bible." In *Women in the Hebrew Bible,* edited by Alice Bach, 273–304. New York: Routledge.

"The Strange Case of the Suspected Sotah (Numbers 5:11–31)." In *Women in the Hebrew Bible,* edited by Alice Bach, 463–74. New York: Routledge.

1998　"Gender and Law: An Introduction." In *Gender and Law in the Hebrew Bible and the Ancient Near East,* edited by Victor Matthews, Bernard Levinson, and Tikva Frymer-Kensky, 17–24. Journal for the Study of the Old Testament, Supplement Series 262. Sheffield, Eng.: Sheffield Academic Press. Reprint, T. & T. Clark, 2004.

"Virginity in the Bible." In *Gender and Law in the Hebrew Bible and the Ancient Near East,* edited by Victor Matthews, Bernard Levinson, and Tikva Frymer-Kensky, 78–96. Journal for the Study of the Old Testament, Supplement Series 262. Sheffield, Eng.: Sheffield Academic Press. Reprint, Edinburgh: T. & T. Clark, 2004.

1997　"The Akedah: The View from the Bible." In *Beginning Anew: A Woman's Companion to the High Holy Days*, edited by Gail Twersky Reimer and Judith A. Kates, 127–44. New York: Touchstone Books.

"Constructing a Theology of Healing." In *Healing and Judaism,* edited by Kerry M. Olinsky and Nancy Weiner, 1–15. New York: The National Center for Jewish Healing.

"Reading Rahab." In *Tehillah Le-Moshe: Biblical and Judaic Studies in Honor of Moshe Greenberg,* edited by Moshe Greenberg, Mordechai Cogan, and Barry L. Eichler, 57–67. Winona Lake, Ind.: Eisenbrauns.

"Sanctifying Torah." In *The Shabbat Series: Excellence in Education for Jewish Women,* edited by Irene Fine, 57–73. San Diego: Woman's Institute for Continuing Jewish Education.

1996　"The Family in the Hebrew Bible." In *Religion, Feminism, and the Family (Studies in Family Religion and Culture),* edited by Anne E. Carr and Mary Stewart Van Leeuwen, 55–73. Louisville, Ky.: Westminster-John Knox Press.

"The Story of Abraham, Sarah, and Hagar: Genesis 16:17–21." In *Talking about Genesis: A Resource Guide,* edited by Bill Moyers, 93–97. New York: Doubleday.

1995   "Goddesses: Biblical Echoes." In *Feminist Approaches to the Bible: Symposium at the Smithsonian Institution September 24, 1994,* edited by Hershel Shanks, 26–44. Washington, D.C.: Biblical Archaeology Society.

"Law and Philosophy: The Case of Sex in the Bible." In *Jewish Explorations of Sexuality,* edited by Jonathan Magonet, 3–16. Providence, R.I.: Berghahn Books.

1994   "The Bible and Women's Studies." In *Feminist Perspectives on Jewish Studies,* edited by Shelly Tanenbaum and Lynn Davidman, 16–39. New Haven, Conn.: Yale University Press.

1992   "A Ritual for Affirming and Accepting Pregnancy." In *Daughters of the King: Women and the Synagogue: A Survey of History, Halakhah, and Contemporary Realities,* edited by Susan Grossman and Rivka Haut, 290–96. Philadelphia: The Jewish Publication Society.

1991   "Woman Jews." In *Women's and Men's Liberation: Testimonies of Spirit,* edited by Leonard Grob, Riffat Hassan, and Haim Gordon, 33–49. New York: Greenwood Press.

1990   "The Sage in the Pentateuch: Soundings." In *The Sage in Israel and the Ancient Near East,* edited by John Gammie and Leo Perdue, 275–87. Winona Lake, Ind.: Eisenbrauns.

1989   "The Ideology of Gender in the Bible and the Ancient Near East." In *dumu-e2-dub-ba-a: Studies in Honor of Ake W. Sjoberg,* edited by Hermann Behrens, Darlene Loding, and Martha T. Roth, 185–192. Philaldelphia: The University Museum. (Occasional Publications of the Samuel Noah Kramer Fund, v. 9).

1987   "Biblical Cosmology." In *Backgrounds for the Bible,* edited by Michael Patrick O'Connor and David Noel Freedman, 231–40. Winona Lake, Ind.: Eisenbrauns.

"The Planting of Man: A Study in Biblical Imagery." In *Love and Death in the Ancient Near East: Essays in Honor of Marvin H. Pope,* edited by John H. Marks and Robert M. Good, 129–36. Guilford, Conn.: Four Quarters Publishing Company.

1986   "Jesus and the Law." In *Jesus in History and Myth,* edited by R. Joseph Hoffman and Gerald Larue, 119–32. Buffalo, N.Y.: Prometheus Books.

1984   "The Relationship between Bible, Oriental Studies, and Archaeology from the Perspective of an Orientalist—A Response to Professor Liverani." In *A Symposium on the Relationship between Bible, Oriental Studies, and Archaeology,* edited by Pheme Perkins, Mario Liverani, and William G. Dever, 24–30.

Berrien Springs, Mich.: Occasional Publications by the Horn Archaeological Museum, no. 3.

1983 "Pollution, Purification, and Purgation in Biblical Israel." In *The Word of the Lord Shall Go Forth: Essays in Honor of David Noel Freedman in Celebration of His 60ᵗʰ Birthday,* edited by Carol L. Meyers and M. O'Connor, 399–414. American Schools of Oriental Research no. 1. Winona Lake, Ind.

1982 "*Atrahasis.*" In *In The Beginning: Creation Myths from Ancient Mesopotamia, Israel, and Greece,* edited by Joan O'Brien and Wilfred Major, 70–87. Chico, Calif.: Scholars Press.

"Linguistic Anthropology: Primate Communication"; "Linguistic Anthropology Approaches to the Study of Language"; "Anthropological Archaeology: Theory of Methods"; "A Survey of Prehistory." In *Anthropological Perspectives,* edited by Honeydew Blumfield. An in-house textbook for the Open University, University College, University of Maryland.

1981 "Suprarational Legal Procedures in Elam and Nuzi." In *Studies on the Civilization and Culture of Nuzi and the Hurrians in Honor of Ernest Lacheman,* edited by M. A. Morrison and D. I. Owen, 115–31. Winona Lake, Ind.: Eisenbrauns.

ENCYCLOPEDIA, DICTIONARY, AND COMMENTARY ENTRIES

1992 "Deuteronomy." In *The Women's Bible Commentary,* edited by Carol Newsom and Sharon H. Ringe, 52–61. Louisville, Ky.: SPCK.

"Sex and Sexuality." In *Anchor Dictionary of the Bible,* vol. 5, edited by David Noel Freedman, 1144–46. New York: Doubleday.

1987 "Adad." In *The Encyclopedia of Religion,* vol. 1, edited by Mircea Eliade, 26–27. New York: Macmillan Publishing.

"Ashur." In *The Encyclopedia of Religion,* vol. 1, edited by Mircea Eliade, 461–62. New York: Macmillan Publishing.

"*Atrahasis.*" In *The Encyclopedia of Religion,* vol. 1, edited by Mircea Eliade, 499–500. New York: Macmillan Publishing.

"Enuma Elish." In *The Encyclopedia of Religion,* vol. 5, edited by Mircea Eliade, 124–26. New York: Macmillan Publishing.

"Israelite Law: The Personal Status and Family Law." In *The Encyclopedia of Religion,* vol. 7, edited by Mircea Eliade, 469–72. New York: Macmillan Publishing.

"Israelite Law: State and Judiciary Law." In *The Encyclopaedia of Religion*, vol. 7, edited by Mircea Eliade, 478–81. New York: Macmillan Publishing.

"Marduk." In *The Encyclopedia of Religion*, vol. 9, edited by Mircea Eliade, 201–2. New York: Macmillan Publishing.

"Nabu." In *The Encyclopaedia of Religion*, vol. 10, edited by Mircea Eliade, 290. New York: Macmillan Publishing.

"Utu." In *The Encyclopaedia of Religion*, vol. 15, edited by Mircea Eliade, 162–63. New York: Macmillan Publishing.

1985 "Women." In *Harper's Bible Dictionary*, edited by Paul J. Achtemeier, 1138–41. San Francisco: Harper & Row.

1976 "Ordeal, Judicial." In *The Interpreter's Dictionary of the Bible: An Illustrated Encyclopaedia*, supplementary volume, edited by Keith R. Crim, 638–40. Nashville, Tenn.: Abingdon Press.

1972 "Ararat"; "Ariel"; "Asherah"; "Ashtoreth"; "Avvim"; "Sacred Groves"; "Hazael"; "Honey"; "Huldah"; "Hushai the Archite"; "Milk." In *Encyclopaedia Judaica*. Israel: Judaica Multimedia, 1997. CD-Rom. Jerusalem: Keter Publishing House.

ARTICLES

2002 "A Jewish Look at Isaiah 2:2–4." *Criterion: A Publication of the University of Chicago Divinity School* 41, no. 3: 20–25.

"Unwrapping the Torah: Making a Symbol Real Again." *Bible Review* 18, no. 5: 26–31, 60–62.

2001 "Dabru Emet (Redet Wahrheit): Eine jüdische Stellungnahme zu Christen und Christentum." *Evangelische Theologie* 61, no. 4: 334–36.

2000 "Dabru Emet: A Jewish Statement on Christians and Christianity." *First Things* 107: 39–41.

"Defining Jewish-Christian Values for a Just Society." *From the Martin Buber House* 27: 47–65.

"Lolita-Inanna." *NiN: Journal of Gender Studies in Antiquity* 1: 91–94.

1998 "Creation Myths Breed Violence: The Chaoskampf Myth of Creation Sets up a Cosmic Cycle of Violence: Can It Ever Bring Peace?" *Bible Review* 14: 17, 47.

"A New Bar/Bat Mitzvah Ritual." *Moment* 23, no. 4: 32–33, 63.

"The Quest for Meaning in Text, Tradition, and Liturgy." *Proceedings of the Cantors Assembly.*

1997 "Forgotten Heroines of the Exodus: The Exclusion of Women from Moses' Vision." *Bible Review* 13: 38–44.

1996 "Jerusalem as the Symbol of the Human Body." *Proceedings of the Rabbinical Assembly* 118: 159–61.

1995 "The Akedah: The View from the Bible." *Mekorot: Sources.*

"Birth Silence and Motherprayer." *Criterion: A Publication of the Divinity School of the University of Chicago* 34, no. 2: 28–34.

"Halakhah, Law, and Feminism." *Conservative Judaism* 47, no. 2: 46–52.

"Towards a Liberal Theory of Halakhah." *Tikkun* 10, no. 4: 42–48, 77.

1994 "Breaking Glass: Power in the Jewish Community." With Chanita Blumfield. *Hadassah Magazine* 76, no. 1: 24–26.

"On Feminine God-Talk." *The Reconstructionist* 59, no. 1: 48–55.

"Judaism and the Health Plan." With Chanita Blumfield. *Hadassah Magazine* 75.

1990 "Bible, Goddesses, and Sex." *Daughters of Sarah* 16, (1990).

1989 "Law and Philosophy: The Case of Sex in the Bible." *Semeia* 45: 89–102.

1988 "A Theology of Catastrophe." *Beer-Sheva* 3: 121–24. (In Hebrew transliteration: Ha-teulogia shel ha-ason: She'elat ha-tsedeq ha-histori.)

1986 "The Trial Before God of an Accused Adulteress." *Bible Review* 2, no. 3: 46–49.

1985 "*Inclusio* in Sumerian." *Revue d'assyriologie et d'archeologie Orientale* 79, no. 1: 93–94.

"Moses and the Cults: The Question of Religious Leadership." *Judaism* 34, no. 4: 444–52.

1984 "The Strange Case of the Suspected Sotah (Numbers 5:11–31)." *Vetus Testamentum* 34, no. 1: 11–26.

1983 "The Tribulations of Marduk: The So-Called 'Marduk Ordeal Text.'" *Journal of the American Oriental Society* 103, no. 1: 131–41.

1982 "God Before the Hebrews: Treasures of Darkness Goes Back to the Mesopotamian Roots of Biblical Religion." *Biblical Archaeology Review* 8, no. 5: 18–25.

1981   "Patriarchal Family Relationships and Near Eastern Law." *Biblical Archeologist* 44, no. 4: 209–13.

1980   "'Tit for Tat': The Principle of Equal Retribution in Near Eastern and Biblical Law." *Biblical Archeologist* 43: 230–34.

1979   "Israel and the Ancient Near East: New Perspectives on the Flood." *Proceedings of the Rabbinical Assembly* 41.

1978   "What the Babylonian Flood Stories Can and Cannot Teach Us about the Genesis Flood." *Biblical Archaeology Review* 4, no. 4: 32–41.

1977   "The *Atrahasis* epic and Its significance for Our Understanding of Genesis 1–9." *Biblical Archeologist* 40, no. 4: 147–55.

        "The Nungal-Hymn and the Ekur-Prison." *Journal of the Economic and Social History of the Orient* 20, Part 1: 78–89.

CPSIA information can be obtained
at www.ICGtesting.com
Printed in the USA
LVHW091923120520
655460LV00006B/73/J